TITAN®
COMICS

STATIX
PRESS

ATLAS & AXIS **VOLUME ONE**
ISBN: 9781782763505

Published by Titan Comics
A division of Titan Publishing Group Ltd.
144 Southwark St., London, SE1 0UP.
Titan Comics is a registered trademark of Titan Publishing Group, Ltd.
All rights reserved.

Originally published in French as: *La Saga d'Atlas & Axis* by Pau.
© Ankama Editions, 2011, 2013.
All rights reserved.

A CIP catalogue record for this title is available from the British Library

10 9 8 7 6 5 4 3 2 1
First Published July 2018

Printed in China.
Titan Comics.

www.titan-comics.com
Follow us on Twitter @ComicsTitan
Visit us at facebook.com/comicstitan

CREATED, WRITTEN AND DRAWN BY
PAU

TITAN COMICS

COLLECTION EDITOR JONATHAN STEVENSON
DESIGNER WILFRIED TSHIKANA-EKUTSHU
MANAGING AND LAUNCH EDITOR ANDREW JAMES
PRODUCTION CONTROLLER PETER JAMES
PRODUCTION SUPERVISOR MARIA PEARSON
SENIOR PRODUCTION CONTROLLER JACKIE FLOOK
ART DIRECTOR OZ BROWNE
SALES MANAGER SANTOSH MAHARAJ
CIRCULATION ASSISTANT FRANCES HALLAM
PRESS OFFICER WILL O'MULLANE

BRAND MANAGER CHRIS THOMPSON
ADS & MARKETING ASSISTANT BELLA HOY
DIRECT SALES & MARKETING MANAGER RICKY CLAYDON
COMMERCIAL MANAGER MICHELLE FAIRLAMB
PUBLISHING MANAGER DARRYL TOTHILL
PUBLISHING DIRECTOR CHRIS TEATHER
OPERATIONS DIRECTOR LEIGH BAULCH
EXECUTIVE DIRECTOR VIVIAN CHEUNG
PUBLISHER NICK LANDAU

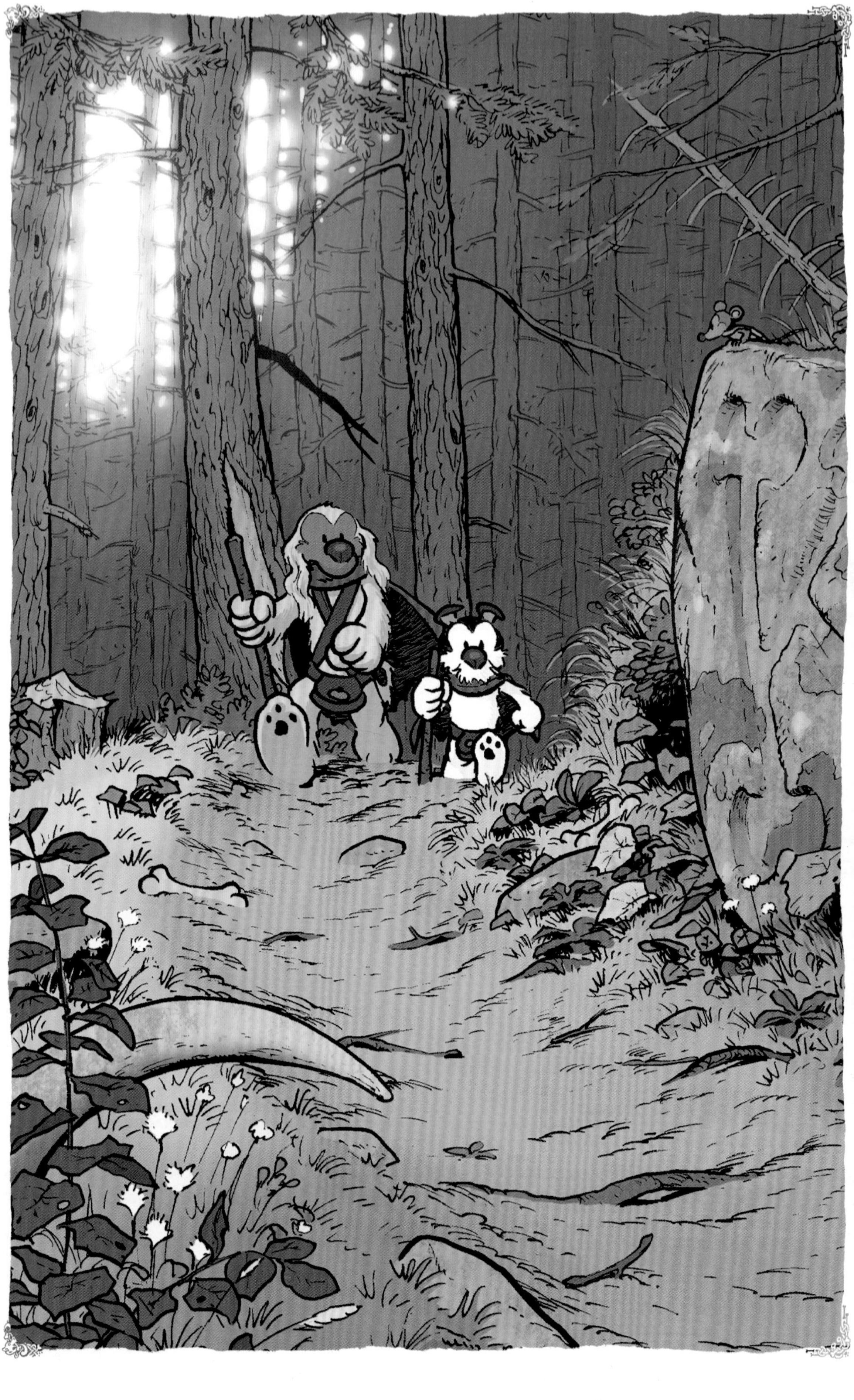

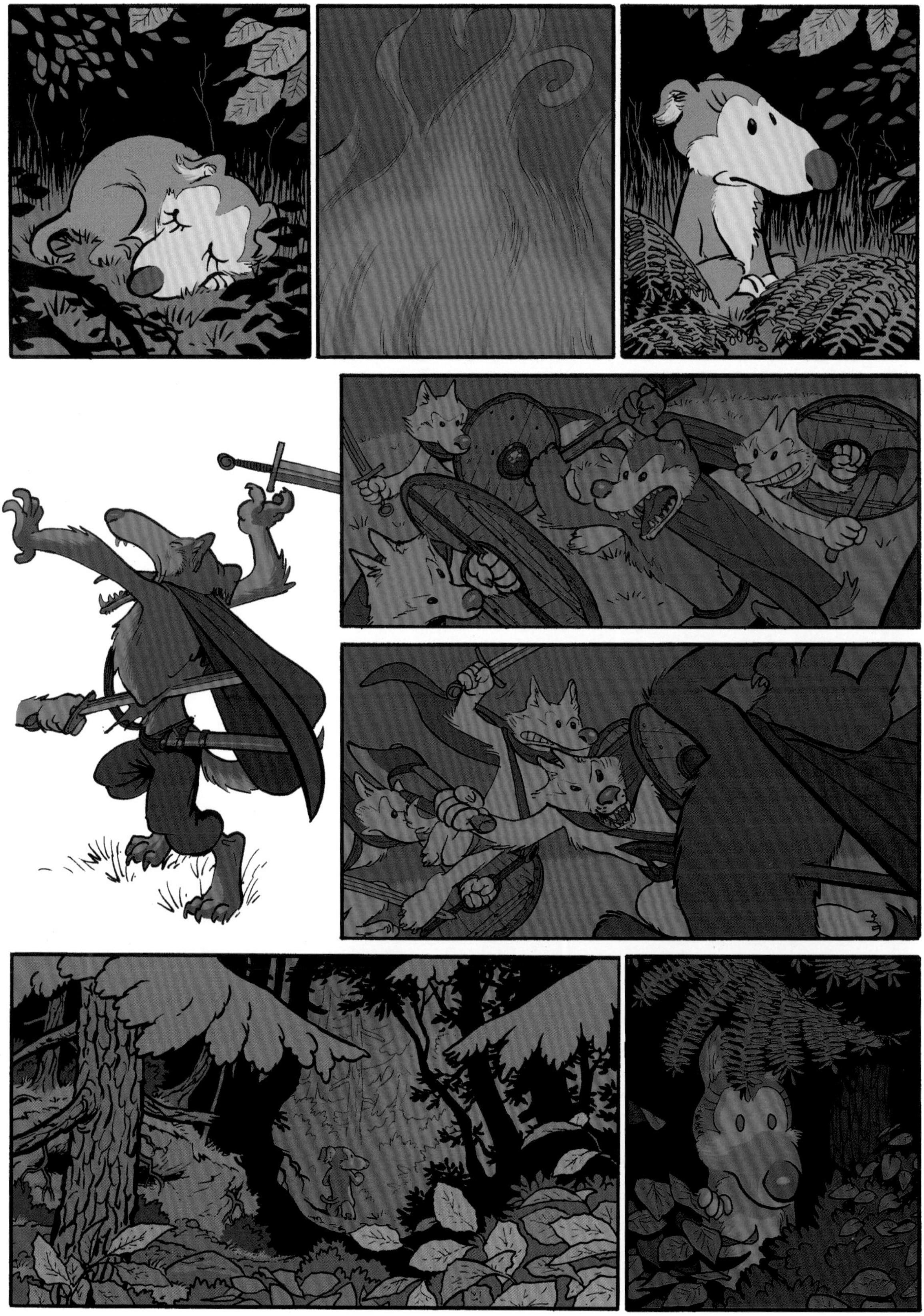

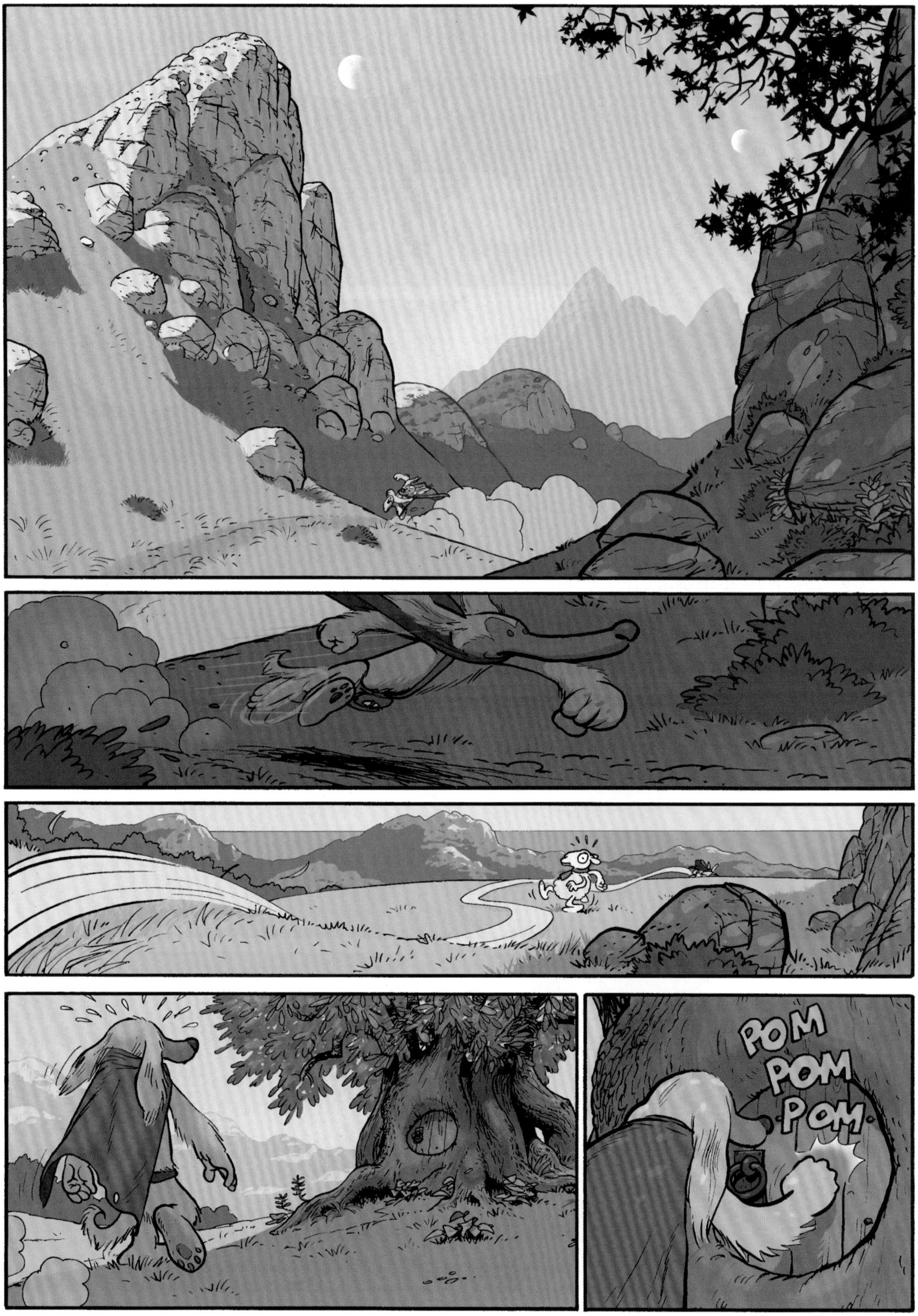
POM POM POM

WOOF!
I LOVE A
GOOD
PUDDLE.

ATLAS!

YOU'RE BACK
WITH CANUTO'S
PARCHMENT
ALREADY?

DID YOU
DOUBT IT FOR A
SECOND?

AND I'VE
BROUGHT IT BACK
TRANSLATED.

I BET
YOU THOUGHT
I WOULDN'T MAKE
IT BACK FOR THE
FEAST, DIDN'T
YOU?

I'M JUST GLAD YOU'RE BACK.
I'VE HAD NOTHING TO DO BUT RUB
MY BUM ON THE CARPET WITHOUT
YOU HERE.

SO WHAT
DOES THE
PARCHMENT
SAY?

ALL I KNOW
IS THAT CANUTO IS
LOOKING INTO SOME
KIND OF LEGEND ABOUT
A MAGIC BONE. AND...
YOU NEED TO GET YOUR
CARPET CLEANED...
SERIOUSLY.

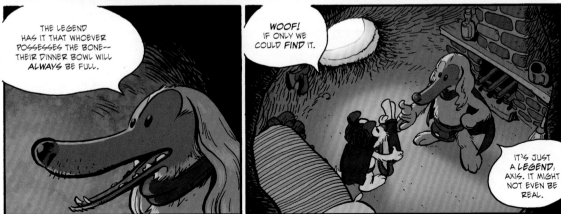

THE LEGEND
HAS IT THAT WHOEVER
POSSESSES THE BONE--
THEIR DINNER BOWL WILL
ALWAYS BE FULL.

WOOF!
IF ONLY WE
COULD FIND IT.

IT'S JUST
A LEGEND,
AXIS. IT MIGHT
NOT EVEN BE
REAL.

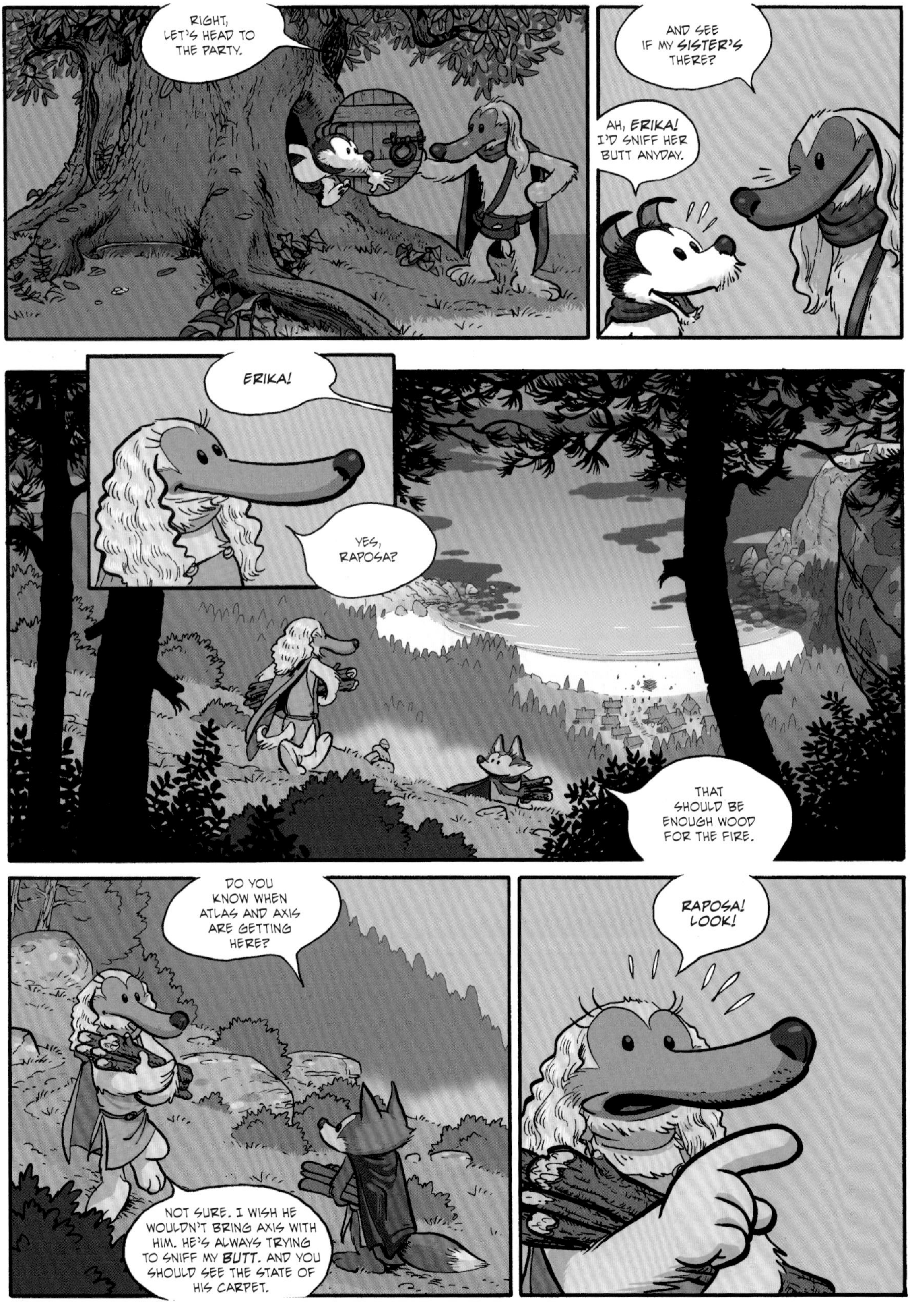
RIGHT, LET'S HEAD TO THE PARTY.
AND SEE IF MY SISTER'S THERE?
AH, ERIKA! I'D SNIFF HER BUTT ANYDAY.
ERIKA!
YES, RAPOSA?
THAT SHOULD BE ENOUGH WOOD FOR THE FIRE.
DO YOU KNOW WHEN ATLAS AND AXIS ARE GETTING HERE?
NOT SURE. I WISH HE WOULDN'T BRING AXIS WITH HIM. HE'S ALWAYS TRYING TO SNIFF MY BUTT. AND YOU SHOULD SEE THE STATE OF HIS CARPET.
RAPOSA! LOOK!

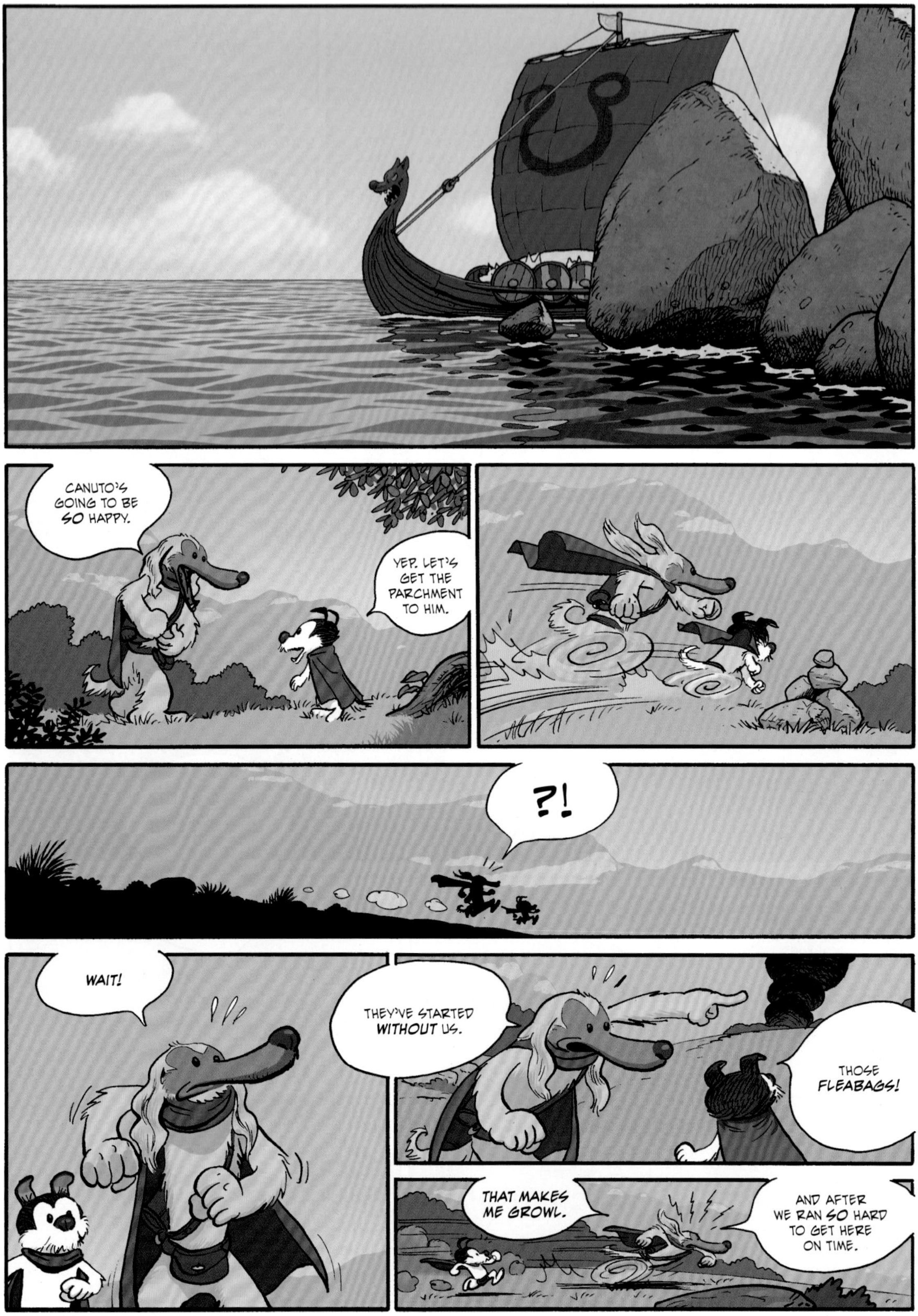
CANUTO'S GOING TO BE *SO* HAPPY.
YEP. LET'S GET THE PARCHMENT TO HIM.
?!
WAIT!
THEY'VE STARTED *WITHOUT* US.
THOSE *FLEABAGS!*
THAT MAKES ME GROWL.
AND AFTER WE RAN *SO* HARD TO GET HERE ON TIME.

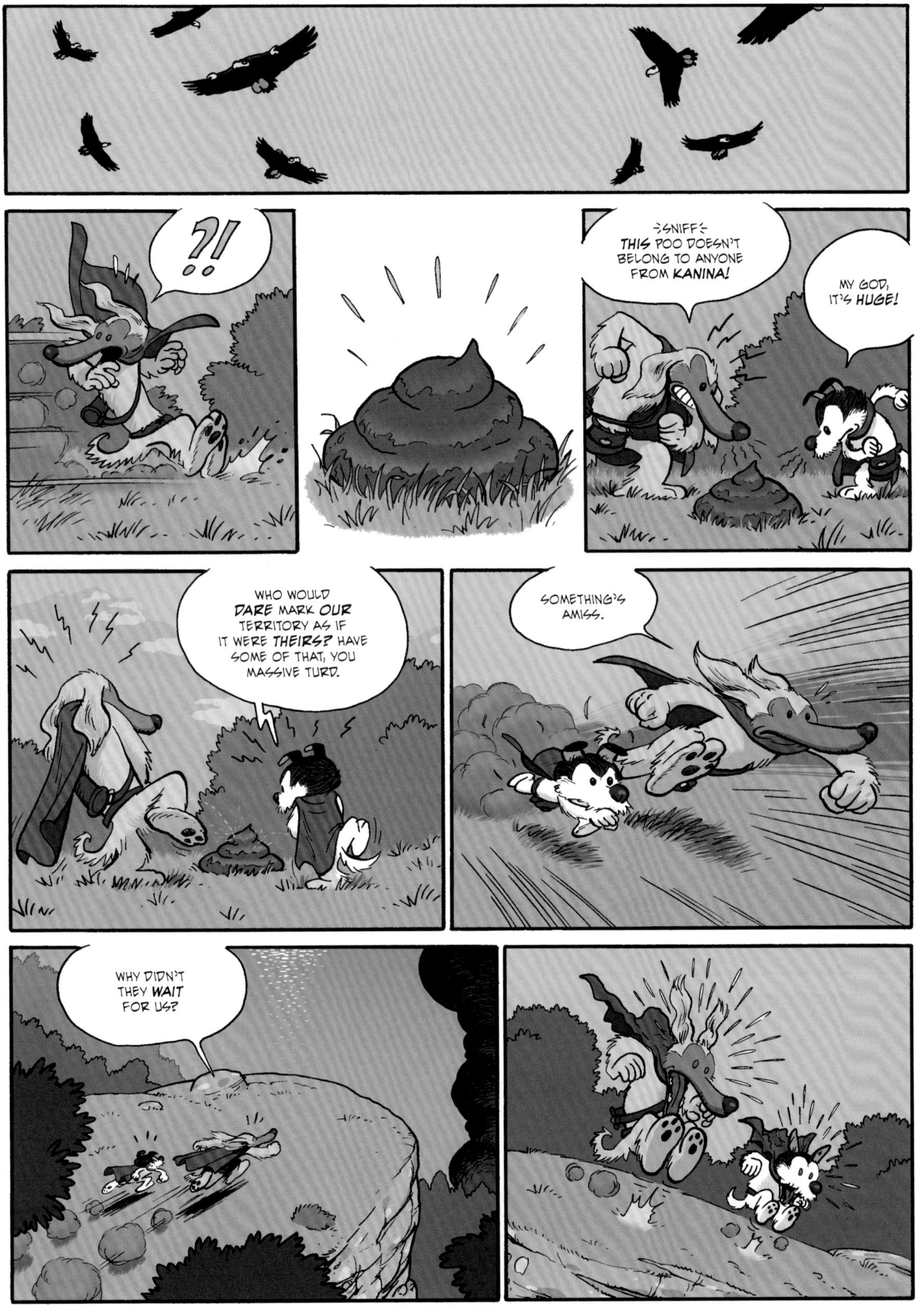
?!
-SNIFF-
THIS POO DOESN'T BELONG TO ANYONE FROM KANINA!
MY GOD, IT'S HUGE!
WHO WOULD DARE MARK OUR TERRITORY AS IF IT WERE THEIRS? HAVE SOME OF THAT, YOU MASSIVE TURD.
SOMETHING'S AMISS.
WHY DIDN'T THEY WAIT FOR US?

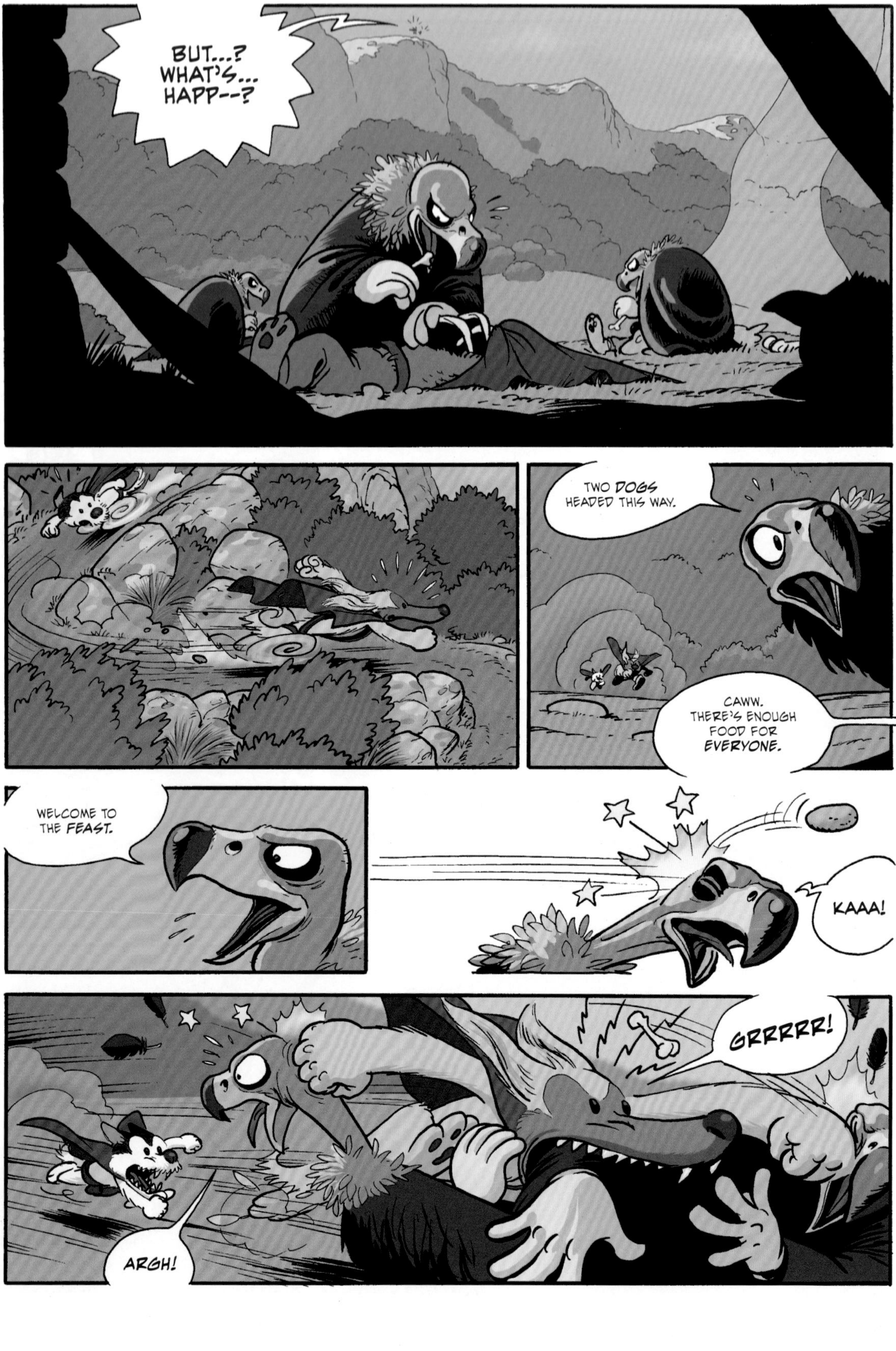
BUT...? WHAT'S... HAPP--?
TWO DOGS HEADED THIS WAY.
CAWW. THERE'S ENOUGH FOOD FOR EVERYONE.
WELCOME TO THE FEAST.
KAAA!
GRRRRR!
ARGH!

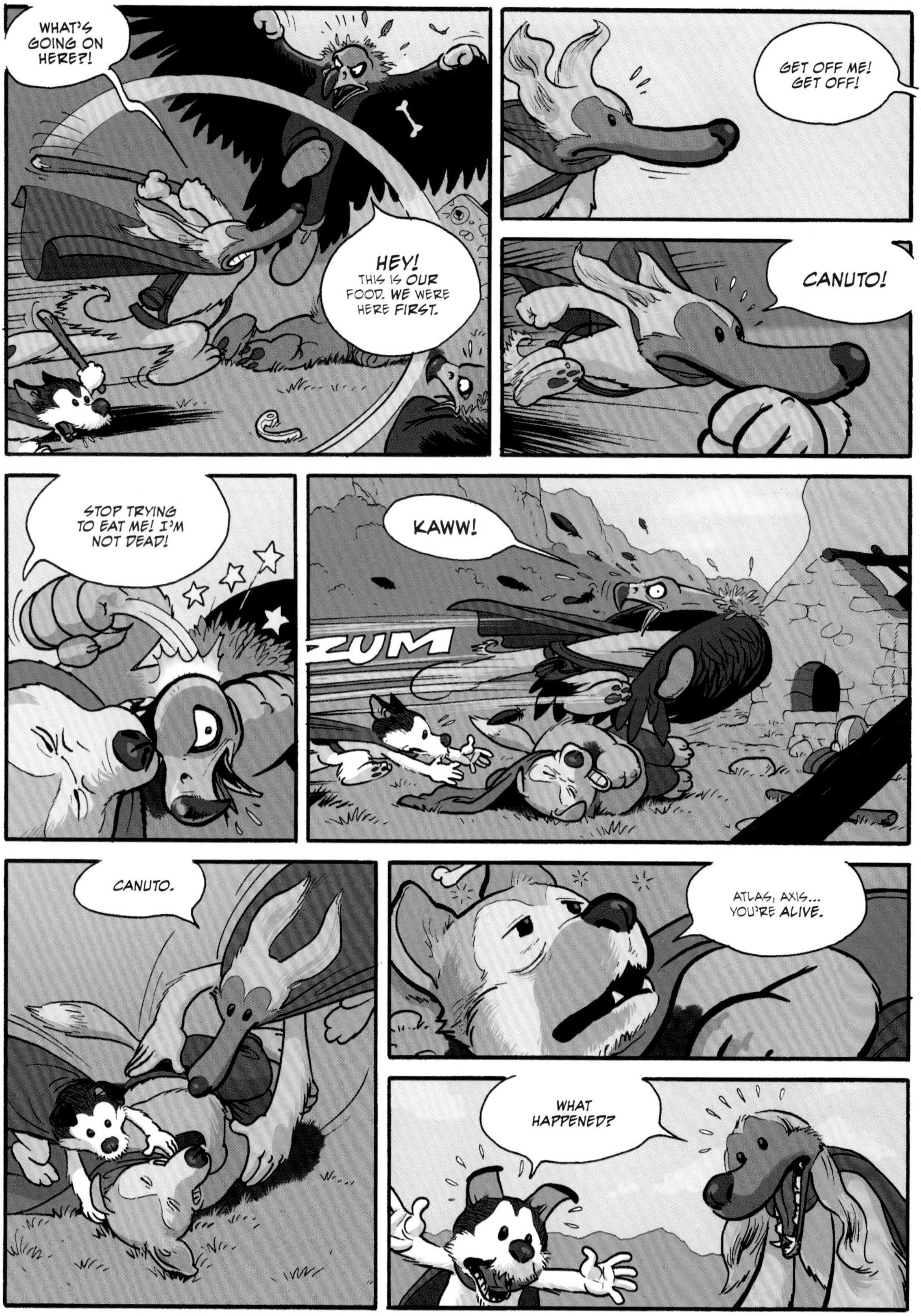
WHAT'S GOING ON HERE?!
HEY! THIS IS OUR FOOD. WE WERE HERE FIRST.
GET OFF ME! GET OFF!
CANUTO!
STOP TRYING TO EAT ME! I'M NOT DEAD!
KAWW!
ZUM
CANUTO.
ATLAS, AXIS... YOU'RE ALIVE.
WHAT HAPPENED?

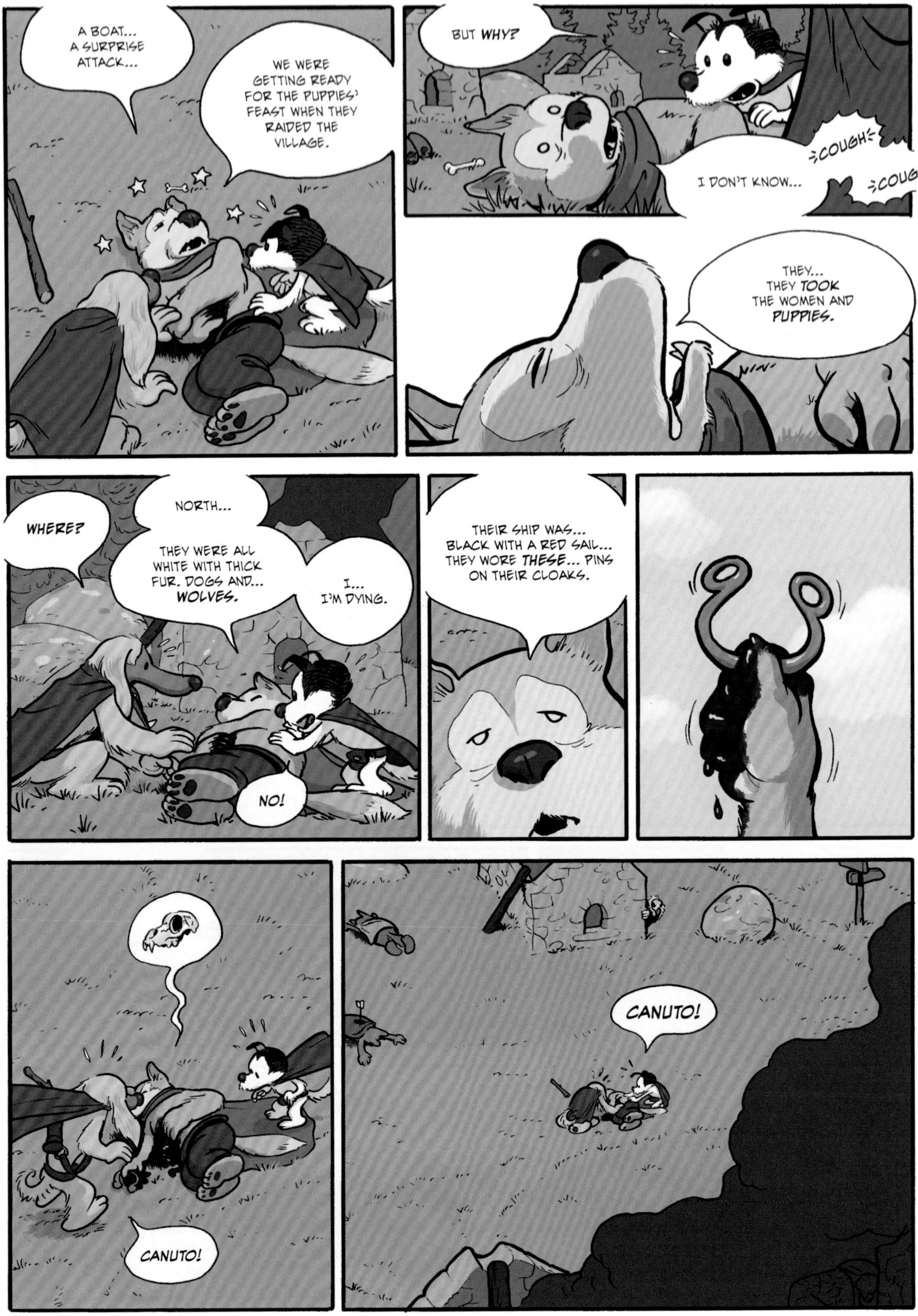
A BOAT... A SURPRISE ATTACK...
WE WERE GETTING READY FOR THE PUPPIES' FEAST WHEN THEY RAIDED THE VILLAGE.
BUT WHY?
I DON'T KNOW...
COUGH
COUGH
THEY... THEY TOOK THE WOMEN AND PUPPIES.
WHERE?
NORTH...
THEY WERE ALL WHITE WITH THICK FUR. DOGS AND... WOLVES.
I... I'M DYING.
NO!
THEIR SHIP WAS... BLACK WITH A RED SAIL... THEY WORE THESE... PINS ON THEIR CLOAKS.
CANUTO!
CANUTO!

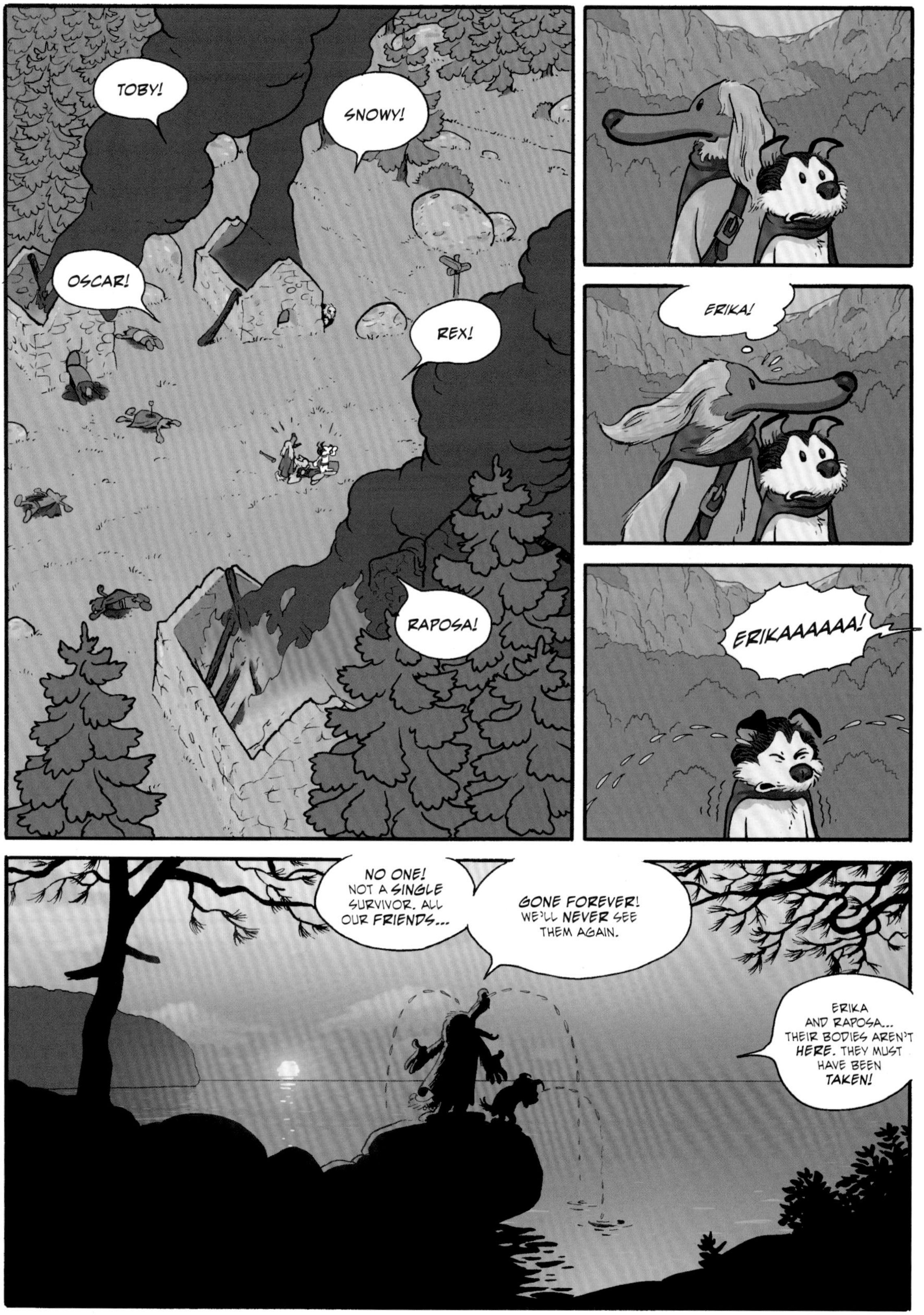
TOBY!
SNOWY!
OSCAR!
REX!
RAPOSA!
ERIKA!
ERIKAAAAAA!
NO ONE! NOT A SINGLE SURVIVOR. ALL OUR FRIENDS...
GONE FOREVER! WE'LL NEVER SEE THEM AGAIN.
ERIKA AND RAPOSA... THEIR BODIES AREN'T HERE. THEY MUST HAVE BEEN TAKEN!

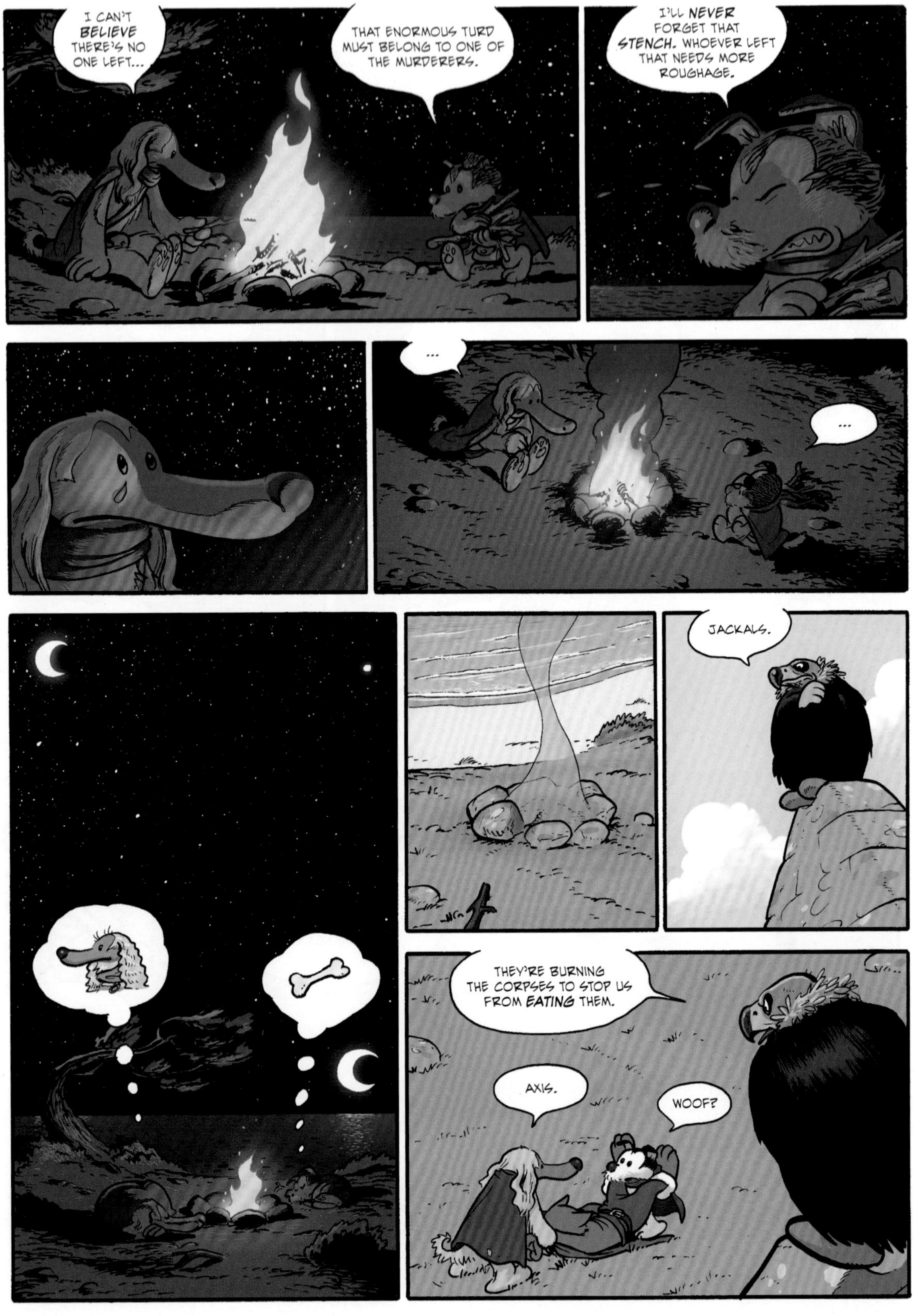
I CAN'T BELIEVE THERE'S NO ONE LEFT...
THAT ENORMOUS TURD MUST BELONG TO ONE OF THE MURDERERS.
I'LL NEVER FORGET THAT STENCH. WHOEVER LEFT THAT NEEDS MORE ROUGHAGE.
...
...
JACKALS.
THEY'RE BURNING THE CORPSES TO STOP US FROM EATING THEM.
AXIS.
WOOF?

WITHOUT OUR *FRIENDS*, THERE'S NOTHING TO KEEP US HERE ANYMORE. THIS IS NO LONGER OUR *HOME*.

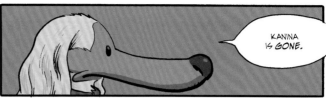

KANINA IS *GONE*.

WE SHOULD HEAD *NORTH* AND LOOK FOR ERIKA AND RAPOSA. IF THEY'RE ALIVE, WE'LL *FIND* THEM.

LET'S GO.

GO TO THE BLACKSMITH. SEE IF YOU CAN FIND SOME *WEAPONS*.

JACKALS!

OKAY.

GOODBYE, MY FRIENDS.

THERE WERE ONLY *SPOONS* LEFT AT THE FORGE. BUT I FOUND *THIS*... MUST HAVE BELONGED TO ONE OF THE *PIRATES*.

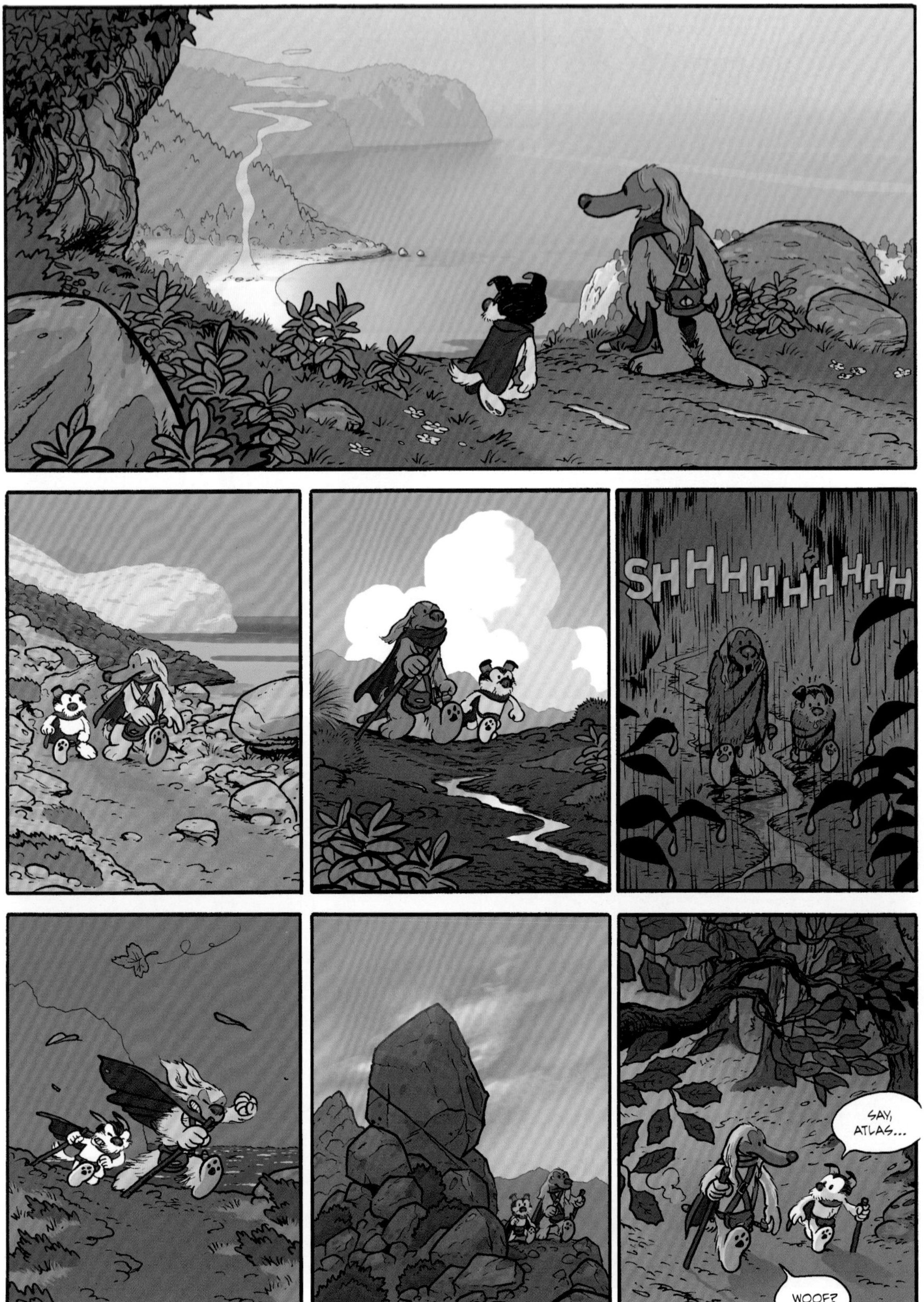
SHHHHHHHHHH
SAY, ATLAS...
WOOF?

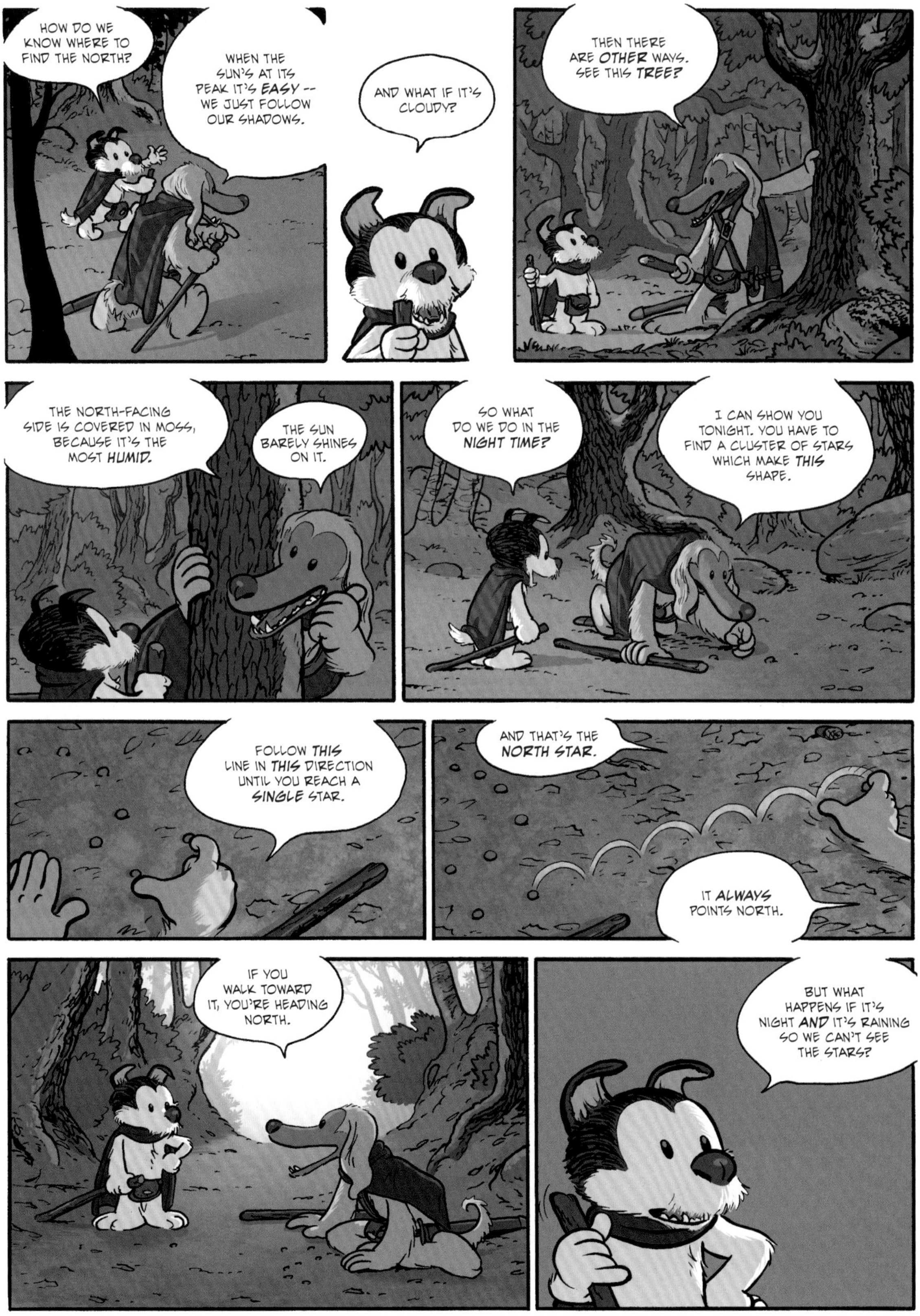
HOW DO WE KNOW WHERE TO FIND THE NORTH?
WHEN THE SUN'S AT ITS PEAK IT'S *EASY* -- WE JUST FOLLOW OUR SHADOWS.
AND WHAT IF IT'S CLOUDY?
THEN THERE ARE *OTHER* WAYS. SEE THIS *TREE?*
THE NORTH-FACING SIDE IS COVERED IN MOSS, BECAUSE IT'S THE MOST *HUMID.*
THE SUN BARELY SHINES ON IT.
SO WHAT DO WE DO IN THE *NIGHT TIME?*
I CAN SHOW YOU TONIGHT. YOU HAVE TO FIND A CLUSTER OF STARS WHICH MAKE *THIS* SHAPE.
FOLLOW *THIS* LINE IN *THIS* DIRECTION UNTIL YOU REACH A *SINGLE* STAR.
AND THAT'S THE *NORTH STAR.*
IT *ALWAYS* POINTS NORTH.
IF YOU WALK TOWARD IT, YOU'RE HEADING NORTH.
BUT WHAT HAPPENS IF IT'S NIGHT *AND* IT'S RAINING SO WE CAN'T SEE THE STARS?

MAYBE YOU SHOULD LET *ME* DO THE THINKING.

GOOD IDEA.

IT'S A GOOD JOB YOU'RE HERE. I WOULD *NEVER* HAVE BEEN ABLE TO FIND THE MURDERERS ON MY *OWN*.

OH AXIS, I DON'T KNOW IF WE'LL BE ABLE TO GET THEM BACK.

ALL WE KNOW IS THAT THEY CAME FROM THE NORTH AND WORE PINS LIKE *THIS*.

AND THERE ARE ONLY *TWO* OF US.

IS THE NORTH VERY BIG?

TLIN TLIN

SOUNDS LIKE *FOOD!*

TLIN

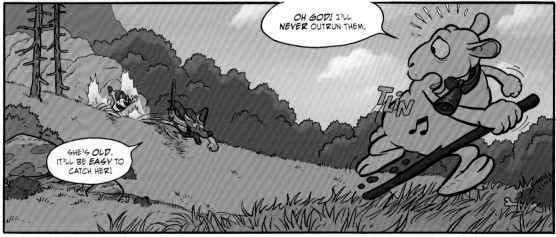

OH GOD! I'LL *NEVER* OUTRUN THEM.

SHE'S *OLD*. IT'LL BE *EASY* TO CATCH HER!

TLIN

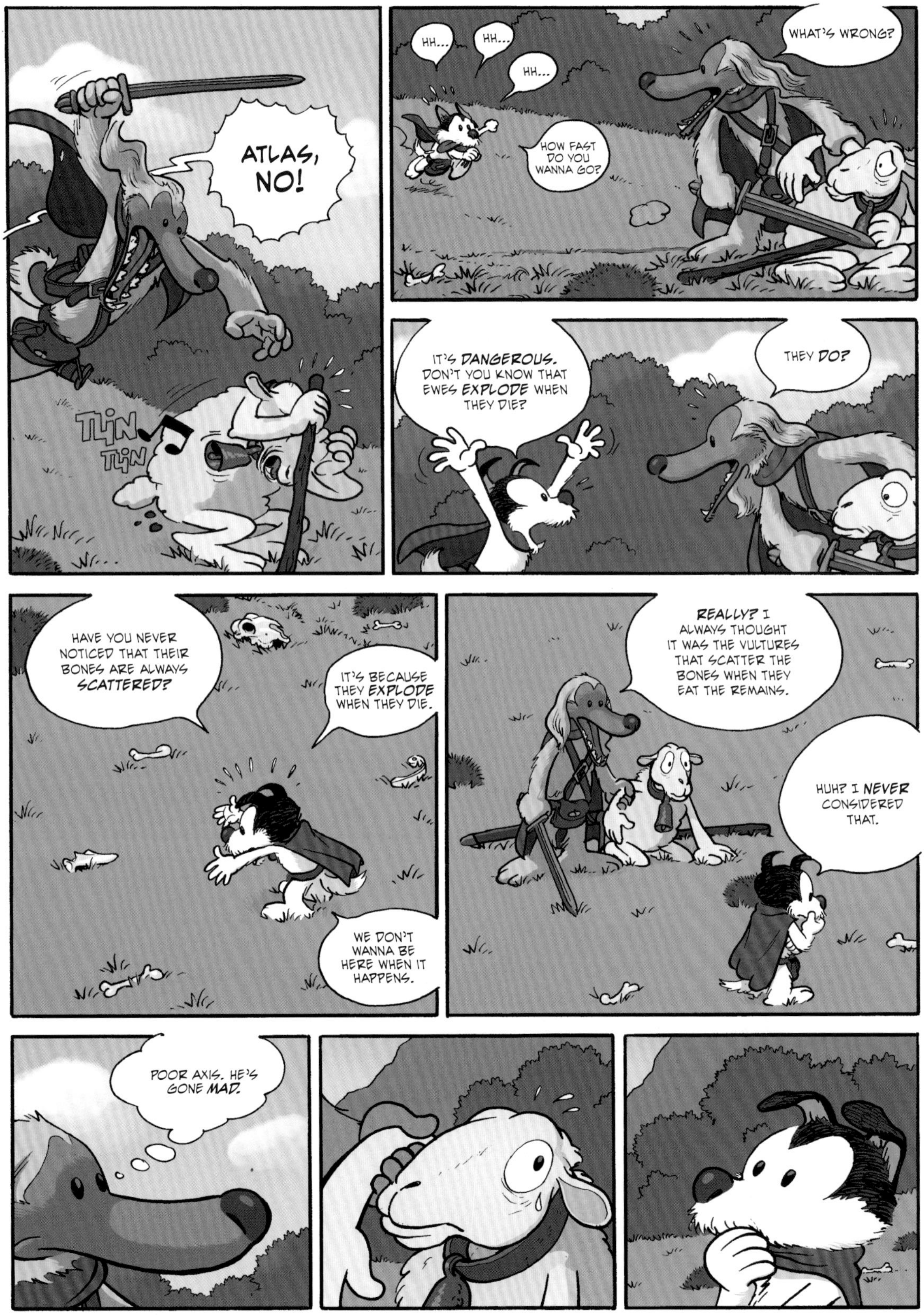
ATLAS, NO!
TLIN TLIN
HH...
HH...
HH...
HOW FAST DO YOU WANNA GO?
WHAT'S WRONG?
IT'S DANGEROUS. DON'T YOU KNOW THAT EWES EXPLODE WHEN THEY DIE?
THEY DO?
HAVE YOU NEVER NOTICED THAT THEIR BONES ARE ALWAYS SCATTERED?
IT'S BECAUSE THEY EXPLODE WHEN THEY DIE.
WE DON'T WANNA BE HERE WHEN IT HAPPENS.
REALLY? I ALWAYS THOUGHT IT WAS THE VULTURES THAT SCATTER THE BONES WHEN THEY EAT THE REMAINS.
HUH? I NEVER CONSIDERED THAT.
POOR AXIS. HE'S GONE MAD.

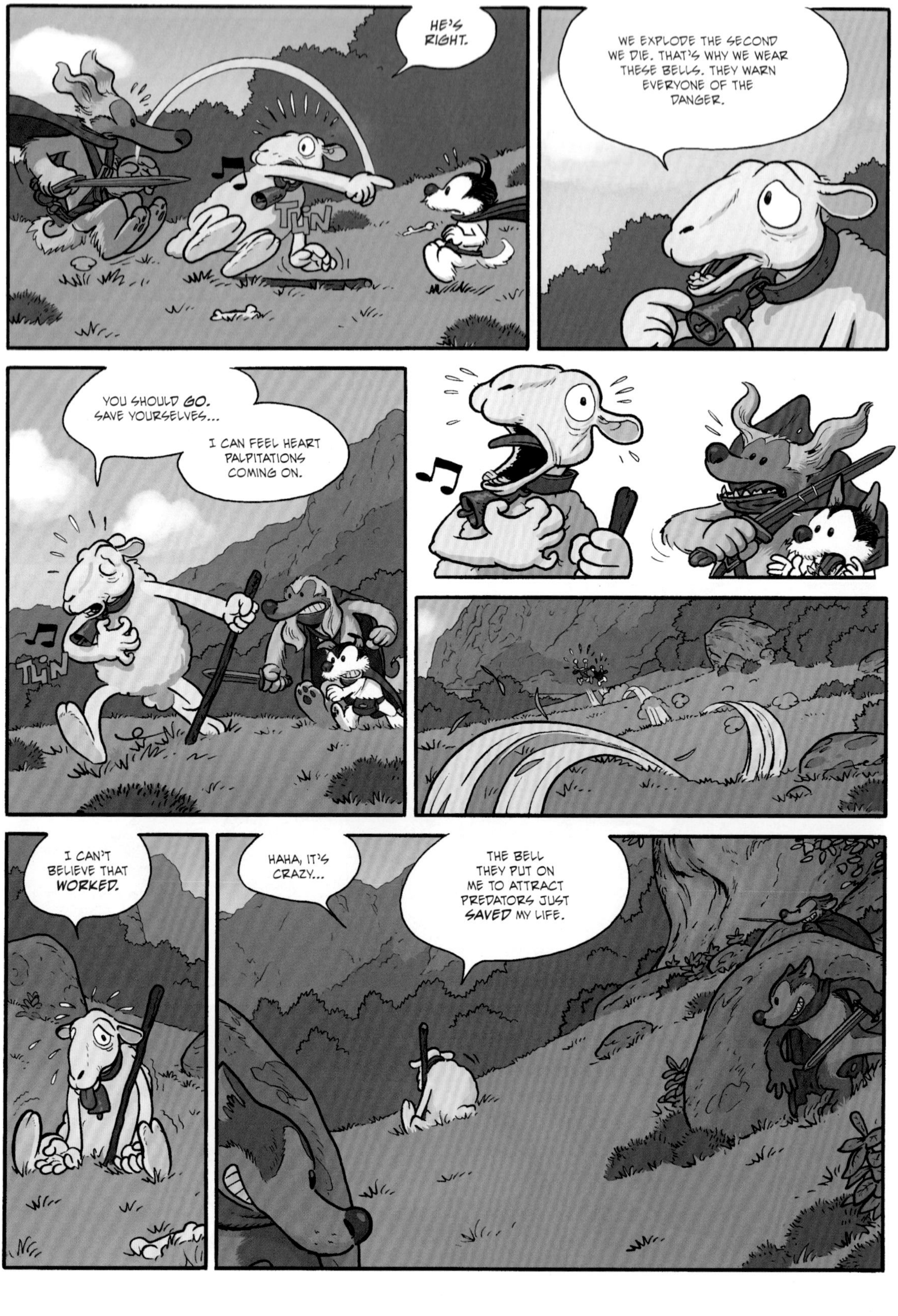
HE'S RIGHT.
TLIN
WE EXPLODE THE SECOND WE DIE. THAT'S WHY WE WEAR THESE BELLS. THEY WARN EVERYONE OF THE DANGER.
YOU SHOULD GO. SAVE YOURSELVES...
I CAN FEEL HEART PALPITATIONS COMING ON.
TLIN
I CAN'T BELIEVE THAT WORKED.
HAHA, IT'S CRAZY...
THE BELL THEY PUT ON ME TO ATTRACT PREDATORS JUST SAVED MY LIFE.

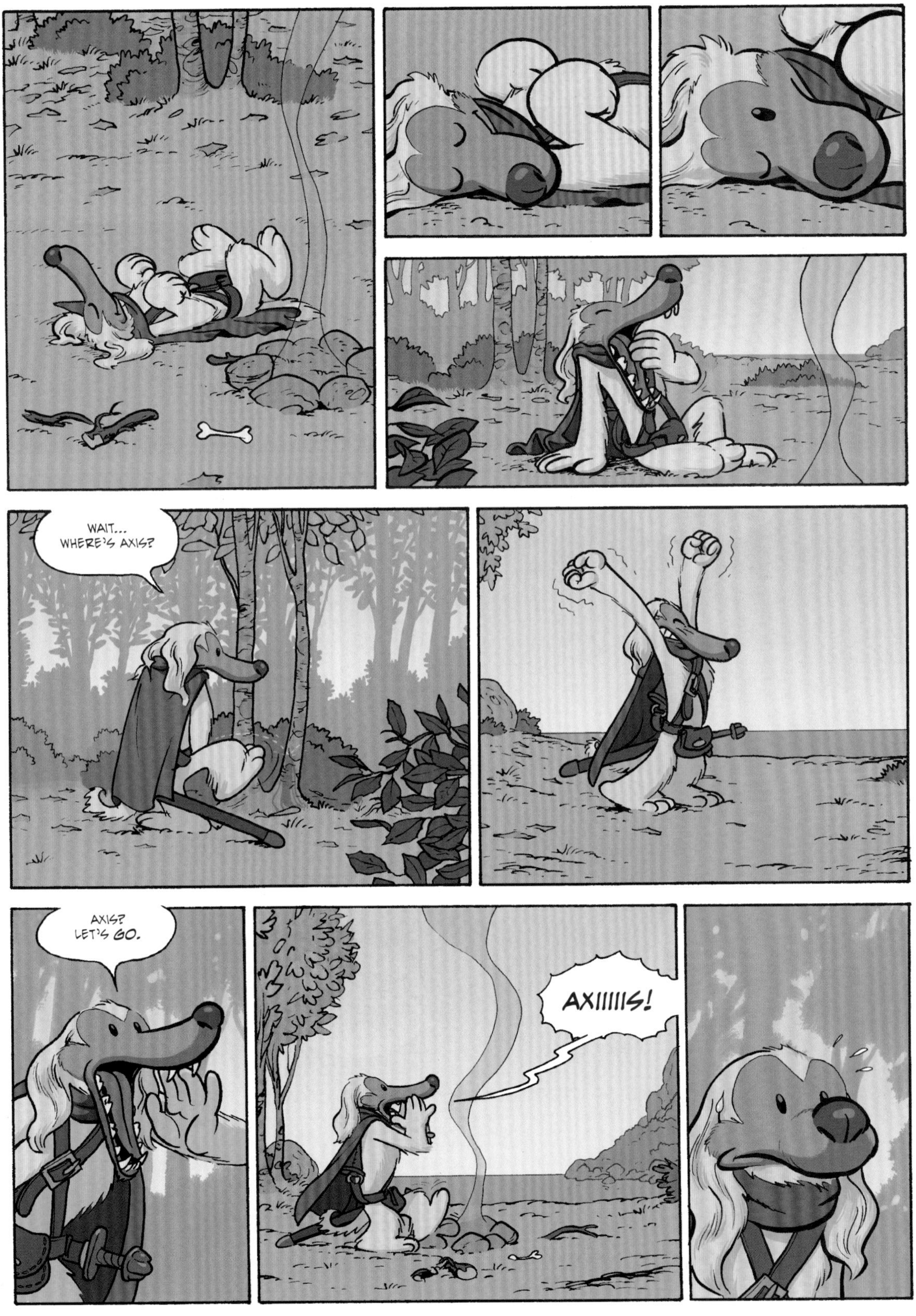
WAIT... WHERE'S AXIS?
AXIS? LET'S GO.
AXIIIIIS!

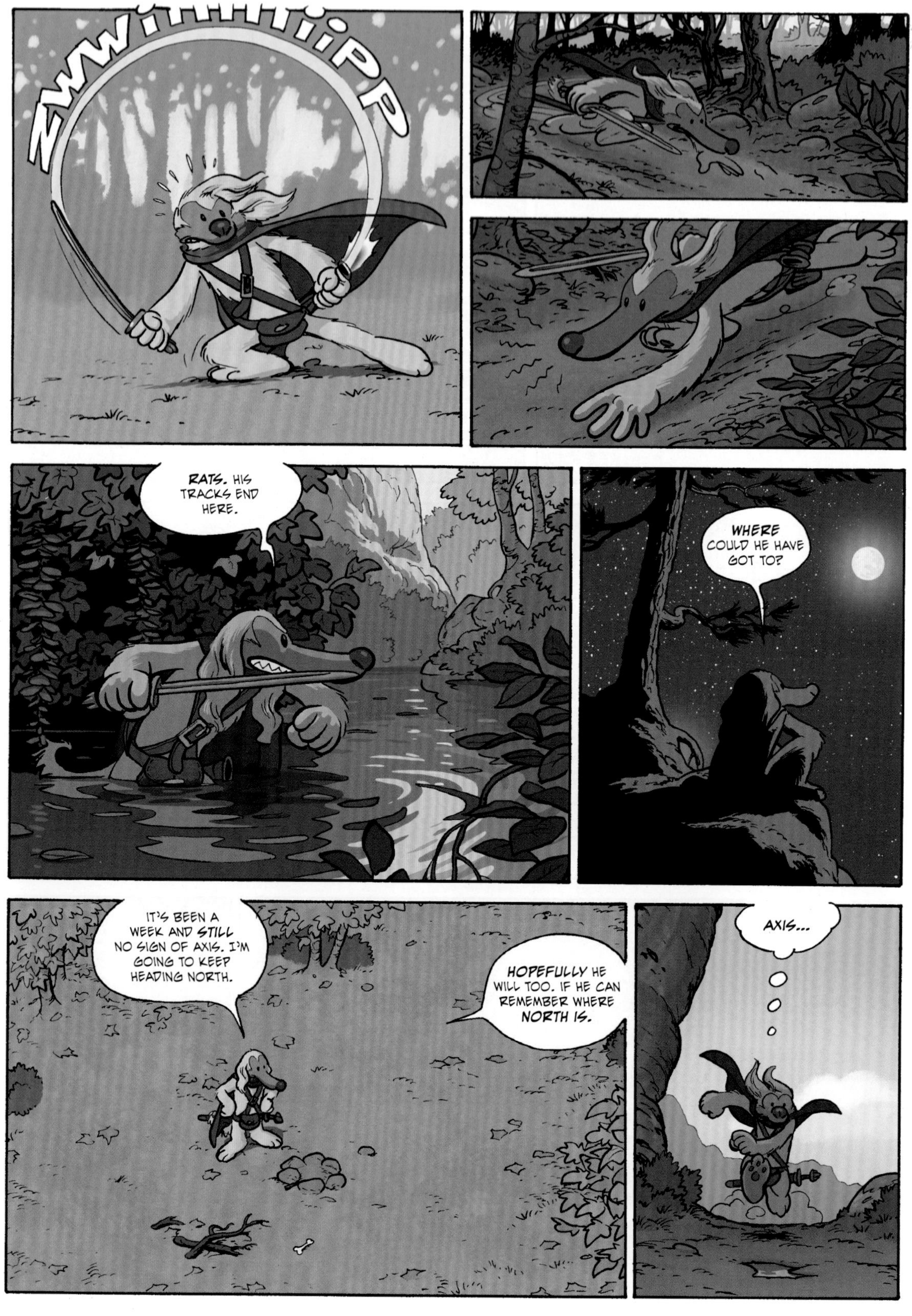
RATS. HIS TRACKS END HERE.
WHERE COULD HE HAVE GOT TO?
IT'S BEEN A WEEK AND STILL NO SIGN OF AXIS. I'M GOING TO KEEP HEADING NORTH.
HOPEFULLY HE WILL TOO. IF HE CAN REMEMBER WHERE NORTH IS.
AXIS...

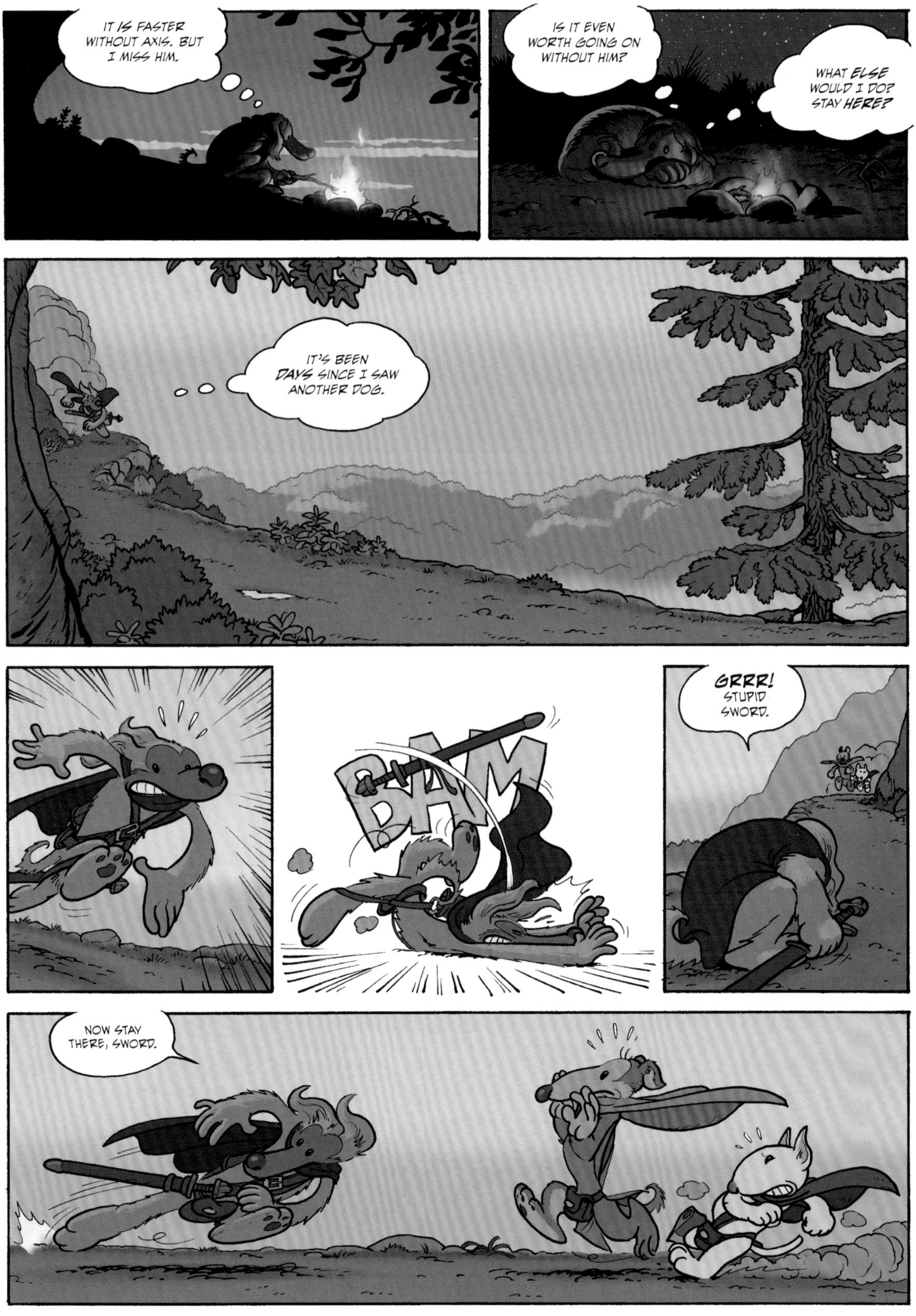
IT IS FASTER WITHOUT AXIS. BUT I MISS HIM.
IS IT EVEN WORTH GOING ON WITHOUT HIM?
WHAT ELSE WOULD I DO? STAY HERE?
IT'S BEEN DAYS SINCE I SAW ANOTHER DOG.
BAM
GRRR! STUPID SWORD.
NOW STAY THERE, SWORD.

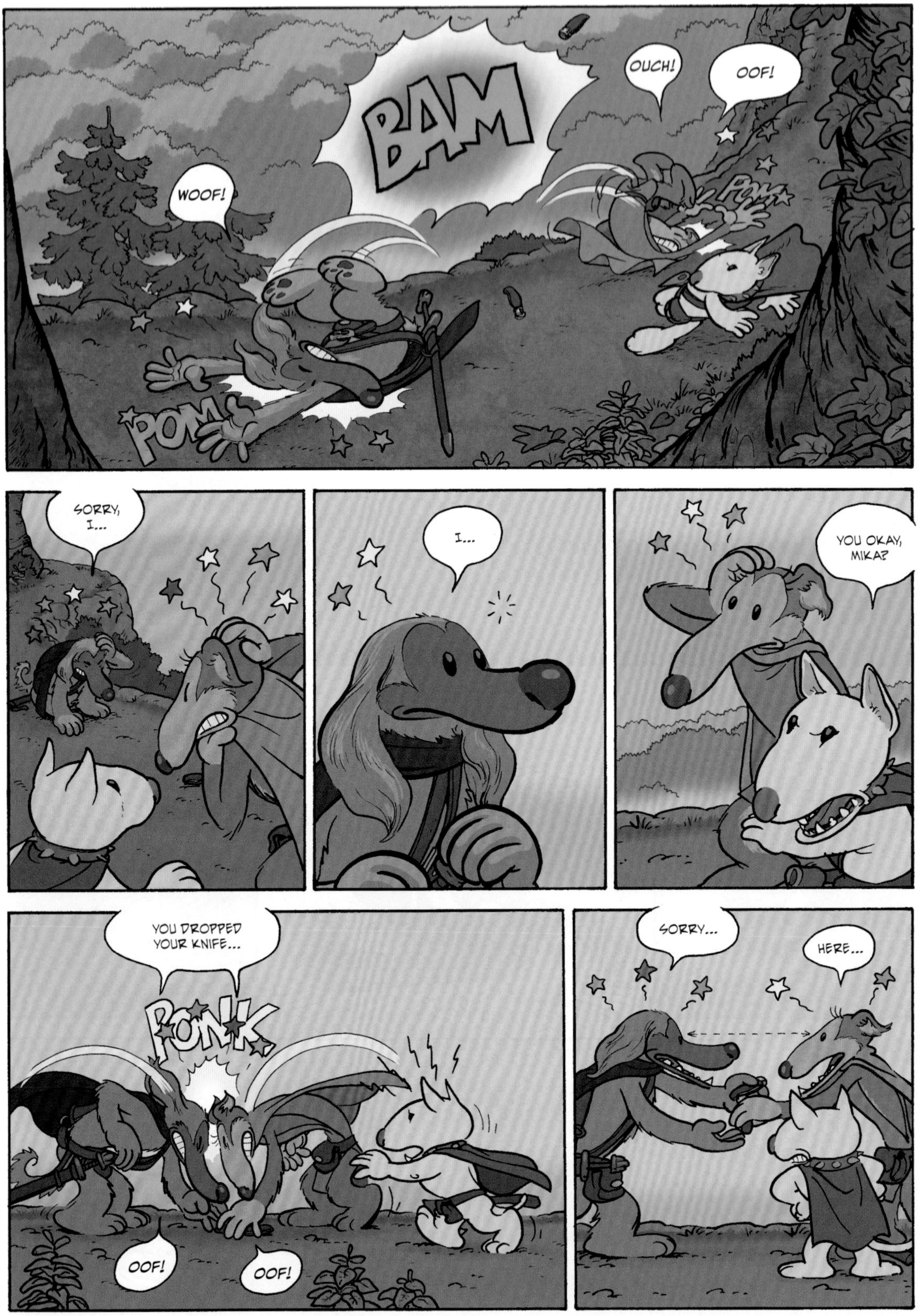
BAM
OUCH!
OOF!
WOOF!
POM
POM
SORRY, I...
I...
YOU OKAY, MIKA?
YOU DROPPED YOUR KNIFE...
PONK
OOF!
OOF!
SORRY...
HERE...

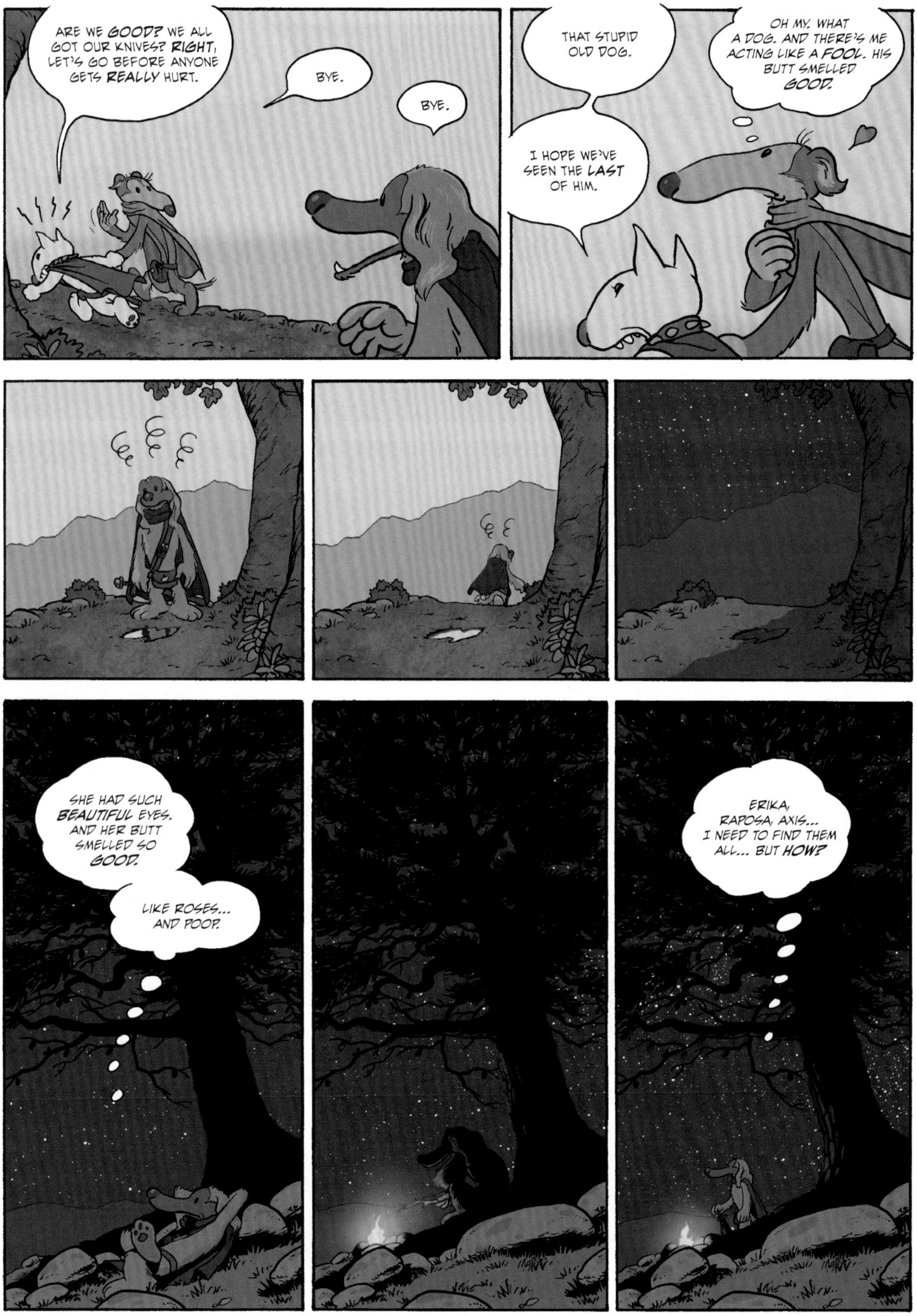
ARE WE GOOD? WE ALL GOT OUR KNIVES? RIGHT, LET'S GO BEFORE ANYONE GETS REALLY HURT.
BYE.
BYE.
THAT STUPID OLD DOG.
I HOPE WE'VE SEEN THE LAST OF HIM.
OH MY. WHAT A DOG. AND THERE'S ME ACTING LIKE A FOOL. HIS BUTT SMELLED GOOD.
SHE HAD SUCH BEAUTIFUL EYES. AND HER BUTT SMELLED SO GOOD.
LIKE ROSES... AND POOP.
ERIKA, RAPOSA, AXIS... I NEED TO FIND THEM ALL... BUT HOW?

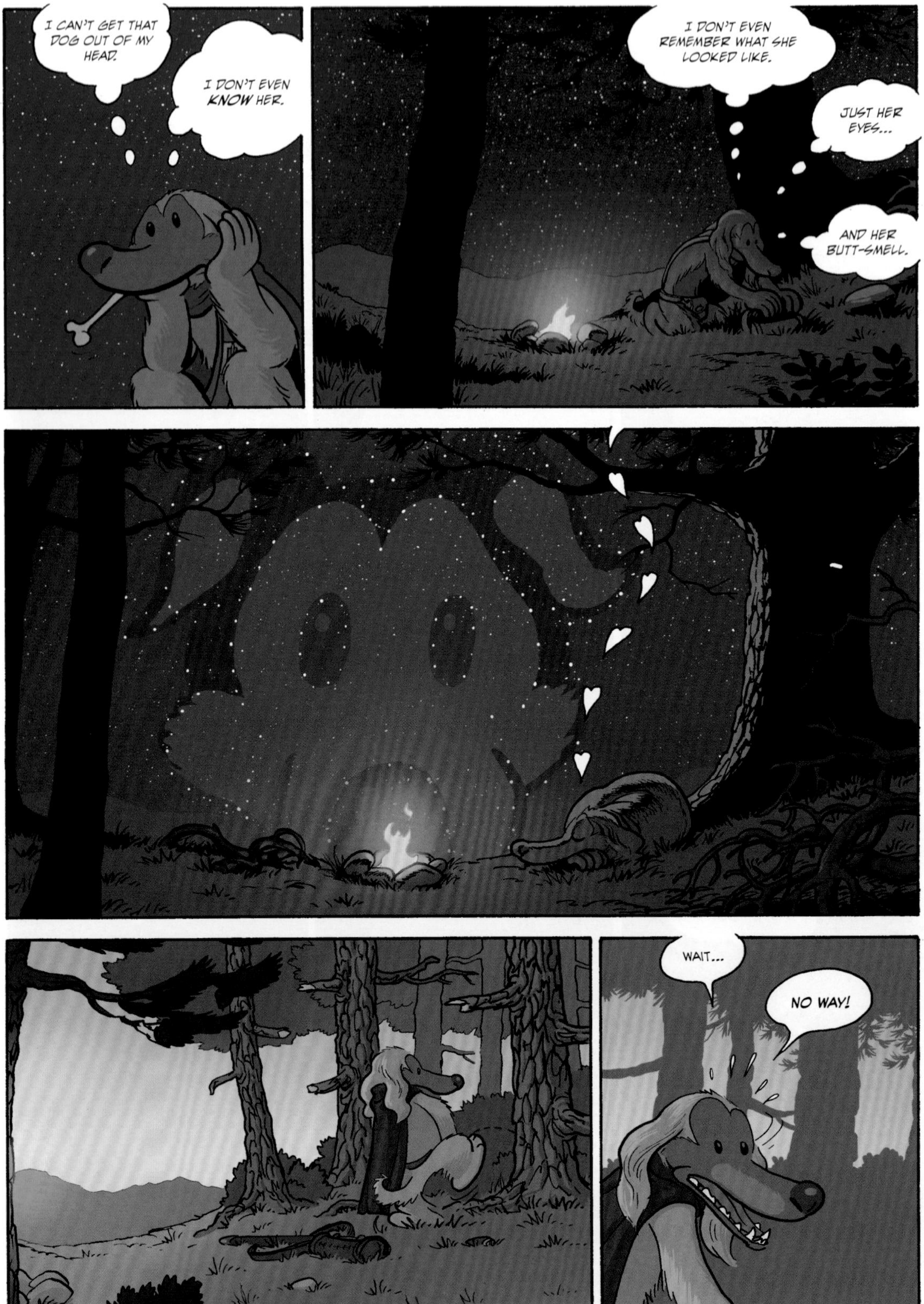
I CAN'T GET THAT DOG OUT OF MY HEAD.
I DON'T EVEN KNOW HER.
I DON'T EVEN REMEMBER WHAT SHE LOOKED LIKE.
JUST HER EYES...
AND HER BUTT-SMELL.
WAIT...
NO WAY!

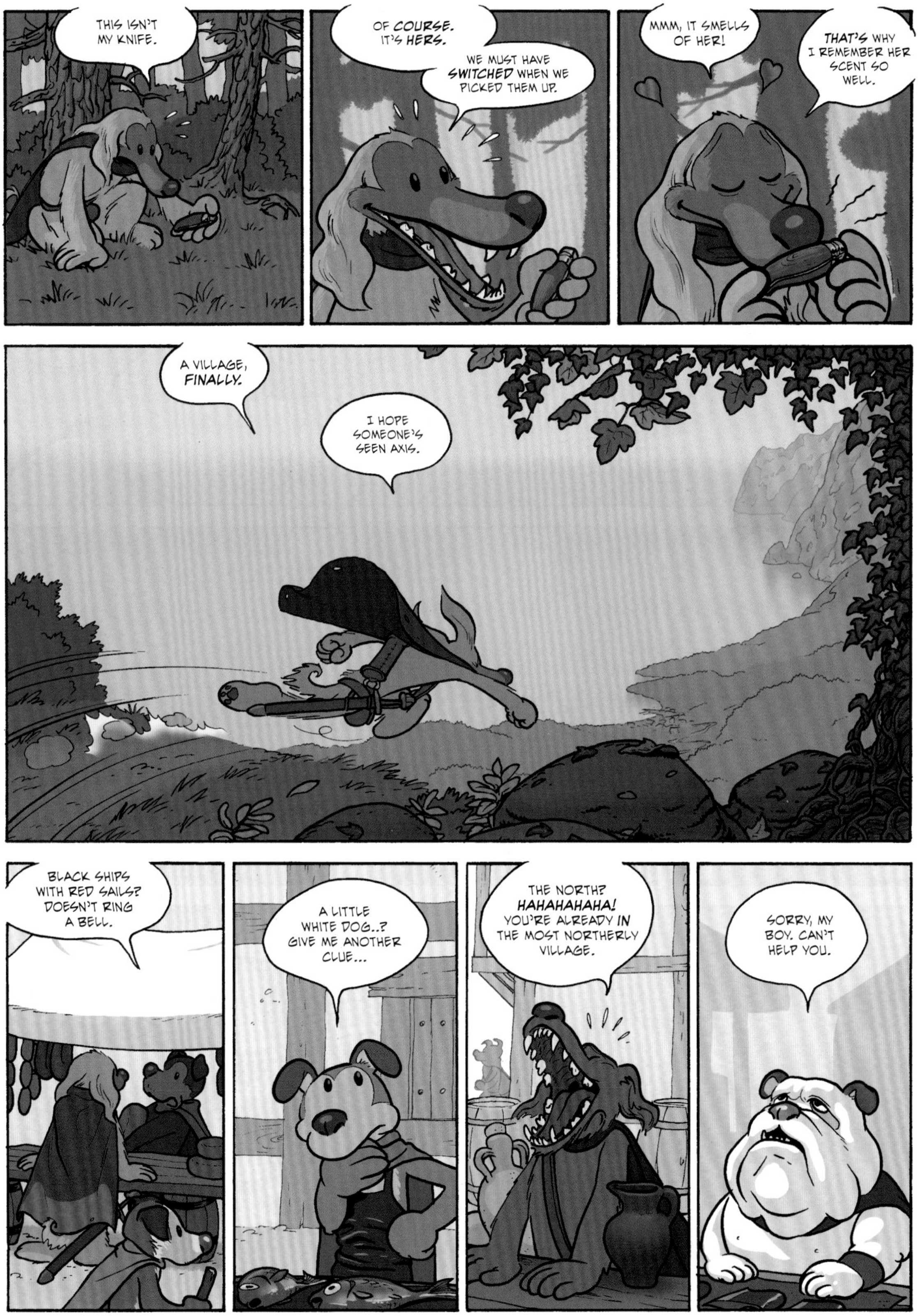
THIS ISN'T MY KNIFE.
OF COURSE. IT'S HERS.
WE MUST HAVE SWITCHED WHEN WE PICKED THEM UP.
MMM, IT SMELLS OF HER!
THAT'S WHY I REMEMBER HER SCENT SO WELL.
A VILLAGE, FINALLY.
I HOPE SOMEONE'S SEEN AXIS.
BLACK SHIPS WITH RED SAILS? DOESN'T RING A BELL.
A LITTLE WHITE DOG..? GIVE ME ANOTHER CLUE...
THE NORTH? HAHAHAHAHA! YOU'RE ALREADY IN THE MOST NORTHERLY VILLAGE.
SORRY, MY BOY. CAN'T HELP YOU.

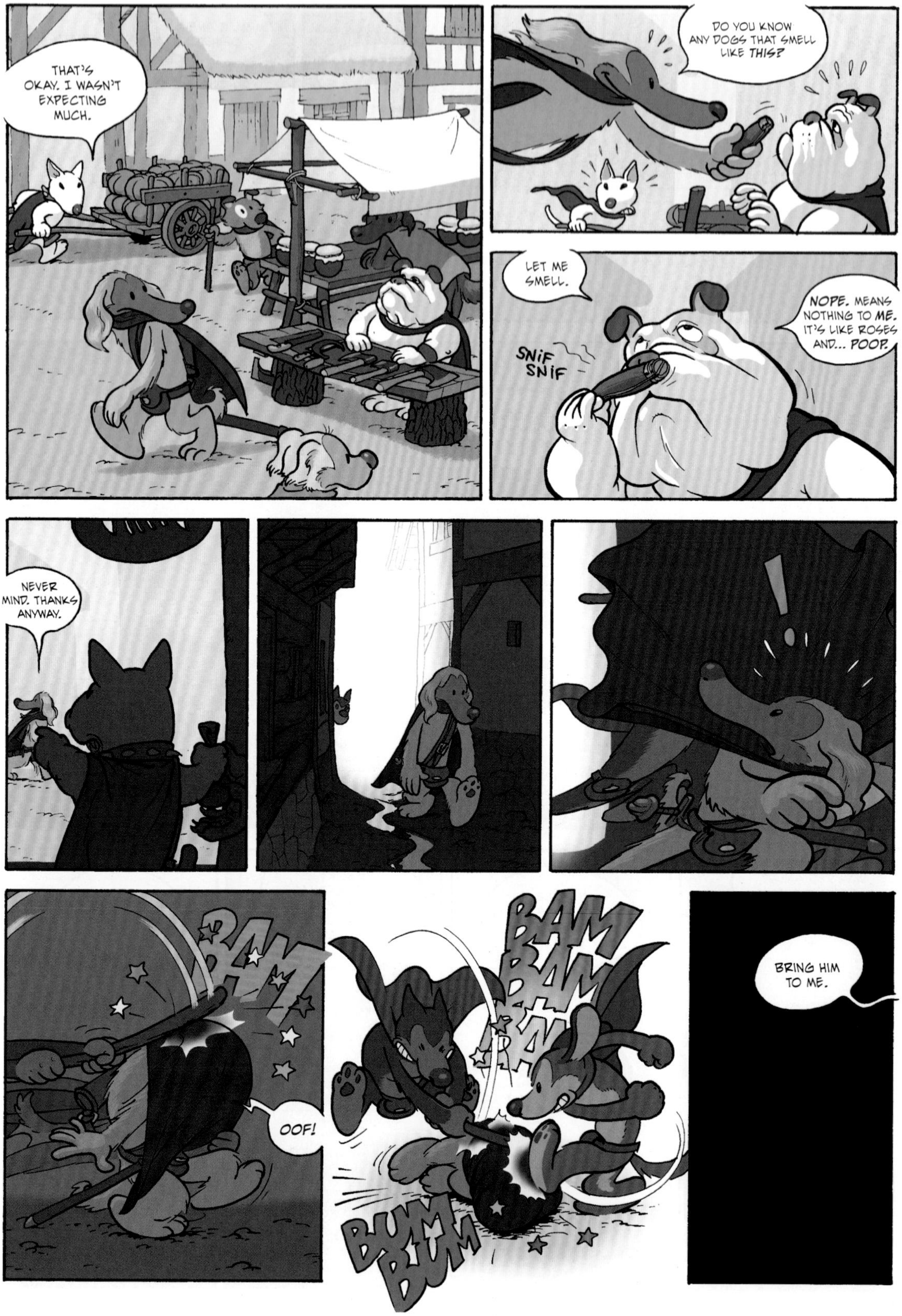
THAT'S OKAY. I WASN'T EXPECTING MUCH.
DO YOU KNOW ANY DOGS THAT SMELL LIKE THIS?
LET ME SMELL.
SNIF SNIF
NOPE. MEANS NOTHING TO ME. IT'S LIKE ROSES AND... POOP.
NEVER MIND. THANKS ANYWAY.
!
BAM
OOF!
BAM BAM
BUM BUM
BRING HIM TO ME.

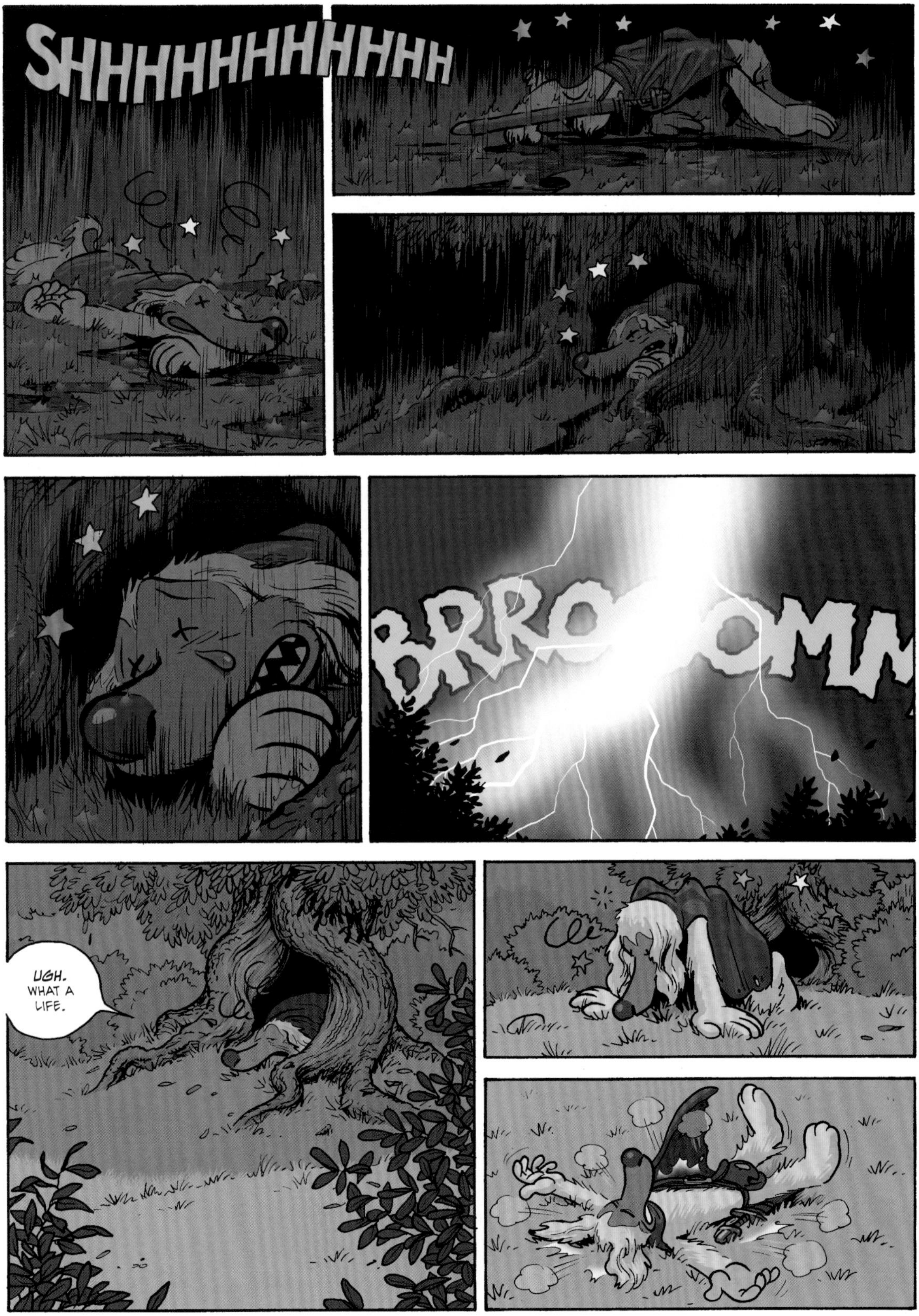
SHHHHHHHHHHH
BRROOOMM
UGH. WHAT A LIFE.

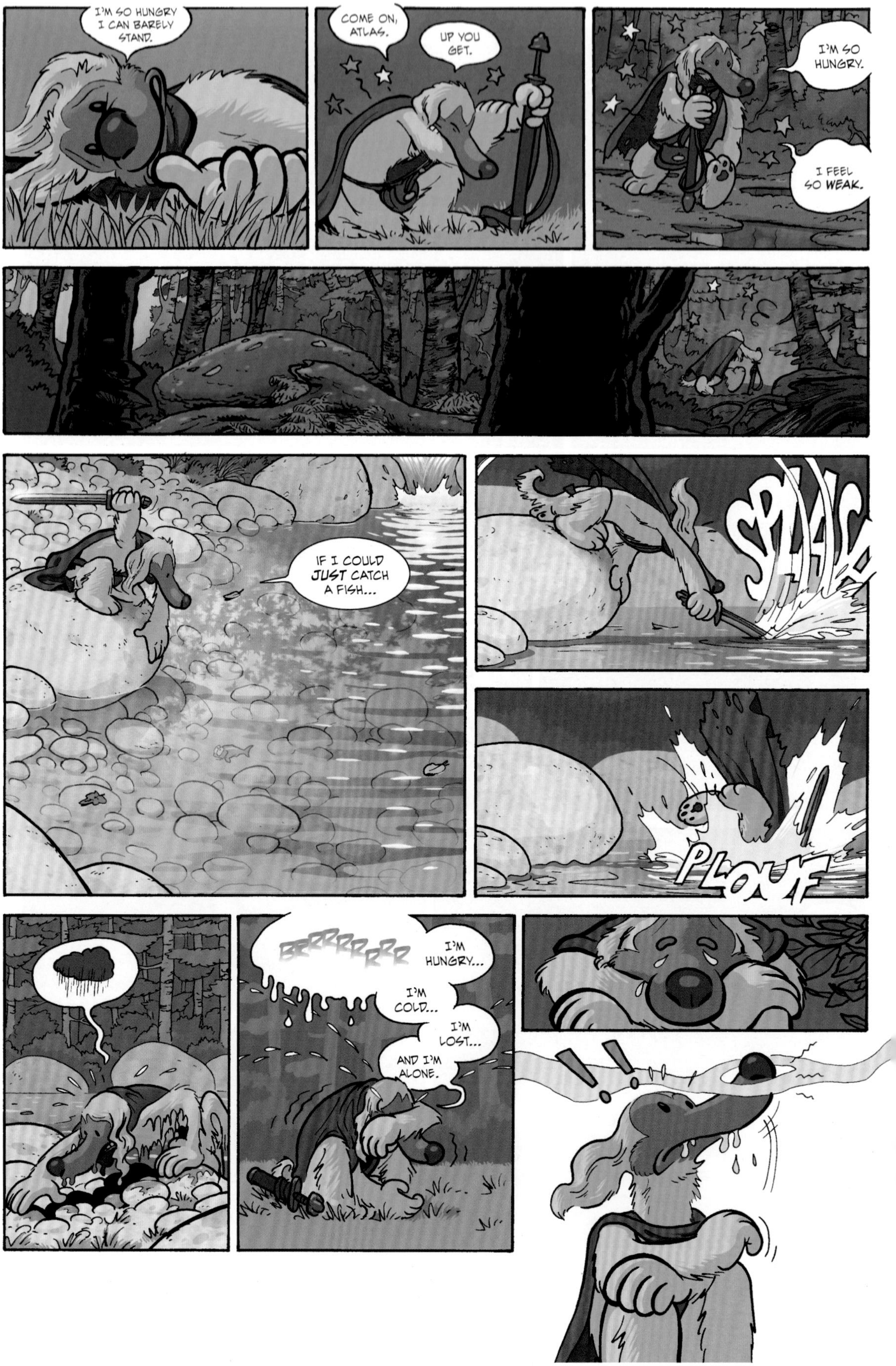
I'M SO HUNGRY I CAN BARELY STAND.
COME ON, ATLAS.
UP YOU GET.
I'M SO HUNGRY.
I FEEL SO WEAK.
IF I COULD JUST CATCH A FISH...
SPLASH
PLOUF
BRRRRRRRR
I'M HUNGRY...
I'M COLD...
I'M LOST...
AND I'M ALONE.

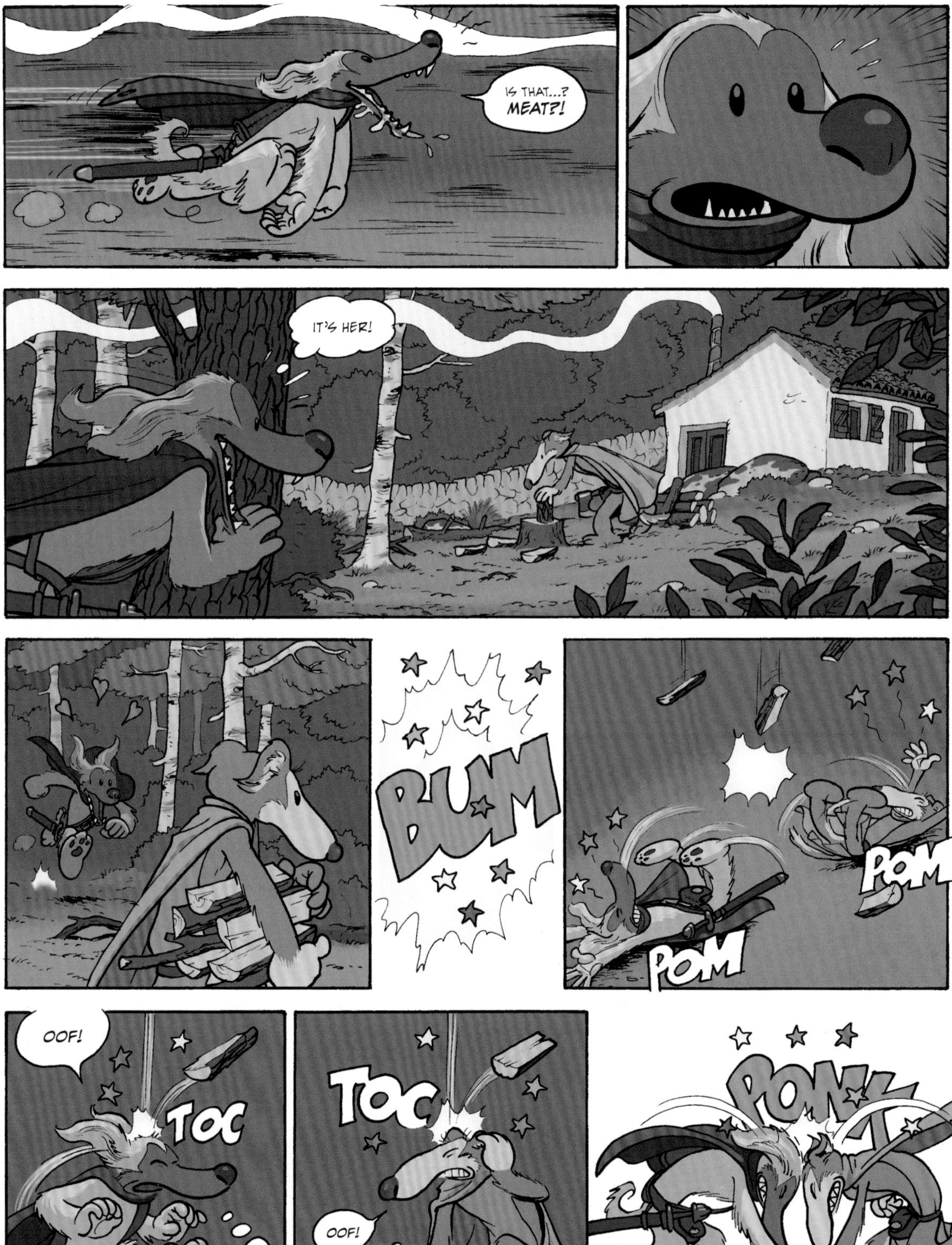
IS THAT...? MEAT?!
IT'S HER!
BUM
POM
POM
OOF!
TOC
OH, NO! ACTING LIKE AN IDIOT AGAIN.
TOC
OOF!
OH, NO! ACTING LIKE AN IDIOT AGAIN.
PONK

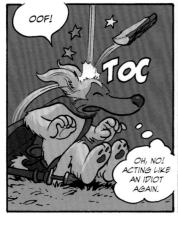

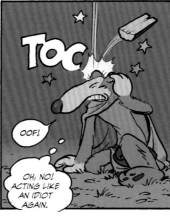

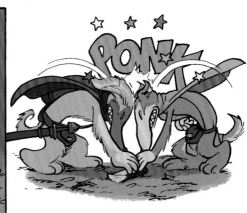

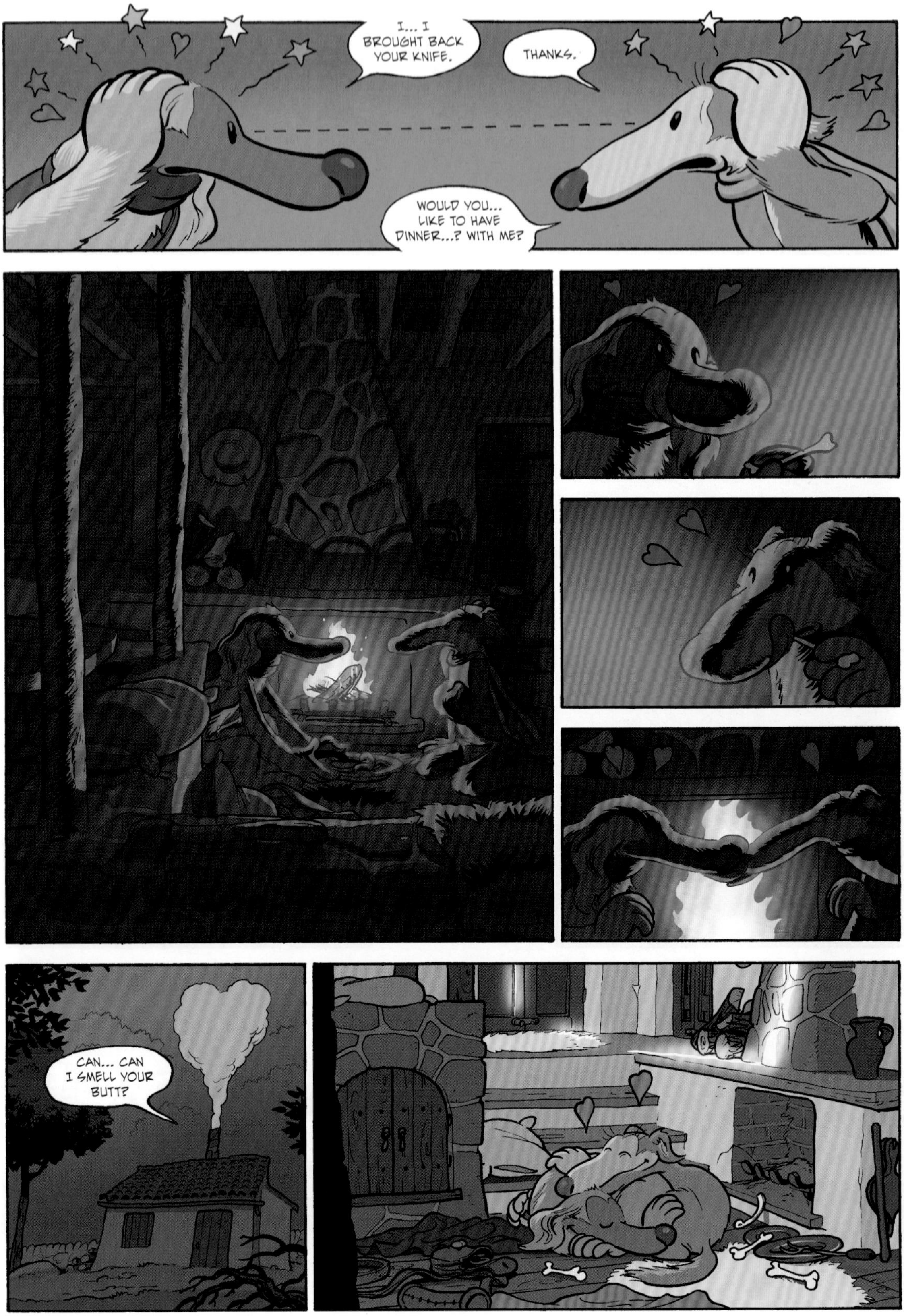
I... I BROUGHT BACK YOUR KNIFE.
THANKS.
WOULD YOU... LIKE TO HAVE DINNER...? WITH ME?
CAN... CAN I SMELL YOUR BUTT?

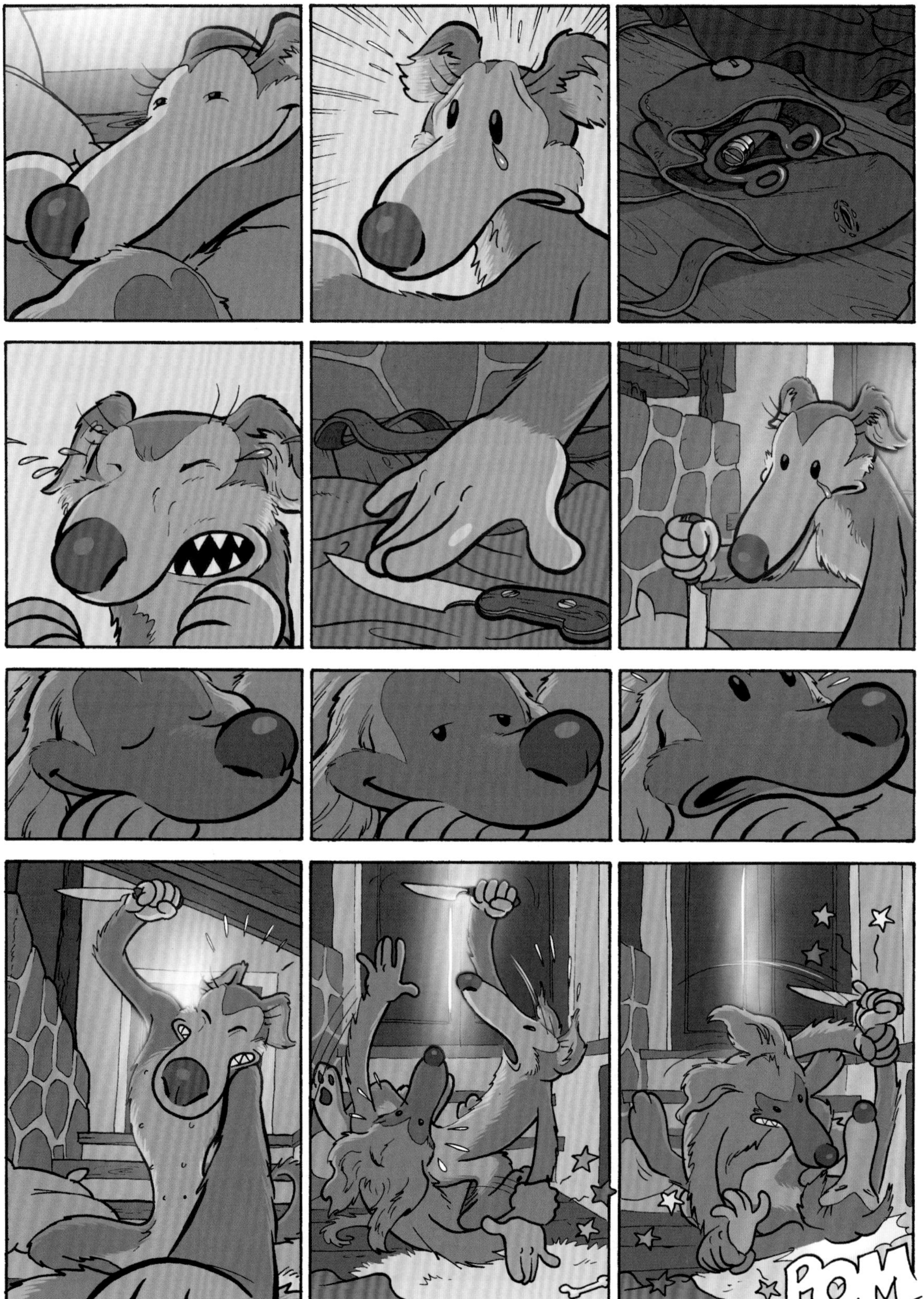
POM

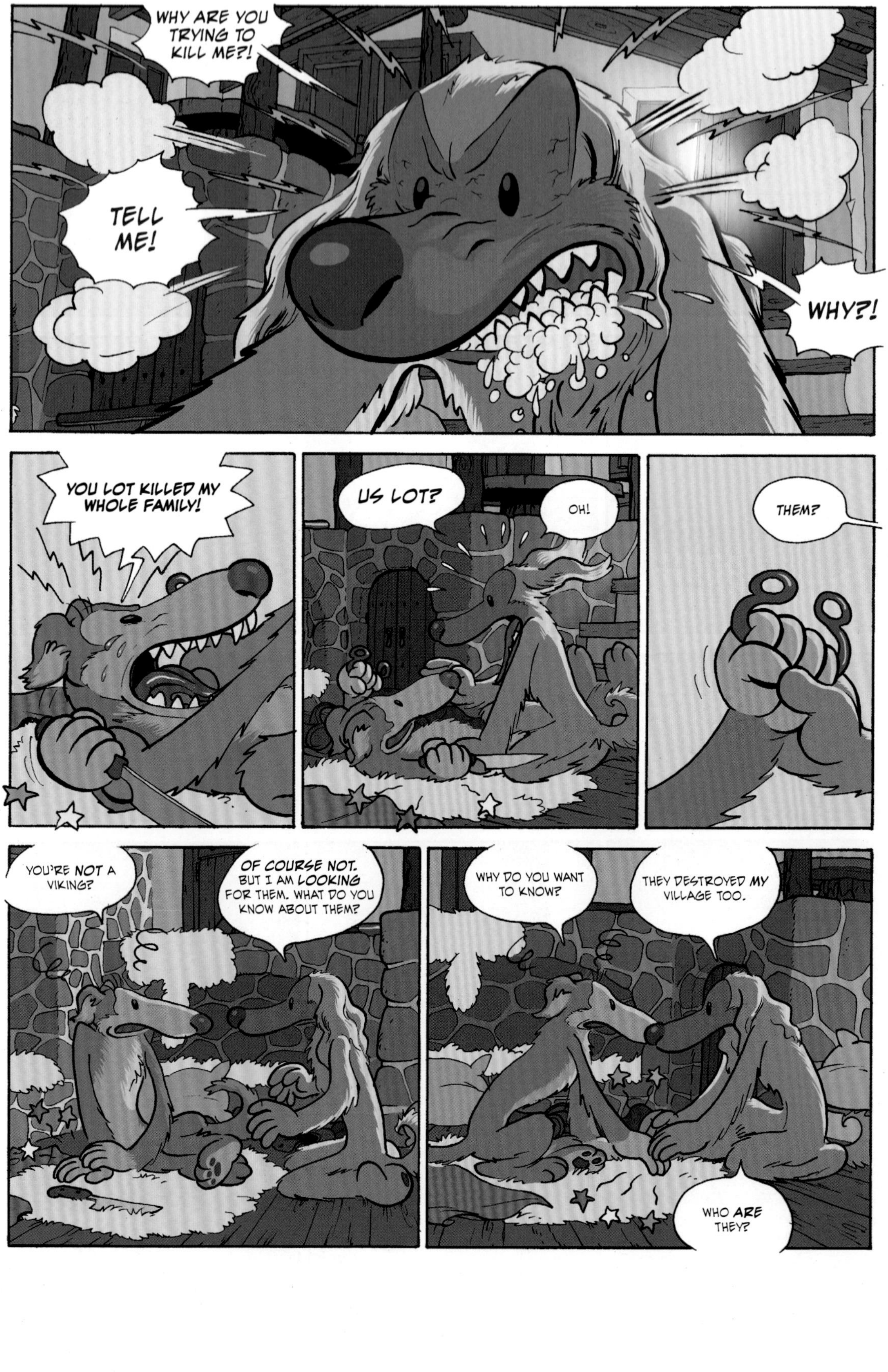

WHY ARE YOU TRYING TO KILL ME?!
TELL ME!
WHY?!
YOU LOT KILLED MY WHOLE FAMILY!
US LOT?
OH!
THEM?
YOU'RE NOT A VIKING?
OF COURSE NOT. BUT I AM LOOKING FOR THEM. WHAT DO YOU KNOW ABOUT THEM?
WHY DO YOU WANT TO KNOW?
THEY DESTROYED MY VILLAGE TOO.
WHO ARE THEY?

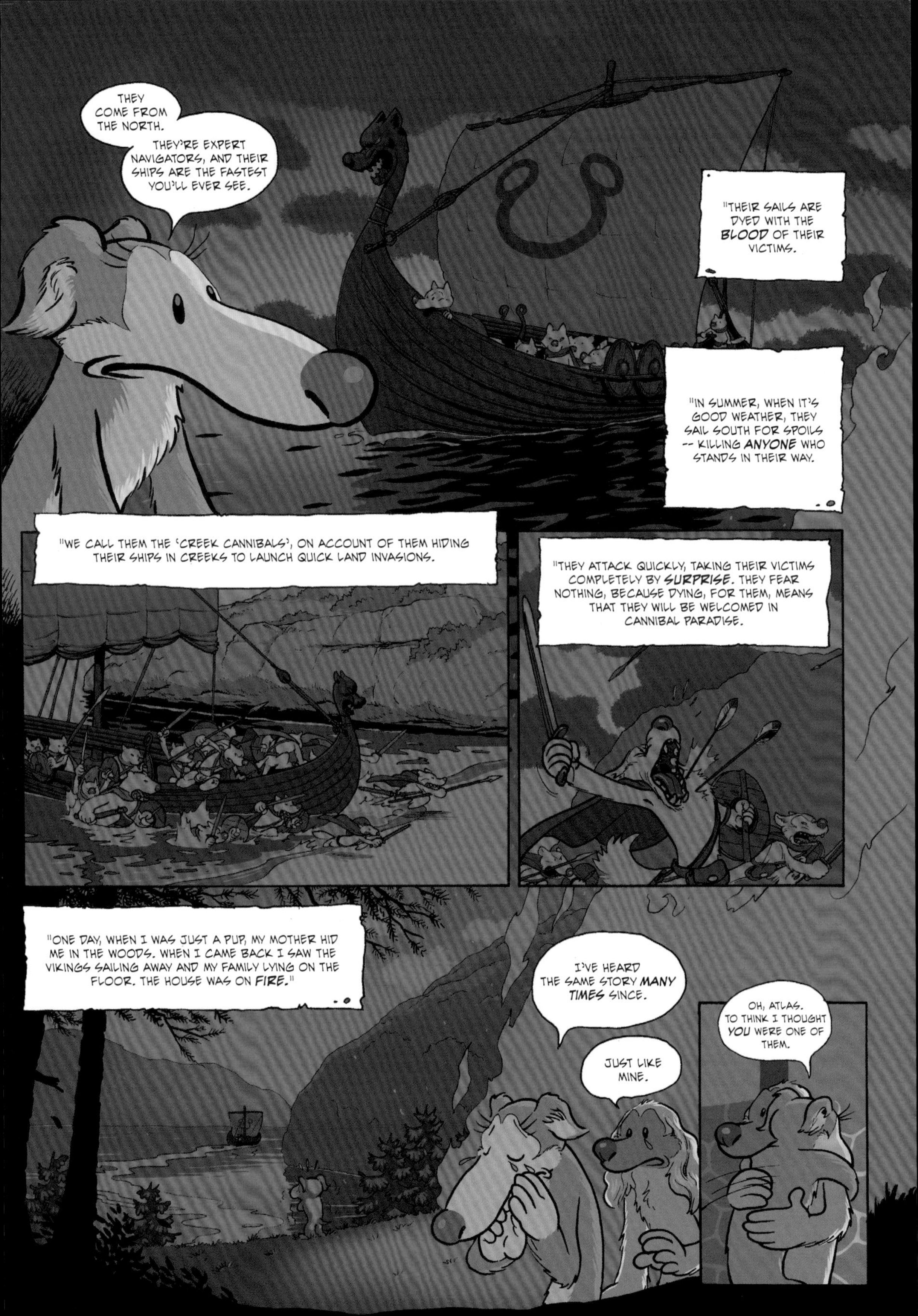
THEY COME FROM THE NORTH.
THEY'RE EXPERT NAVIGATORS, AND THEIR SHIPS ARE THE FASTEST YOU'LL EVER SEE.
"THEIR SAILS ARE DYED WITH THE BLOOD OF THEIR VICTIMS.
"IN SUMMER, WHEN IT'S GOOD WEATHER, THEY SAIL SOUTH FOR SPOILS -- KILLING ANYONE WHO STANDS IN THEIR WAY.
"WE CALL THEM THE 'CREEK CANNIBALS', ON ACCOUNT OF THEM HIDING THEIR SHIPS IN CREEKS TO LAUNCH QUICK LAND INVASIONS.
"THEY ATTACK QUICKLY, TAKING THEIR VICTIMS COMPLETELY BY SURPRISE. THEY FEAR NOTHING, BECAUSE DYING, FOR THEM, MEANS THAT THEY WILL BE WELCOMED IN CANNIBAL PARADISE.
"ONE DAY, WHEN I WAS JUST A PUP, MY MOTHER HID ME IN THE WOODS. WHEN I CAME BACK I SAW THE VIKINGS SAILING AWAY AND MY FAMILY LYING ON THE FLOOR. THE HOUSE WAS ON FIRE."
I'VE HEARD THE SAME STORY MANY TIMES SINCE.
JUST LIKE MINE.
OH, ATLAS. TO THINK I THOUGHT YOU WERE ONE OF THEM.

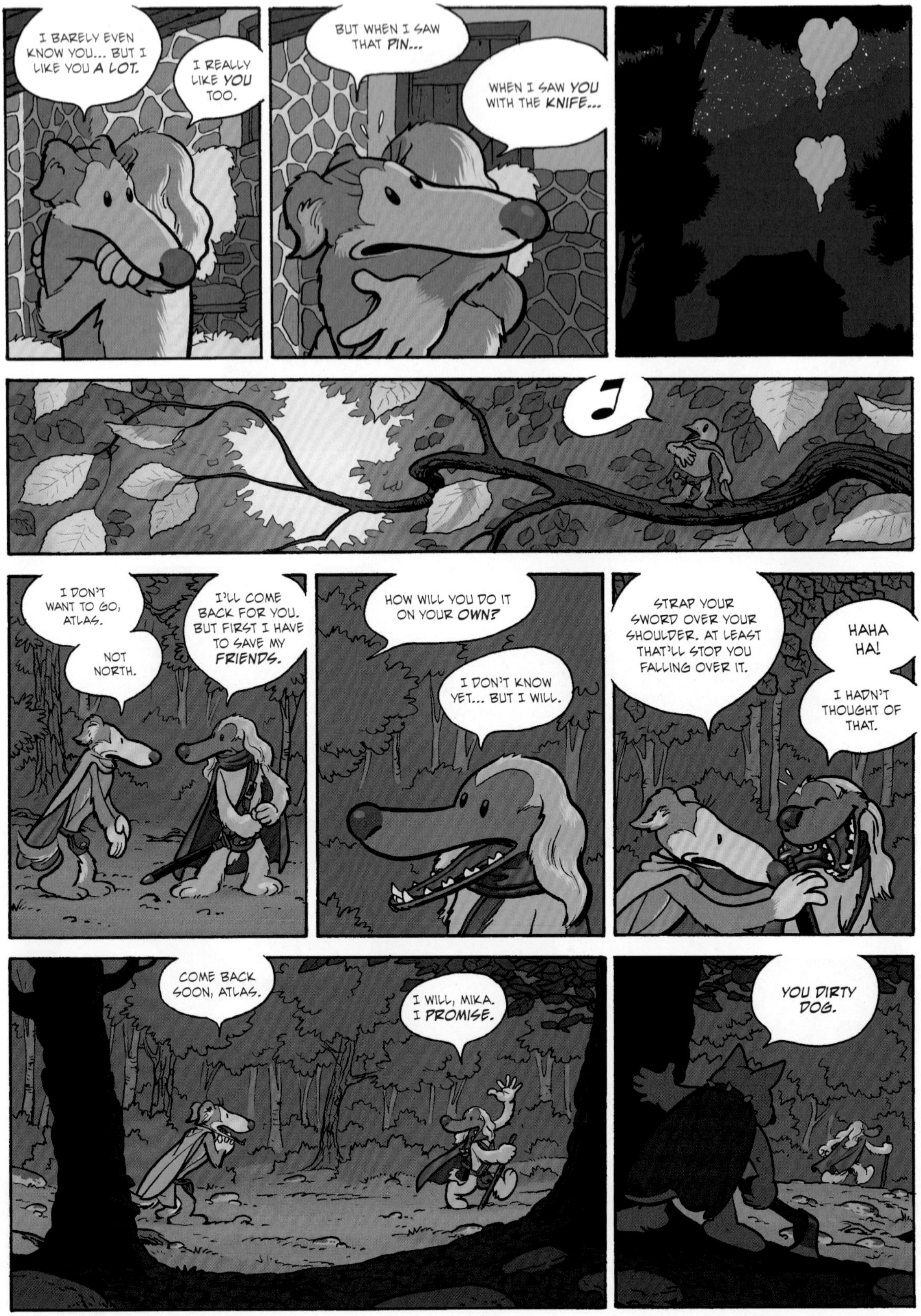
I BARELY EVEN KNOW YOU... BUT I LIKE YOU A LOT.
I REALLY LIKE YOU TOO.
BUT WHEN I SAW THAT PIN...
WHEN I SAW YOU WITH THE KNIFE...
♪
I DON'T WANT TO GO, ATLAS.
NOT NORTH.
I'LL COME BACK FOR YOU. BUT FIRST I HAVE TO SAVE MY FRIENDS.
HOW WILL YOU DO IT ON YOUR OWN?
I DON'T KNOW YET... BUT I WILL.
STRAP YOUR SWORD OVER YOUR SHOULDER. AT LEAST THAT'LL STOP YOU FALLING OVER IT.
HAHA HA!
I HADN'T THOUGHT OF THAT.
COME BACK SOON, ATLAS.
I WILL, MIKA. I PROMISE.
YOU DIRTY DOG.

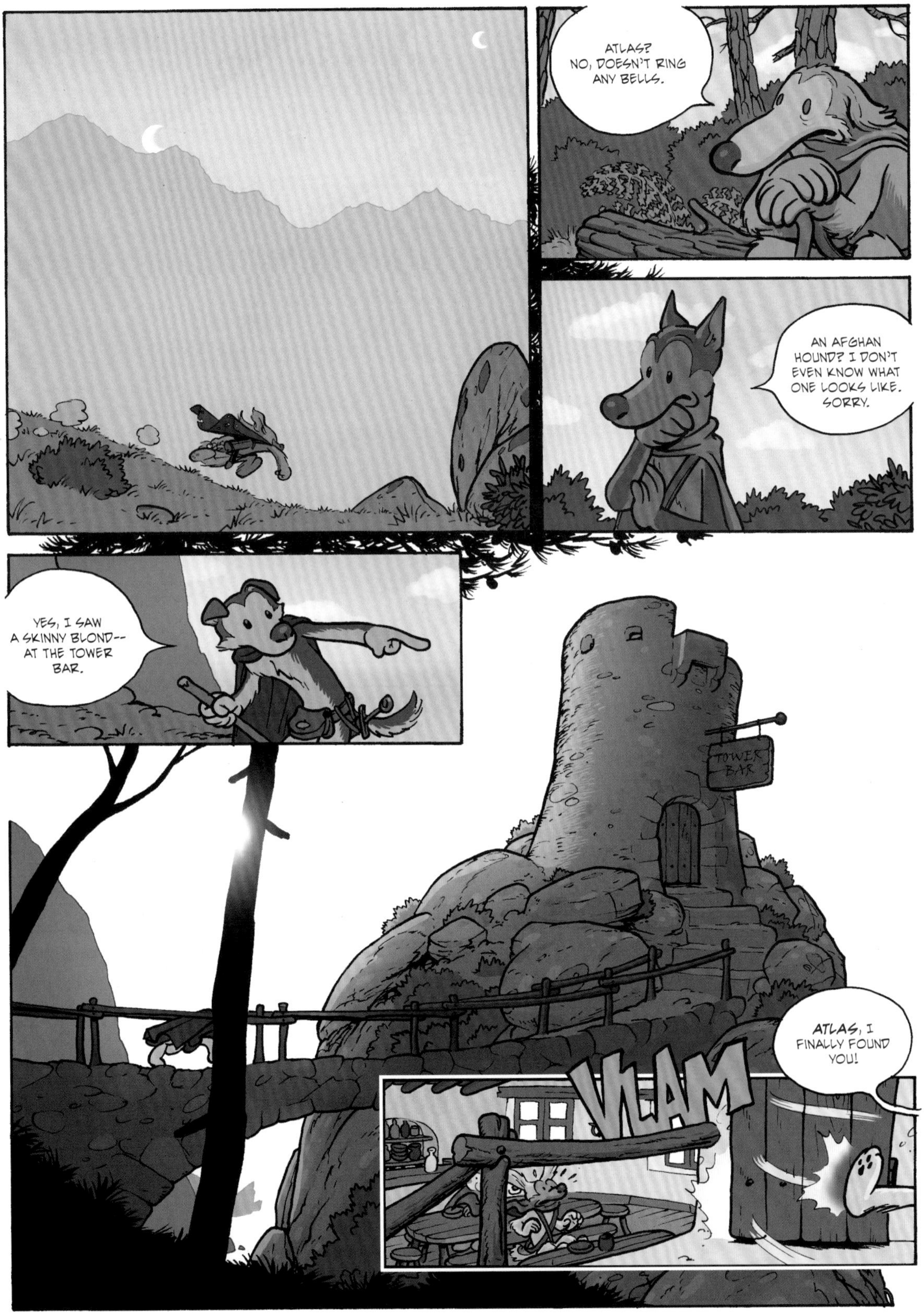
ATLAS?
NO, DOESN'T RING ANY BELLS.
AN AFGHAN HOUND? I DON'T EVEN KNOW WHAT ONE LOOKS LIKE. SORRY.
YES, I SAW A SKINNY BLOND-- AT THE TOWER BAR.
TOWER BAR
ATLAS, I FINALLY FOUND YOU!
VLAM

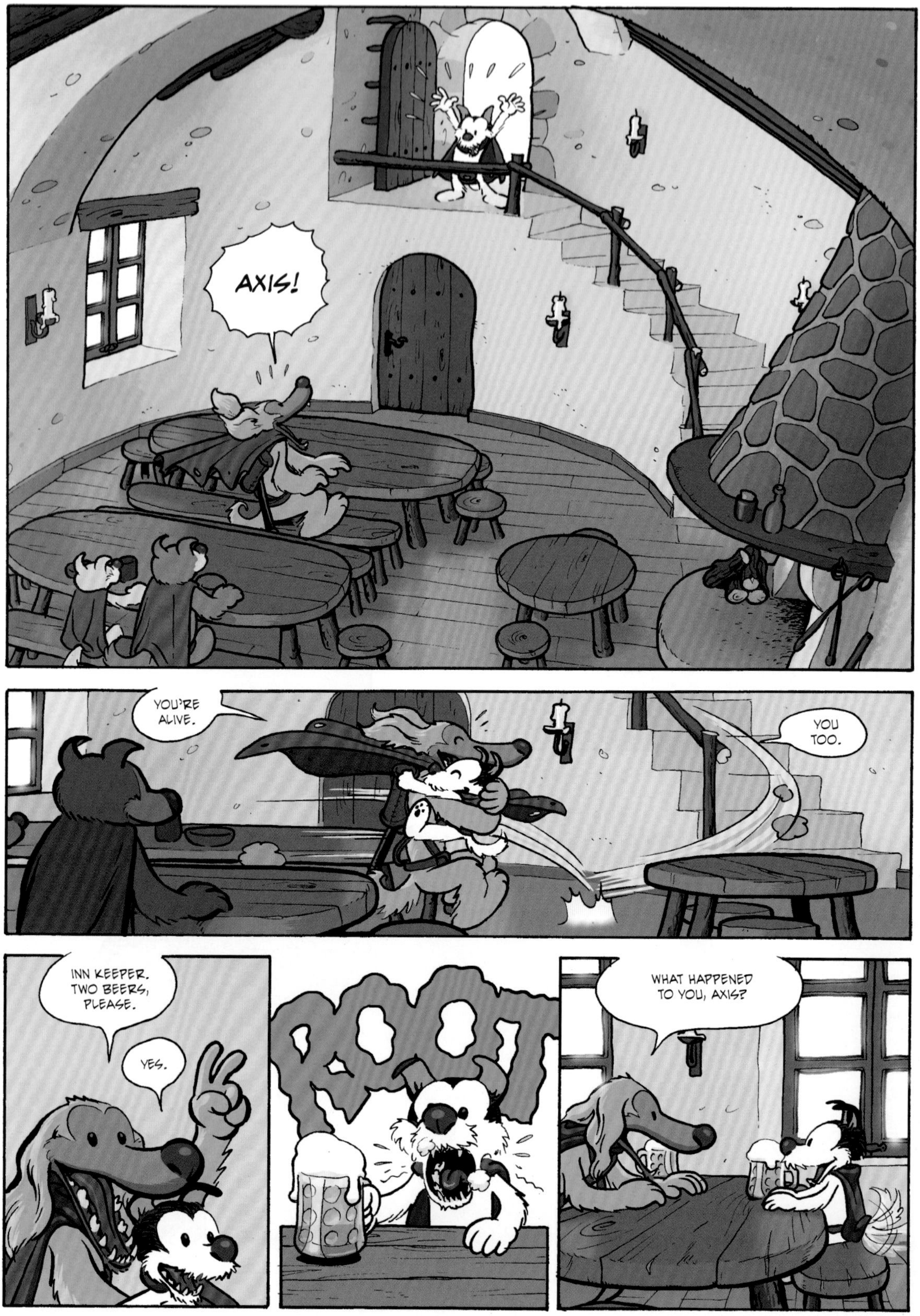
AXIS!
YOU'RE ALIVE.
YOU TOO.
INN KEEPER. TWO BEERS, PLEASE.
YES.
BOOT
WHAT HAPPENED TO YOU, AXIS?

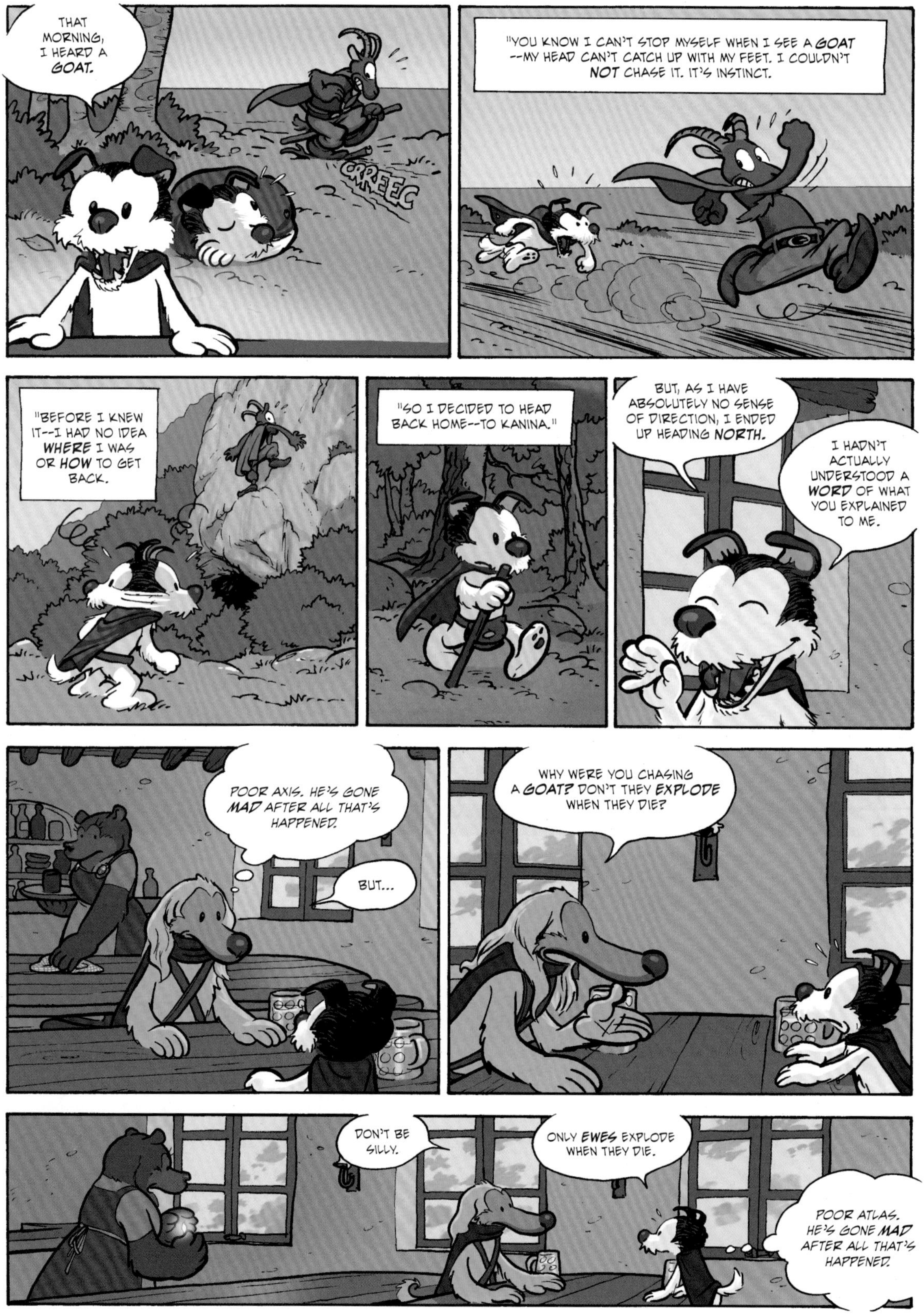
THAT MORNING, I HEARD A GOAT.
CRREEC
"YOU KNOW I CAN'T STOP MYSELF WHEN I SEE A GOAT --MY HEAD CAN'T CATCH UP WITH MY FEET. I COULDN'T NOT CHASE IT. IT'S INSTINCT.
"BEFORE I KNEW IT--I HAD NO IDEA WHERE I WAS OR HOW TO GET BACK.
"SO I DECIDED TO HEAD BACK HOME--TO KANINA."
BUT, AS I HAVE ABSOLUTELY NO SENSE OF DIRECTION, I ENDED UP HEADING NORTH.
I HADN'T ACTUALLY UNDERSTOOD A WORD OF WHAT YOU EXPLAINED TO ME.
POOR AXIS. HE'S GONE MAD AFTER ALL THAT'S HAPPENED.
BUT...
WHY WERE YOU CHASING A GOAT? DON'T THEY EXPLODE WHEN THEY DIE?
DON'T BE SILLY.
ONLY EWES EXPLODE WHEN THEY DIE.
POOR ATLAS. HE'S GONE MAD AFTER ALL THAT'S HAPPENED.

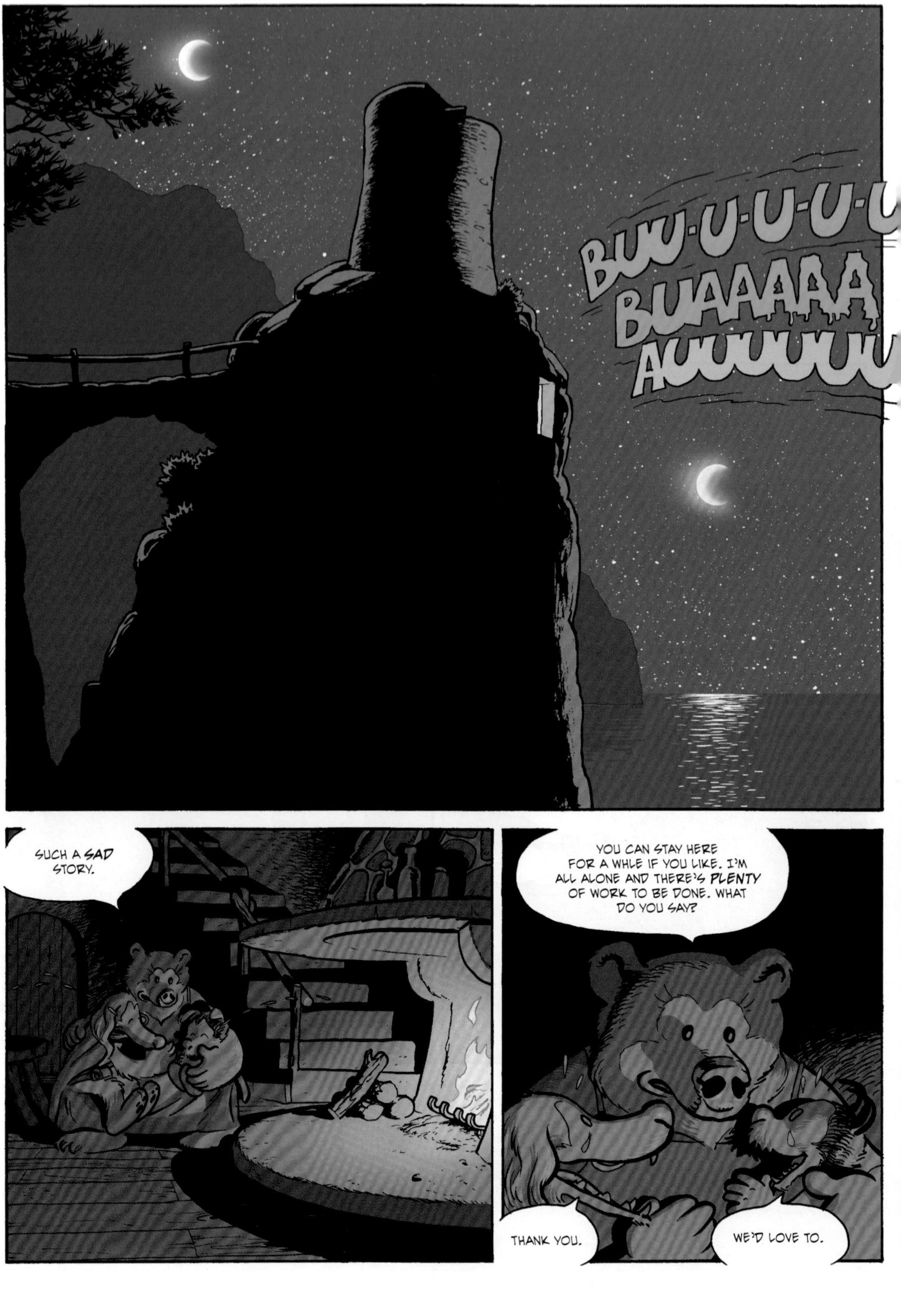
BUU-U-U-U-U
BUAAAAA
AUUUUUU
SUCH A SAD STORY.
YOU CAN STAY HERE FOR A WHLE IF YOU LIKE. I'M ALL ALONE AND THERE'S PLENTY OF WORK TO BE DONE. WHAT DO YOU SAY?
THANK YOU.
WE'D LOVE TO.

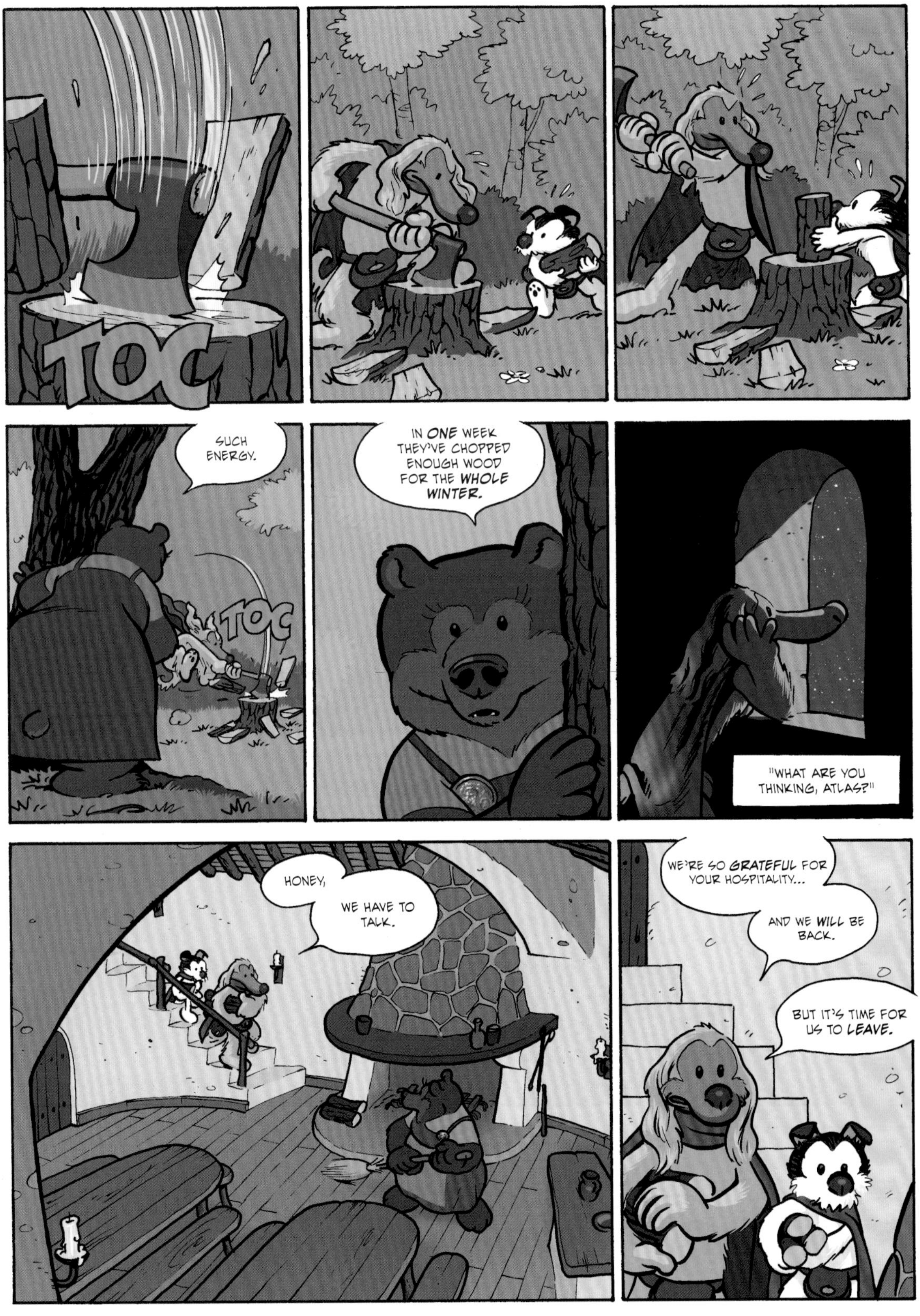
TOC
SUCH ENERGY.
TOC
IN ONE WEEK THEY'VE CHOPPED ENOUGH WOOD FOR THE WHOLE WINTER.
"WHAT ARE YOU THINKING, ATLAS?"
HONEY,
WE HAVE TO TALK.
WE'RE SO GRATEFUL FOR YOUR HOSPITALITY...
AND WE WILL BE BACK.
BUT IT'S TIME FOR US TO LEAVE.

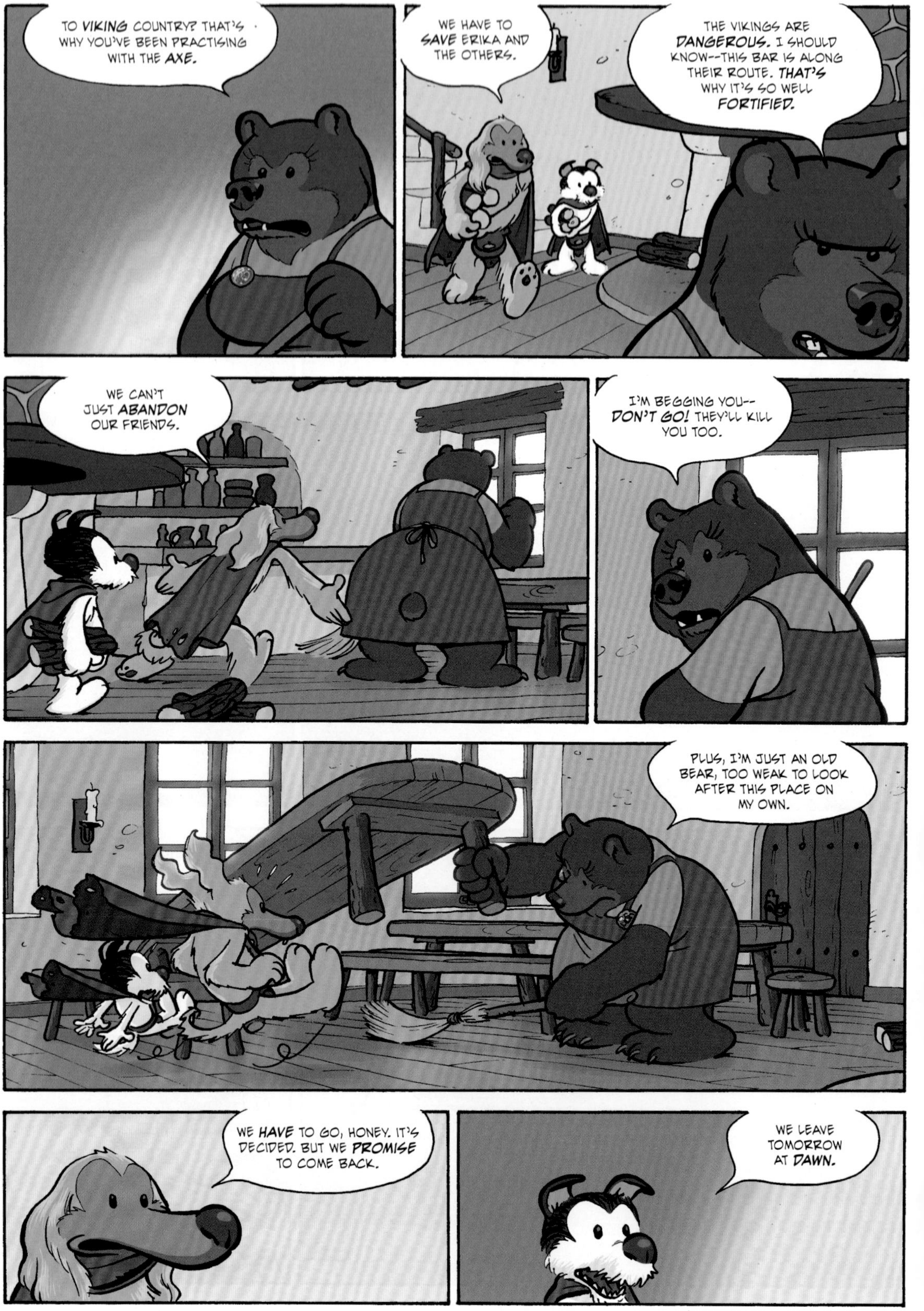
TO VIKING COUNTRY? THAT'S WHY YOU'VE BEEN PRACTISING WITH THE AXE.
WE HAVE TO SAVE ERIKA AND THE OTHERS.
THE VIKINGS ARE DANGEROUS. I SHOULD KNOW--THIS BAR IS ALONG THEIR ROUTE. THAT'S WHY IT'S SO WELL FORTIFIED.
WE CAN'T JUST ABANDON OUR FRIENDS.
I'M BEGGING YOU-- DON'T GO! THEY'LL KILL YOU TOO.
PLUS, I'M JUST AN OLD BEAR, TOO WEAK TO LOOK AFTER THIS PLACE ON MY OWN.
WE HAVE TO GO, HONEY. IT'S DECIDED. BUT WE PROMISE TO COME BACK.
WE LEAVE TOMORROW AT DAWN.

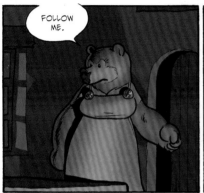

FOLLOW ME.

THIS IS A VERY **LONG** STAIRCASE.

MY HEAD'S SPINNING.

IT GOES RIGHT DOWN TO THE SEA.

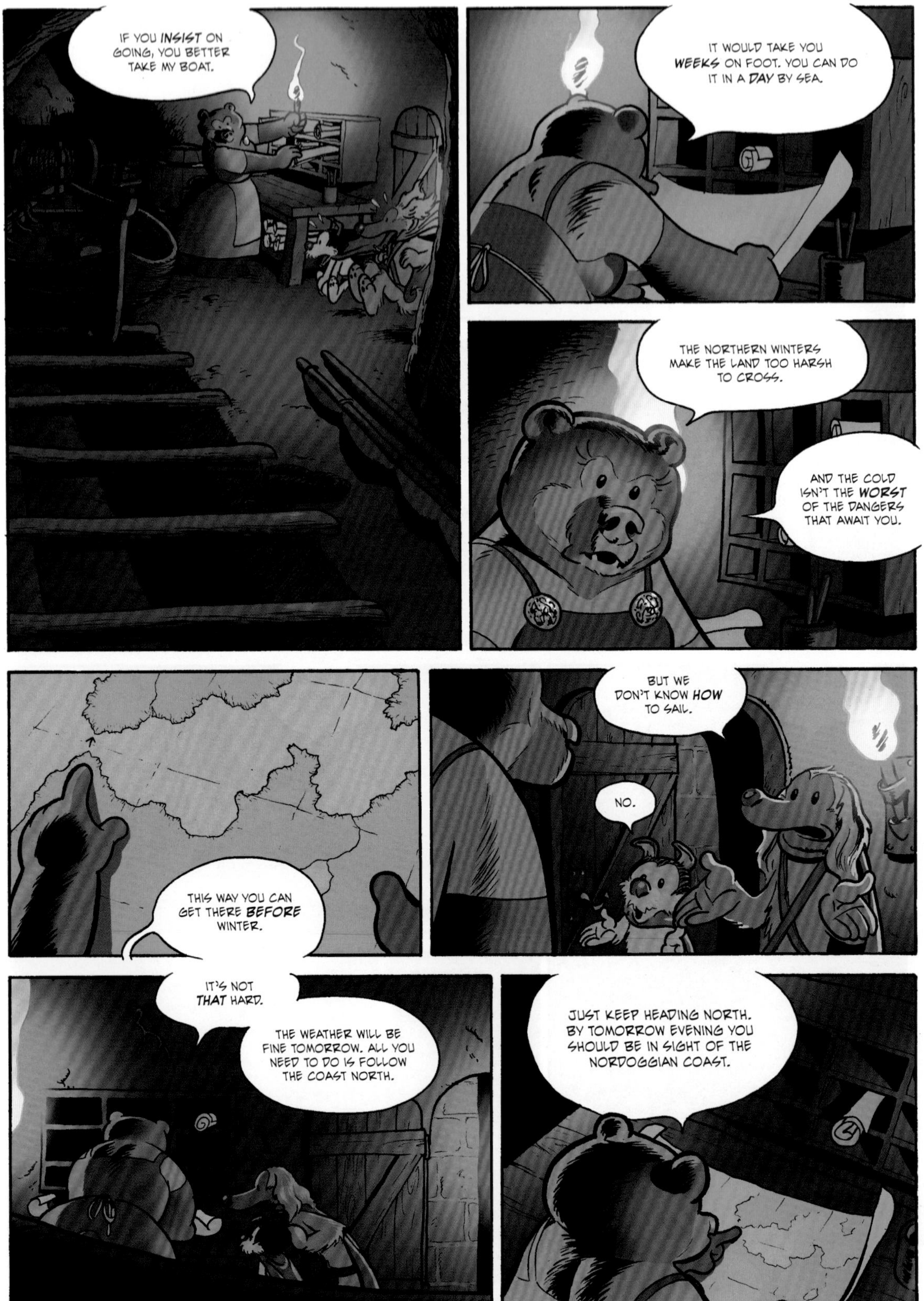
IF YOU INSIST ON GOING, YOU BETTER TAKE MY BOAT.
IT WOULD TAKE YOU WEEKS ON FOOT. YOU CAN DO IT IN A DAY BY SEA.
THE NORTHERN WINTERS MAKE THE LAND TOO HARSH TO CROSS.
AND THE COLD ISN'T THE WORST OF THE DANGERS THAT AWAIT YOU.
THIS WAY YOU CAN GET THERE BEFORE WINTER.
BUT WE DON'T KNOW HOW TO SAIL.
NO.
IT'S NOT THAT HARD.
THE WEATHER WILL BE FINE TOMORROW. ALL YOU NEED TO DO IS FOLLOW THE COAST NORTH.
JUST KEEP HEADING NORTH. BY TOMORROW EVENING YOU SHOULD BE IN SIGHT OF THE NORDOGGIAN COAST.

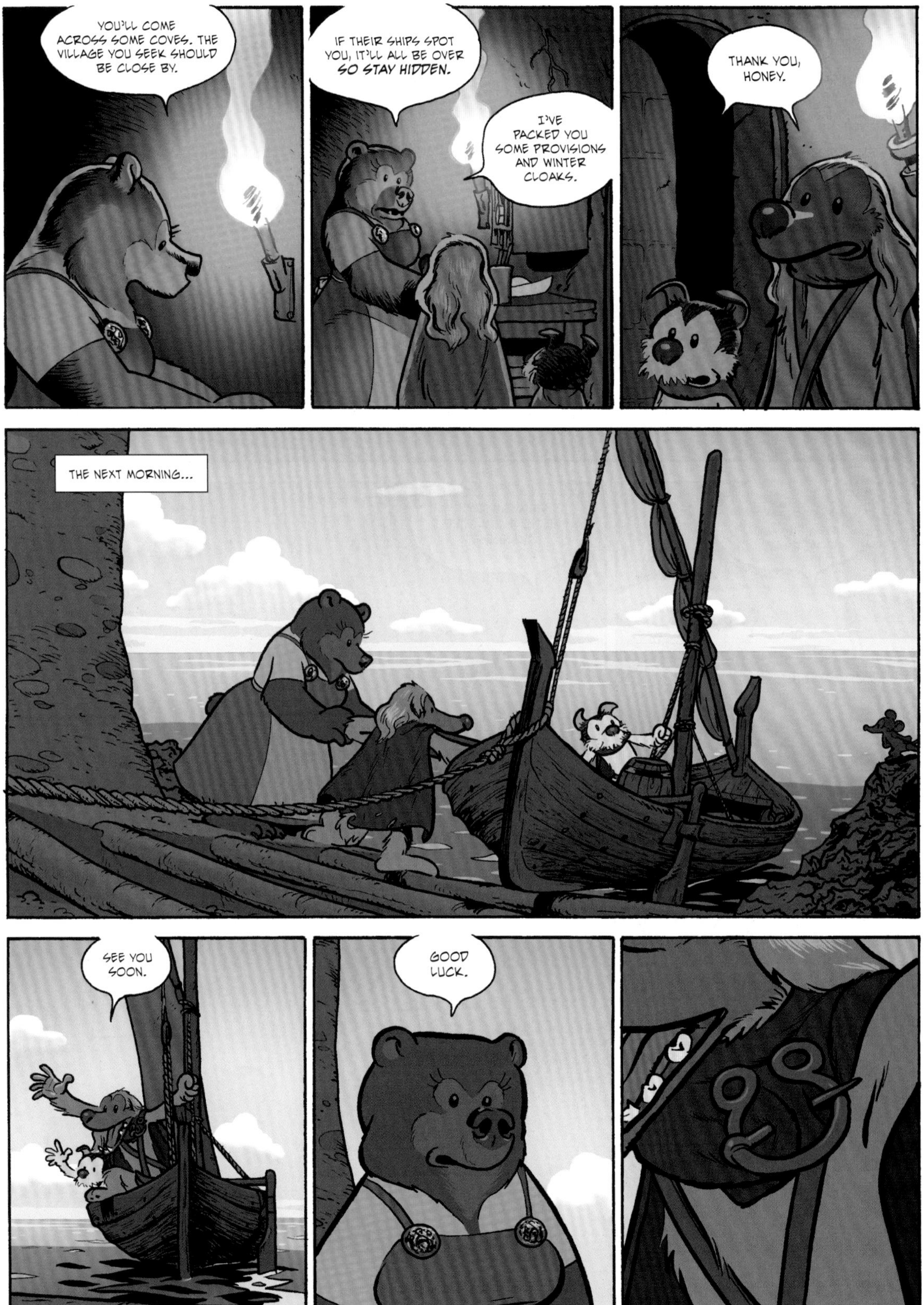
YOU'LL COME ACROSS SOME COVES. THE VILLAGE YOU SEEK SHOULD BE CLOSE BY.
IF THEIR SHIPS SPOT YOU, IT'LL ALL BE OVER **SO STAY HIDDEN.**
I'VE PACKED YOU SOME PROVISIONS AND WINTER CLOAKS.
THANK YOU, HONEY.
THE NEXT MORNING...
SEE YOU SOON.
GOOD LUCK.

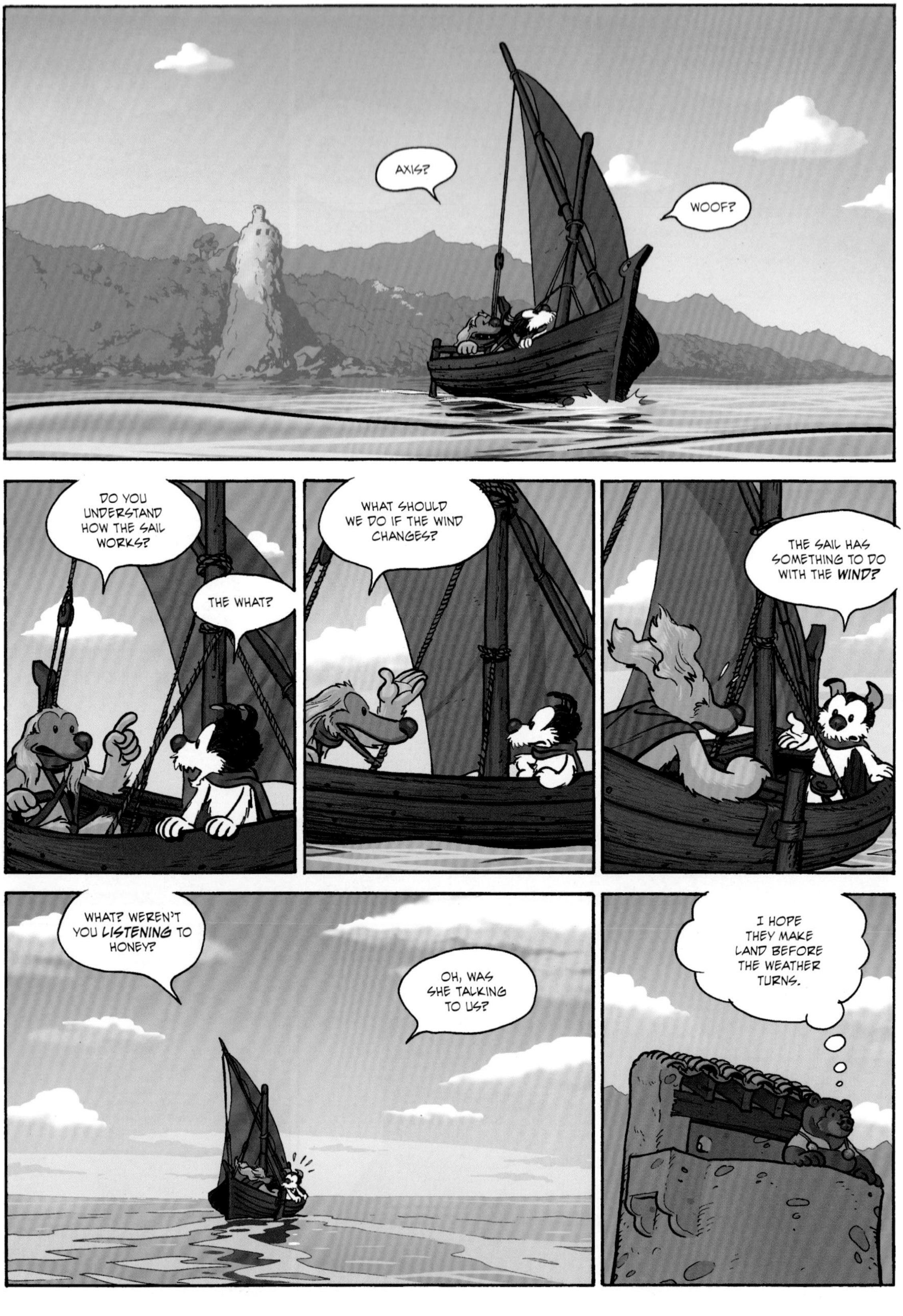
AXIS?
WOOF?
DO YOU UNDERSTAND HOW THE SAIL WORKS?
THE WHAT?
WHAT SHOULD WE DO IF THE WIND CHANGES?
THE SAIL HAS SOMETHING TO DO WITH THE **WIND?**
WHAT? WEREN'T YOU **LISTENING** TO HONEY?
OH, WAS SHE TALKING TO US?
I HOPE THEY MAKE LAND BEFORE THE WEATHER TURNS.

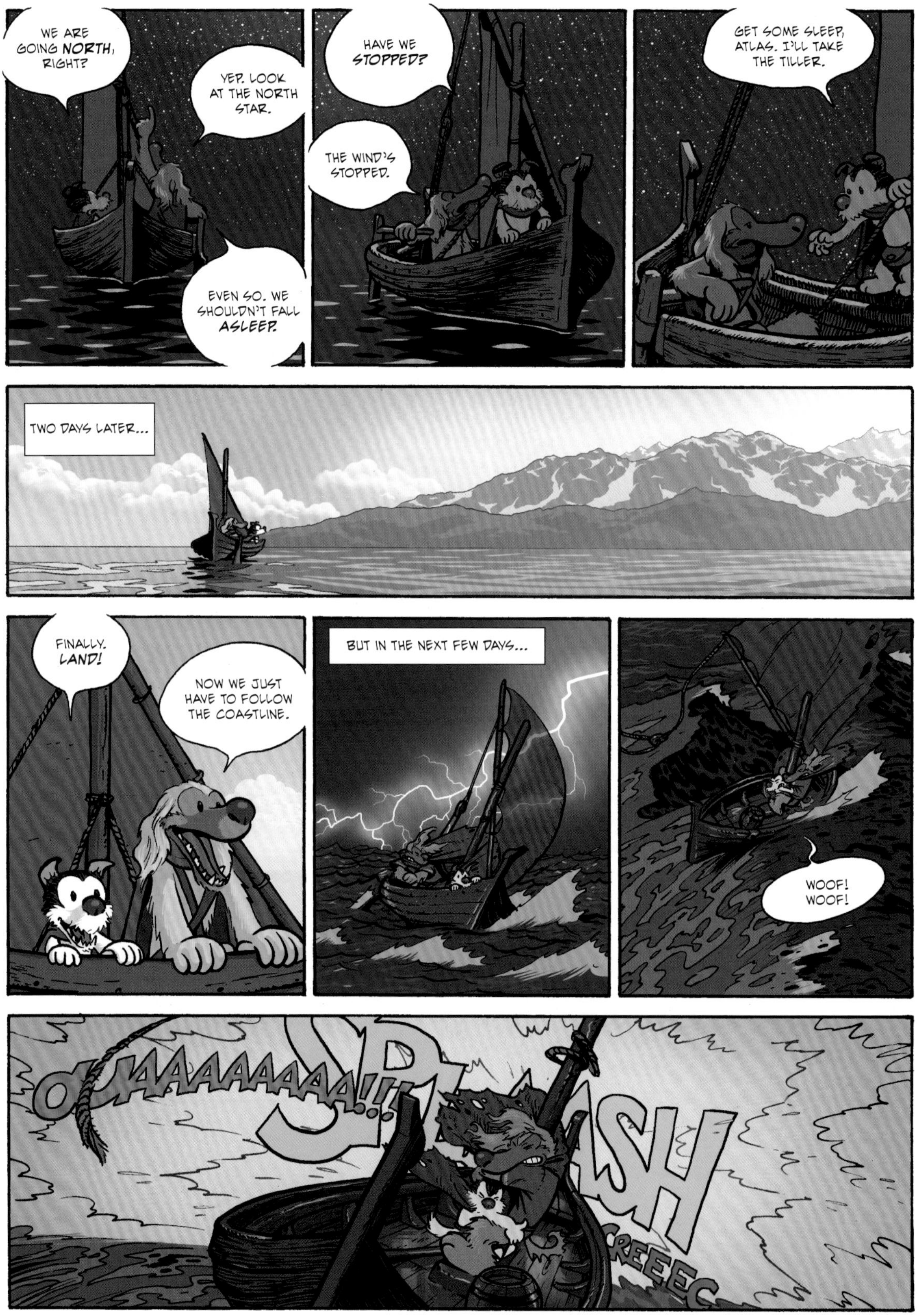
WE ARE GOING NORTH, RIGHT?
YEP. LOOK AT THE NORTH STAR.
EVEN SO. WE SHOULDN'T FALL ASLEEP.
HAVE WE STOPPED?
THE WIND'S STOPPED.
GET SOME SLEEP, ATLAS. I'LL TAKE THE TILLER.
TWO DAYS LATER...
FINALLY. LAND!
NOW WE JUST HAVE TO FOLLOW THE COASTLINE.
BUT IN THE NEXT FEW DAYS...
WOOF! WOOF!
OUAAAAAAAAA!!!
SPLASH
CREEEC

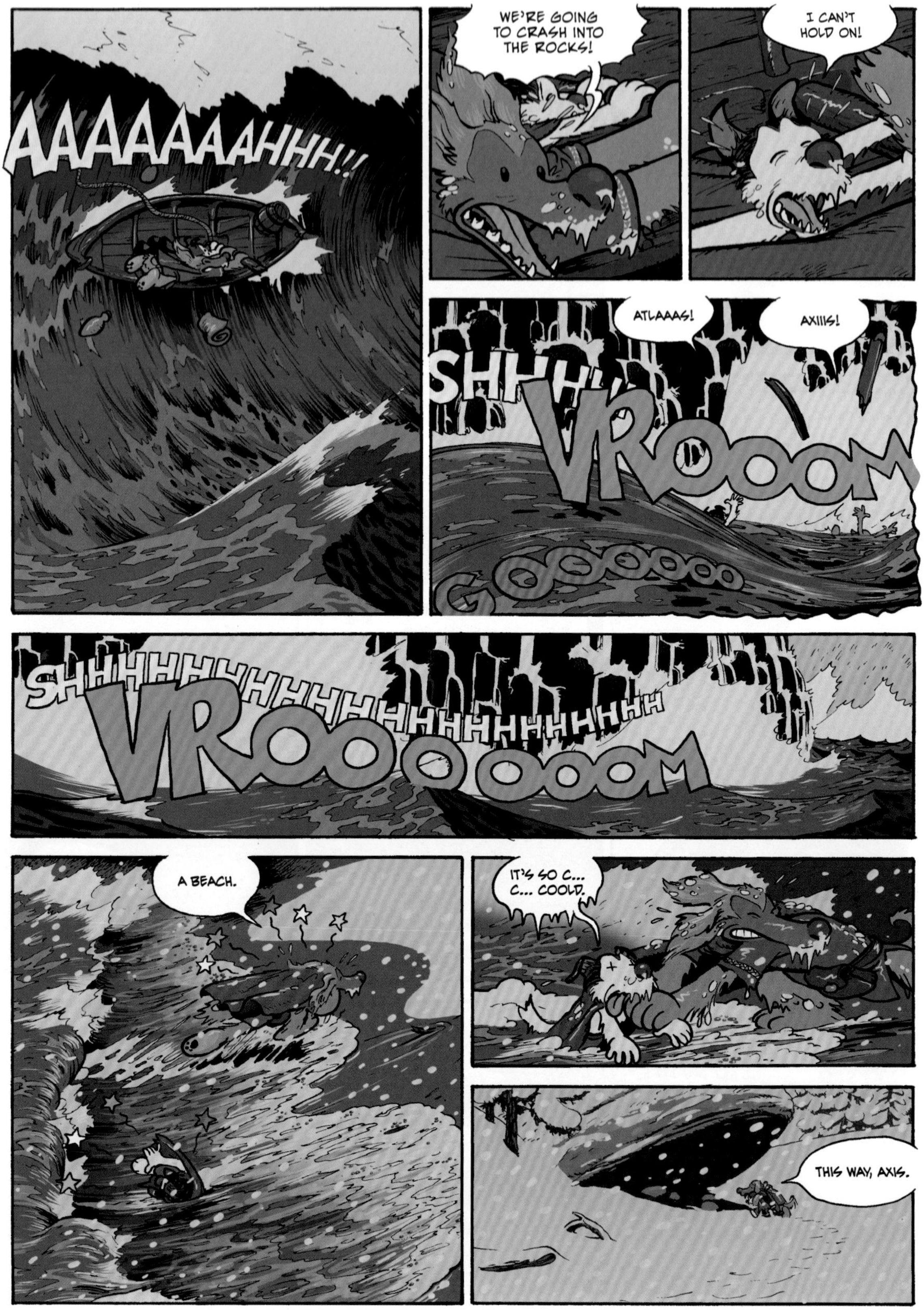
AAAAAAAHHH!!
WE'RE GOING TO CRASH INTO THE ROCKS!
I CAN'T HOLD ON!
ATLAAAS!
AXIIIS!
SHH'H
VROOOM
GOOOOOO
SHHHHHHHHHHHHHHHHHHHHHHH
VROOOOOOM
A BEACH.
IT'S SO C... C... COOLD.
THIS WAY, AXIS.

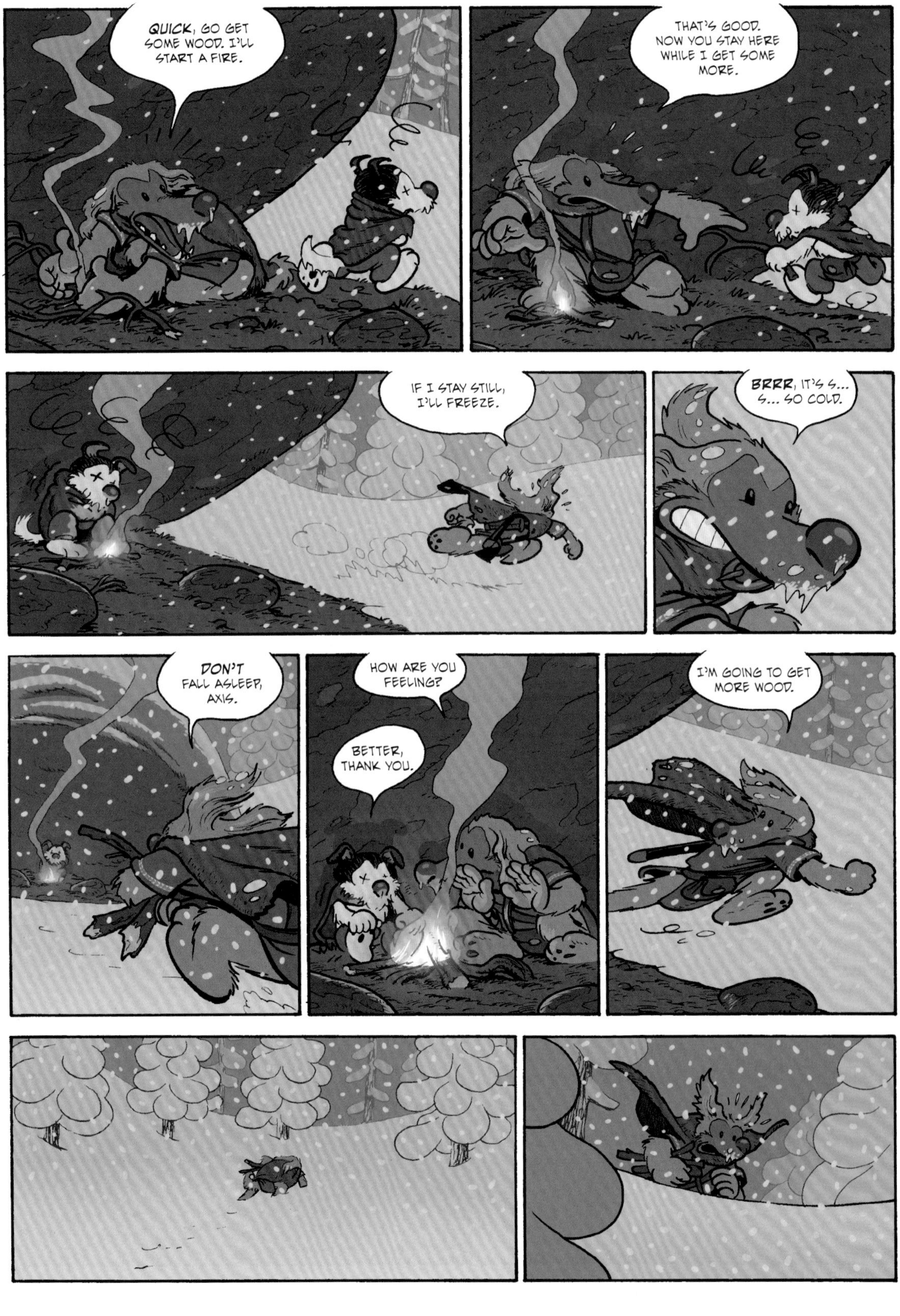

QUICK, GO GET SOME WOOD. I'LL START A FIRE.
THAT'S GOOD. NOW YOU STAY HERE WHILE I GET SOME MORE.
IF I STAY STILL, I'LL FREEZE.
BRRR, IT'S S... S... SO COLD.
DON'T FALL ASLEEP, AXIS.
HOW ARE YOU FEELING?
BETTER, THANK YOU.
I'M GOING TO GET MORE WOOD.

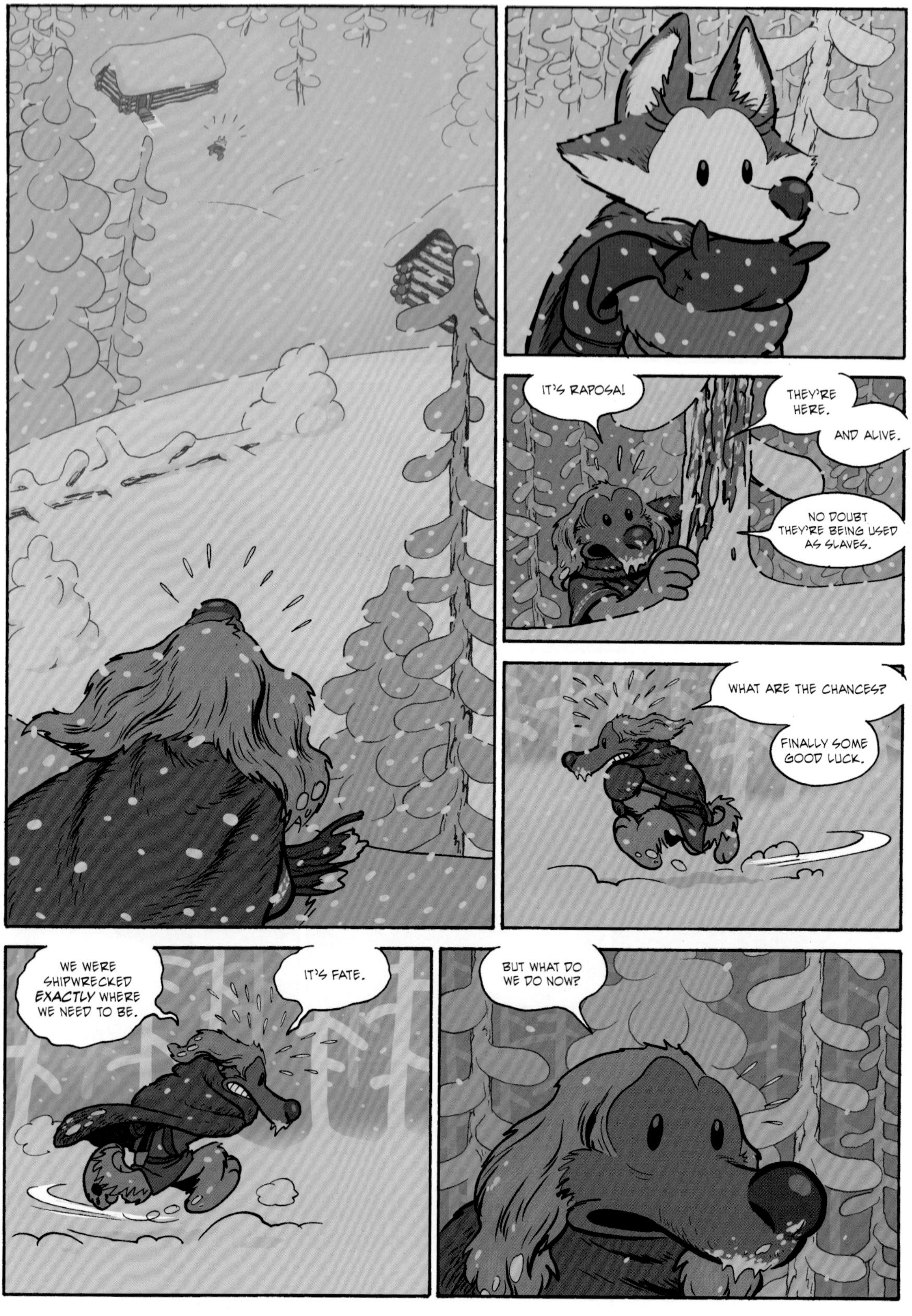
IT'S RAPOSA!
THEY'RE HERE.
AND ALIVE.
NO DOUBT THEY'RE BEING USED AS SLAVES.
WHAT ARE THE CHANCES?
FINALLY SOME GOOD LUCK.
WE WERE SHIPWRECKED *EXACTLY* WHERE WE NEED TO BE.
IT'S FATE.
BUT WHAT DO WE DO NOW?

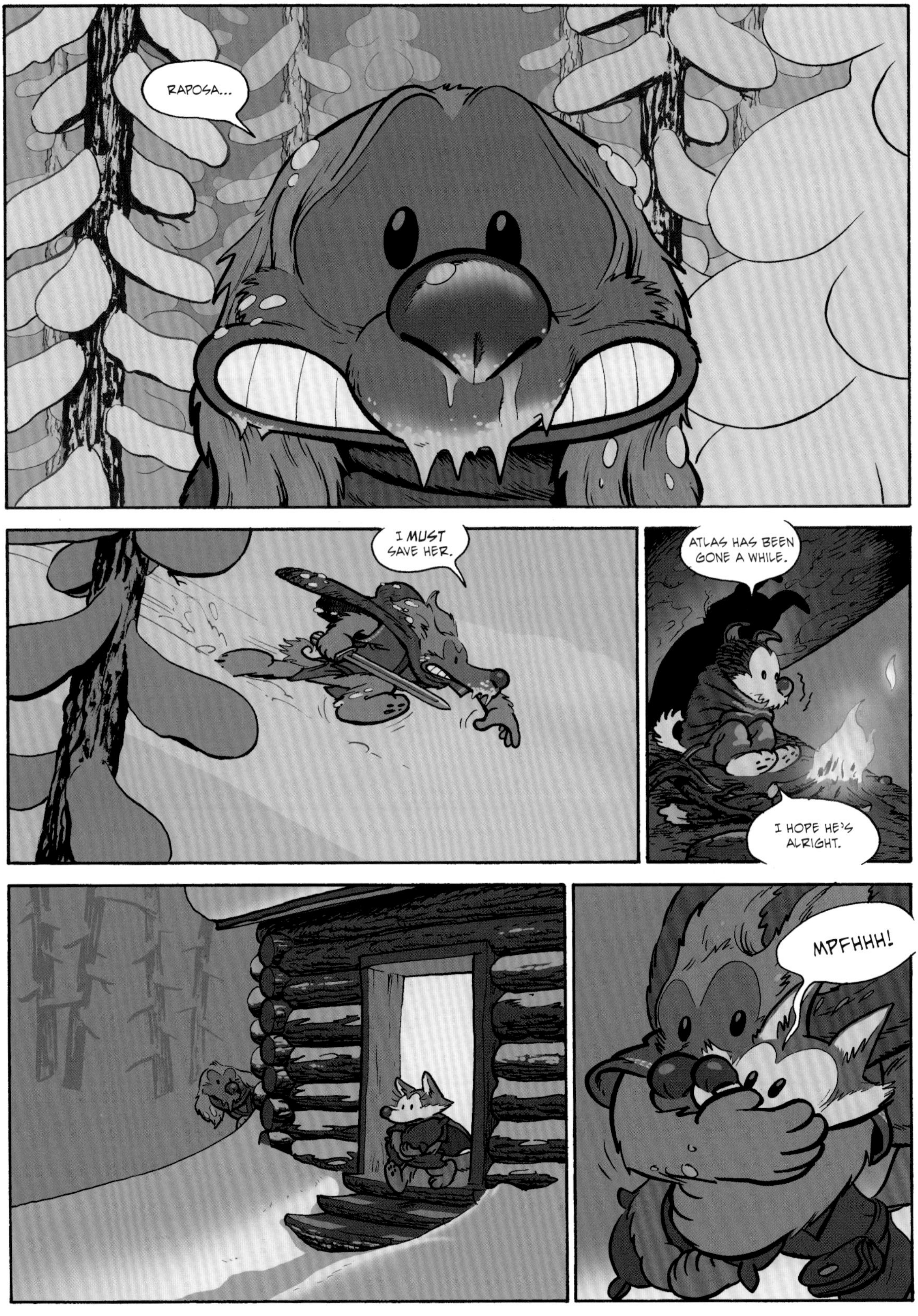
RAPOSA...
I MUST SAVE HER.
ATLAS HAS BEEN GONE A WHILE.
I HOPE HE'S ALRIGHT.
MPFHHH!

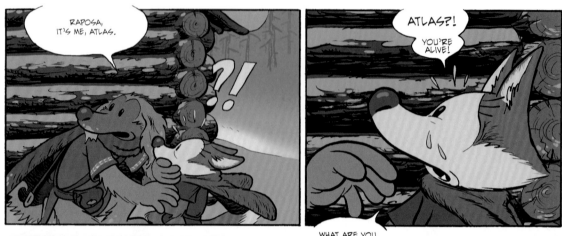

RAPOSA, IT'S ME, ATLAS.

?!

ATLAS?! YOU'RE ALIVE!

WHAT ARE YOU DOING HERE? IT'S DANGEROUS.

WE'RE HERE TO SAVE YOU. WHERE ARE ERIKA AND THE OTHERS?

HOW... HOW MANY OF YOU ARE THERE?

JUST ME AND AXIS. HE'S ON THE BEACH.

GO BACK AND ACT LIKE YOU NEVER SAW ME.

WE WILL SAVE YOU.

WHERE'S ERIKA?

SHE... SHE'S IN THAT CABIN OVER THERE.

ATLAS AND AXIS...

THEY'RE ALIVE!

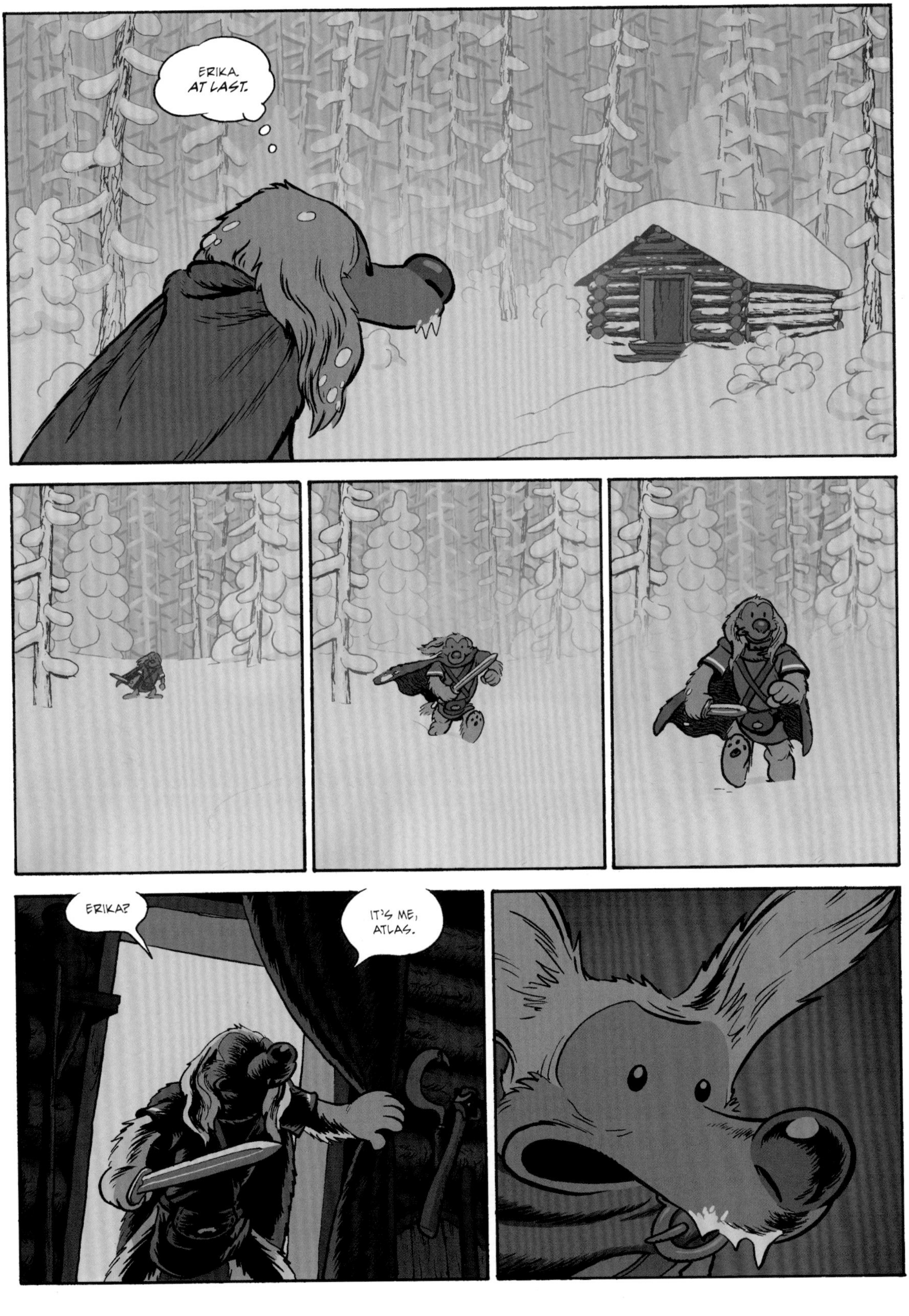
ERIKA.
AT LAST.
ERIKA?
IT'S ME, ATLAS.

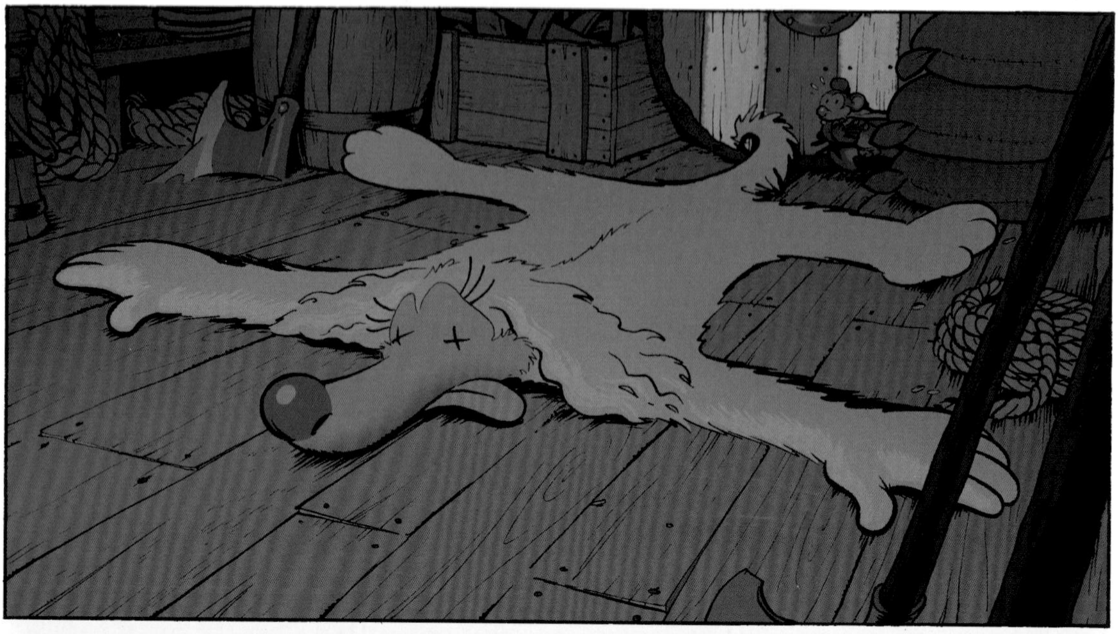

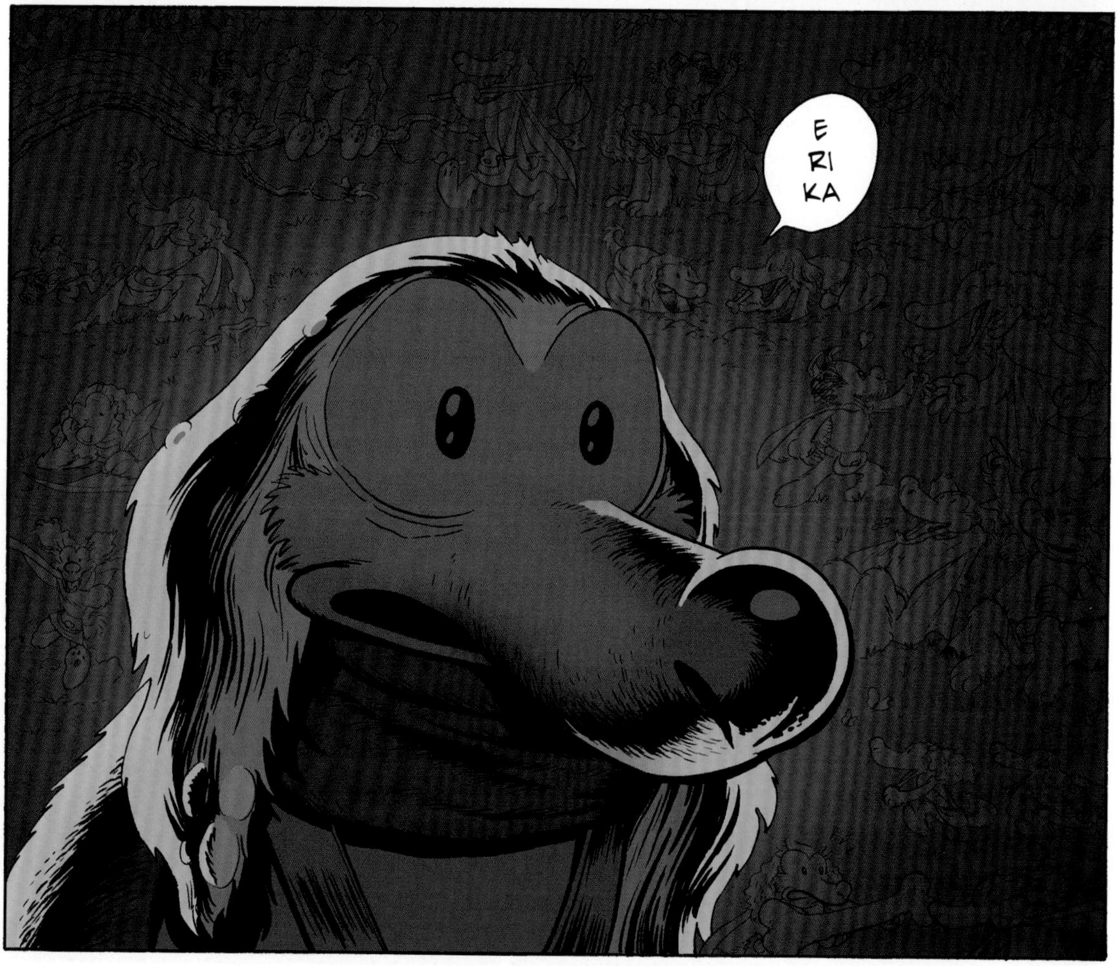
E RI KA

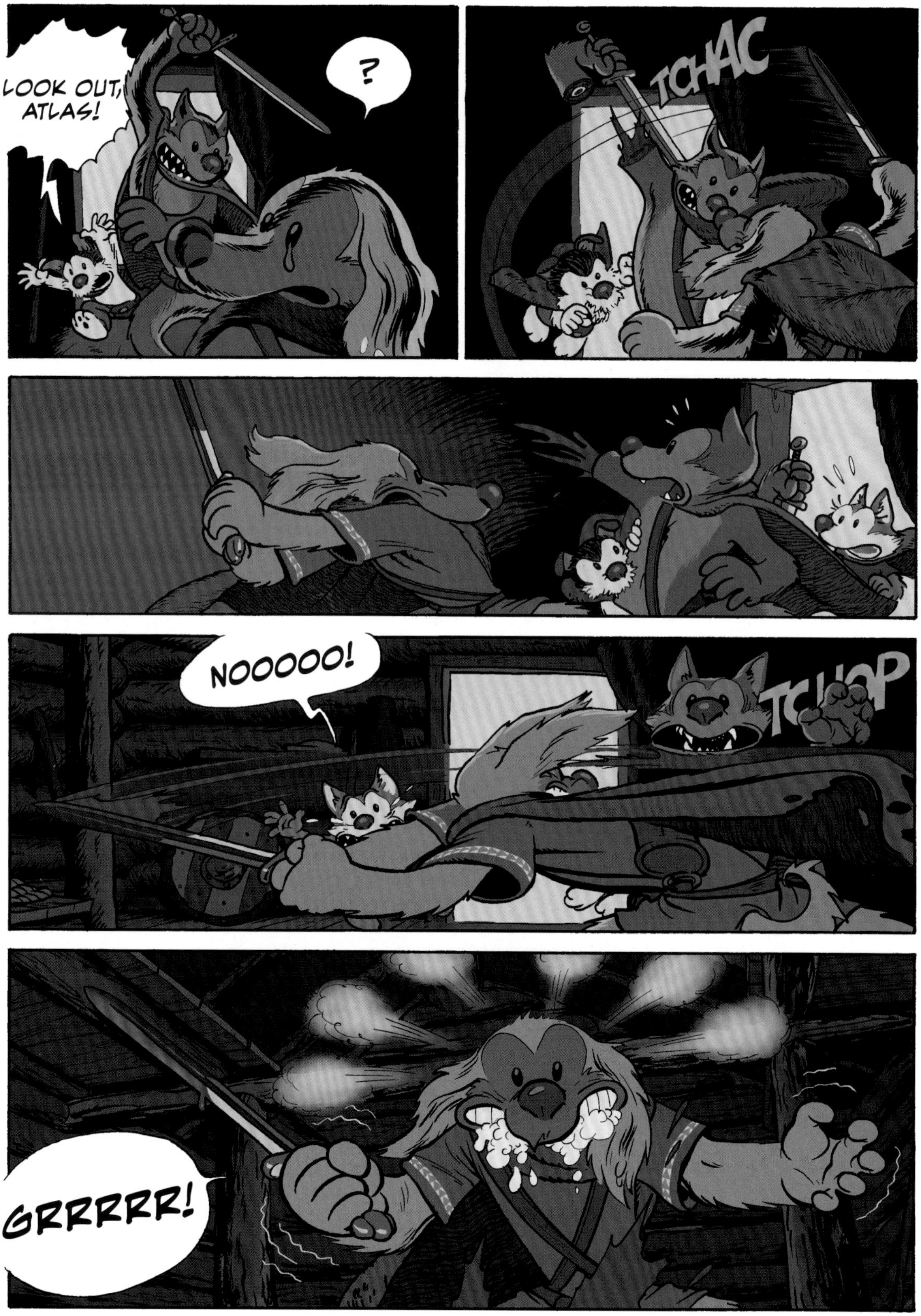
LOOK OUT, ATLAS!
?
TCHAC
NOOOOO!
GRRRRR!

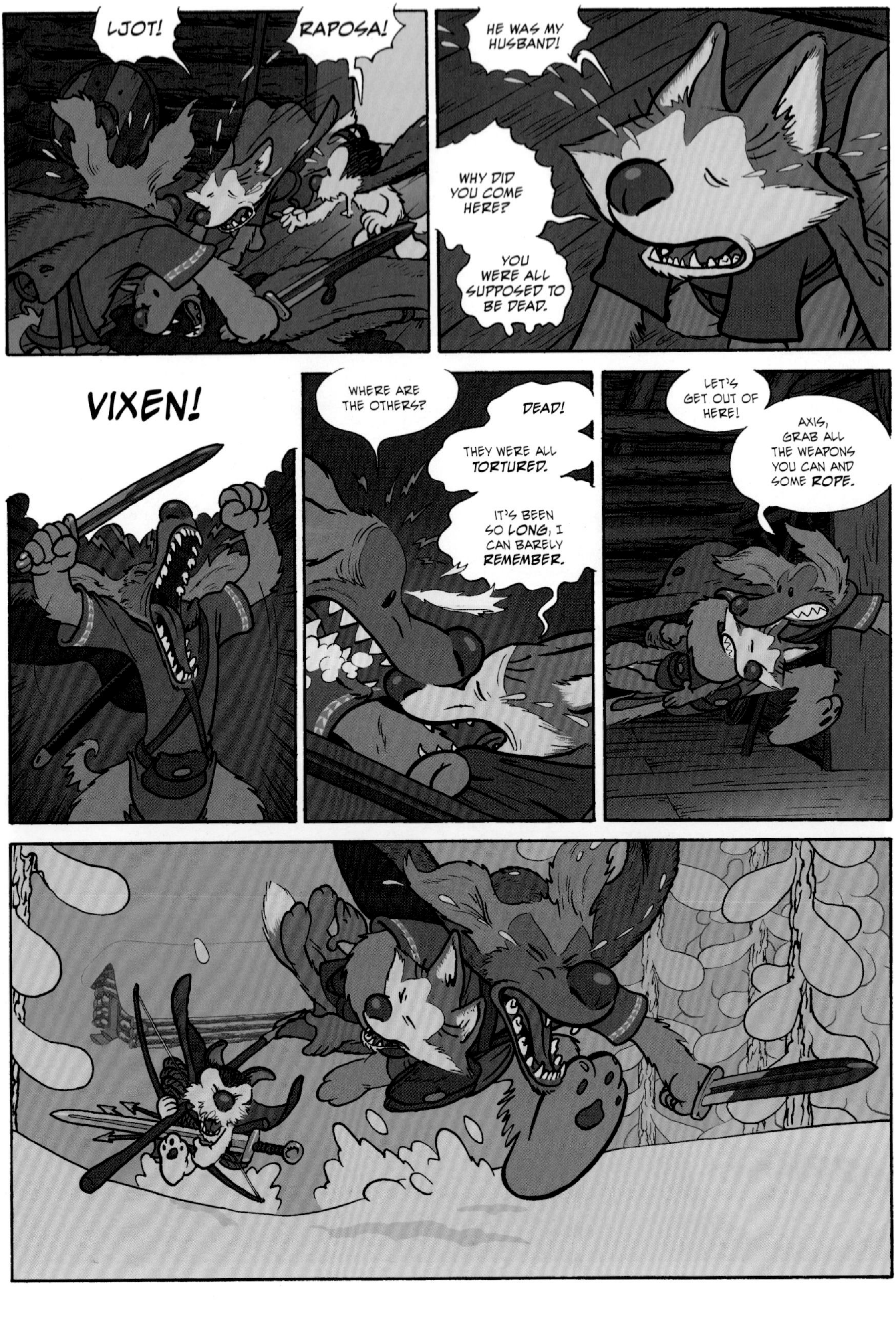
LJOT!
RAPOSA!
HE WAS MY HUSBAND!
WHY DID YOU COME HERE?
YOU WERE ALL SUPPOSED TO BE DEAD.
VIXEN!
WHERE ARE THE OTHERS?
DEAD!
THEY WERE ALL TORTURED.
IT'S BEEN SO LONG, I CAN BARELY REMEMBER.
LET'S GET OUT OF HERE!
AXIS, GRAB ALL THE WEAPONS YOU CAN AND SOME ROPE.

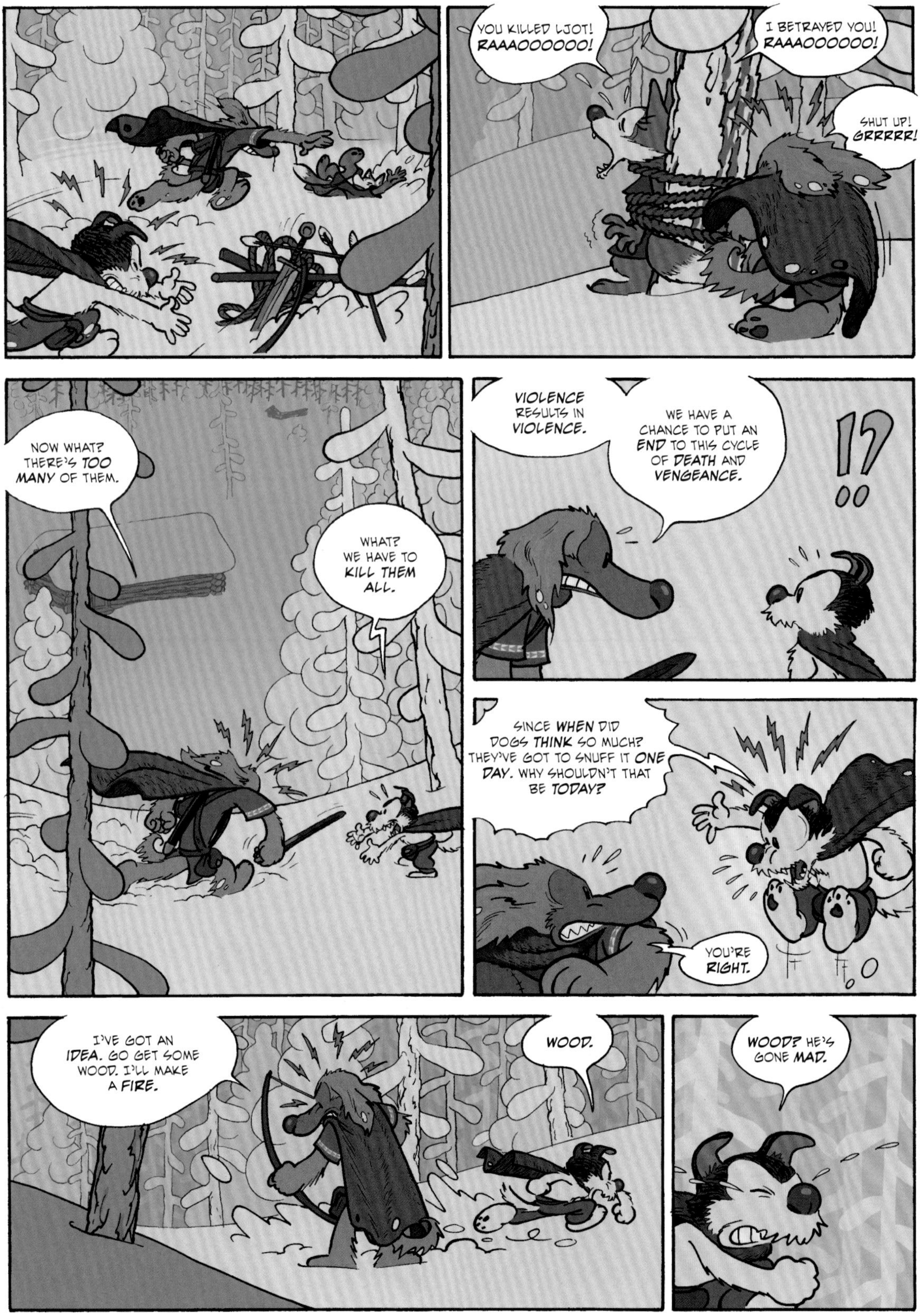

YOU KILLED LJOT! RAAAOOOOOO!
I BETRAYED YOU! RAAAOOOOOO!
SHUT UP! GRRRRR!
NOW WHAT? THERE'S TOO MANY OF THEM.
WHAT? WE HAVE TO KILL THEM ALL.
VIOLENCE RESULTS IN VIOLENCE.
WE HAVE A CHANCE TO PUT AN END TO THIS CYCLE OF DEATH AND VENGEANCE.
!?
SINCE WHEN DID DOGS THINK SO MUCH? THEY'VE GOT TO SNUFF IT ONE DAY. WHY SHOULDN'T THAT BE TODAY?
YOU'RE RIGHT.
I'VE GOT AN IDEA. GO GET SOME WOOD. I'LL MAKE A FIRE.
WOOD.
WOOD? HE'S GONE MAD.

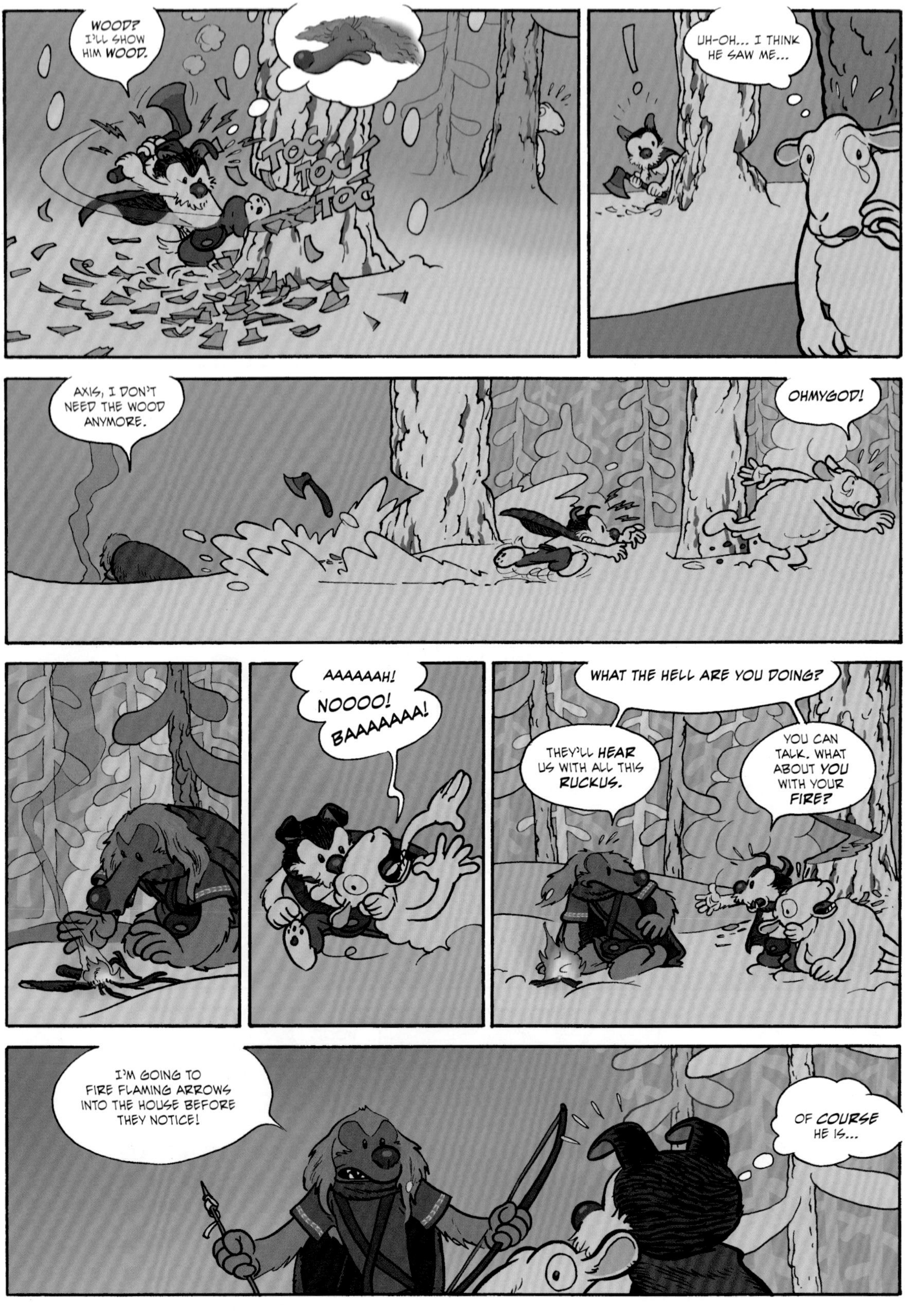

WOOD? I'LL SHOW HIM WOOD.
TOC TOC TOC
UH-OH... I THINK HE SAW ME...
!
AXIS, I DON'T NEED THE WOOD ANYMORE.
OHMYGOD!
AAAAAAH!
NOOOO!
BAAAAAAA!
WHAT THE HELL ARE YOU DOING?
THEY'LL HEAR US WITH ALL THIS RUCKUS.
YOU CAN TALK. WHAT ABOUT YOU WITH YOUR FIRE?
I'M GOING TO FIRE FLAMING ARROWS INTO THE HOUSE BEFORE THEY NOTICE!
OF COURSE HE IS...

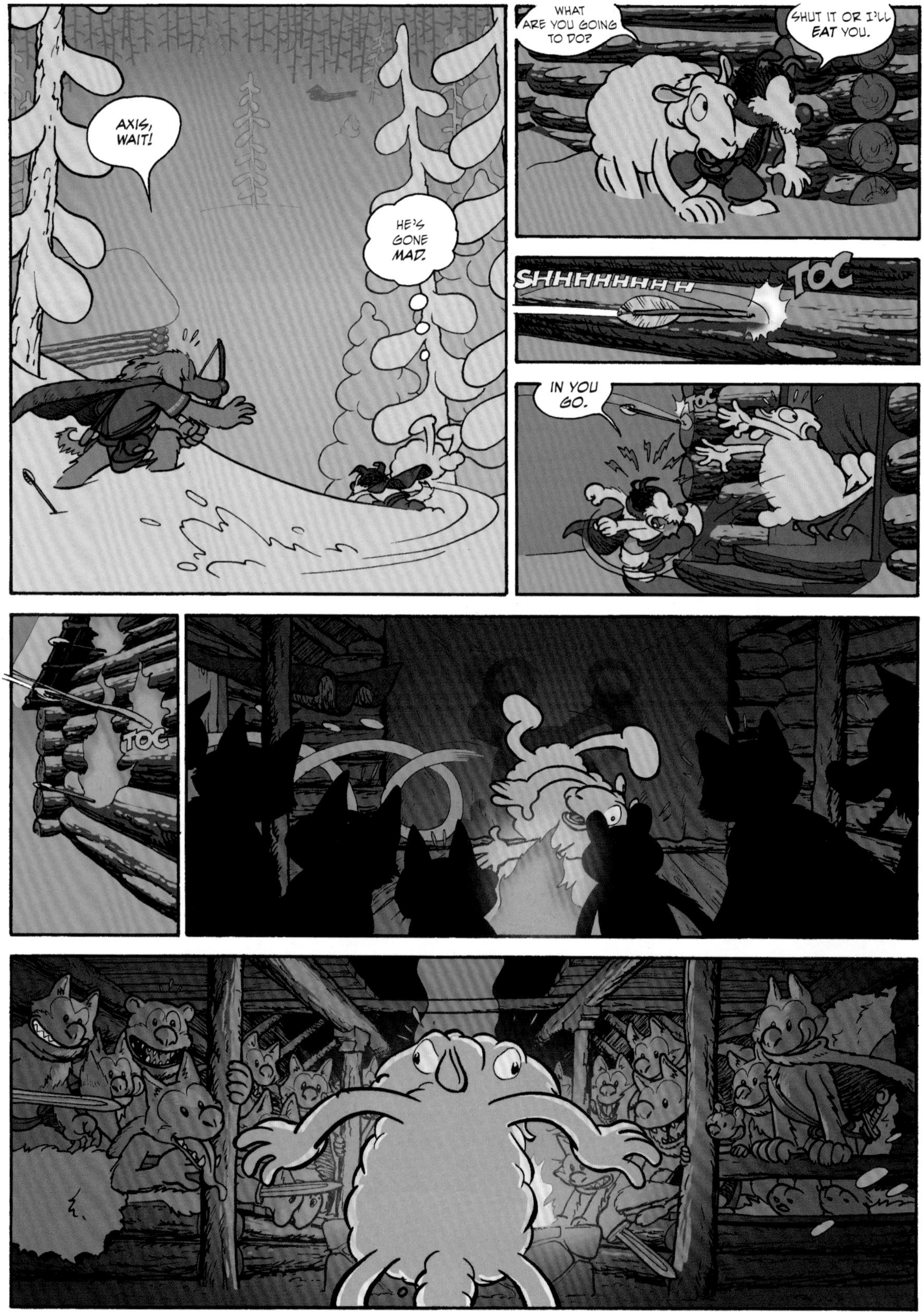
AXIS, WAIT!
HE'S GONE MAD.
WHAT ARE YOU GOING TO DO?
SHUT IT OR I'LL EAT YOU.
SHHHHHHHHH
TOC
IN YOU GO.
TOC
TOC

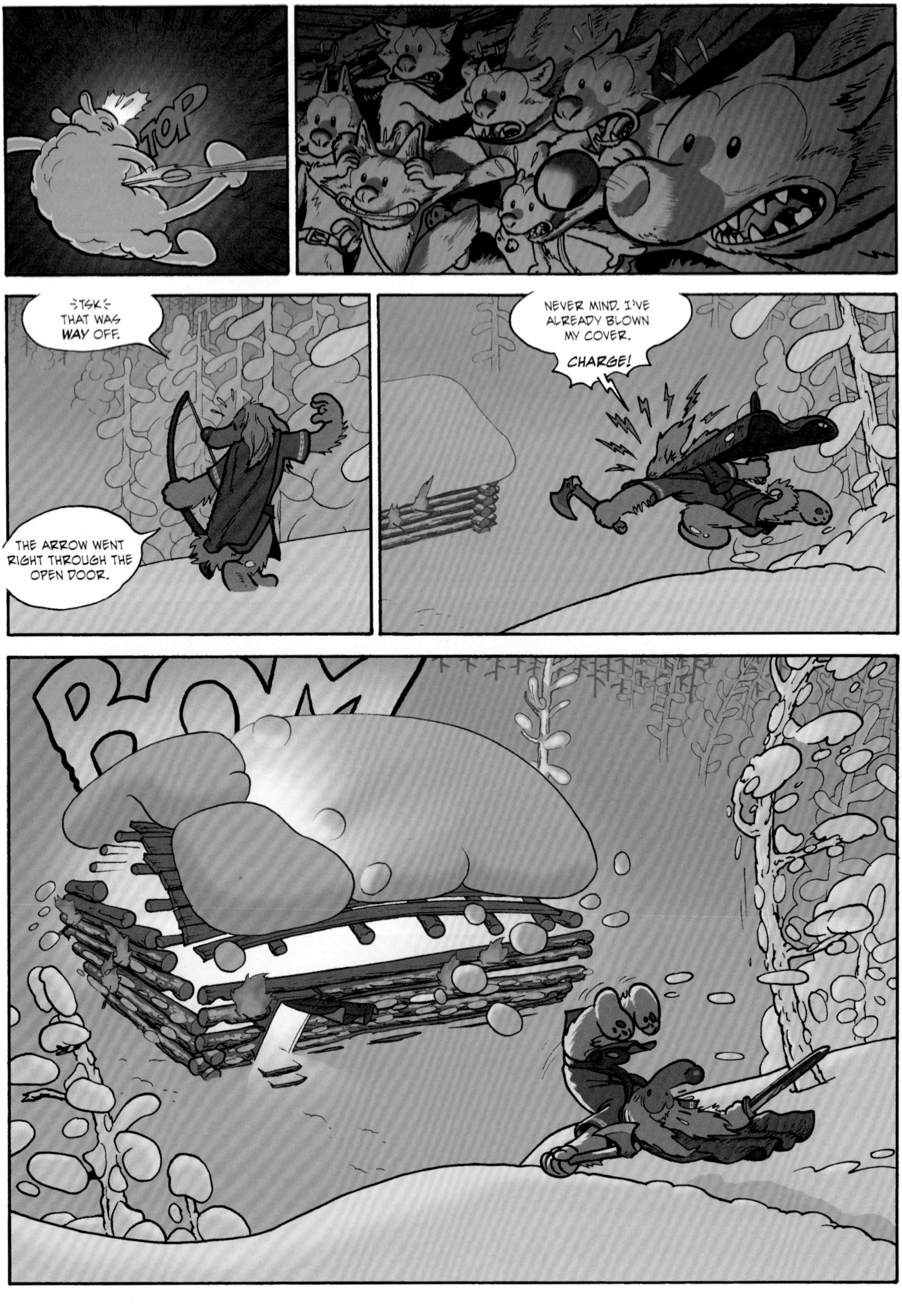
TOP
-TSK-
THAT WAS **WAY** OFF.
THE ARROW WENT RIGHT THROUGH THE OPEN DOOR.
NEVER MIND. I'VE ALREADY BLOWN MY COVER.
CHARGE!

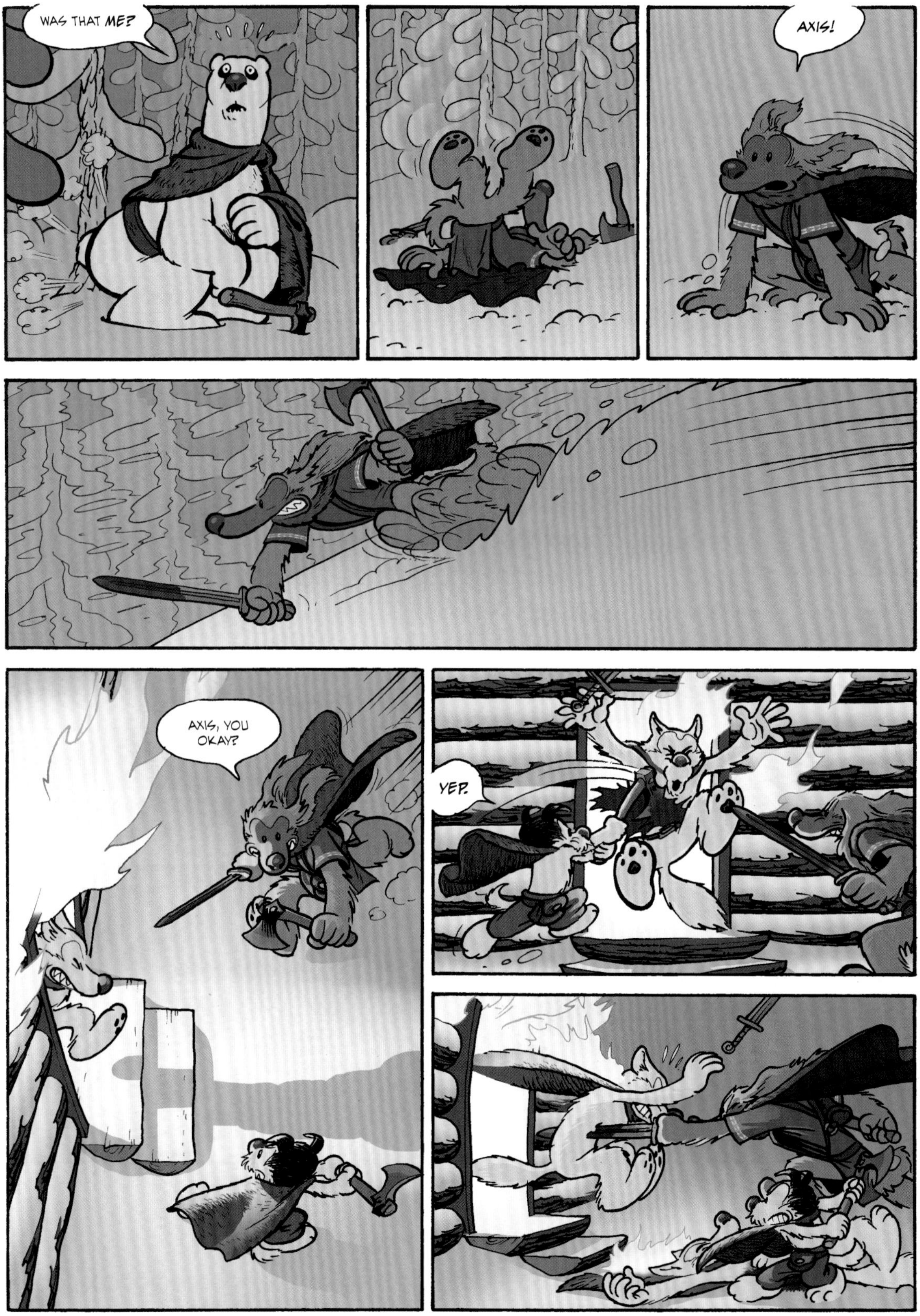
WAS THAT ME?
AXIS!
AXIS, YOU OKAY?
YEP.

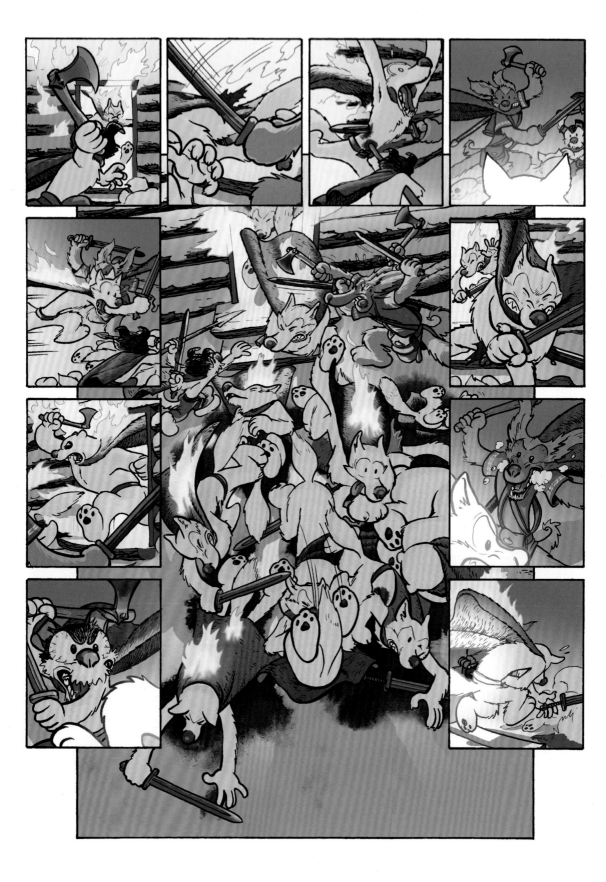

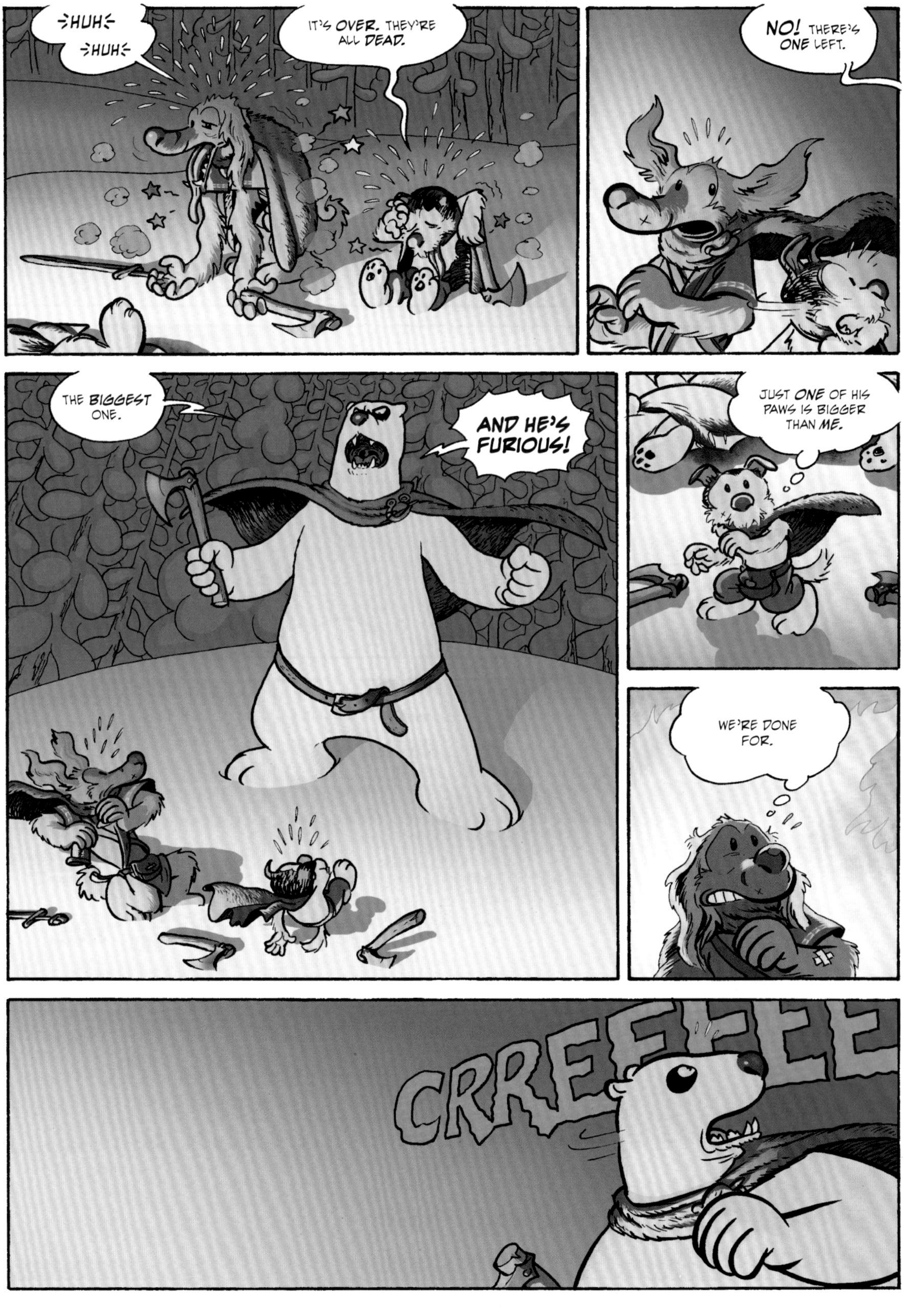
HUH
HUH
IT'S OVER. THEY'RE ALL DEAD.
NO! THERE'S ONE LEFT.
THE BIGGEST ONE.
AND HE'S FURIOUS!
JUST ONE OF HIS PAWS IS BIGGER THAN ME.
WE'RE DONE FOR.
CRREEEEE

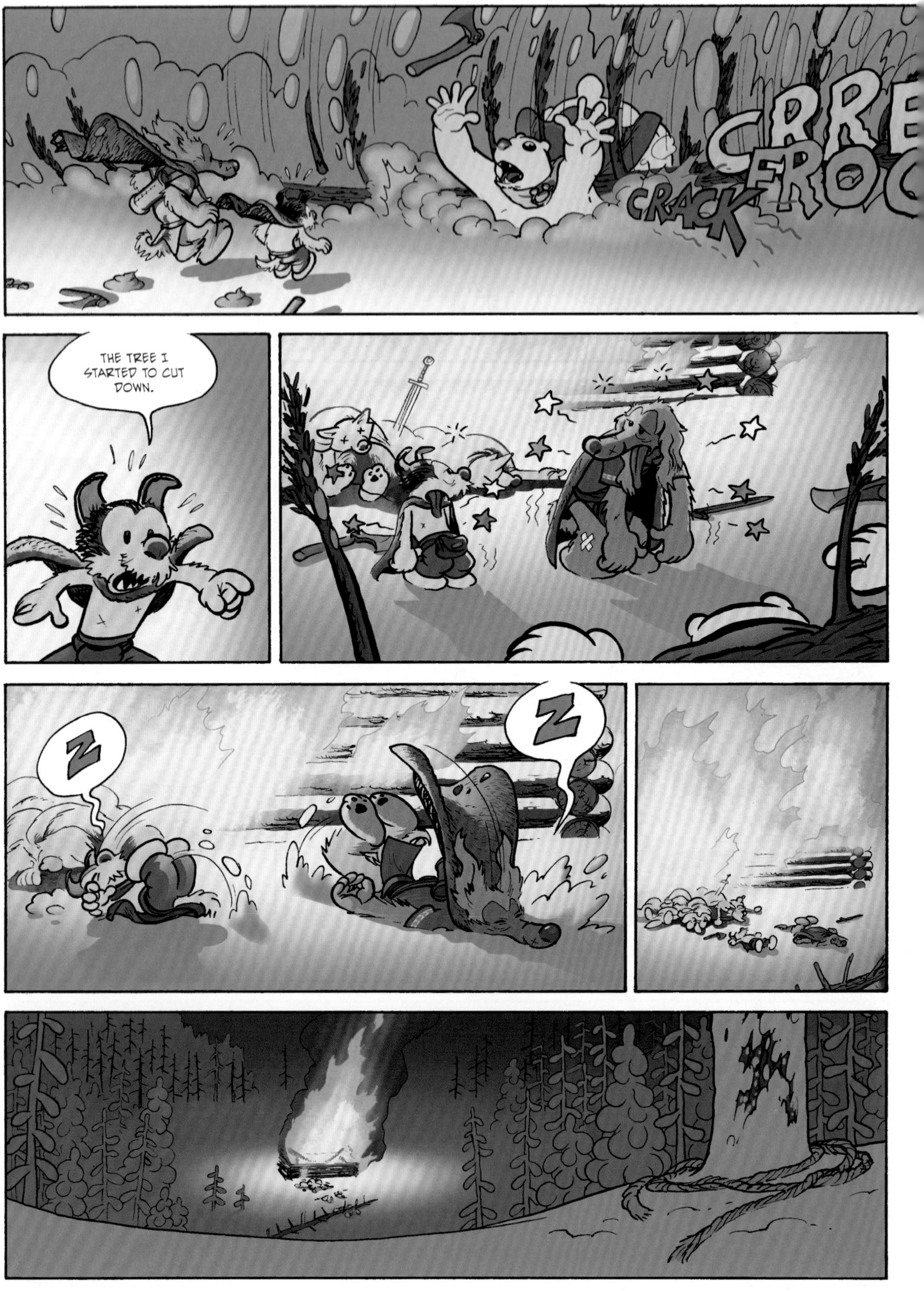
CRRE
FROC
CRACK
THE TREE I STARTED TO CUT DOWN.
Z
Z

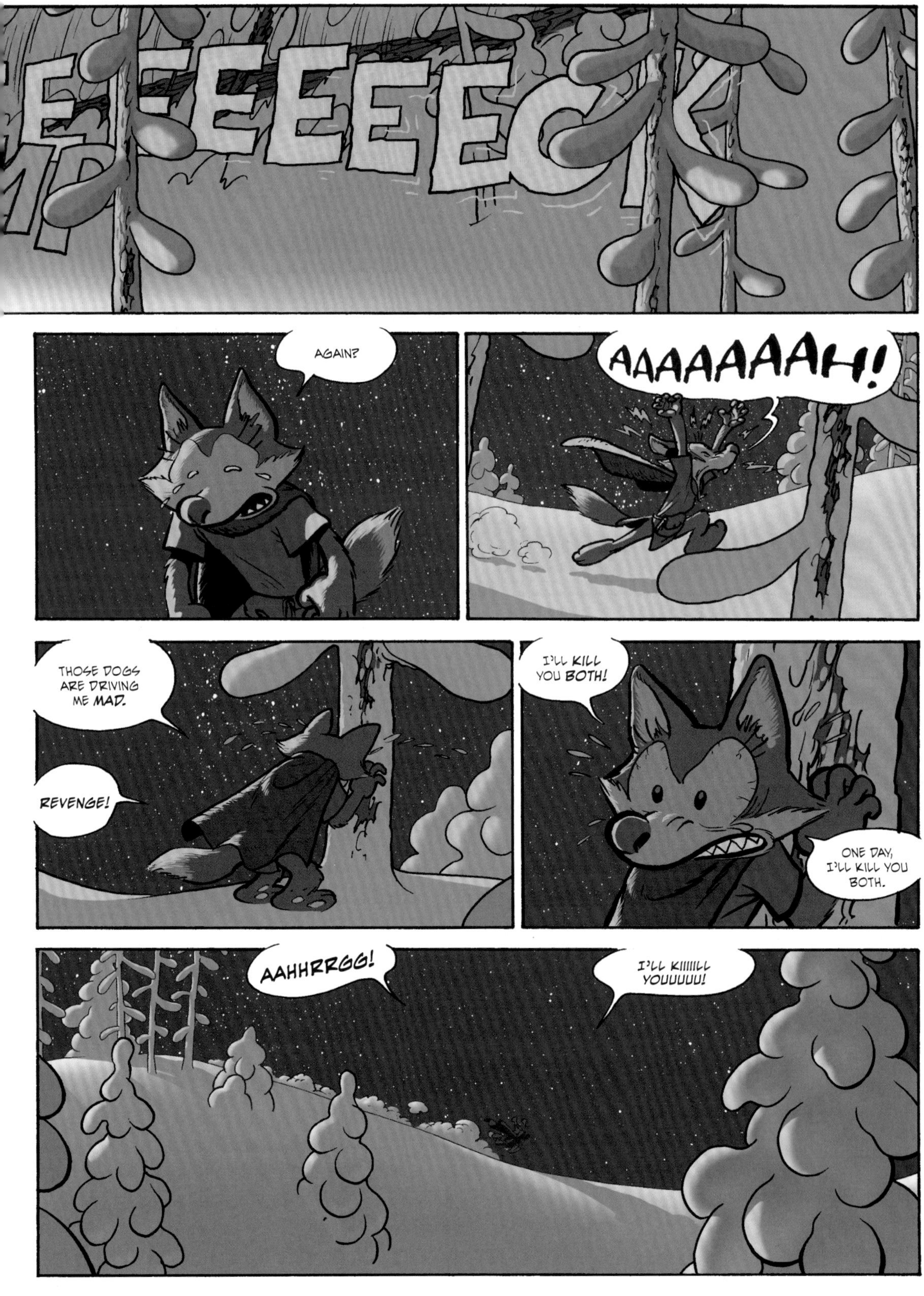
EEEEEEECK
AGAIN?
AAAAAAAH!
THOSE DOGS ARE DRIVING ME MAD.
REVENGE!
I'LL KILL YOU BOTH!
ONE DAY, I'LL KILL YOU BOTH.
AAHHRRGG!
I'LL KIIIIILL YOUUUUU!

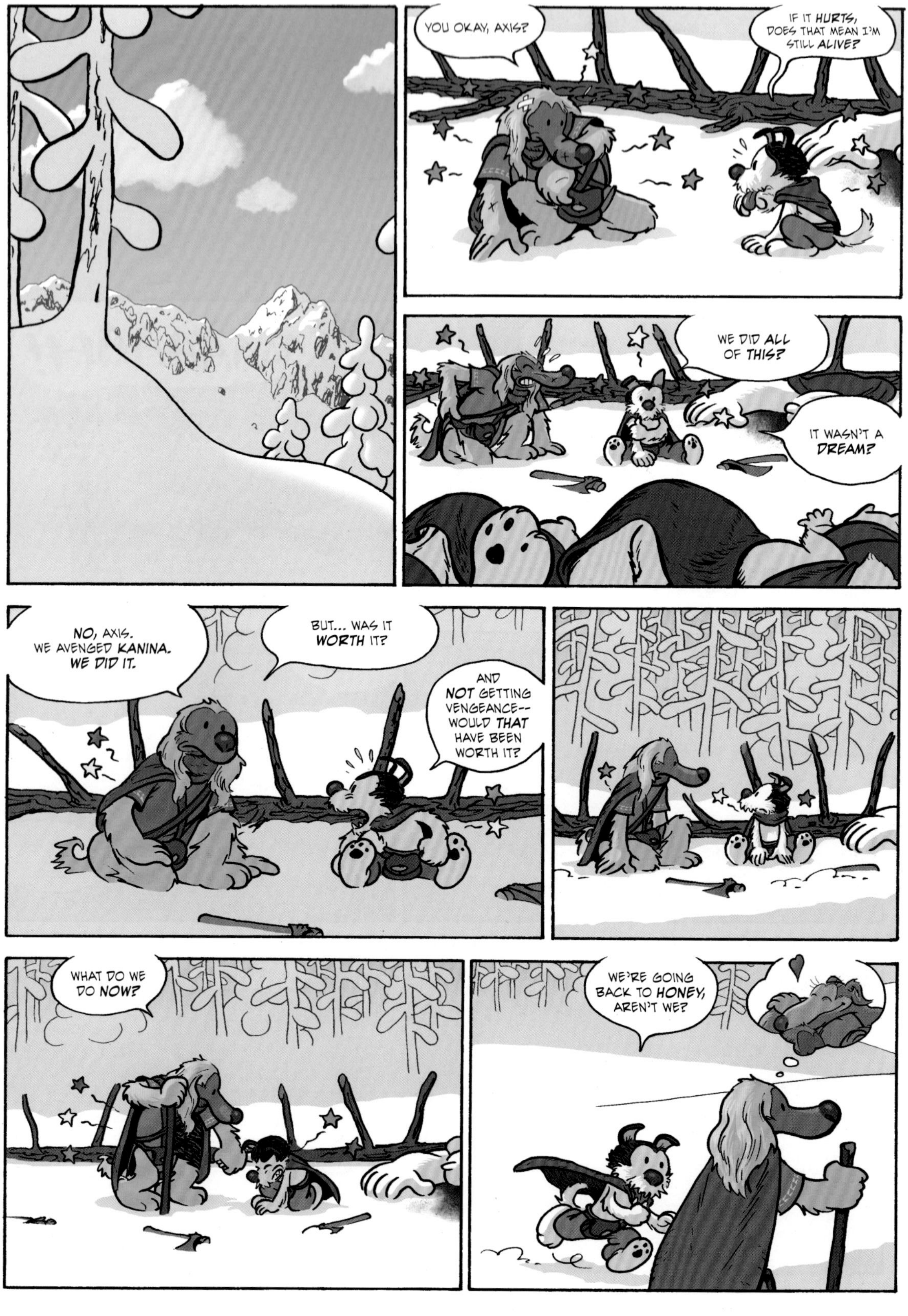
YOU OKAY, AXIS?
IF IT HURTS, DOES THAT MEAN I'M STILL ALIVE?
WE DID ALL OF THIS?
IT WASN'T A DREAM?
NO, AXIS. WE AVENGED KANINA. WE DID IT.
BUT... WAS IT WORTH IT?
AND NOT GETTING VENGEANCE-- WOULD THAT HAVE BEEN WORTH IT?
WHAT DO WE DO NOW?
WE'RE GOING BACK TO HONEY, AREN'T WE?

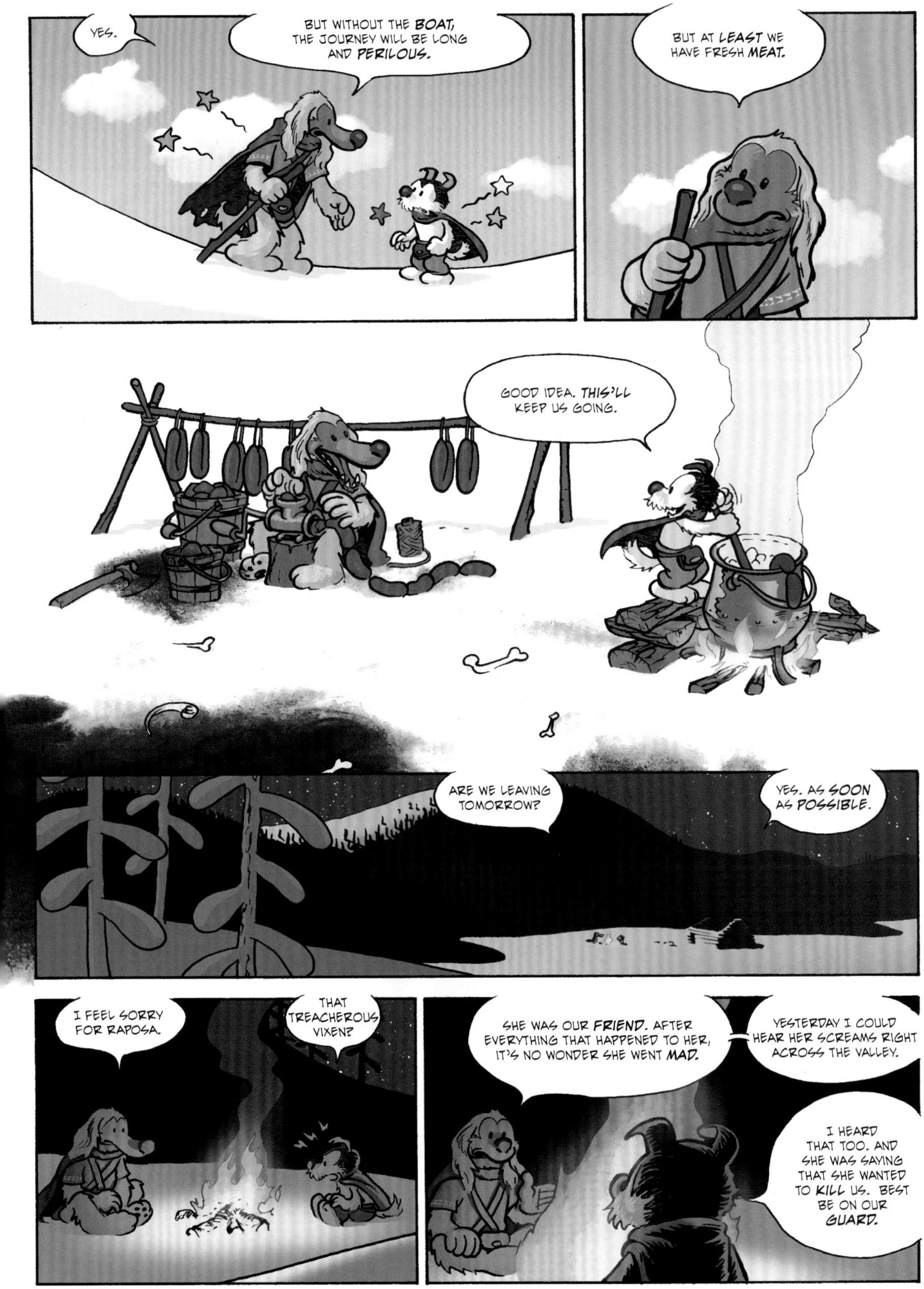
YES.
BUT WITHOUT THE BOAT, THE JOURNEY WILL BE LONG AND PERILOUS.
BUT AT LEAST WE HAVE FRESH MEAT.
GOOD IDEA. THIS'LL KEEP US GOING.
ARE WE LEAVING TOMORROW?
YES. AS SOON AS POSSIBLE.
I FEEL SORRY FOR RAPOSA.
THAT TREACHEROUS VIXEN?
SHE WAS OUR FRIEND. AFTER EVERYTHING THAT HAPPENED TO HER, IT'S NO WONDER SHE WENT MAD.
YESTERDAY I COULD HEAR HER SCREAMS RIGHT ACROSS THE VALLEY.
I HEARD THAT TOO. AND SHE WAS SAYING THAT SHE WANTED TO KILL US. BEST BE ON OUR GUARD.

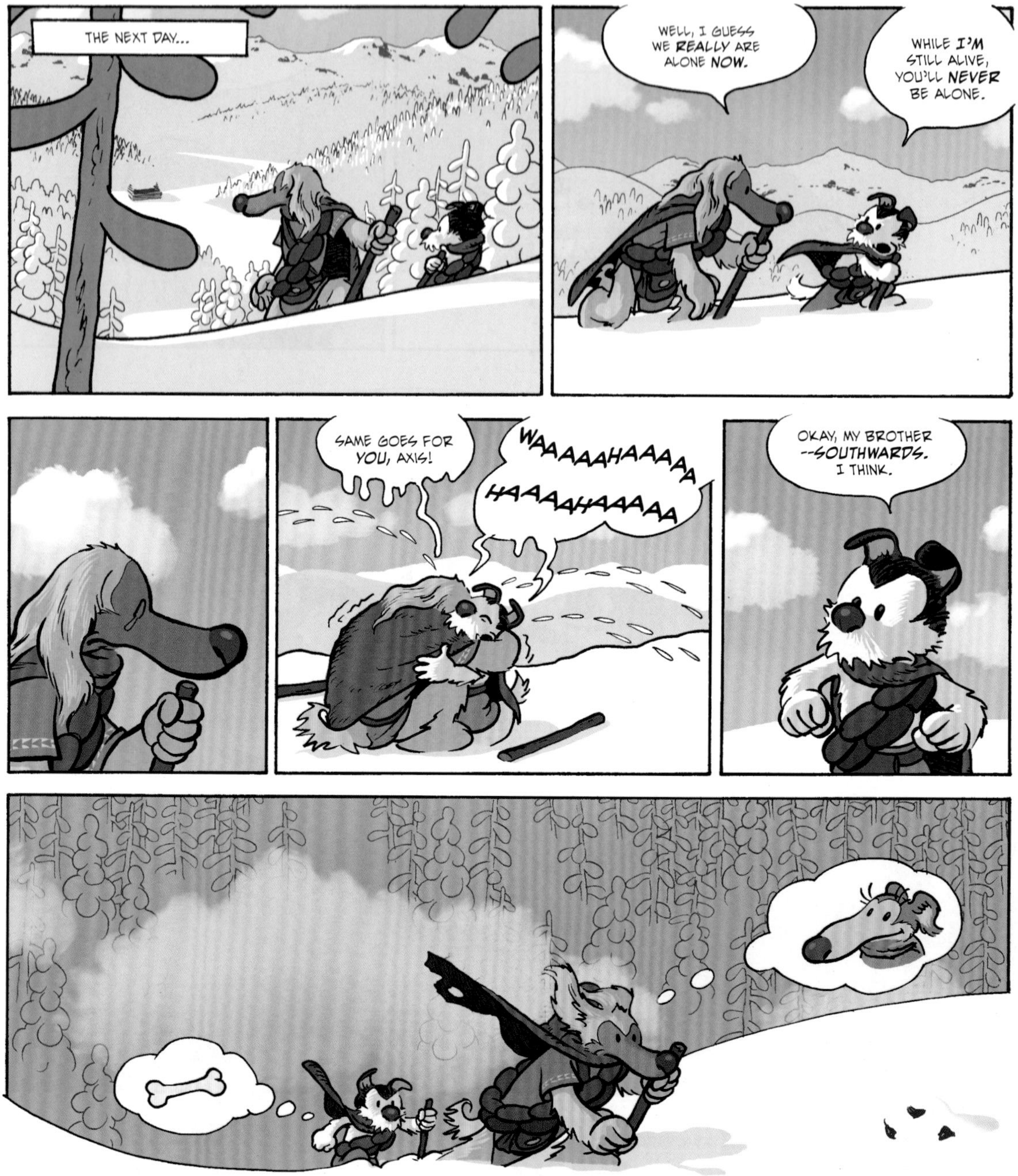
THE NEXT DAY...
WELL, I GUESS WE REALLY ARE ALONE NOW.
WHILE I'M STILL ALIVE, YOU'LL NEVER BE ALONE.
SAME GOES FOR YOU, AXIS!
WAAAAAHAAAAA HAAAAHAAAAA
OKAY, MY BROTHER --SOUTHWARDS. I THINK.

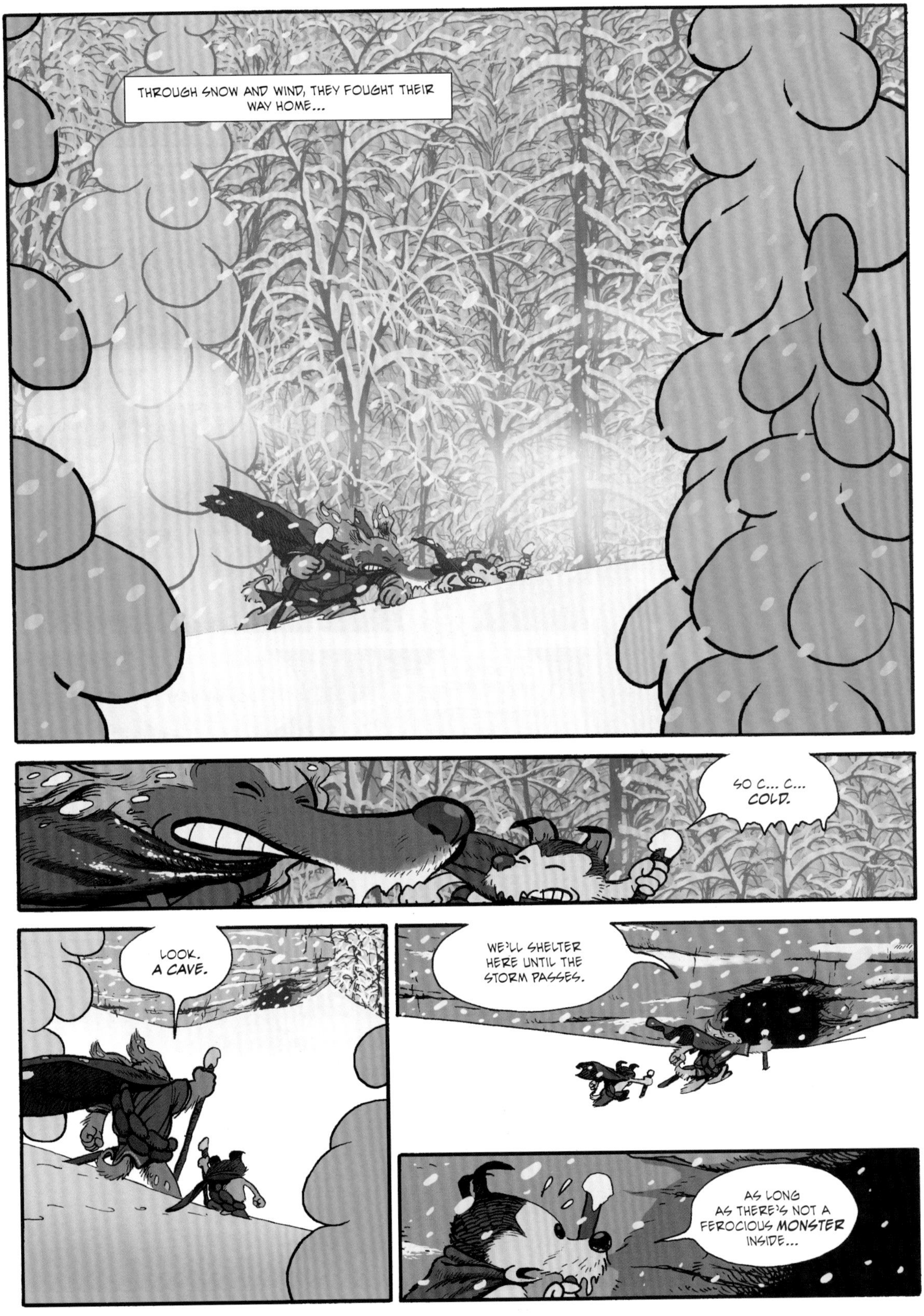
THROUGH SNOW AND WIND, THEY FOUGHT THEIR WAY HOME...
SO C... C... COLD.
LOOK. A CAVE.
WE'LL SHELTER HERE UNTIL THE STORM PASSES.
AS LONG AS THERE'S NOT A FEROCIOUS MONSTER INSIDE...

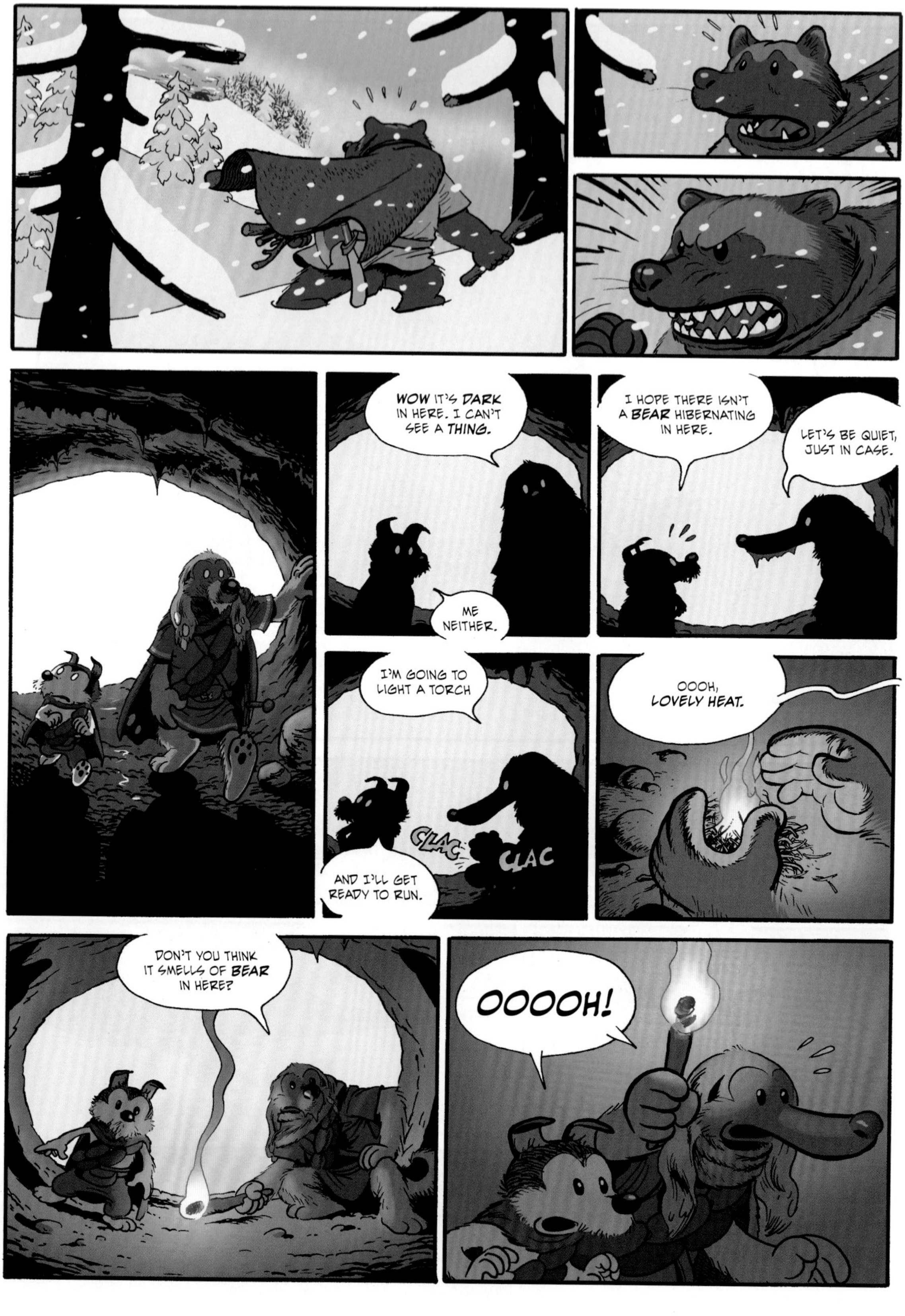
WOW IT'S DARK IN HERE. I CAN'T SEE A THING.
ME NEITHER.
I HOPE THERE ISN'T A BEAR HIBERNATING IN HERE.
LET'S BE QUIET, JUST IN CASE.
I'M GOING TO LIGHT A TORCH
CLAC
CLAC
AND I'LL GET READY TO RUN.
OOOH, LOVELY HEAT.
DON'T YOU THINK IT SMELLS OF BEAR IN HERE?
OOOOH!

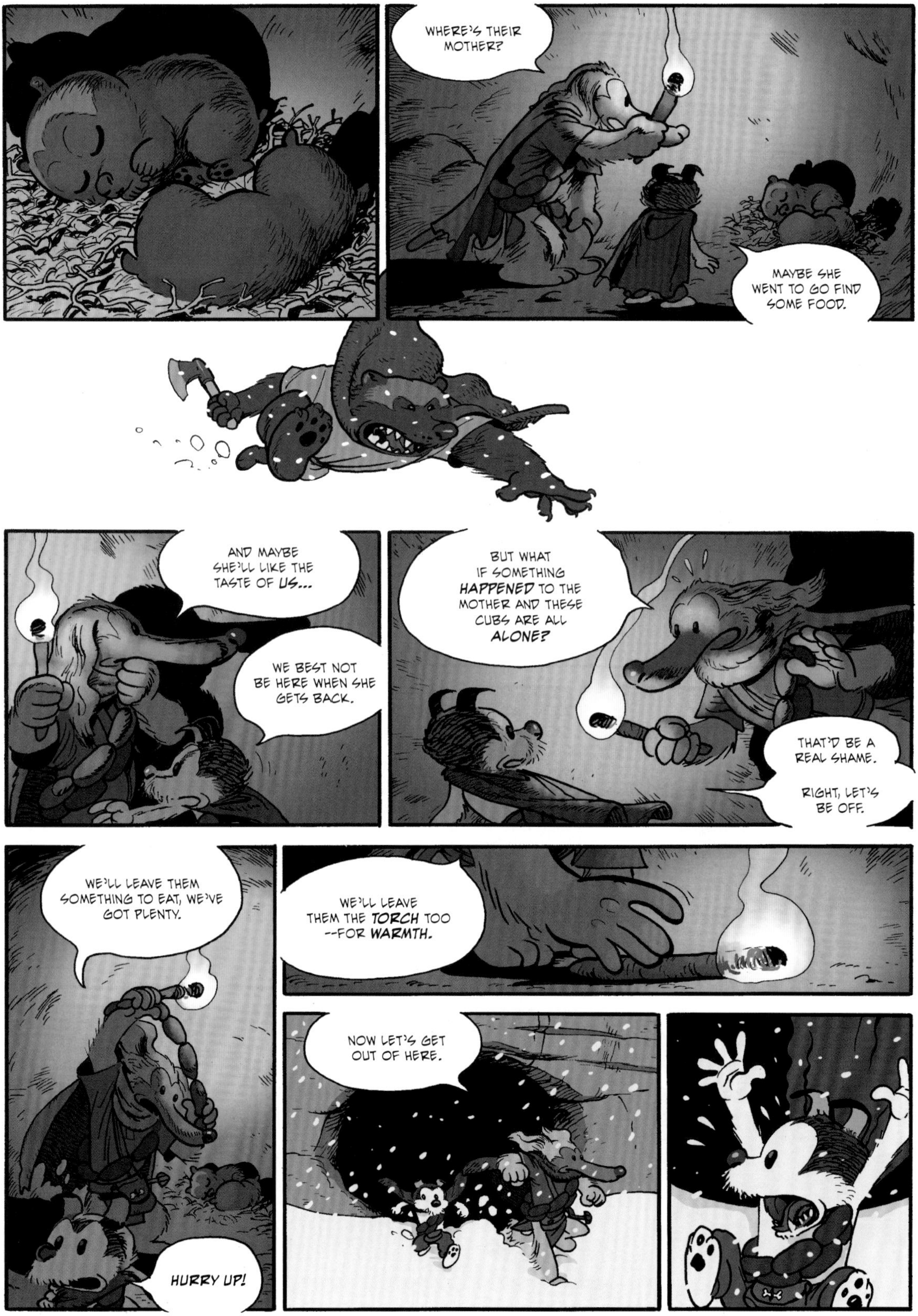
WHERE'S THEIR MOTHER?
MAYBE SHE WENT TO GO FIND SOME FOOD.
AND MAYBE SHE'LL LIKE THE TASTE OF US...
WE BEST NOT BE HERE WHEN SHE GETS BACK.
BUT WHAT IF SOMETHING HAPPENED TO THE MOTHER AND THESE CUBS ARE ALL ALONE?
THAT'D BE A REAL SHAME.
RIGHT, LET'S BE OFF.
WE'LL LEAVE THEM SOMETHING TO EAT, WE'VE GOT PLENTY.
HURRY UP!
WE'LL LEAVE THEM THE TORCH TOO --FOR WARMTH.
NOW LET'S GET OUT OF HERE.

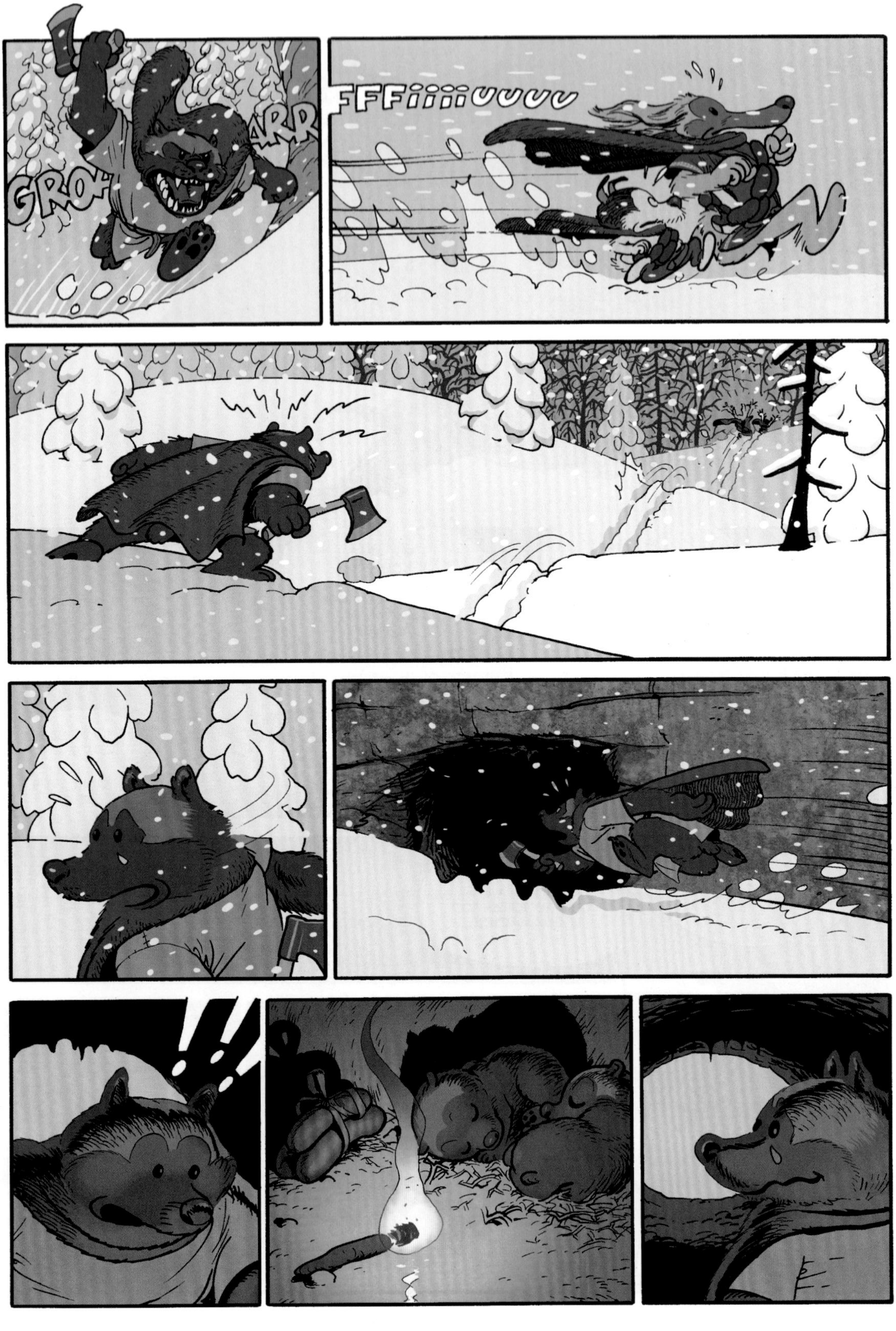
GROHARR
FFFiiiiUUUU
!!

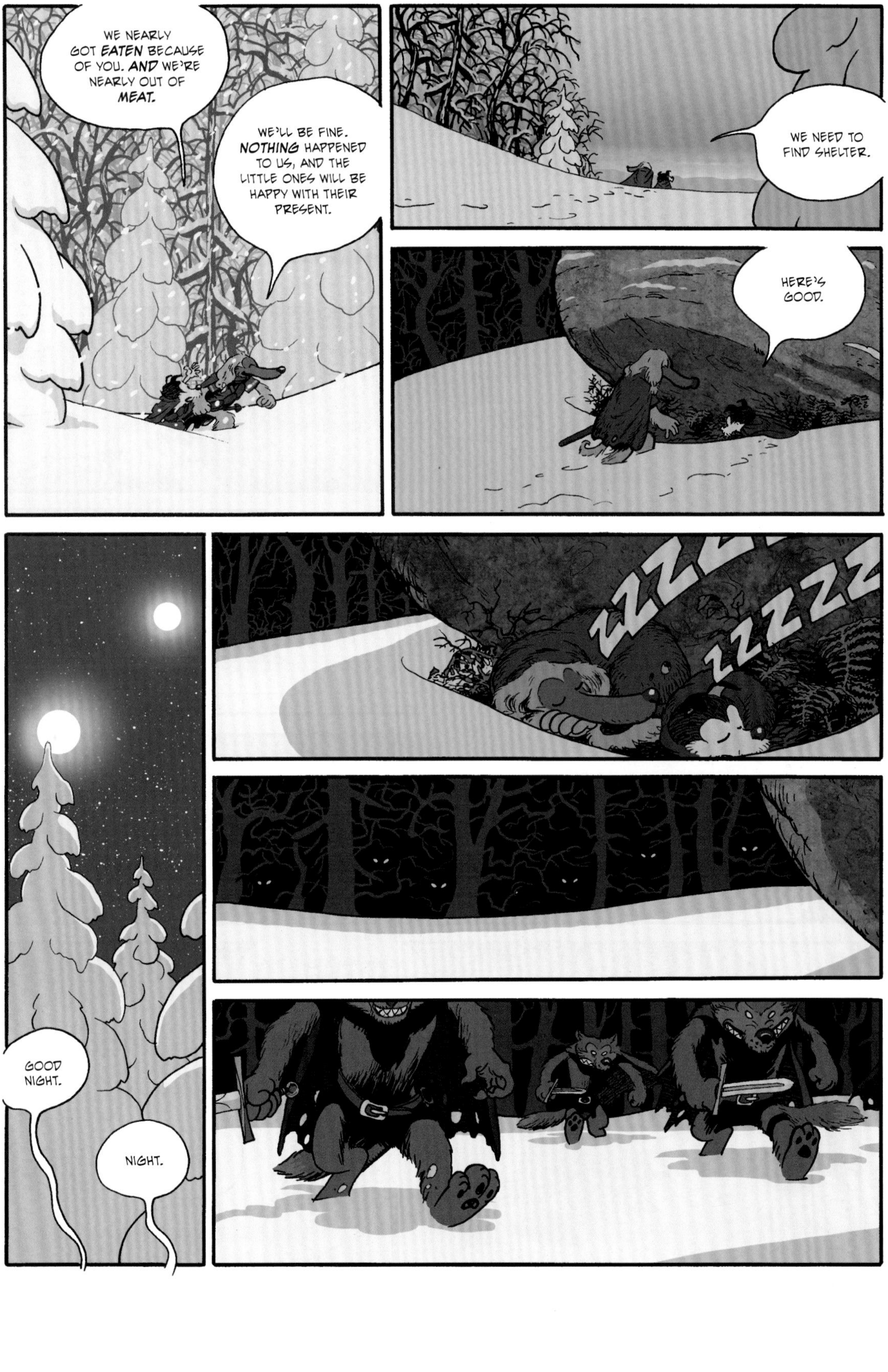
WE NEARLY GOT EATEN BECAUSE OF YOU. AND WE'RE NEARLY OUT OF MEAT.
WE'LL BE FINE. NOTHING HAPPENED TO US, AND THE LITTLE ONES WILL BE HAPPY WITH THEIR PRESENT.
WE NEED TO FIND SHELTER.
HERE'S GOOD.
GOOD NIGHT.
NIGHT.
ZZZZZ
ZZZZZ

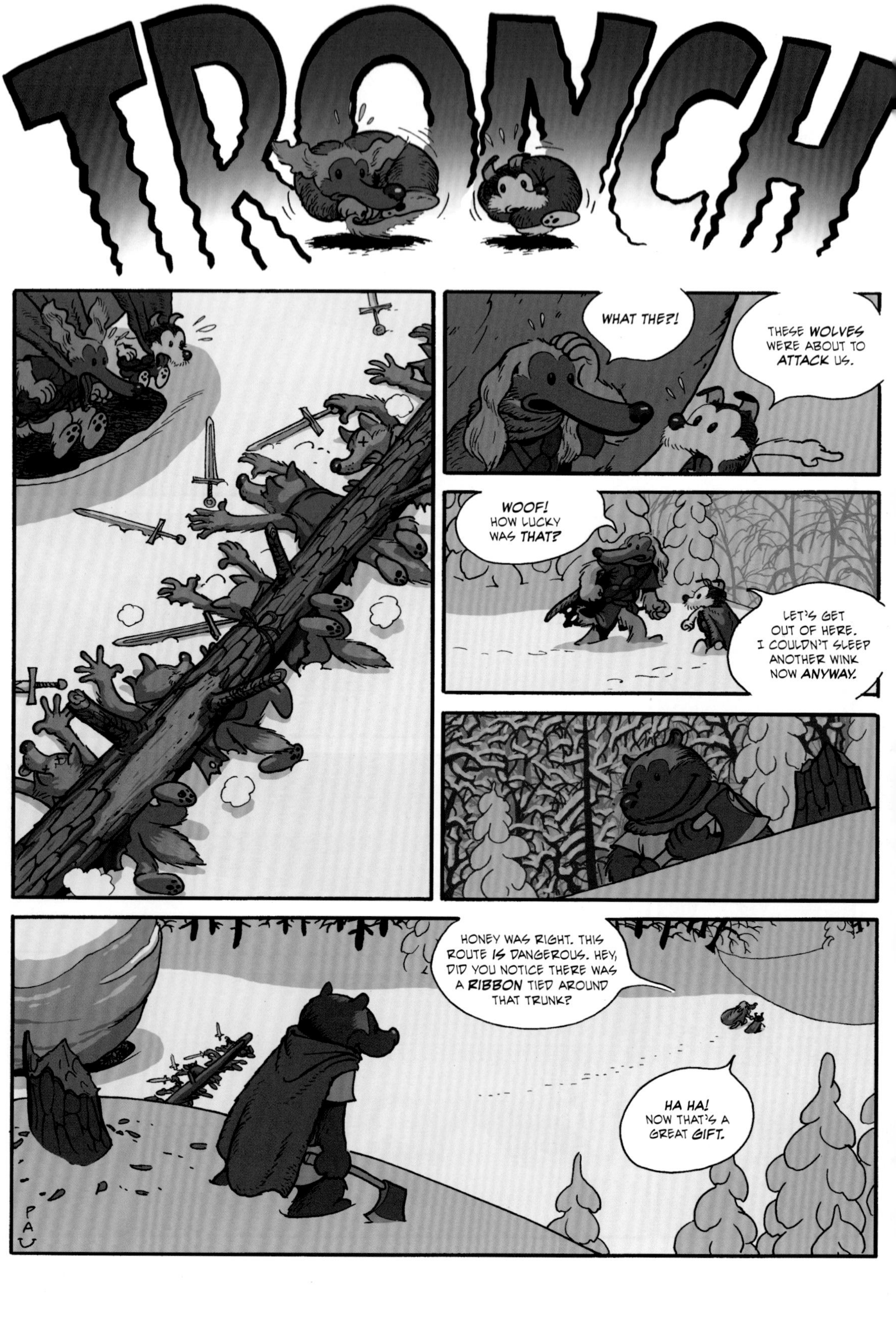
TRONCH
WHAT THE?!
THESE WOLVES WERE ABOUT TO ATTACK US.
WOOF! HOW LUCKY WAS THAT?
LET'S GET OUT OF HERE. I COULDN'T SLEEP ANOTHER WINK NOW ANYWAY.
HONEY WAS RIGHT. THIS ROUTE IS DANGEROUS. HEY, DID YOU NOTICE THERE WAS A RIBBON TIED AROUND THAT TRUNK?
HA HA! NOW THAT'S A GREAT GIFT.

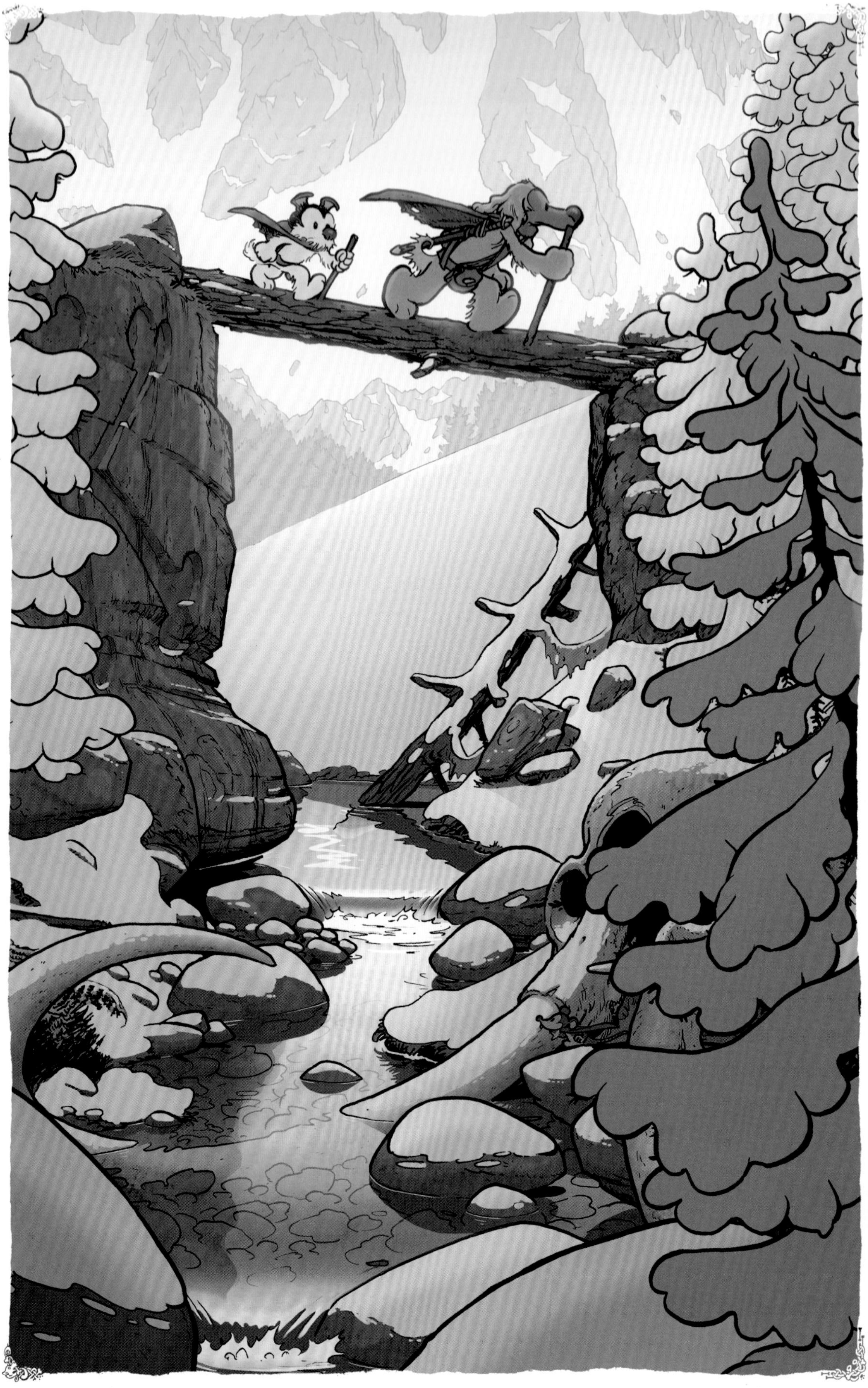

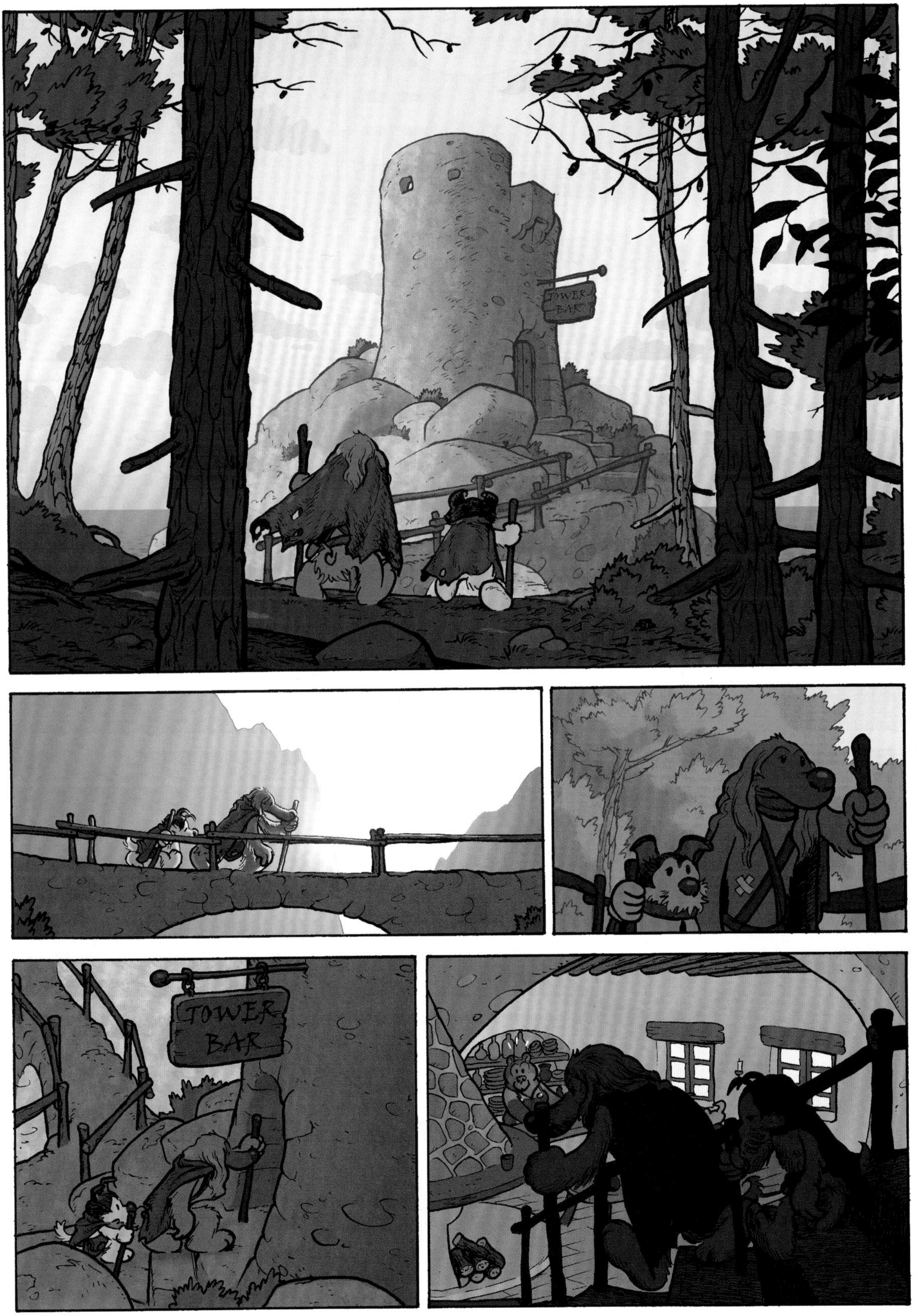
TOWER BAR
TOWER BAR

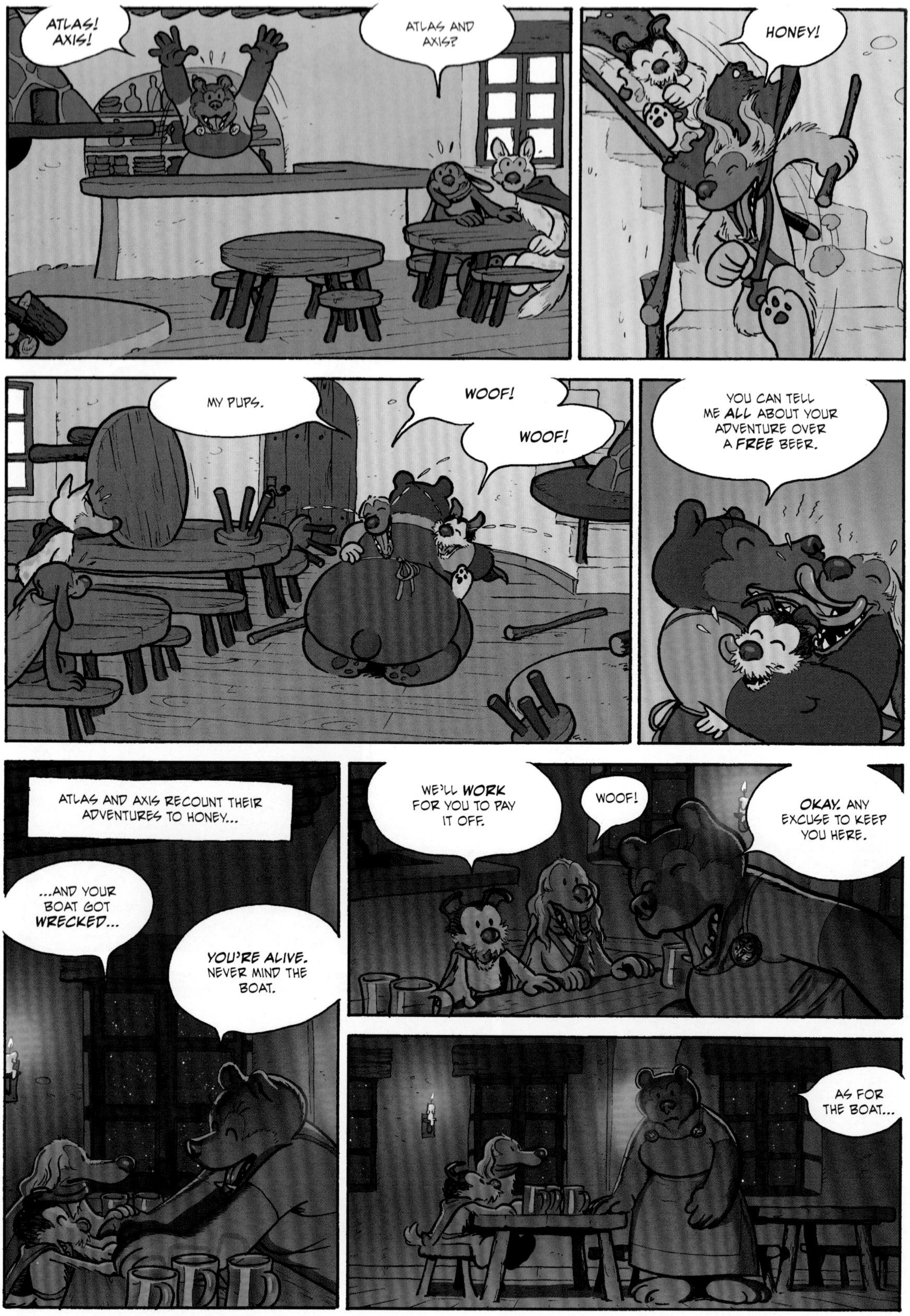
ATLAS! AXIS!
ATLAS AND AXIS?
HONEY!
MY PUPS.
WOOF!
WOOF!
YOU CAN TELL ME ALL ABOUT YOUR ADVENTURE OVER A FREE BEER.
ATLAS AND AXIS RECOUNT THEIR ADVENTURES TO HONEY...
...AND YOUR BOAT GOT WRECKED...
YOU'RE ALIVE. NEVER MIND THE BOAT.
WE'LL WORK FOR YOU TO PAY IT OFF.
WOOF!
OKAY. ANY EXCUSE TO KEEP YOU HERE.
AS FOR THE BOAT...

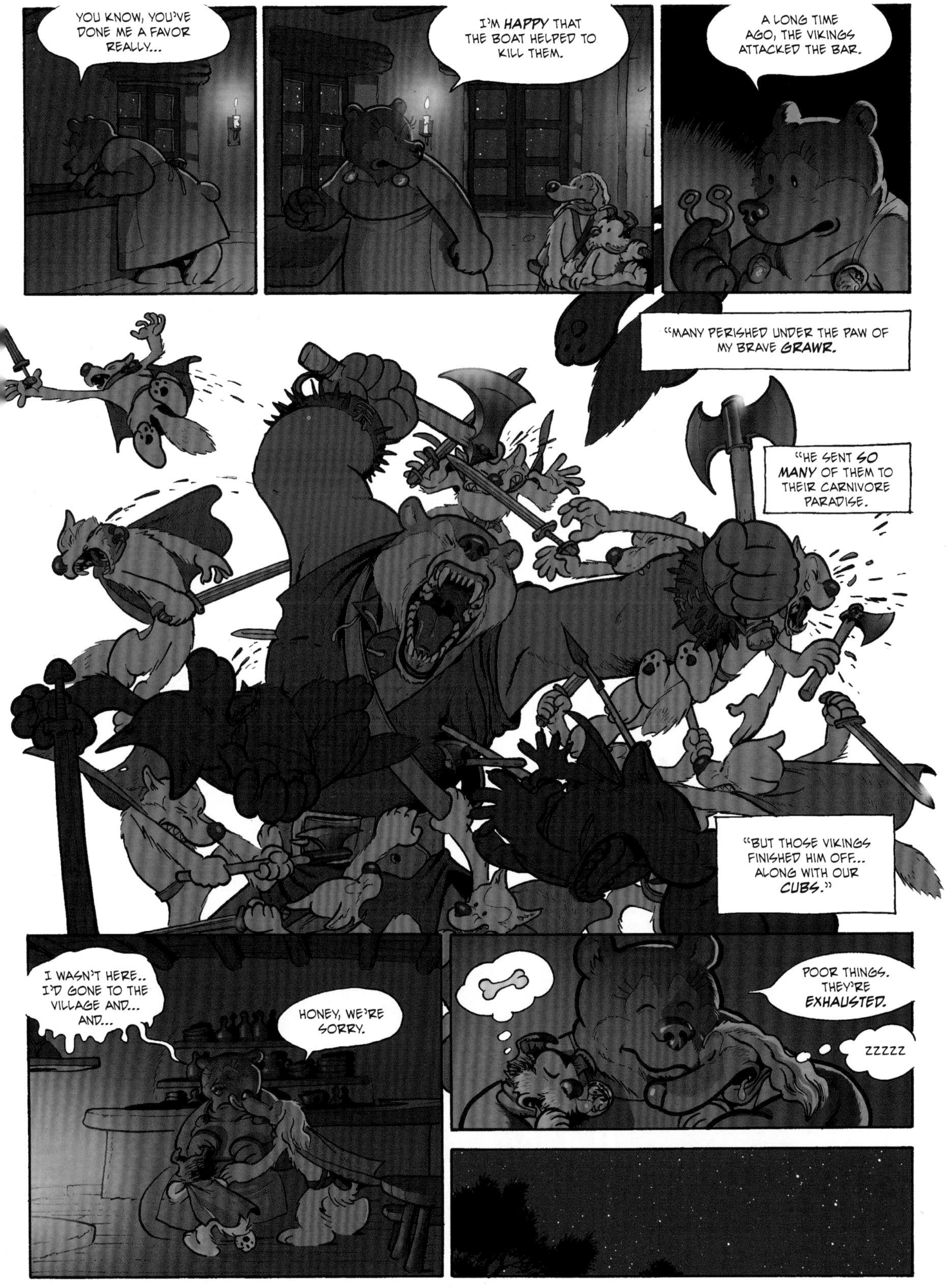
YOU KNOW, YOU'VE DONE ME A FAVOR REALLY...
I'M HAPPY THAT THE BOAT HELPED TO KILL THEM.
A LONG TIME AGO, THE VIKINGS ATTACKED THE BAR.
"MANY PERISHED UNDER THE PAW OF MY BRAVE GRAWR.
"HE SENT SO MANY OF THEM TO THEIR CARNIVORE PARADISE.
"BUT THOSE VIKINGS FINISHED HIM OFF... ALONG WITH OUR CUBS."
I WASN'T HERE.. I'D GONE TO THE VILLAGE AND... AND...
HONEY, WE'RE SORRY.
POOR THINGS. THEY'RE EXHAUSTED.
ZZZZZ

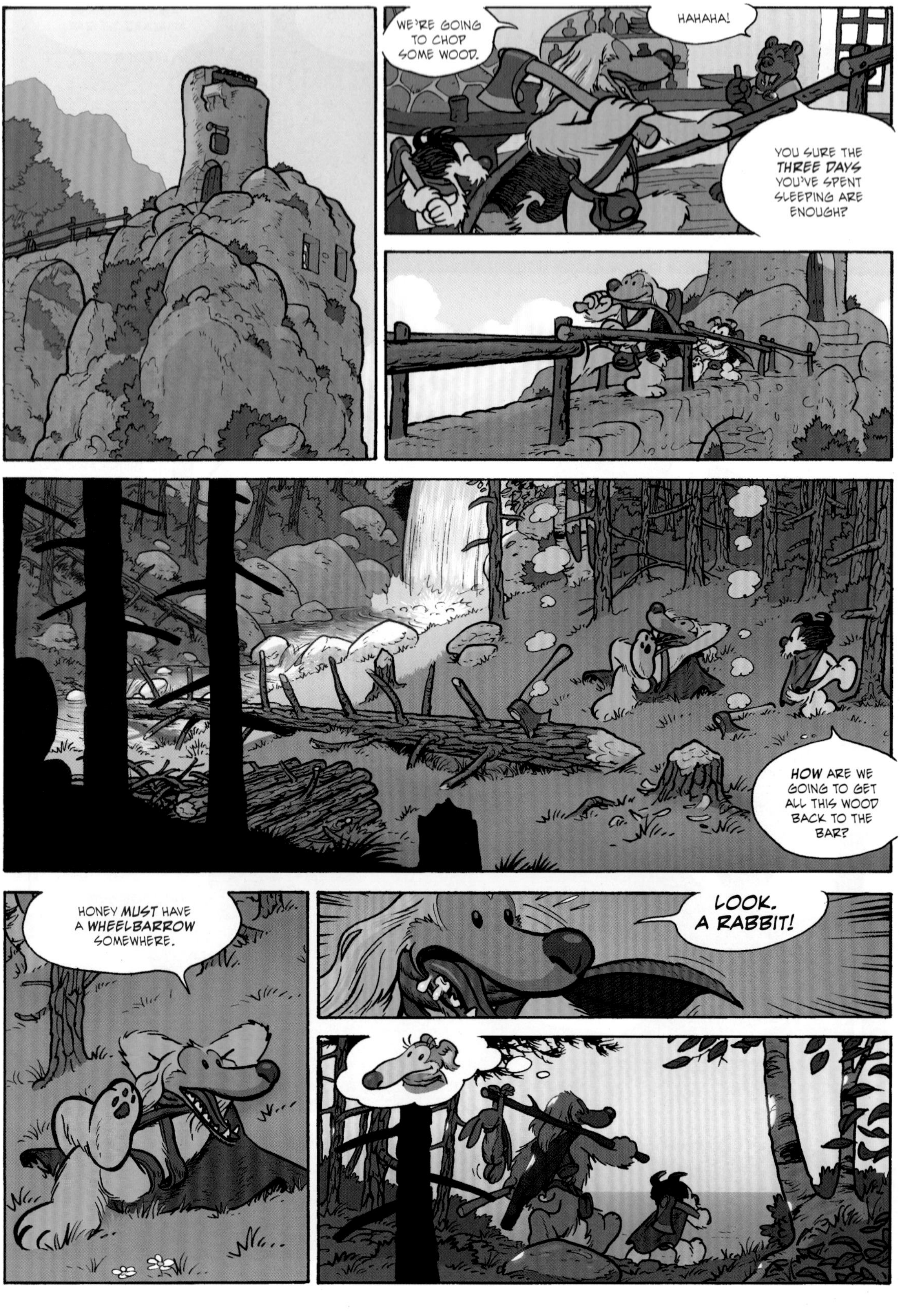
WE'RE GOING TO CHOP SOME WOOD.
HAHAHA!
YOU SURE THE THREE DAYS YOU'VE SPENT SLEEPING ARE ENOUGH?
HOW ARE WE GOING TO GET ALL THIS WOOD BACK TO THE BAR?
HONEY MUST HAVE A WHEELBARROW SOMEWHERE.
LOOK. A RABBIT!

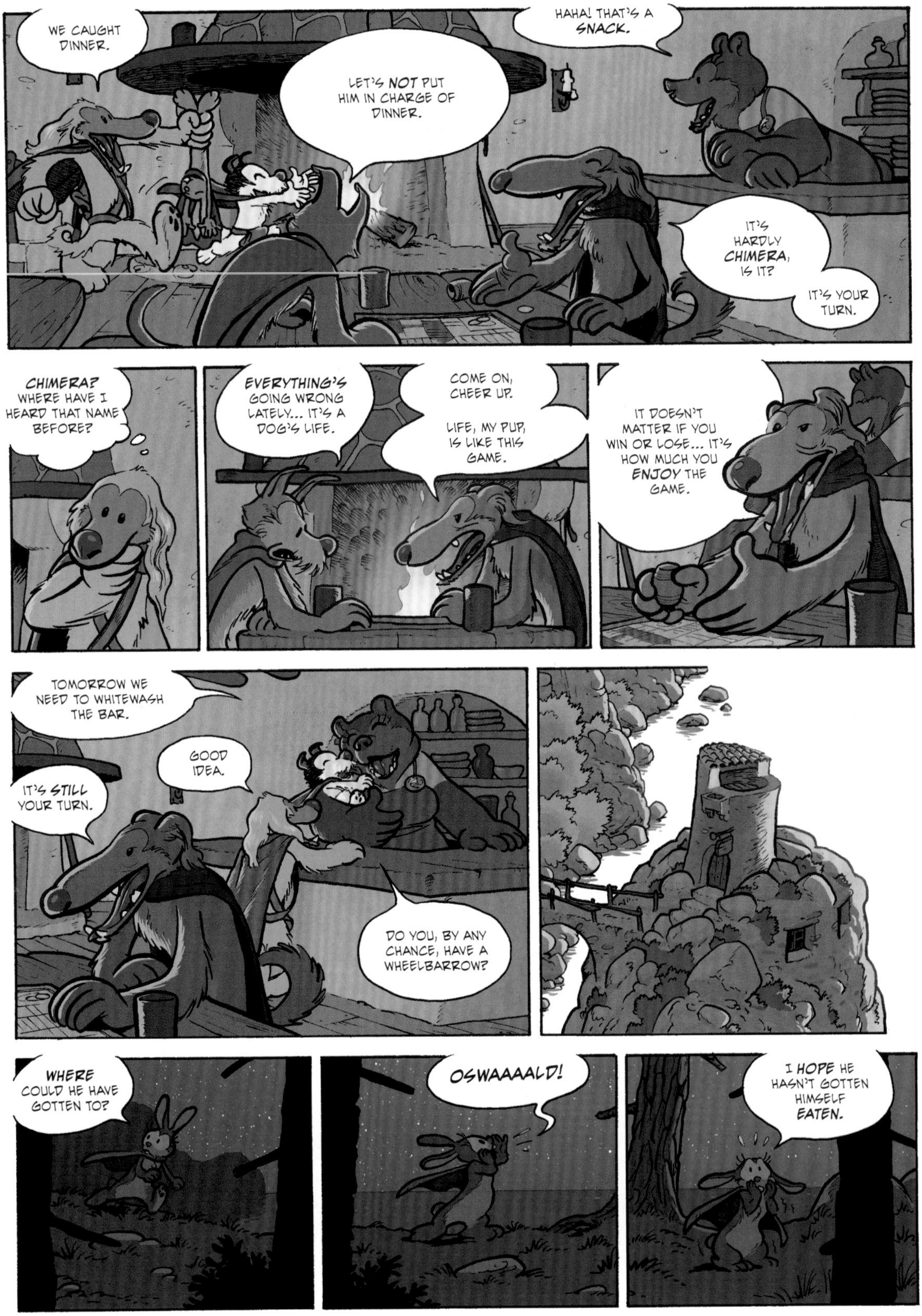
WE CAUGHT DINNER.
LET'S NOT PUT HIM IN CHARGE OF DINNER.
HAHA! THAT'S A SNACK.
IT'S HARDLY CHIMERA, IS IT?
IT'S YOUR TURN.
CHIMERA? WHERE HAVE I HEARD THAT NAME BEFORE?
EVERYTHING'S GOING WRONG LATELY... IT'S A DOG'S LIFE.
COME ON, CHEER UP.
LIFE, MY PUP, IS LIKE THIS GAME.
IT DOESN'T MATTER IF YOU WIN OR LOSE... IT'S HOW MUCH YOU ENJOY THE GAME.
TOMORROW WE NEED TO WHITEWASH THE BAR.
GOOD IDEA.
IT'S STILL YOUR TURN.
DO YOU, BY ANY CHANCE, HAVE A WHEELBARROW?
WHERE COULD HE HAVE GOTTEN TO?
OSWAAAALD!
I HOPE HE HASN'T GOTTEN HIMSELF EATEN.

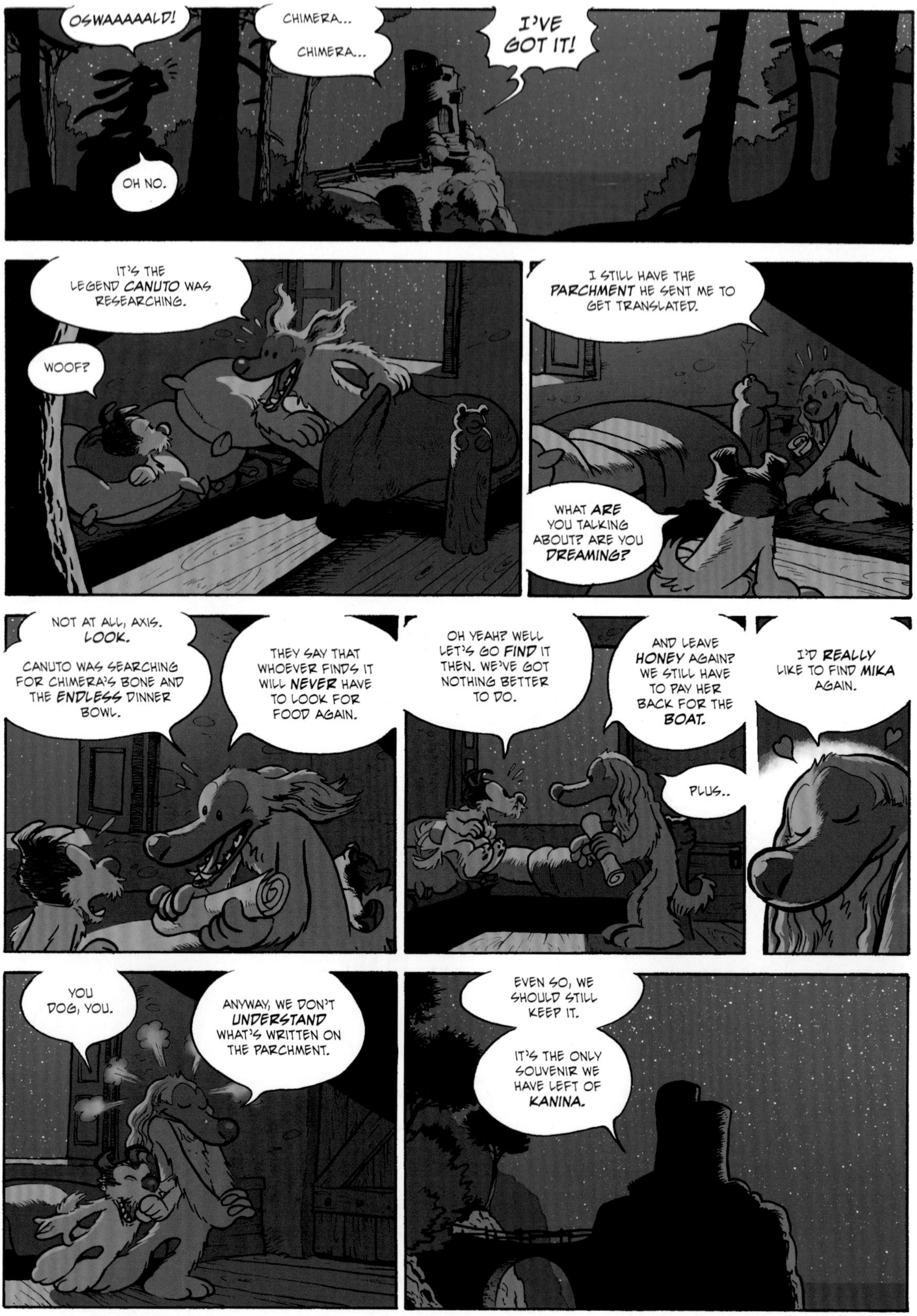
OSWAAAAALD!
OH NO.
CHIMERA...
CHIMERA...
I'VE GOT IT!
IT'S THE LEGEND CANUTO WAS RESEARCHING.
WOOF?
I STILL HAVE THE PARCHMENT HE SENT ME TO GET TRANSLATED.
WHAT ARE YOU TALKING ABOUT? ARE YOU DREAMING?
NOT AT ALL, AXIS. LOOK.
CANUTO WAS SEARCHING FOR CHIMERA'S BONE AND THE ENDLESS DINNER BOWL.
THEY SAY THAT WHOEVER FINDS IT WILL NEVER HAVE TO LOOK FOR FOOD AGAIN.
OH YEAH? WELL LET'S GO FIND IT THEN. WE'VE GOT NOTHING BETTER TO DO.
AND LEAVE HONEY AGAIN? WE STILL HAVE TO PAY HER BACK FOR THE BOAT.
PLUS..
I'D REALLY LIKE TO FIND MIKA AGAIN.
YOU DOG, YOU.
ANYWAY, WE DON'T UNDERSTAND WHAT'S WRITTEN ON THE PARCHMENT.
EVEN SO, WE SHOULD STILL KEEP IT.
IT'S THE ONLY SOUVENIR WE HAVE LEFT OF KANINA.

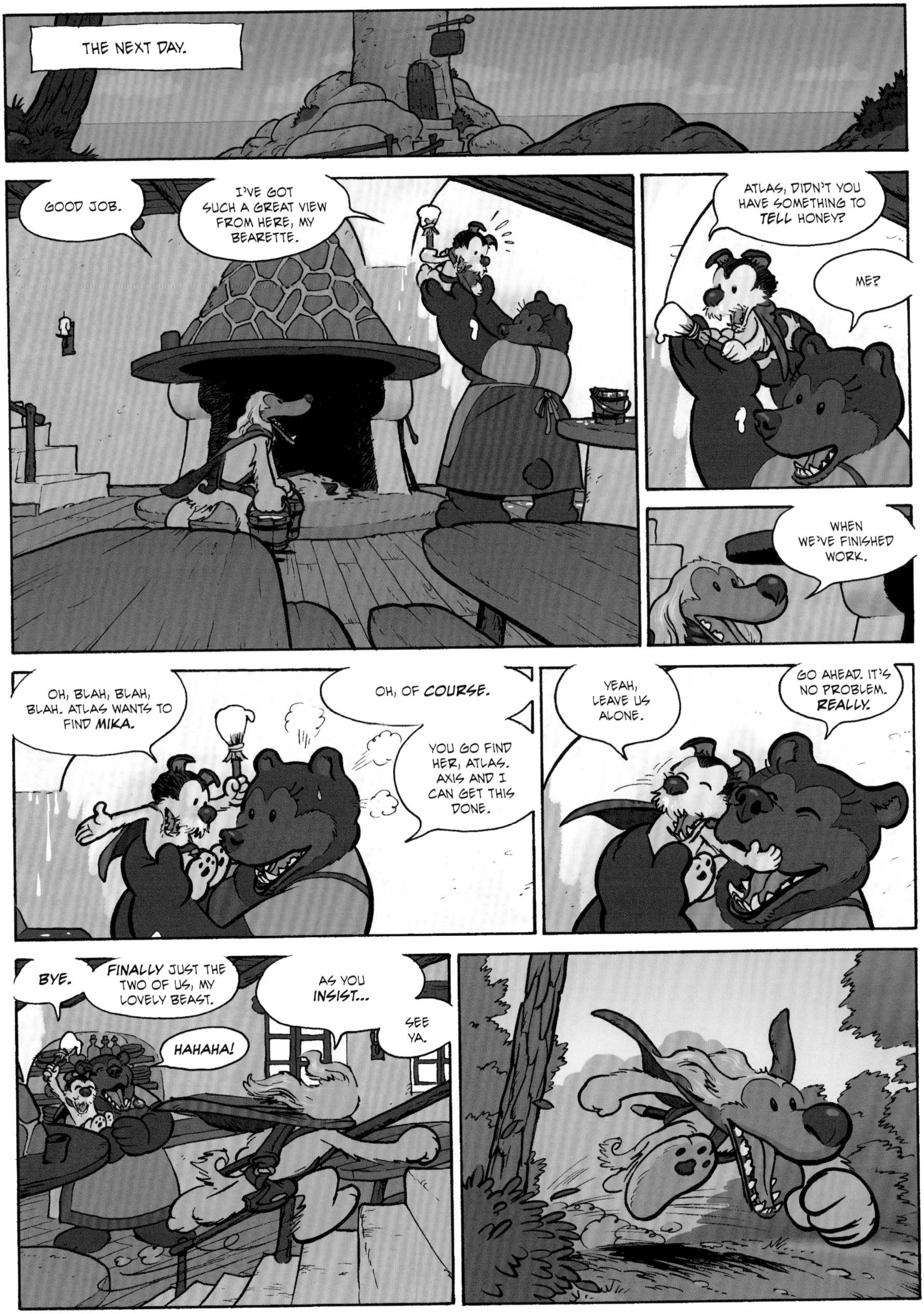

THE NEXT DAY.
GOOD JOB.
I'VE GOT SUCH A GREAT VIEW FROM HERE, MY BEARETTE.
ATLAS, DIDN'T YOU HAVE SOMETHING TO *TELL* HONEY?
ME?
WHEN WE'VE FINISHED WORK.
OH, BLAH, BLAH, BLAH. ATLAS WANTS TO FIND *MIKA.*
OH, OF *COURSE.*
YOU GO FIND HER, ATLAS. AXIS AND I CAN GET THIS DONE.
YEAH, LEAVE US ALONE.
GO AHEAD. IT'S NO PROBLEM. *REALLY.*
BYE.
FINALLY JUST THE TWO OF US, MY LOVELY BEAST.
HAHAHA!
AS YOU *INSIST...*
SEE YA.

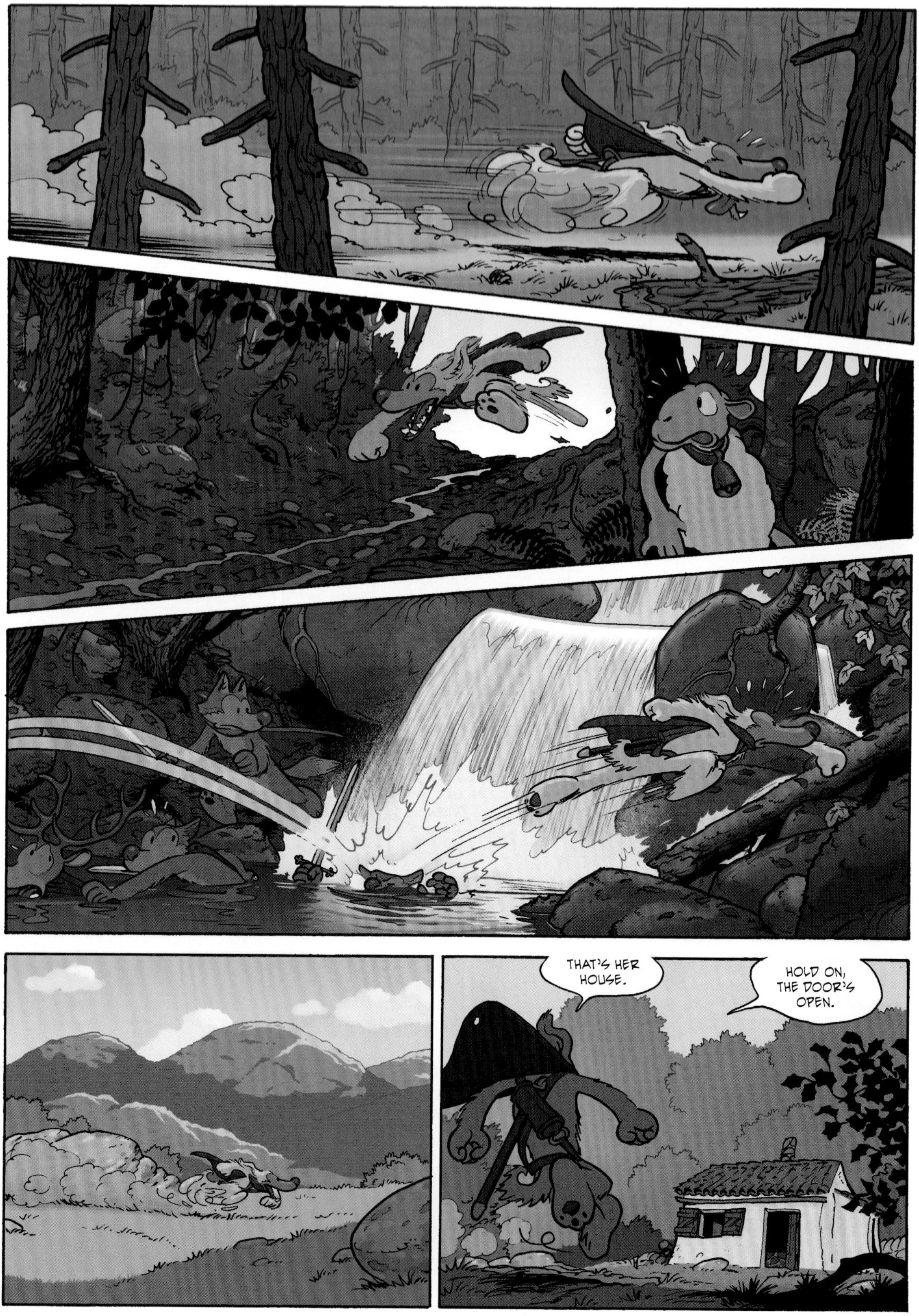
THAT'S HER HOUSE.
HOLD ON, THE DOOR'S OPEN.

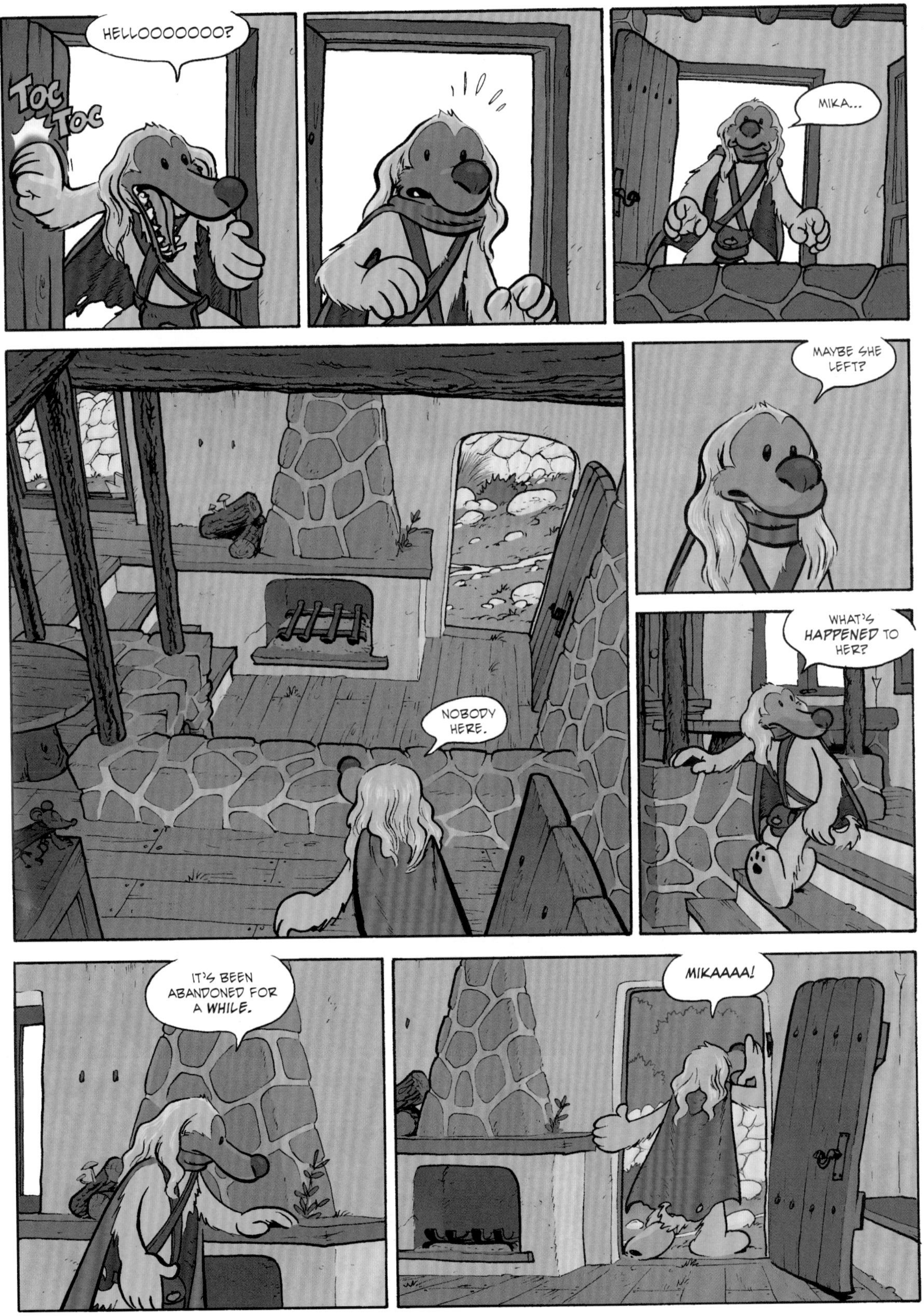
HELLOOOOOOOO?
TOC TOC
MIKA...
NOBODY HERE.
MAYBE SHE LEFT?
WHAT'S HAPPENED TO HER?
IT'S BEEN ABANDONED FOR A WHILE.
MIKAAAA!

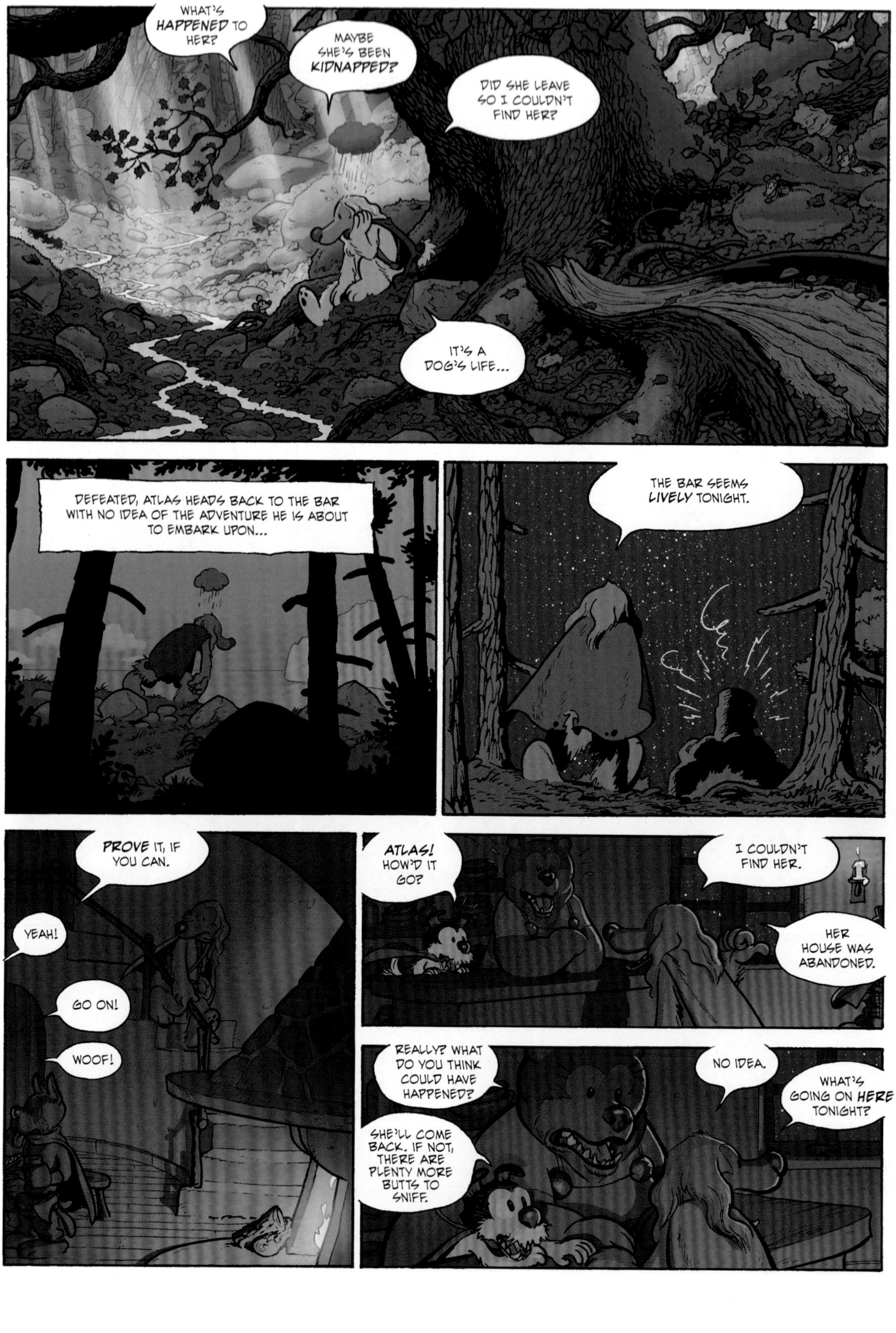
WHAT'S HAPPENED TO HER?
MAYBE SHE'S BEEN KIDNAPPED?
DID SHE LEAVE SO I COULDN'T FIND HER?
IT'S A DOG'S LIFE...
DEFEATED, ATLAS HEADS BACK TO THE BAR WITH NO IDEA OF THE ADVENTURE HE IS ABOUT TO EMBARK UPON...
THE BAR SEEMS LIVELY TONIGHT.
PROVE IT, IF YOU CAN.
YEAH!
GO ON!
WOOF!
ATLAS! HOW'D IT GO?
I COULDN'T FIND HER.
HER HOUSE WAS ABANDONED.
REALLY? WHAT DO YOU THINK COULD HAVE HAPPENED?
NO IDEA.
WHAT'S GOING ON HERE TONIGHT?
SHE'LL COME BACK. IF NOT, THERE ARE PLENTY MORE BUTTS TO SNIFF.

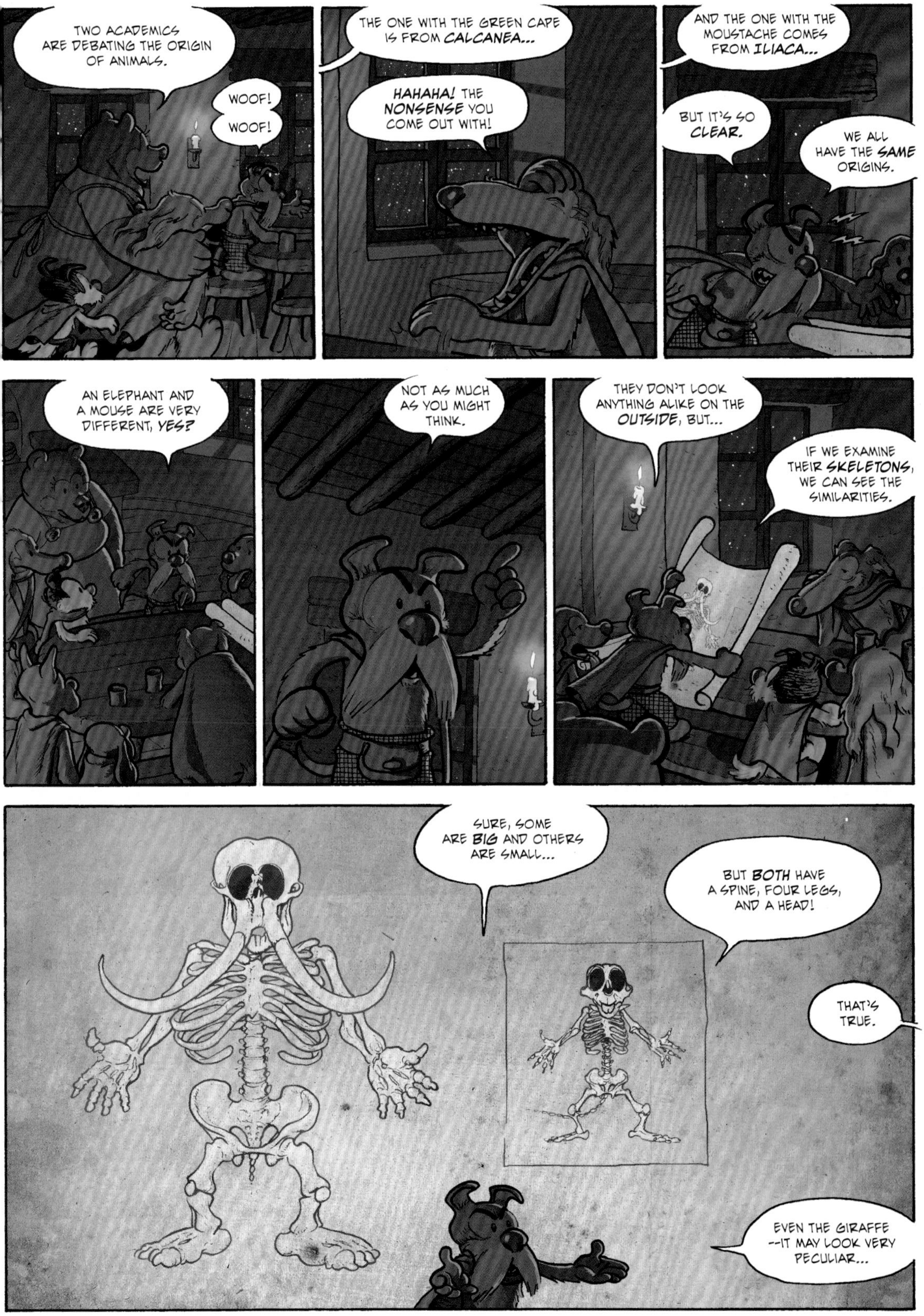
TWO ACADEMICS ARE DEBATING THE ORIGIN OF ANIMALS.
WOOF!
WOOF!
THE ONE WITH THE GREEN CAPE IS FROM CALCANEA...
HAHAHA! THE NONSENSE YOU COME OUT WITH!
AND THE ONE WITH THE MOUSTACHE COMES FROM ILIACA...
BUT IT'S SO CLEAR.
WE ALL HAVE THE SAME ORIGINS.
AN ELEPHANT AND A MOUSE ARE VERY DIFFERENT, YES?
NOT AS MUCH AS YOU MIGHT THINK.
THEY DON'T LOOK ANYTHING ALIKE ON THE OUTSIDE, BUT...
IF WE EXAMINE THEIR SKELETONS, WE CAN SEE THE SIMILARITIES.
SURE, SOME ARE BIG AND OTHERS ARE SMALL...
BUT BOTH HAVE A SPINE, FOUR LEGS, AND A HEAD!
THAT'S TRUE.
EVEN THE GIRAFFE --IT MAY LOOK VERY PECULIAR...

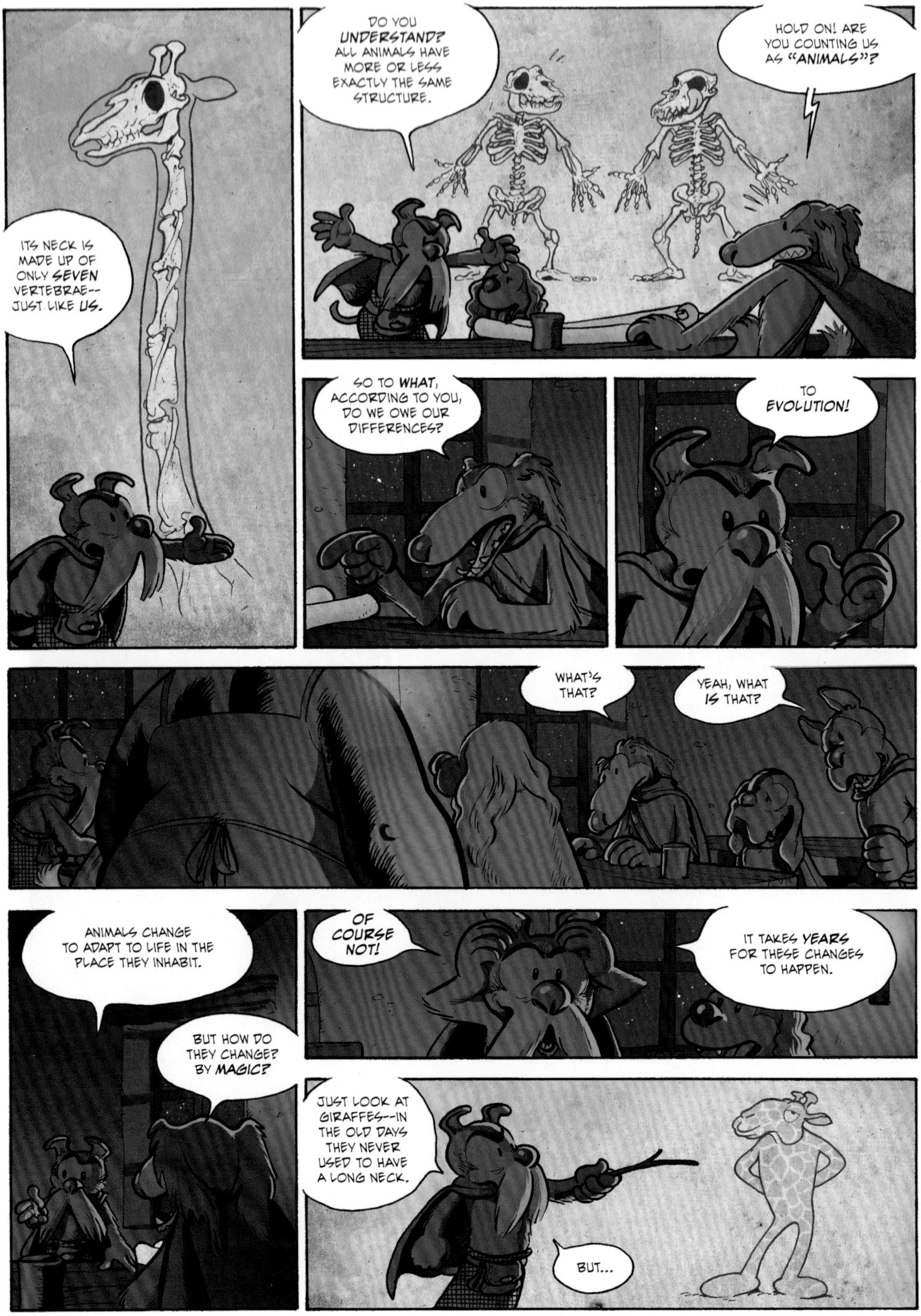
ITS NECK IS MADE UP OF ONLY SEVEN VERTEBRAE--JUST LIKE US.
DO YOU UNDERSTAND? ALL ANIMALS HAVE MORE OR LESS EXACTLY THE SAME STRUCTURE.
HOLD ON! ARE YOU COUNTING US AS "ANIMALS"?
SO TO WHAT, ACCORDING TO YOU, DO WE OWE OUR DIFFERENCES?
TO EVOLUTION!
WHAT'S THAT?
YEAH, WHAT IS THAT?
ANIMALS CHANGE TO ADAPT TO LIFE IN THE PLACE THEY INHABIT.
BUT HOW DO THEY CHANGE? BY MAGIC?
OF COURSE NOT!
IT TAKES YEARS FOR THESE CHANGES TO HAPPEN.
JUST LOOK AT GIRAFFES--IN THE OLD DAYS THEY NEVER USED TO HAVE A LONG NECK.
BUT...

"THERE CAME A TIME WHEN THERE WASN'T ENOUGH FOOD TO GO ROUND.

"SO SOME OF THEM STARTED TO STARVE.

"WHICH ONES? THOSE WITH THE **SHORTEST** NECKS BECAUSE THEY COULDN'T REACH THE TOP BRANCHES WHERE THERE WAS STILL FOOD."

THE ONES WHO WERE BEST SUITED **SURVIVED** AND HAD CHILDREN WITH THE SAME LONG NECKS.

AND SO GIRAFFES EVOLVED LONGER AND LONGER NECKS.

HAHAHA! **STOP!** I'M GOING TO DIE FROM LAUGHING SO MUCH.

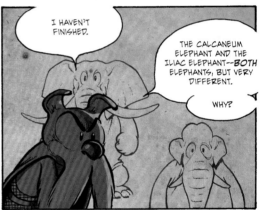

I HAVEN'T FINISHED.

THE CALCANEUM ELEPHANT AND THE ILIAC ELEPHANT--**BOTH** ELEPHANTS, BUT VERY DIFFERENT.

WHY?

BECAUSE THEY'RE **BOTH** DESCENDED FROM THE SAME ANIMAL--**THE WOOLLY MAMMOTH**--BUT THEY'VE HAD TO EVOLVE TO ADAPT TO THE DIFFERENT CONDITIONS IN **CALCANEA** AND **ILIACA**.

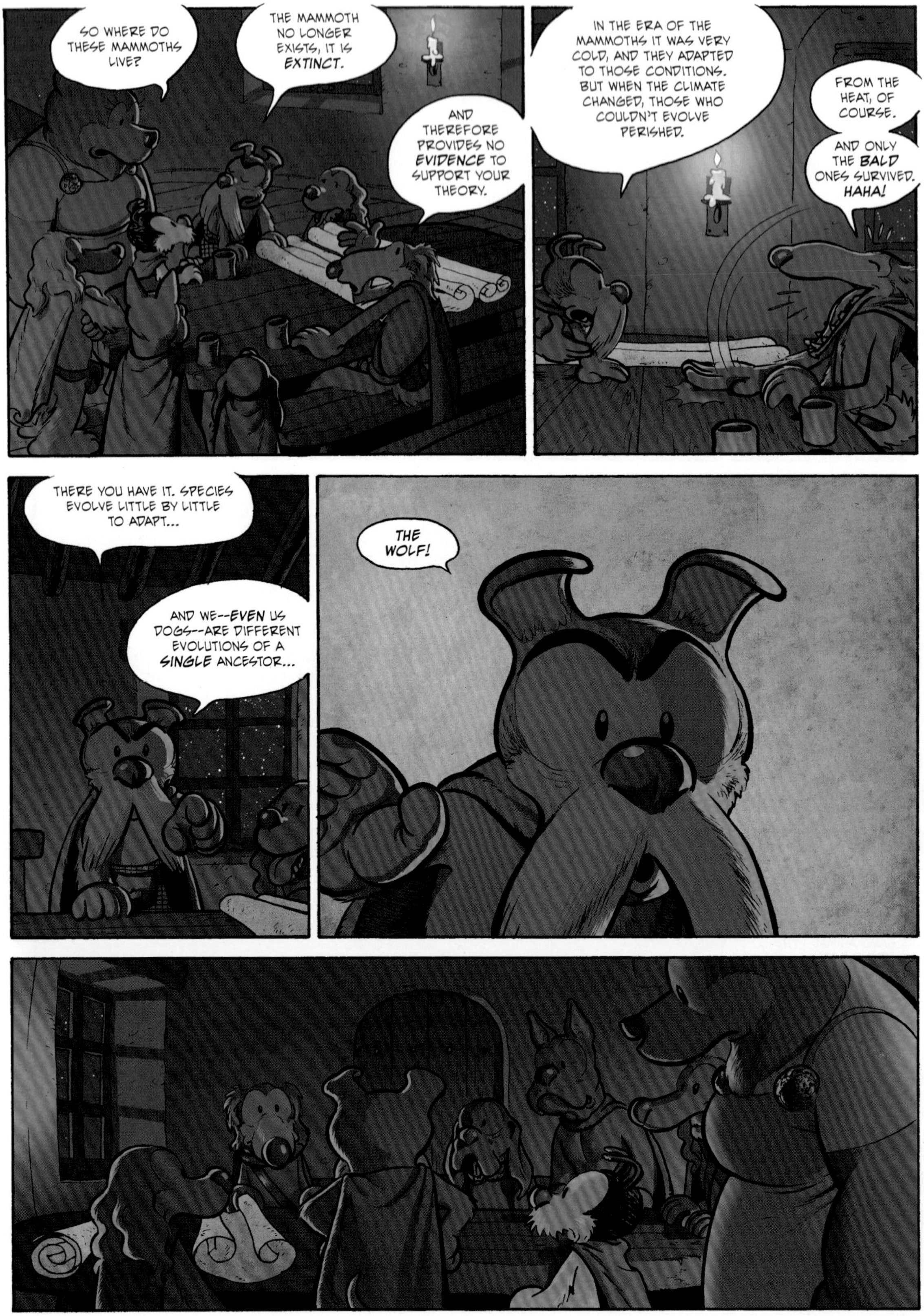
SO WHERE DO THESE MAMMOTHS LIVE?
THE MAMMOTH NO LONGER EXISTS, IT IS EXTINCT.
AND THEREFORE PROVIDES NO EVIDENCE TO SUPPORT YOUR THEORY.
IN THE ERA OF THE MAMMOTHS IT WAS VERY COLD, AND THEY ADAPTED TO THOSE CONDITIONS. BUT WHEN THE CLIMATE CHANGED, THOSE WHO COULDN'T EVOLVE PERISHED.
FROM THE HEAT, OF COURSE.
AND ONLY THE BALD ONES SURVIVED. HAHA!
THERE YOU HAVE IT. SPECIES EVOLVE LITTLE BY LITTLE TO ADAPT...
AND WE--EVEN US DOGS--ARE DIFFERENT EVOLUTIONS OF A SINGLE ANCESTOR...
THE WOLF!

YOU'RE **MAD!**

WHAT ARE YOU GOING ON ABOUT?

DESCENDED FROM THE **WOLF?!**

WOLVES ARE SAVAGE BEASTS.

THEY DON'T EVEN WEAR CLOTHES.

PLUS, DOGS LOOK **NOTHING** LIKE WOLVES.

BECAUSE WE'VE EVOLVED SO MUCH. AND WITH TIME, OUR DESCENDANTS WILL LOOK EVEN **LESS** LIKE WOLVES.

LOOK, THE WOLF HAS SEPARATED INTO SEVERAL DIFFERENT TYPES OF DOG: BLOODHOUNDS, FIGHTERS, RUNNERS, PACK DOGS, GUARD DOGS...

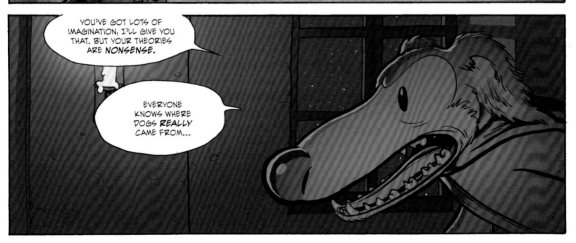

YOU'VE GOT LOTS OF IMAGINATION, I'LL GIVE YOU THAT. BUT YOUR THEORIES ARE **NONSENSE.**

EVERYONE KNOWS WHERE DOGS **REALLY** CAME FROM...

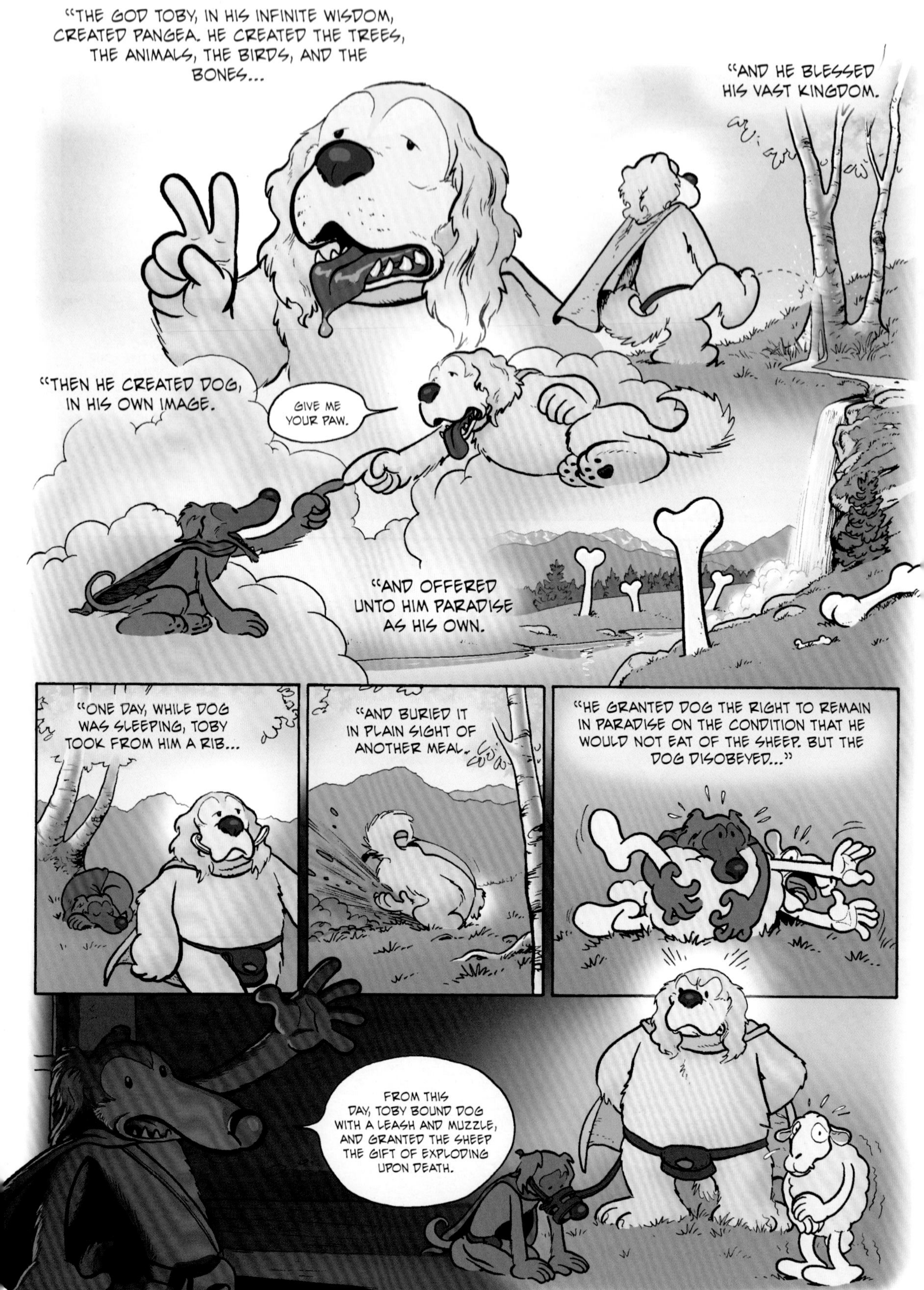
"THE GOD TOBY, IN HIS INFINITE WISDOM, CREATED PANGEA. HE CREATED THE TREES, THE ANIMALS, THE BIRDS, AND THE BONES...
"AND HE BLESSED HIS VAST KINGDOM.
"THEN HE CREATED DOG, IN HIS OWN IMAGE.
GIVE ME YOUR PAW.
"AND OFFERED UNTO HIM PARADISE AS HIS OWN.
"ONE DAY, WHILE DOG WAS SLEEPING, TOBY TOOK FROM HIM A RIB...
"AND BURIED IT IN PLAIN SIGHT OF ANOTHER MEAL.
"HE GRANTED DOG THE RIGHT TO REMAIN IN PARADISE ON THE CONDITION THAT HE WOULD NOT EAT OF THE SHEEP. BUT THE DOG DISOBEYED..."
FROM THIS DAY, TOBY BOUND DOG WITH A LEASH AND MUZZLE, AND GRANTED THE SHEEP THE GIFT OF EXPLODING UPON DEATH.

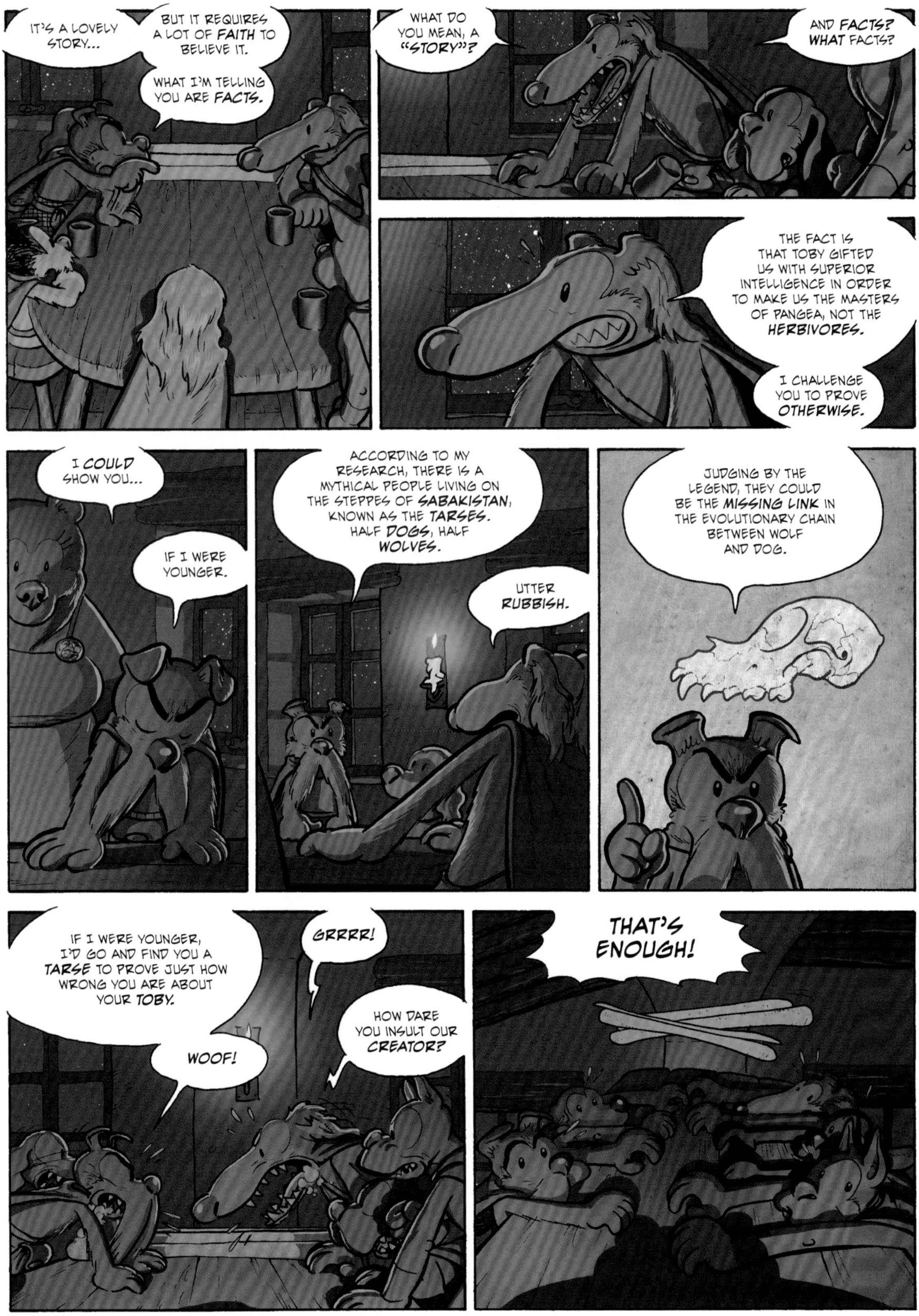
IT'S A LOVELY STORY...
BUT IT REQUIRES A LOT OF FAITH TO BELIEVE IT.
WHAT I'M TELLING YOU ARE FACTS.
WHAT DO YOU MEAN, A "STORY"?
AND FACTS? WHAT FACTS?
THE FACT IS THAT TOBY GIFTED US WITH SUPERIOR INTELLIGENCE IN ORDER TO MAKE US THE MASTERS OF PANGEA, NOT THE HERBIVORES.
I CHALLENGE YOU TO PROVE OTHERWISE.
I COULD SHOW YOU...
IF I WERE YOUNGER.
ACCORDING TO MY RESEARCH, THERE IS A MYTHICAL PEOPLE LIVING ON THE STEPPES OF SABAKISTAN, KNOWN AS THE TARSES. HALF DOGS, HALF WOLVES.
UTTER RUBBISH.
JUDGING BY THE LEGEND, THEY COULD BE THE MISSING LINK IN THE EVOLUTIONARY CHAIN BETWEEN WOLF AND DOG.
IF I WERE YOUNGER, I'D GO AND FIND YOU A TARSE TO PROVE JUST HOW WRONG YOU ARE ABOUT YOUR TOBY.
GRRRR!
WOOF!
HOW DARE YOU INSULT OUR CREATOR?
THAT'S ENOUGH!

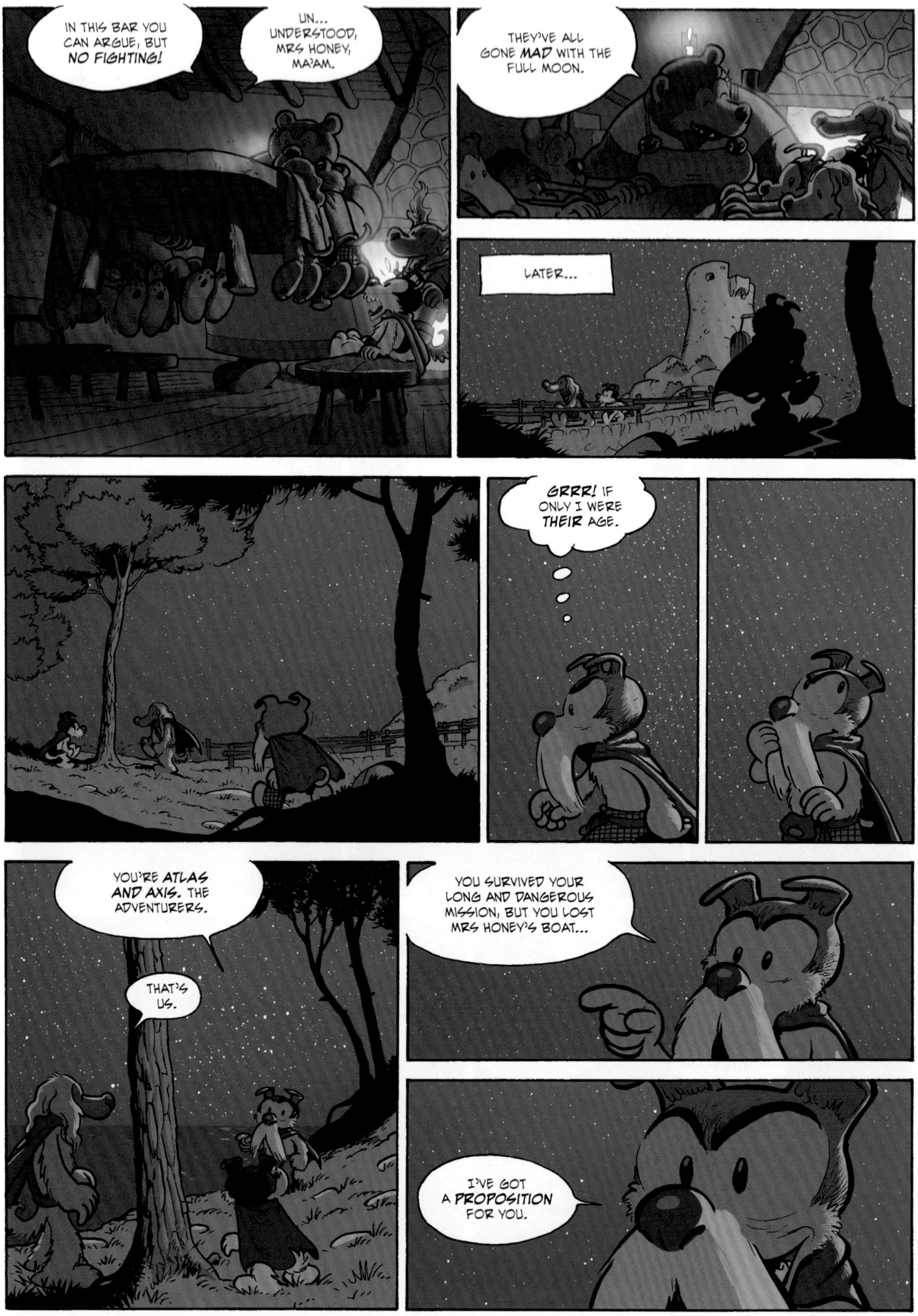
IN THIS BAR YOU CAN ARGUE, BUT **NO FIGHTING!**
UN... UNDERSTOOD, MRS HONEY, MA'AM.
THEY'VE ALL GONE **MAD** WITH THE FULL MOON.
LATER...
GRRR! IF ONLY I WERE **THEIR** AGE.
YOU'RE **ATLAS AND AXIS.** THE ADVENTURERS.
THAT'S US.
YOU SURVIVED YOUR LONG AND DANGEROUS MISSION, BUT YOU LOST MRS HONEY'S BOAT...
I'VE GOT A **PROPOSITION** FOR YOU.

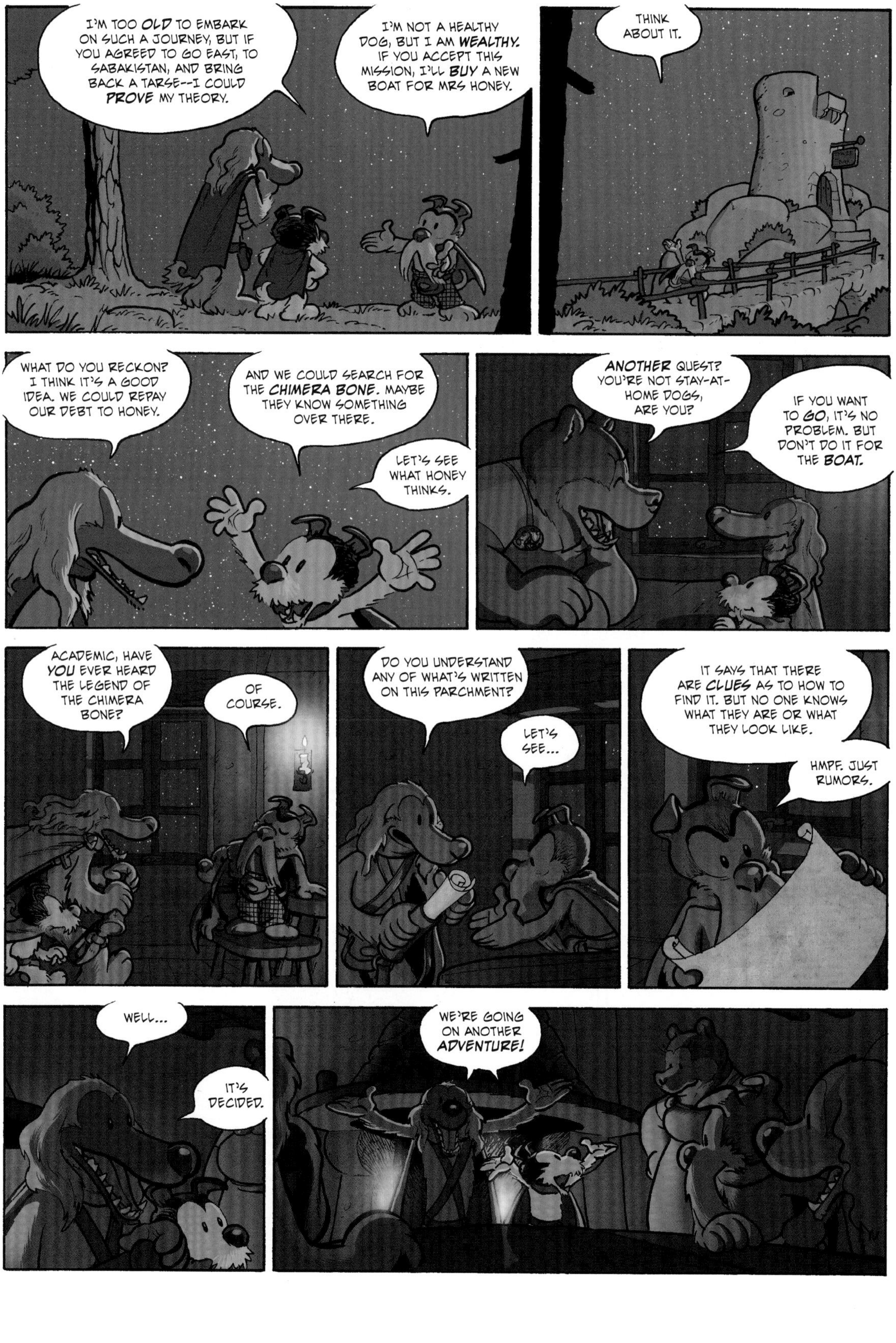
I'M TOO *OLD* TO EMBARK ON SUCH A JOURNEY, BUT IF YOU AGREED TO GO EAST, TO SABAKISTAN, AND BRING BACK A TARSE--I COULD *PROVE* MY THEORY.
I'M NOT A HEALTHY DOG, BUT I AM *WEALTHY.* IF YOU ACCEPT THIS MISSION, I'LL *BUY* A NEW BOAT FOR MRS HONEY.
THINK ABOUT IT.
WHAT DO YOU RECKON? I THINK IT'S A GOOD IDEA. WE COULD REPAY OUR DEBT TO HONEY.
AND WE COULD SEARCH FOR THE *CHIMERA BONE.* MAYBE THEY KNOW SOMETHING OVER THERE.
LET'S SEE WHAT HONEY THINKS.
ANOTHER QUEST? YOU'RE NOT STAY-AT-HOME DOGS, ARE YOU?
IF YOU WANT TO *GO,* IT'S NO PROBLEM. BUT DON'T DO IT FOR THE *BOAT.*
ACADEMIC, HAVE *YOU* EVER HEARD THE LEGEND OF THE CHIMERA BONE?
OF COURSE.
DO YOU UNDERSTAND ANY OF WHAT'S WRITTEN ON THIS PARCHMENT?
LET'S SEE...
IT SAYS THAT THERE ARE *CLUES* AS TO HOW TO FIND IT. BUT NO ONE KNOWS WHAT THEY ARE OR WHAT THEY LOOK LIKE.
HMPF. JUST RUMORS.
WELL...
IT'S DECIDED.
WE'RE GOING ON ANOTHER *ADVENTURE!*

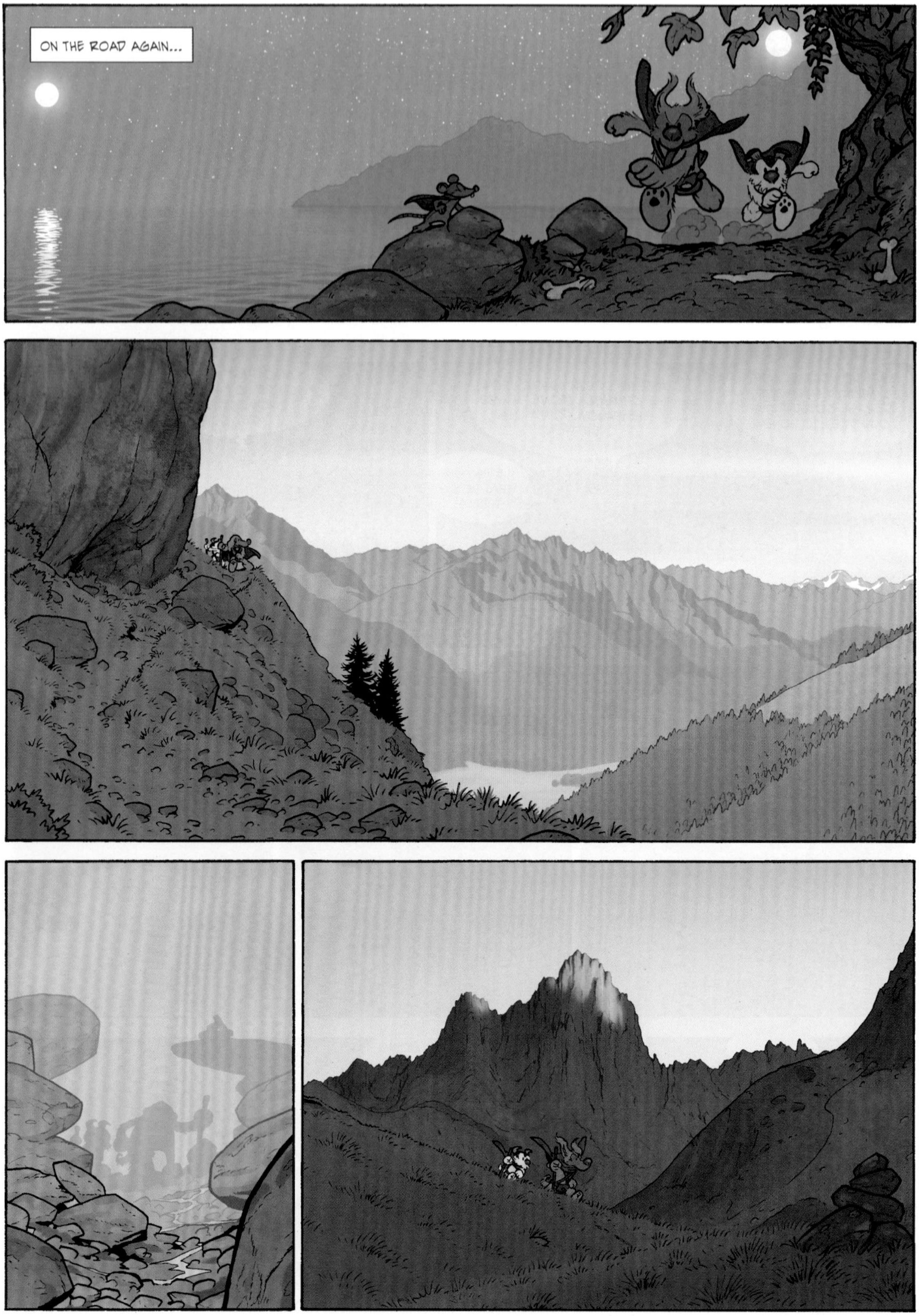
ON THE ROAD AGAIN...

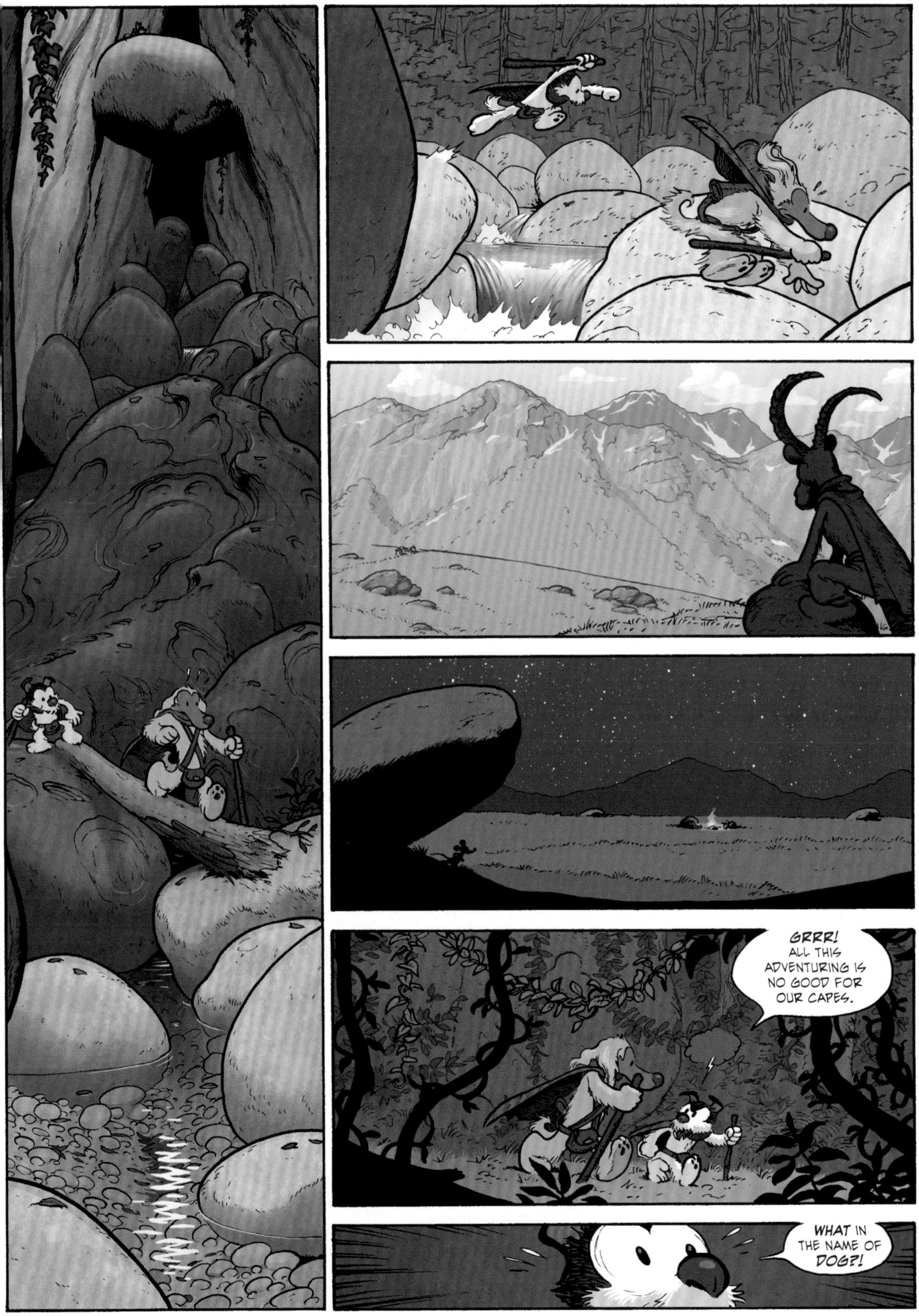
GRRR! ALL THIS ADVENTURING IS NO GOOD FOR OUR CAPES.
WHAT IN THE NAME OF DOG?!

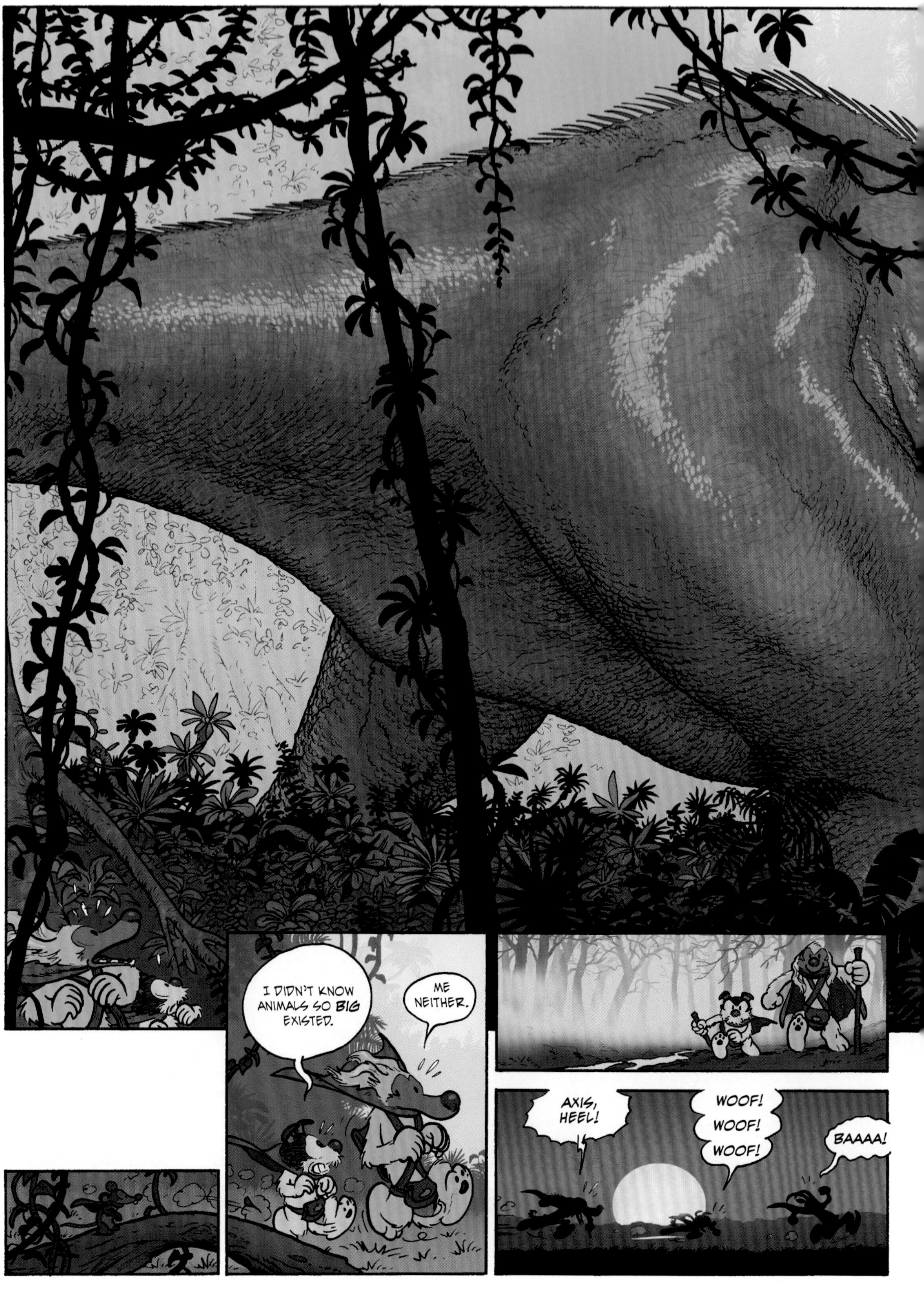
I DIDN'T KNOW ANIMALS SO BIG EXISTED.
ME NEITHER.
AXIS, HEEL!
WOOF! WOOF! WOOF!
BAAAA!

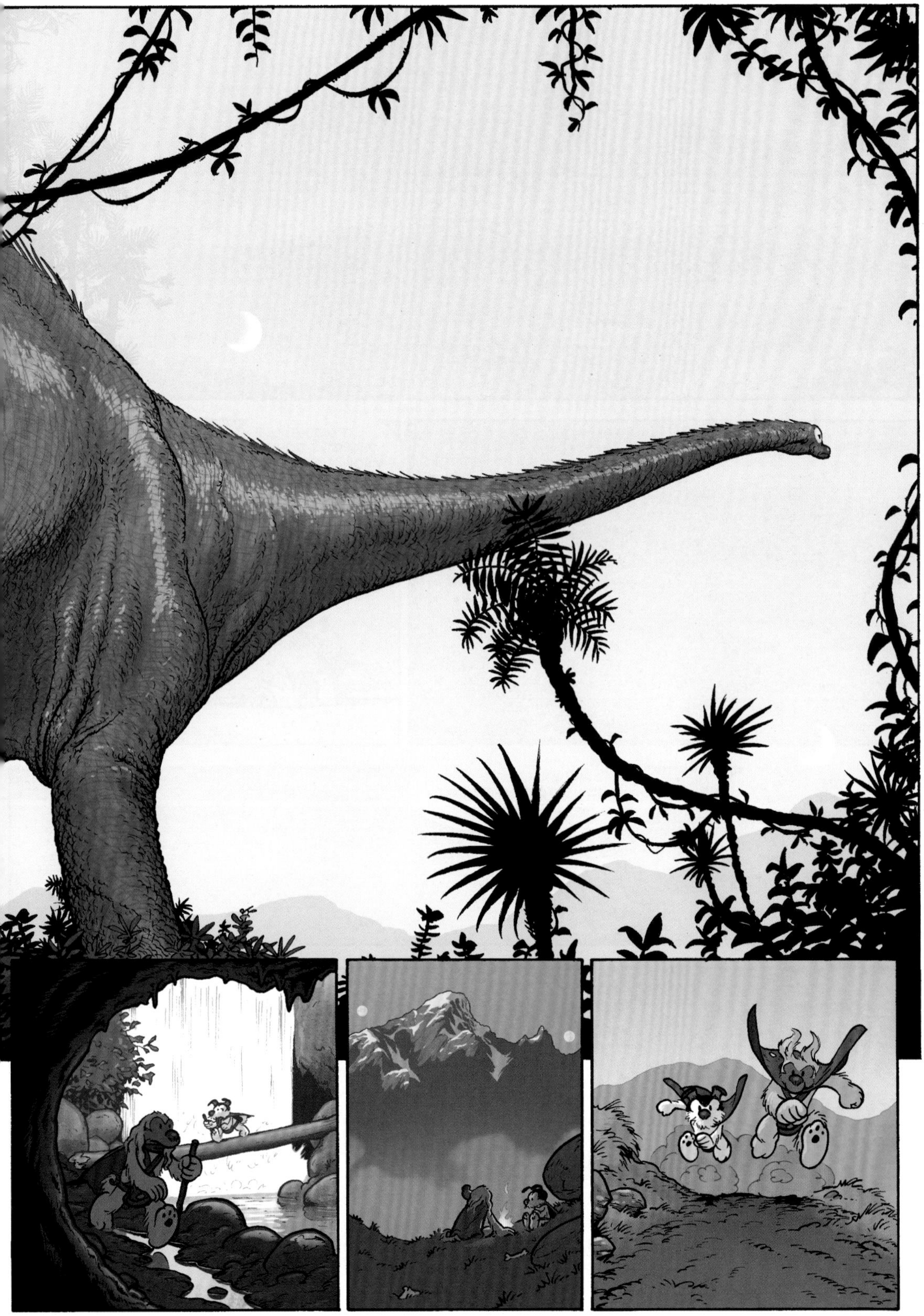

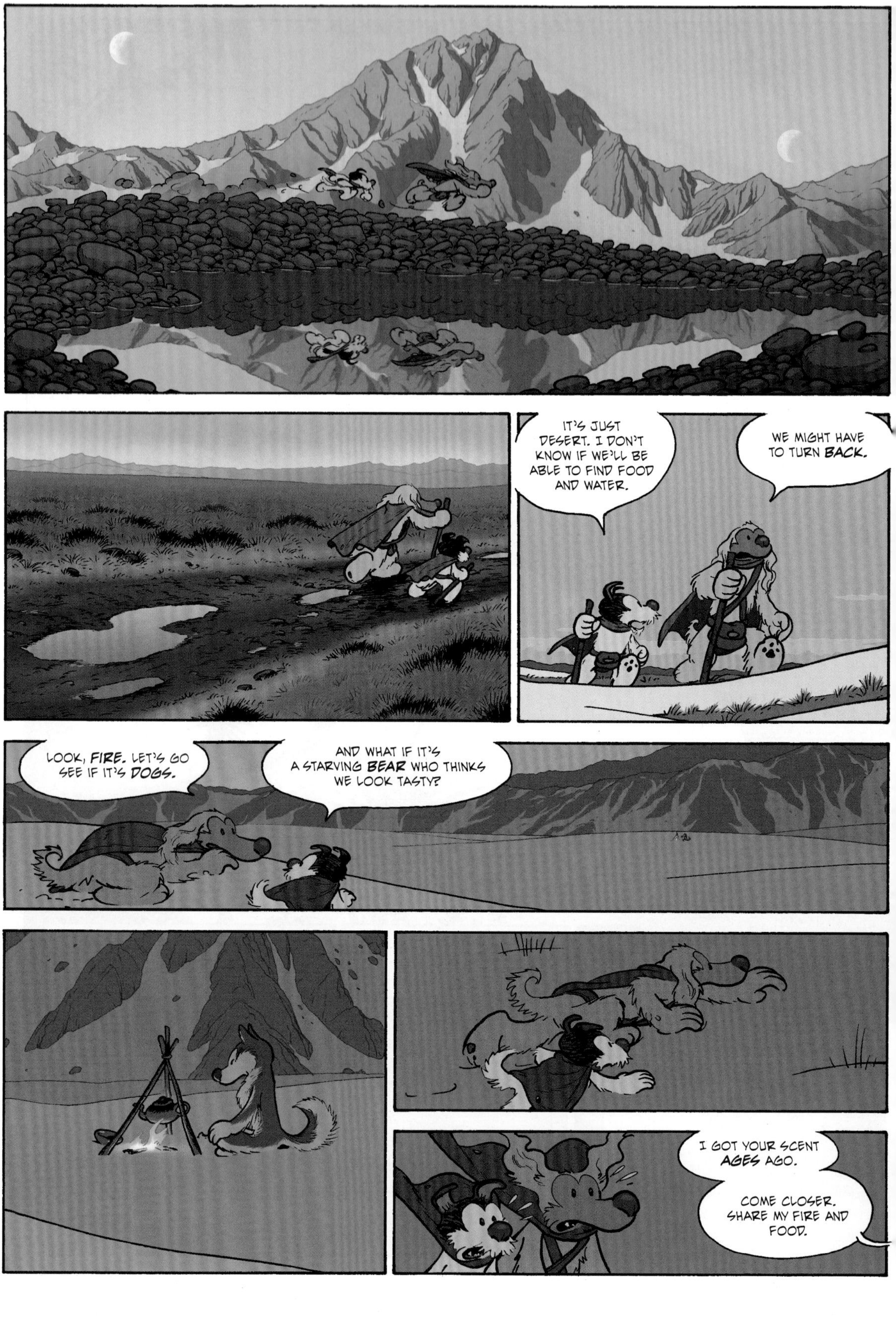
IT'S JUST DESERT. I DON'T KNOW IF WE'LL BE ABLE TO FIND FOOD AND WATER.
WE MIGHT HAVE TO TURN BACK.
LOOK, FIRE. LET'S GO SEE IF IT'S DOGS.
AND WHAT IF IT'S A STARVING BEAR WHO THINKS WE LOOK TASTY?
I GOT YOUR SCENT AGES AGO.
COME CLOSER. SHARE MY FIRE AND FOOD.

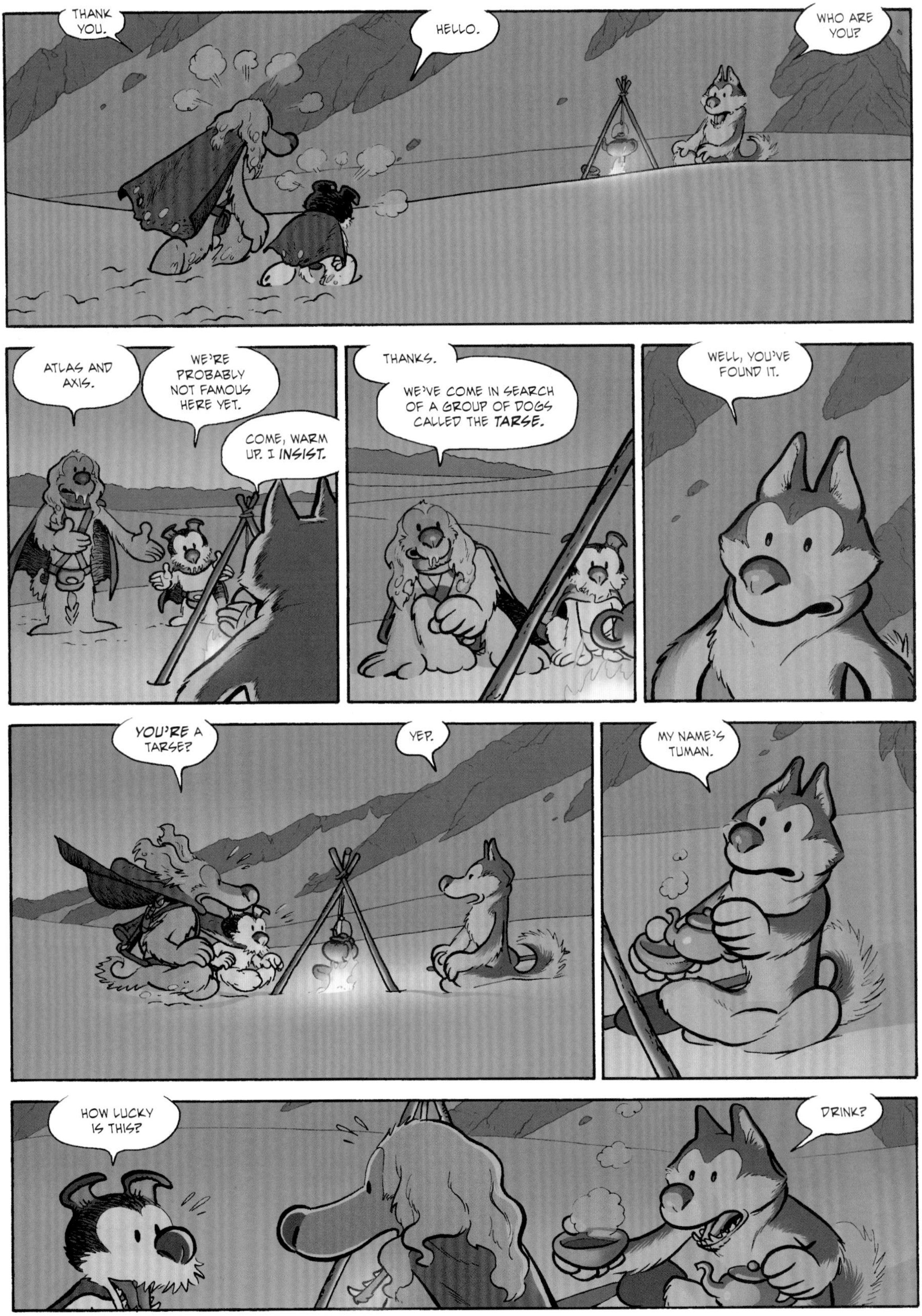
THANK YOU.
HELLO.
WHO ARE YOU?
ATLAS AND AXIS.
WE'RE PROBABLY NOT FAMOUS HERE YET.
COME, WARM UP. I *INSIST.*
THANKS.
WE'VE COME IN SEARCH OF A GROUP OF DOGS CALLED THE *TARSE.*
WELL, YOU'VE FOUND IT.
YOU'RE A TARSE?
YEP.
MY NAME'S TUMAN.
HOW LUCKY IS THIS?
DRINK?

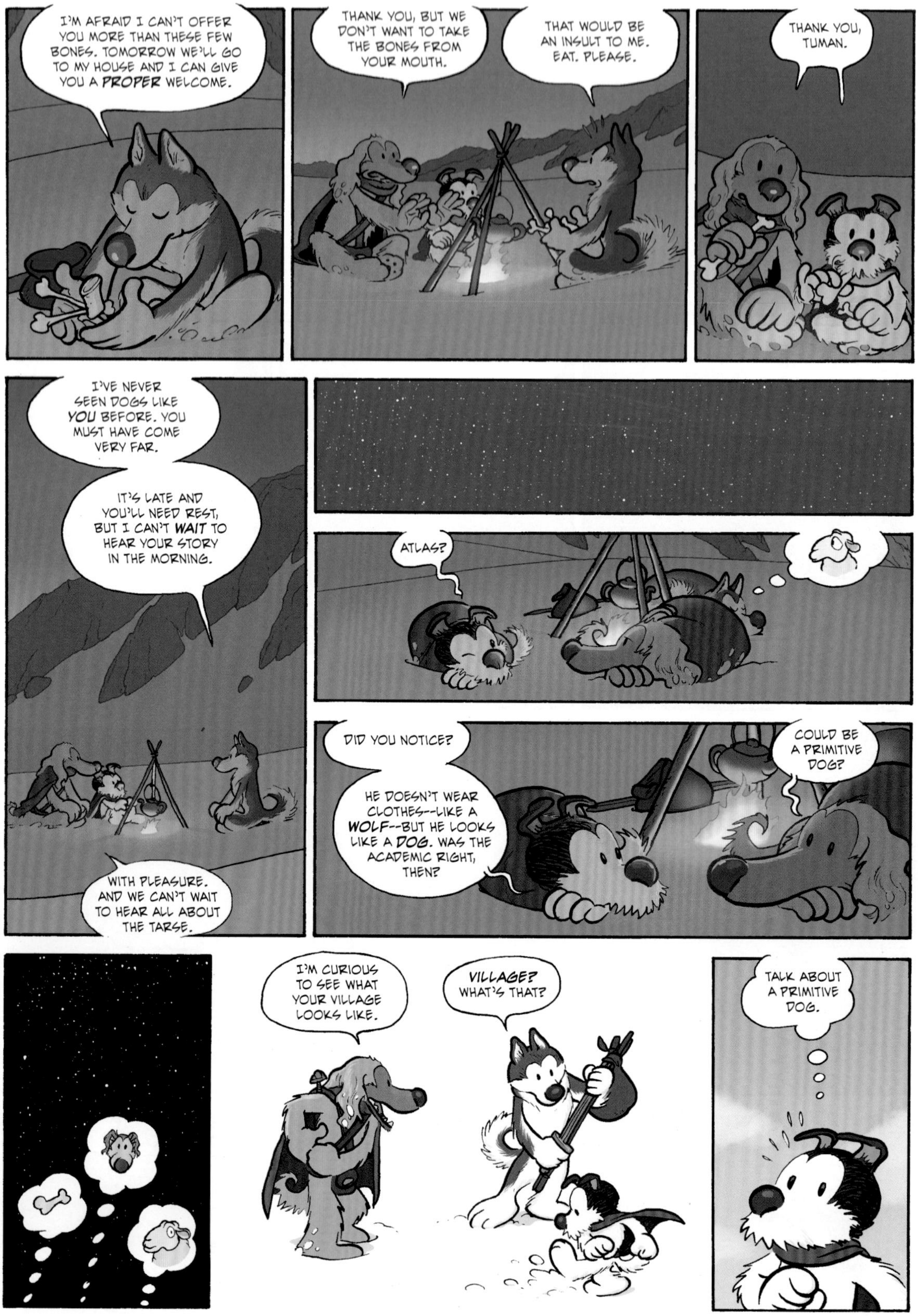

I'M AFRAID I CAN'T OFFER YOU MORE THAN THESE FEW BONES. TOMORROW WE'LL GO TO MY HOUSE AND I CAN GIVE YOU A PROPER WELCOME.
THANK YOU, BUT WE DON'T WANT TO TAKE THE BONES FROM YOUR MOUTH.
THAT WOULD BE AN INSULT TO ME. EAT. PLEASE.
THANK YOU, TUMAN.
I'VE NEVER SEEN DOGS LIKE YOU BEFORE. YOU MUST HAVE COME VERY FAR.
IT'S LATE AND YOU'LL NEED REST, BUT I CAN'T WAIT TO HEAR YOUR STORY IN THE MORNING.
WITH PLEASURE. AND WE CAN'T WAIT TO HEAR ALL ABOUT THE TARSE.
ATLAS?
DID YOU NOTICE?
HE DOESN'T WEAR CLOTHES--LIKE A WOLF--BUT HE LOOKS LIKE A DOG. WAS THE ACADEMIC RIGHT, THEN?
COULD BE A PRIMITIVE DOG?
I'M CURIOUS TO SEE WHAT YOUR VILLAGE LOOKS LIKE.
VILLAGE? WHAT'S THAT?
TALK ABOUT A PRIMITIVE DOG.

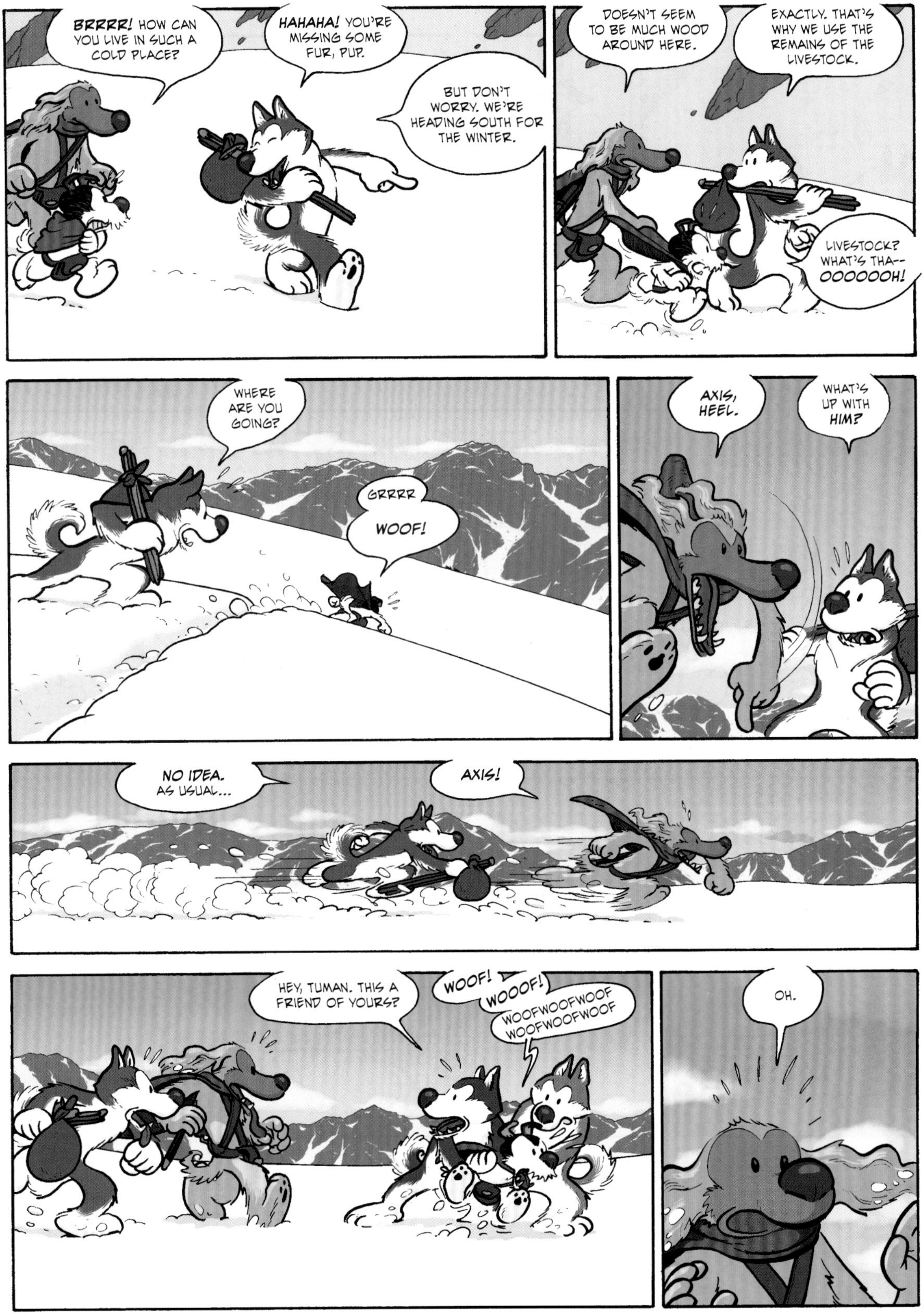
BRRRR! HOW CAN YOU LIVE IN SUCH A COLD PLACE?
HAHAHA! YOU'RE MISSING SOME FUR, PUP.
BUT DON'T WORRY. WE'RE HEADING SOUTH FOR THE WINTER.
DOESN'T SEEM TO BE MUCH WOOD AROUND HERE.
EXACTLY. THAT'S WHY WE USE THE REMAINS OF THE LIVESTOCK.
LIVESTOCK? WHAT'S THA-- OOOOOOH!
WHERE ARE YOU GOING?
GRRRR
WOOF!
AXIS, HEEL.
WHAT'S UP WITH HIM?
NO IDEA. AS USUAL...
AXIS!
HEY, TUMAN. THIS A FRIEND OF YOURS?
WOOF!
WOOOF!
WOOFWOOFWOOF WOOFWOOFWOOF
OH.

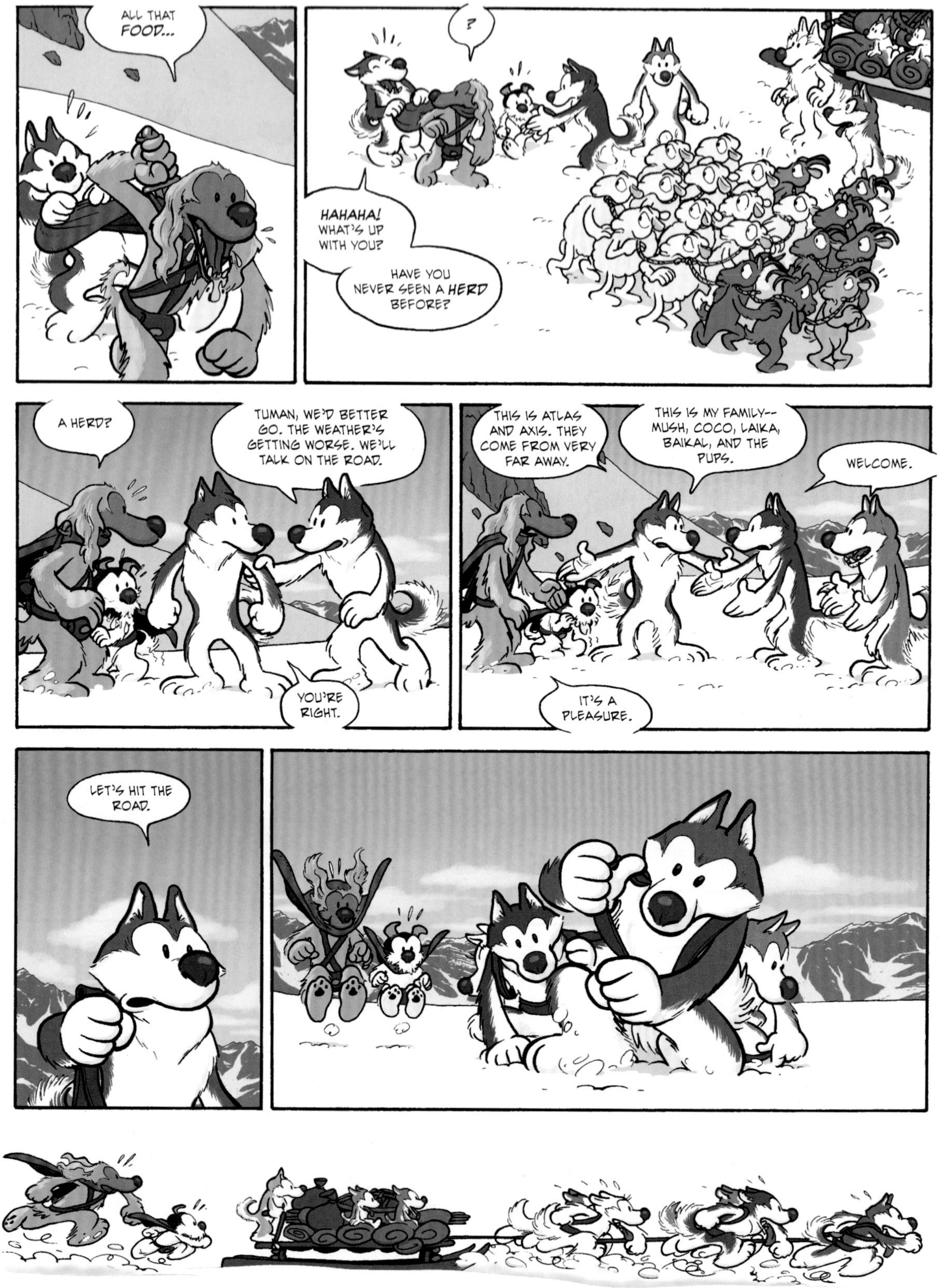

ALL THAT FOOD...
?
HAHAHA! WHAT'S UP WITH YOU?
HAVE YOU NEVER SEEN A HERD BEFORE?
A HERD?
TUMAN, WE'D BETTER GO. THE WEATHER'S GETTING WORSE. WE'LL TALK ON THE ROAD.
YOU'RE RIGHT.
THIS IS ATLAS AND AXIS. THEY COME FROM VERY FAR AWAY.
THIS IS MY FAMILY-- MUSH, COCO, LAIKA, BAIKAL, AND THE PUPS.
WELCOME.
IT'S A PLEASURE.
LET'S HIT THE ROAD.

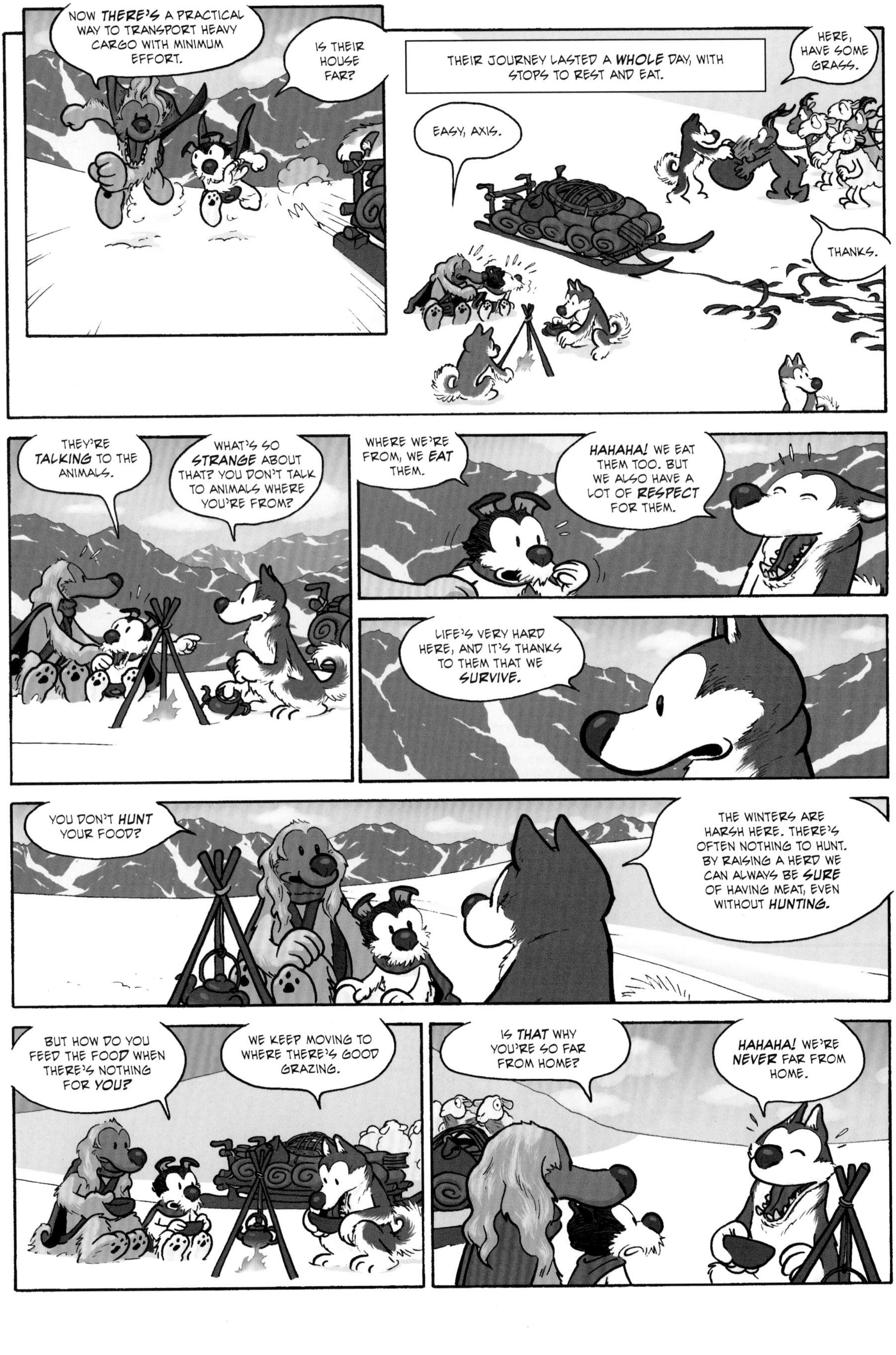
NOW THERE'S A PRACTICAL WAY TO TRANSPORT HEAVY CARGO WITH MINIMUM EFFORT.
IS THEIR HOUSE FAR?
THEIR JOURNEY LASTED A WHOLE DAY, WITH STOPS TO REST AND EAT.
EASY, AXIS.
HERE, HAVE SOME GRASS.
THANKS.
THEY'RE TALKING TO THE ANIMALS.
WHAT'S SO STRANGE ABOUT THAT? YOU DON'T TALK TO ANIMALS WHERE YOU'RE FROM?
WHERE WE'RE FROM, WE EAT THEM.
HAHAHA! WE EAT THEM TOO. BUT WE ALSO HAVE A LOT OF RESPECT FOR THEM.
LIFE'S VERY HARD HERE, AND IT'S THANKS TO THEM THAT WE SURVIVE.
YOU DON'T HUNT YOUR FOOD?
THE WINTERS ARE HARSH HERE. THERE'S OFTEN NOTHING TO HUNT. BY RAISING A HERD WE CAN ALWAYS BE SURE OF HAVING MEAT, EVEN WITHOUT HUNTING.
BUT HOW DO YOU FEED THE FOOD WHEN THERE'S NOTHING FOR YOU?
WE KEEP MOVING TO WHERE THERE'S GOOD GRAZING.
IS THAT WHY YOU'RE SO FAR FROM HOME?
HAHAHA! WE'RE NEVER FAR FROM HOME.

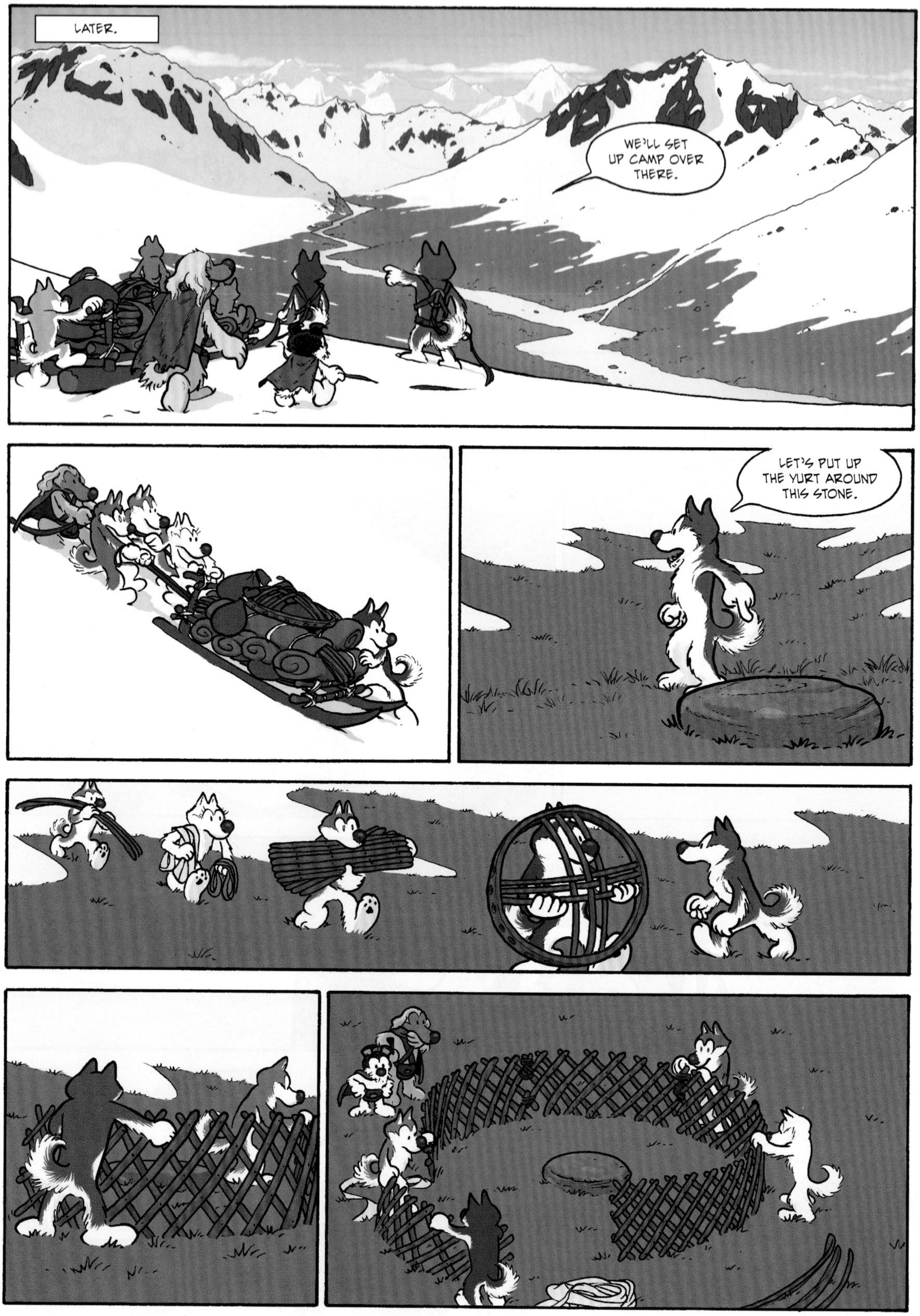
LATER.
WE'LL SET UP CAMP OVER THERE.
LET'S PUT UP THE YURT AROUND THIS STONE.

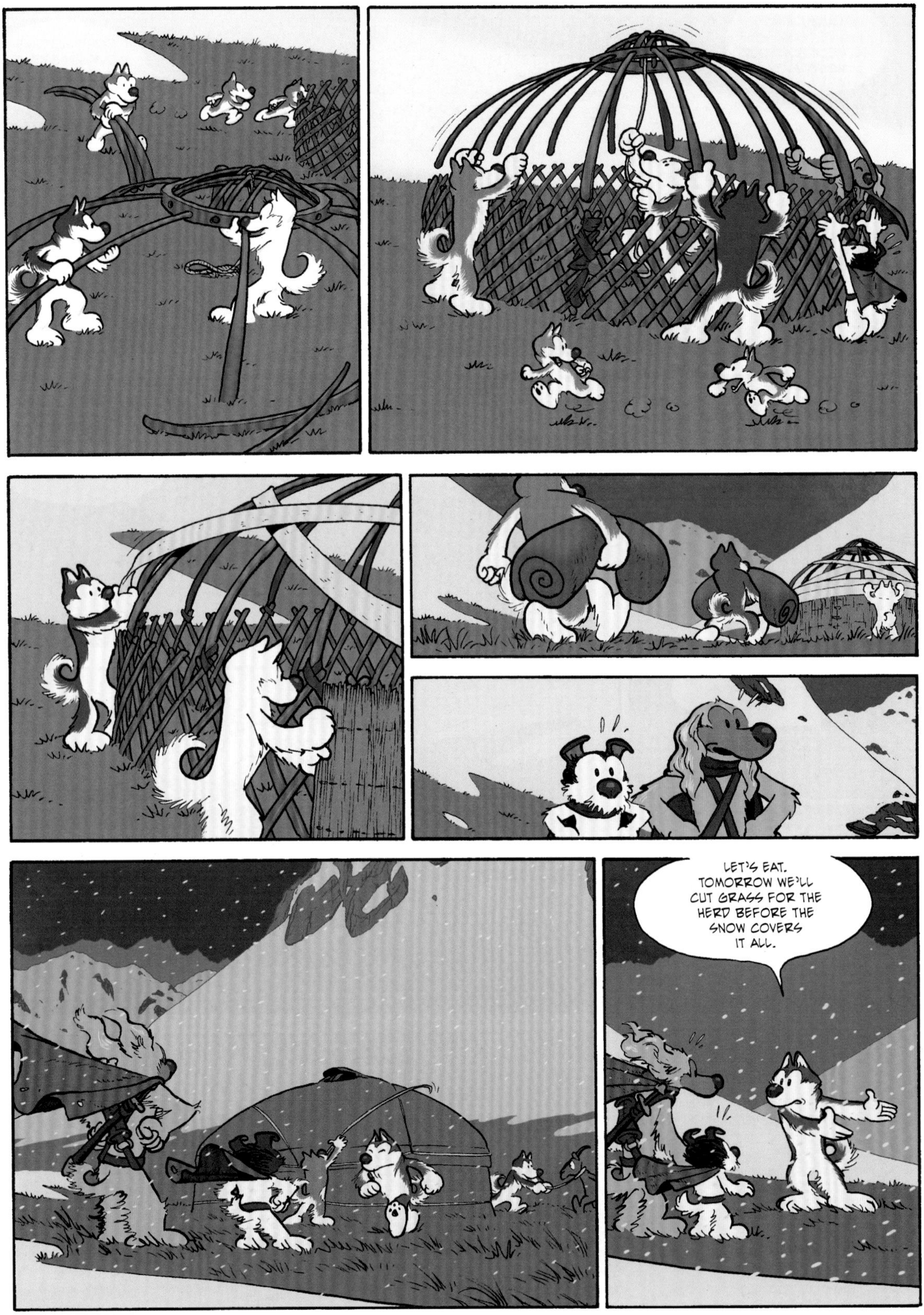
LET'S EAT. TOMORROW WE'LL CUT GRASS FOR THE HERD BEFORE THE SNOW COVERS IT ALL.

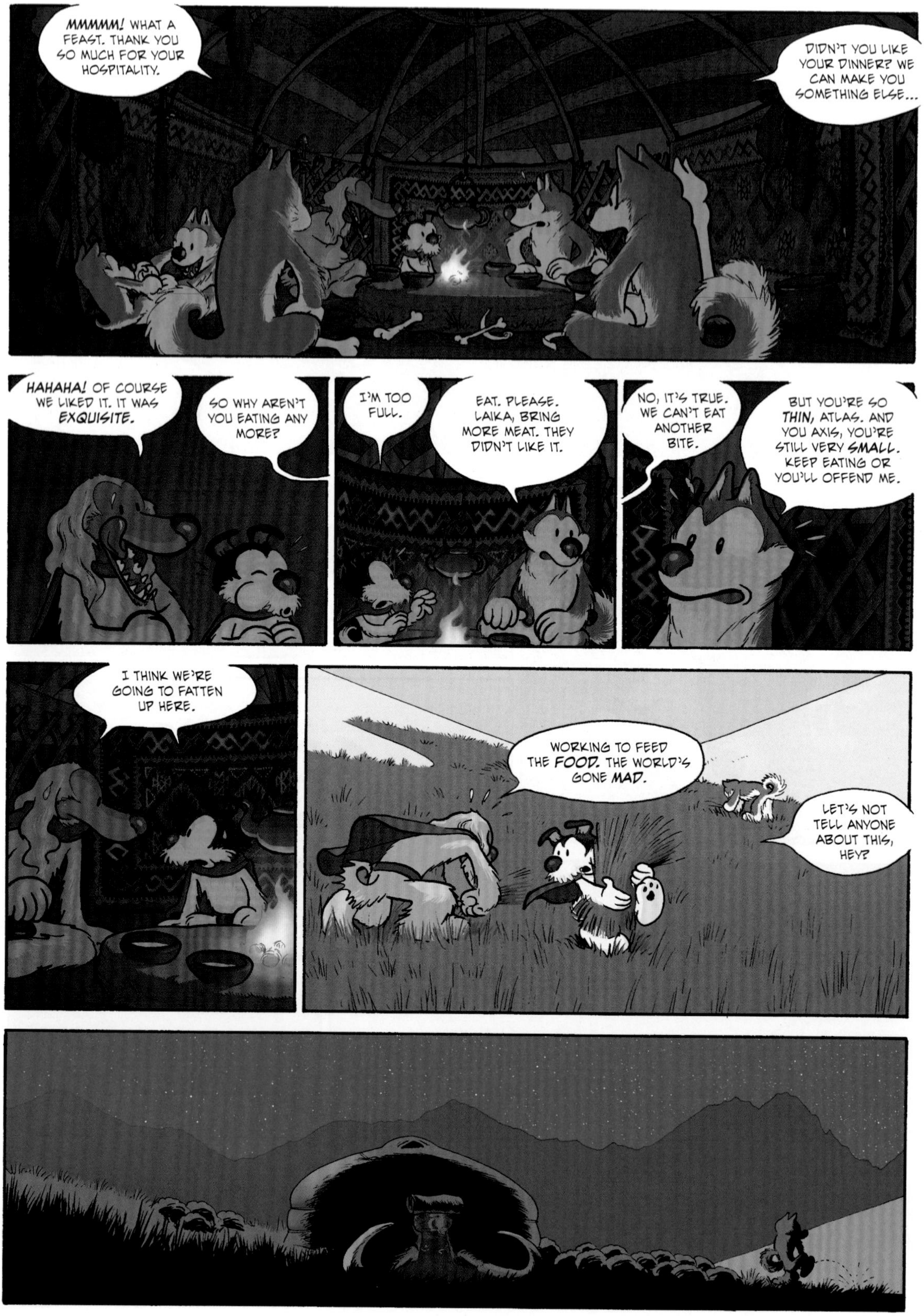
MMMMM! WHAT A FEAST. THANK YOU SO MUCH FOR YOUR HOSPITALITY.
DIDN'T YOU LIKE YOUR DINNER? WE CAN MAKE YOU SOMETHING ELSE...
HAHAHA! OF COURSE WE LIKED IT. IT WAS EXQUISITE.
SO WHY AREN'T YOU EATING ANY MORE?
I'M TOO FULL.
EAT. PLEASE. LAIKA, BRING MORE MEAT. THEY DIDN'T LIKE IT.
NO, IT'S TRUE. WE CAN'T EAT ANOTHER BITE.
BUT YOU'RE SO THIN, ATLAS. AND YOU AXIS, YOU'RE STILL VERY SMALL. KEEP EATING OR YOU'LL OFFEND ME.
I THINK WE'RE GOING TO FATTEN UP HERE.
WORKING TO FEED THE FOOD. THE WORLD'S GONE MAD.
LET'S NOT TELL ANYONE ABOUT THIS, HEY?

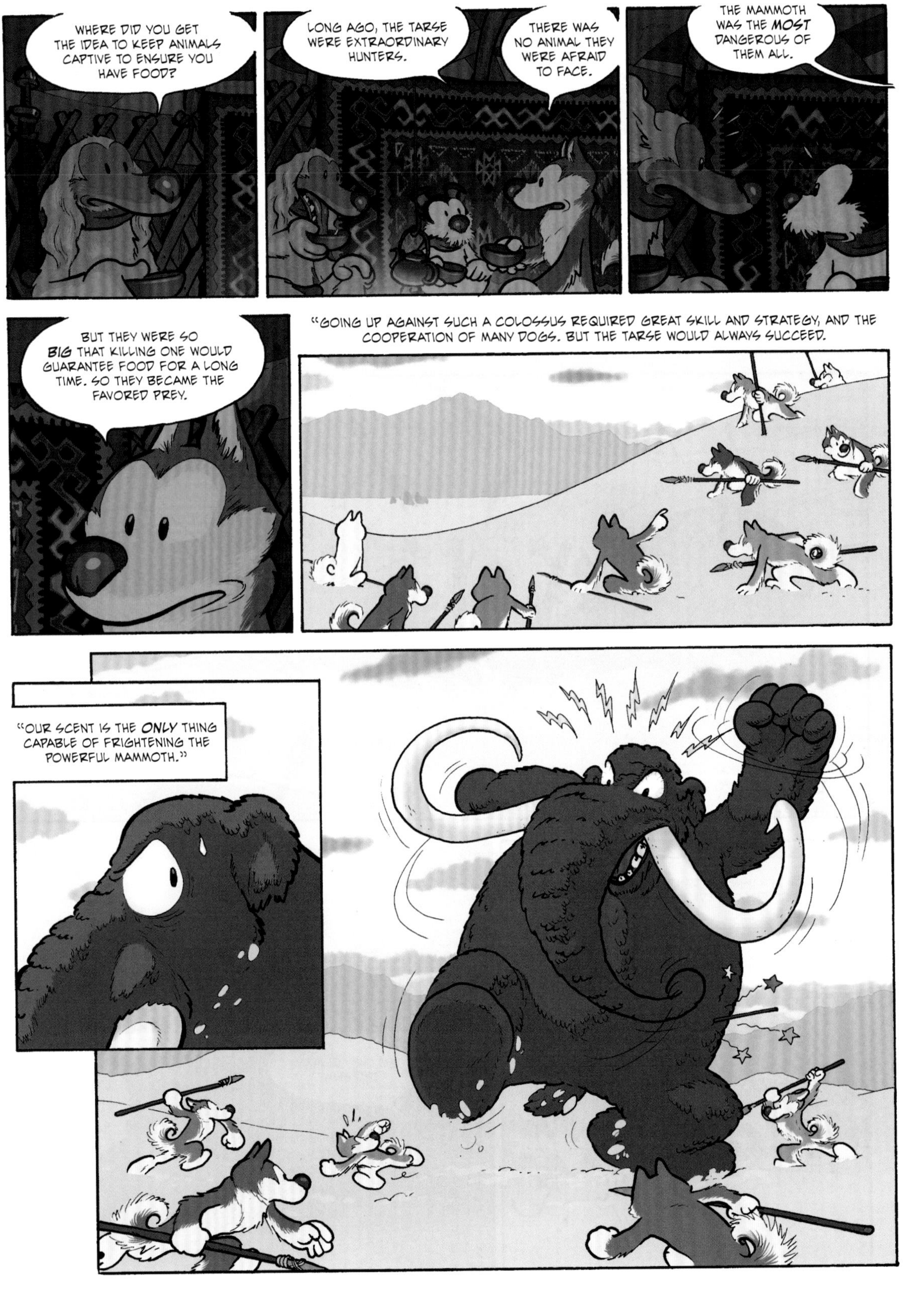
WHERE DID YOU GET THE IDEA TO KEEP ANIMALS CAPTIVE TO ENSURE YOU HAVE FOOD?
LONG AGO, THE TARSE WERE EXTRAORDINARY HUNTERS.
THERE WAS NO ANIMAL THEY WERE AFRAID TO FACE.
THE MAMMOTH WAS THE **MOST** DANGEROUS OF THEM ALL.
BUT THEY WERE SO **BIG** THAT KILLING ONE WOULD GUARANTEE FOOD FOR A LONG TIME. SO THEY BECAME THE FAVORED PREY.
"GOING UP AGAINST SUCH A COLOSSUS REQUIRED GREAT SKILL AND STRATEGY, AND THE COOPERATION OF MANY DOGS. BUT THE TARSE WOULD ALWAYS SUCCEED.
"OUR SCENT IS THE **ONLY** THING CAPABLE OF FRIGHTENING THE POWERFUL MAMMOTH."

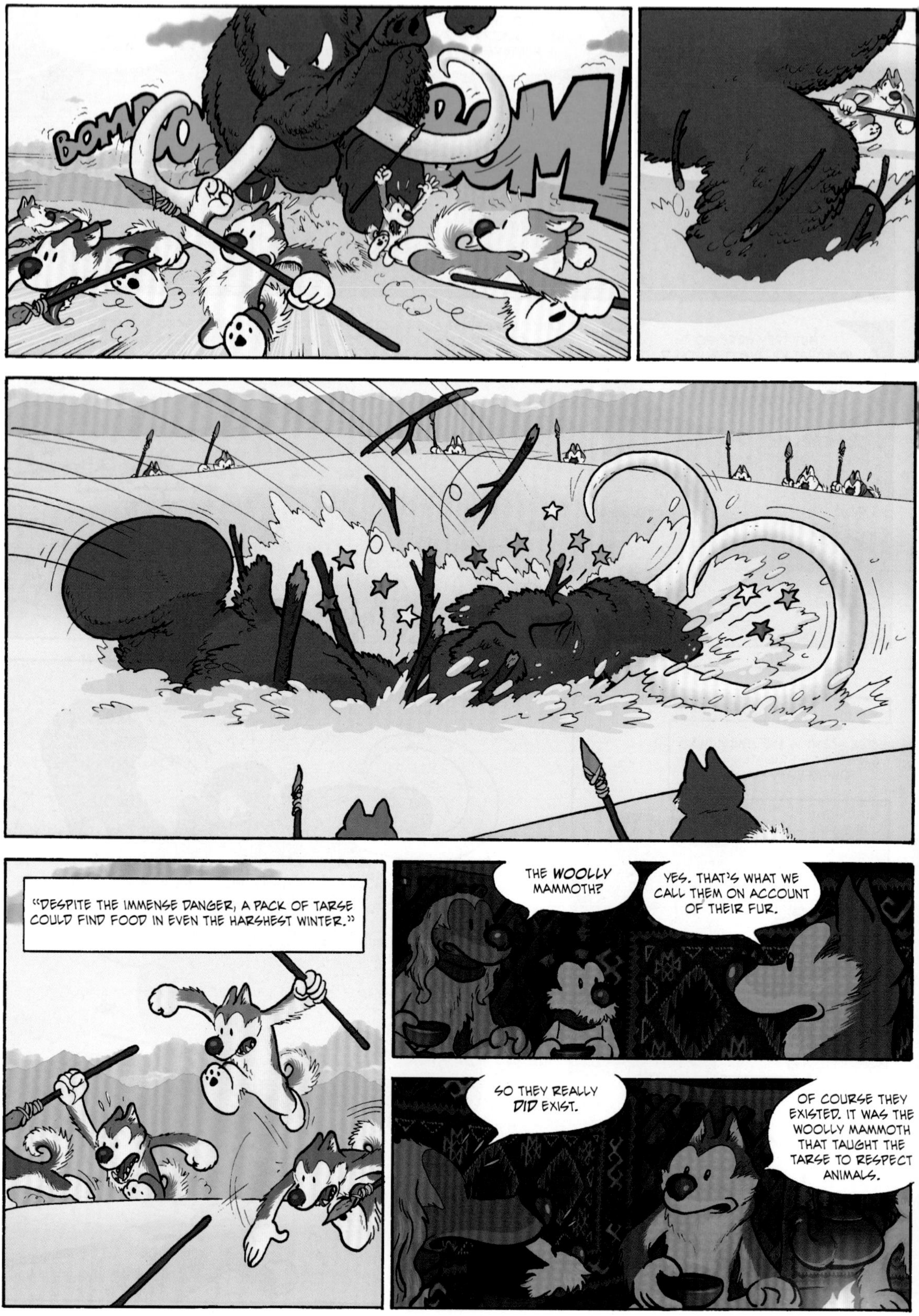
BOMP
BOOM!
"DESPITE THE IMMENSE DANGER, A PACK OF TARSE COULD FIND FOOD IN EVEN THE HARSHEST WINTER."
THE WOOLLY MAMMOTH?
YES. THAT'S WHAT WE CALL THEM ON ACCOUNT OF THEIR FUR.
SO THEY REALLY DID EXIST.
OF COURSE THEY EXISTED. IT WAS THE WOOLLY MAMMOTH THAT TAUGHT THE TARSE TO RESPECT ANIMALS.

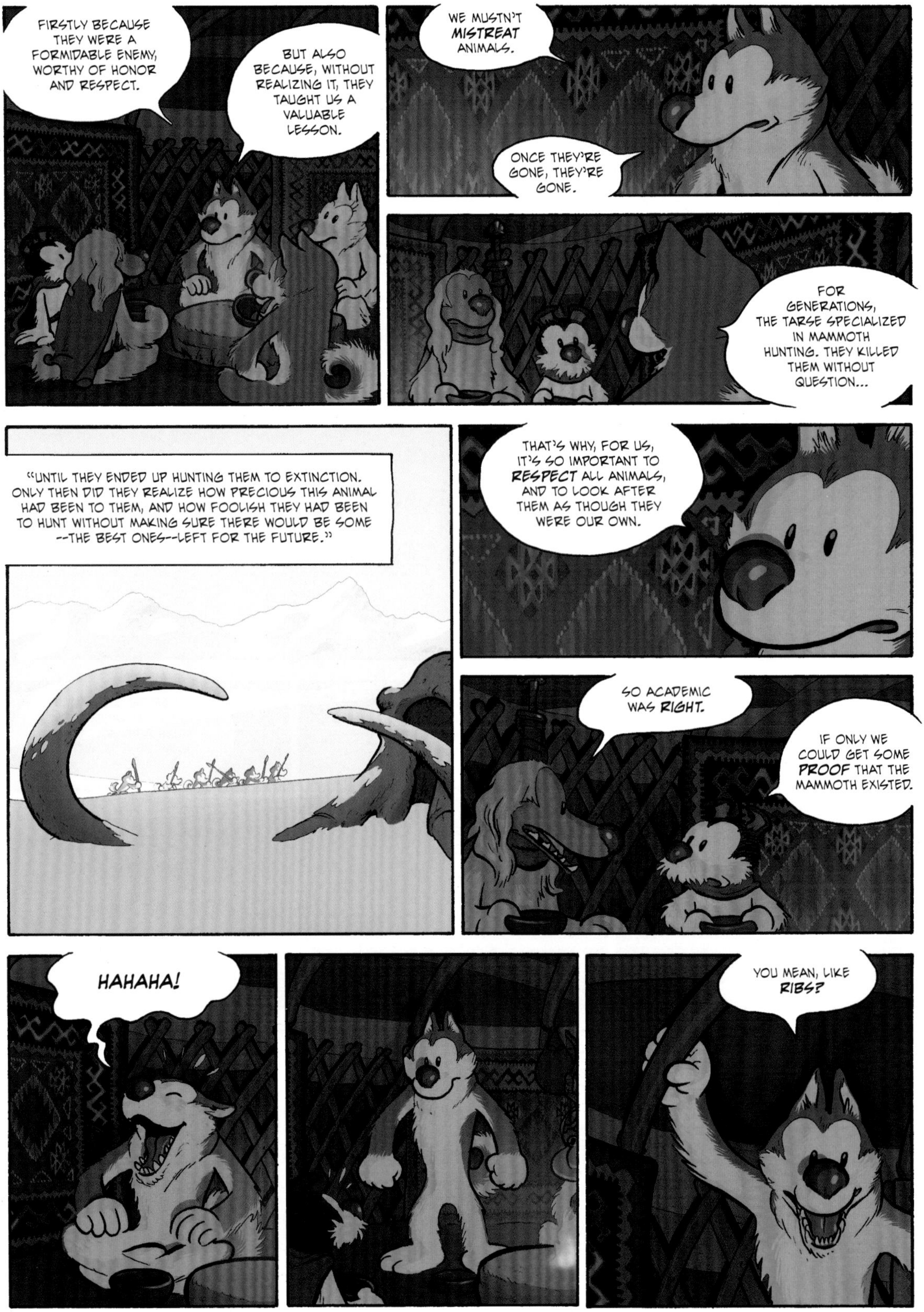
FIRSTLY BECAUSE THEY WERE A FORMIDABLE ENEMY, WORTHY OF HONOR AND RESPECT.
BUT ALSO BECAUSE, WITHOUT REALIZING IT, THEY TAUGHT US A VALUABLE LESSON.
WE MUSTN'T **MISTREAT** ANIMALS.
ONCE THEY'RE GONE, THEY'RE GONE.
FOR GENERATIONS, THE TARSE SPECIALIZED IN MAMMOTH HUNTING. THEY KILLED THEM WITHOUT QUESTION...
"UNTIL THEY ENDED UP HUNTING THEM TO EXTINCTION. ONLY THEN DID THEY REALIZE HOW PRECIOUS THIS ANIMAL HAD BEEN TO THEM, AND HOW FOOLISH THEY HAD BEEN TO HUNT WITHOUT MAKING SURE THERE WOULD BE SOME --THE BEST ONES--LEFT FOR THE FUTURE."
THAT'S WHY, FOR US, IT'S SO IMPORTANT TO **RESPECT** ALL ANIMALS, AND TO LOOK AFTER THEM AS THOUGH THEY WERE OUR OWN.
SO ACADEMIC WAS **RIGHT.**
IF ONLY WE COULD GET SOME **PROOF** THAT THE MAMMOTH EXISTED.
HAHAHA!
YOU MEAN, LIKE **RIBS?**

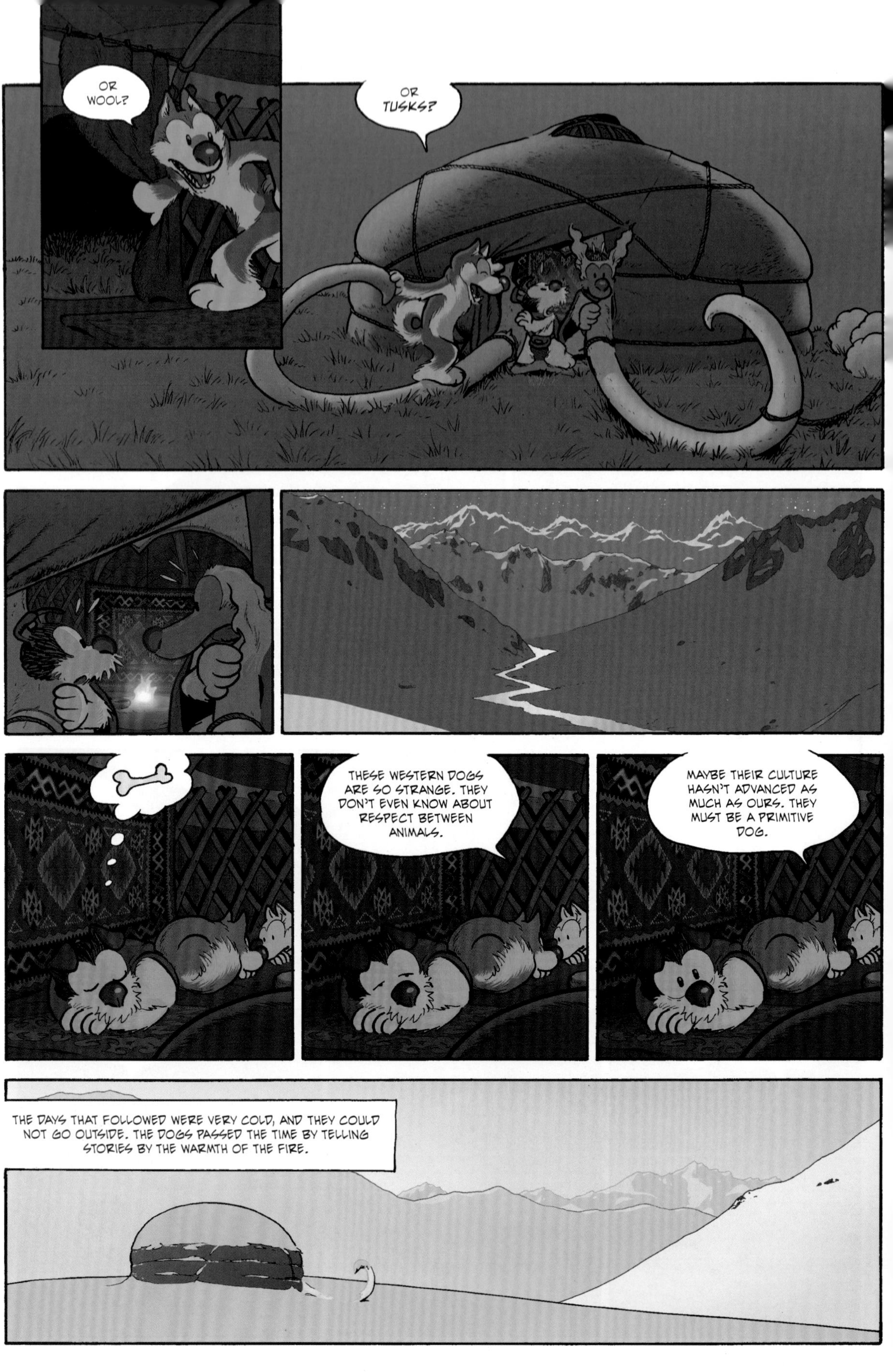
OR WOOL?
OR TUSKS?
THESE WESTERN DOGS ARE SO STRANGE. THEY DON'T EVEN KNOW ABOUT RESPECT BETWEEN ANIMALS.
MAYBE THEIR CULTURE HASN'T ADVANCED AS MUCH AS OURS. THEY MUST BE A PRIMITIVE DOG.
THE DAYS THAT FOLLOWED WERE VERY COLD, AND THEY COULD NOT GO OUTSIDE. THE DOGS PASSED THE TIME BY TELLING STORIES BY THE WARMTH OF THE FIRE.

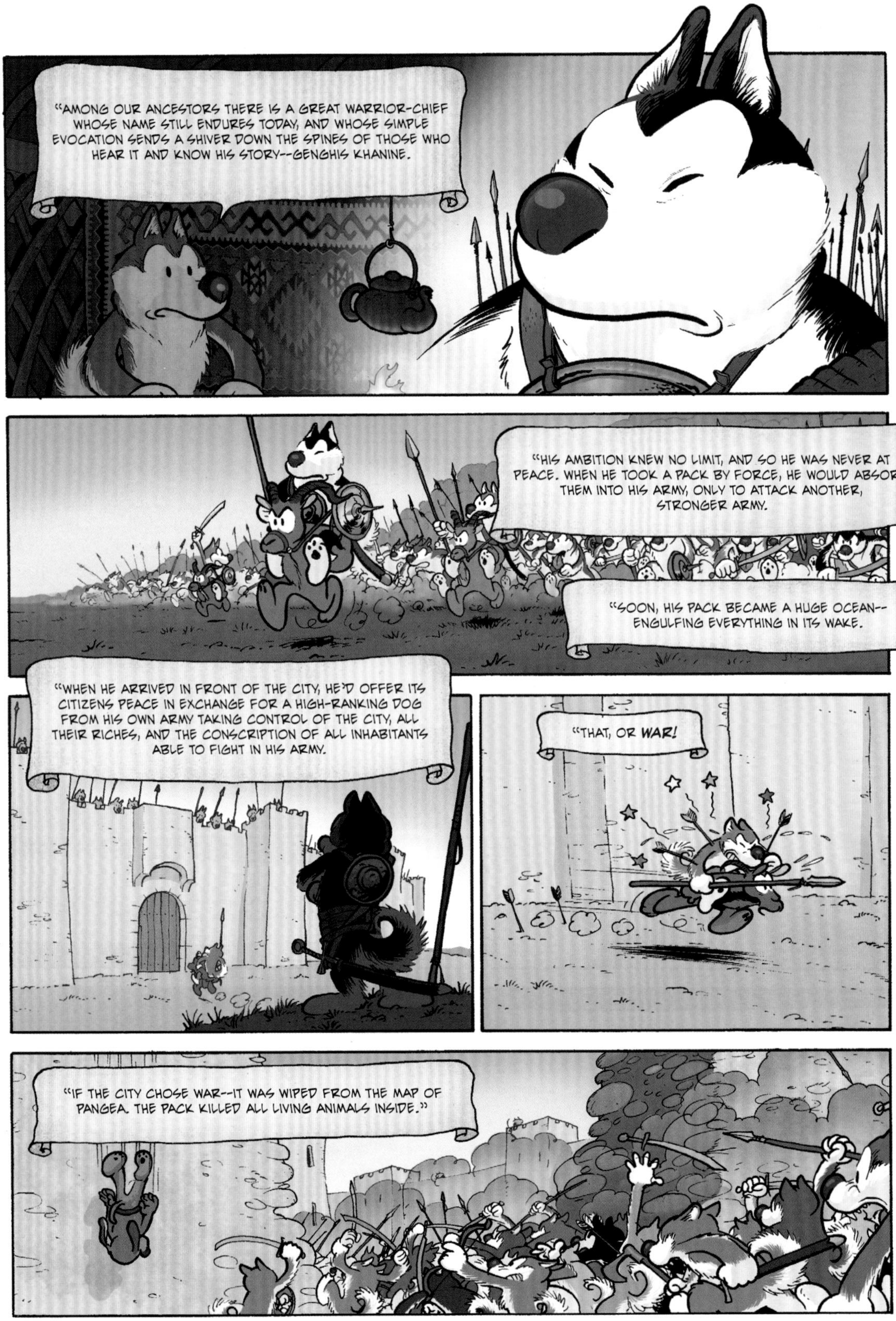
"AMONG OUR ANCESTORS THERE IS A GREAT WARRIOR-CHIEF WHOSE NAME STILL ENDURES TODAY, AND WHOSE SIMPLE EVOCATION SENDS A SHIVER DOWN THE SPINES OF THOSE WHO HEAR IT AND KNOW HIS STORY--GENGHIS KHANINE.
"HIS AMBITION KNEW NO LIMIT, AND SO HE WAS NEVER AT PEACE. WHEN HE TOOK A PACK BY FORCE, HE WOULD ABSORB THEM INTO HIS ARMY, ONLY TO ATTACK ANOTHER, STRONGER ARMY.
"SOON, HIS PACK BECAME A HUGE OCEAN--ENGULFING EVERYTHING IN ITS WAKE.
"WHEN HE ARRIVED IN FRONT OF THE CITY, HE'D OFFER ITS CITIZENS PEACE IN EXCHANGE FOR A HIGH-RANKING DOG FROM HIS OWN ARMY TAKING CONTROL OF THE CITY, ALL THEIR RICHES, AND THE CONSCRIPTION OF ALL INHABITANTS ABLE TO FIGHT IN HIS ARMY.
"THAT, OR WAR!
"IF THE CITY CHOSE WAR--IT WAS WIPED FROM THE MAP OF PANGEA. THE PACK KILLED ALL LIVING ANIMALS INSIDE."

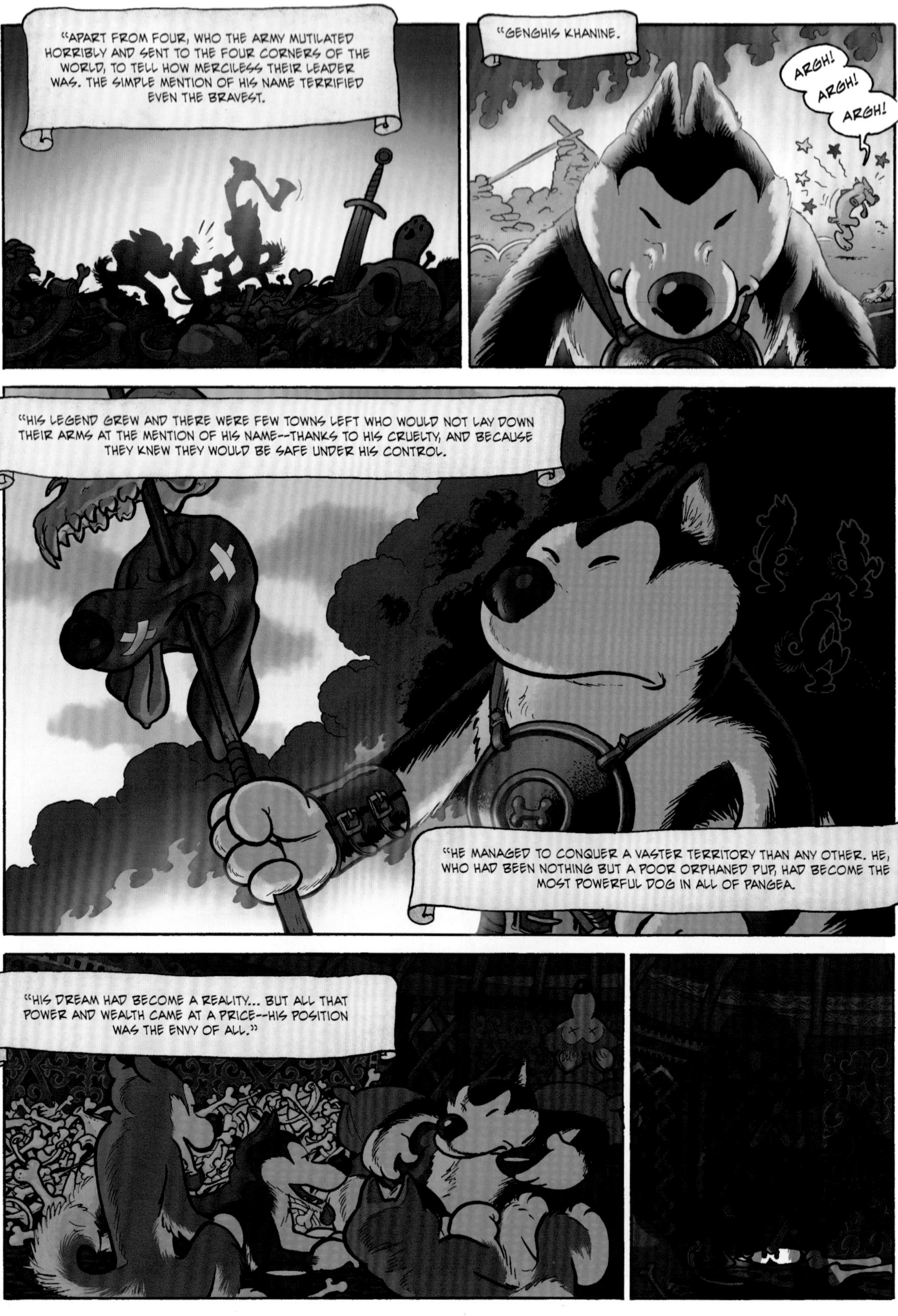
"APART FROM FOUR, WHO THE ARMY MUTILATED HORRIBLY AND SENT TO THE FOUR CORNERS OF THE WORLD, TO TELL HOW MERCILESS THEIR LEADER WAS. THE SIMPLE MENTION OF HIS NAME TERRIFIED EVEN THE BRAVEST.
"GENGHIS KHANINE.
ARGH!
ARGH!
ARGH!
"HIS LEGEND GREW AND THERE WERE FEW TOWNS LEFT WHO WOULD NOT LAY DOWN THEIR ARMS AT THE MENTION OF HIS NAME--THANKS TO HIS CRUELTY, AND BECAUSE THEY KNEW THEY WOULD BE SAFE UNDER HIS CONTROL.
"HE MANAGED TO CONQUER A VASTER TERRITORY THAN ANY OTHER. HE, WHO HAD BEEN NOTHING BUT A POOR ORPHANED PUP, HAD BECOME THE MOST POWERFUL DOG IN ALL OF PANGEA.
"HIS DREAM HAD BECOME A REALITY... BUT ALL THAT POWER AND WEALTH CAME AT A PRICE--HIS POSITION WAS THE ENVY OF ALL."

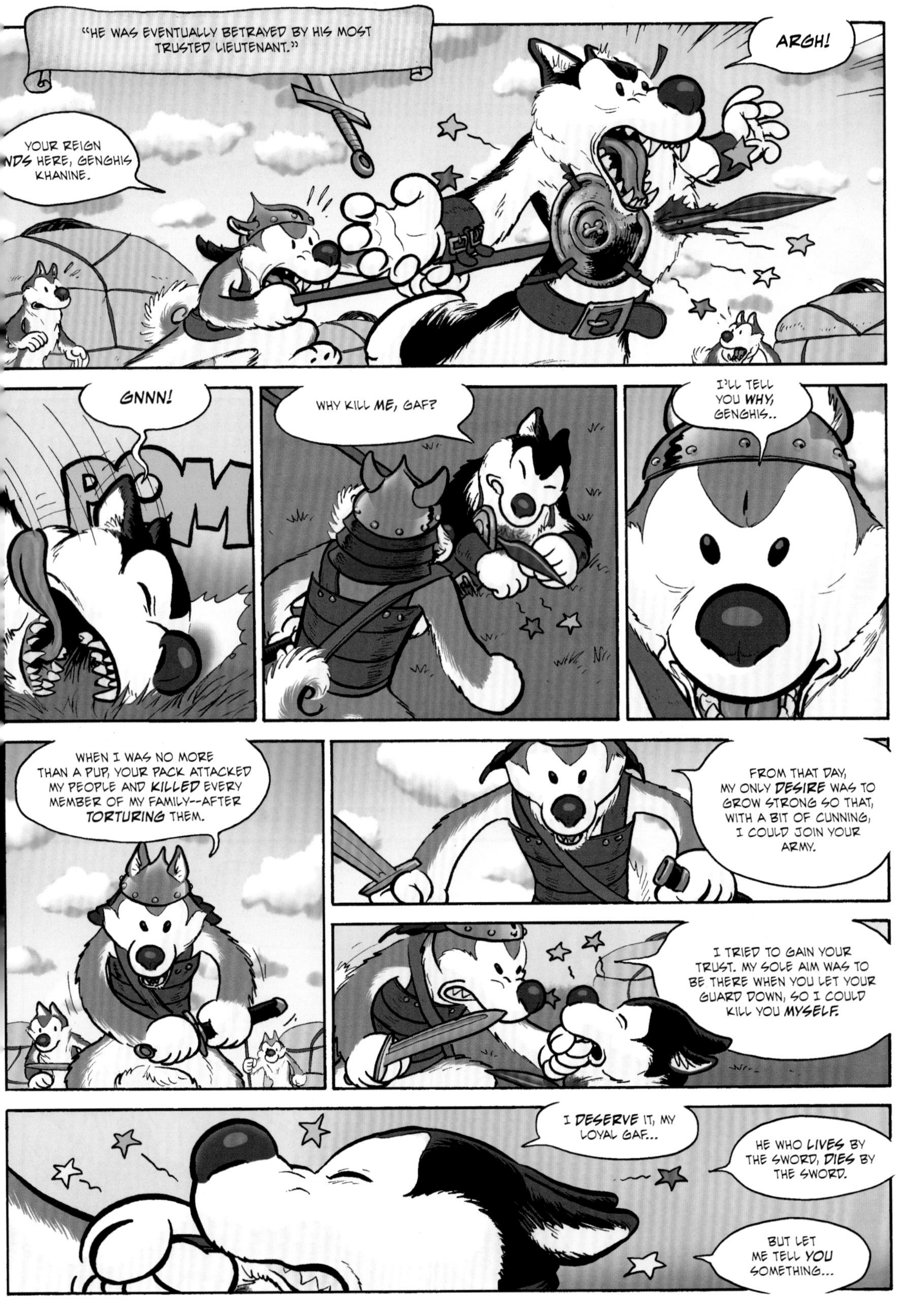
"HE WAS EVENTUALLY BETRAYED BY HIS MOST TRUSTED LIEUTENANT."
ARGH!
YOUR REIGN ENDS HERE, GENGHIS KHANINE.
GNNN!
POM
WHY KILL ME, GAF?
I'LL TELL YOU WHY, GENGHIS..
WHEN I WAS NO MORE THAN A PUP, YOUR PACK ATTACKED MY PEOPLE AND KILLED EVERY MEMBER OF MY FAMILY--AFTER TORTURING THEM.
FROM THAT DAY, MY ONLY DESIRE WAS TO GROW STRONG SO THAT, WITH A BIT OF CUNNING, I COULD JOIN YOUR ARMY.
I TRIED TO GAIN YOUR TRUST. MY SOLE AIM WAS TO BE THERE WHEN YOU LET YOUR GUARD DOWN, SO I COULD KILL YOU MYSELF.
I DESERVE IT, MY LOYAL GAF...
HE WHO LIVES BY THE SWORD, DIES BY THE SWORD.
BUT LET ME TELL YOU SOMETHING...

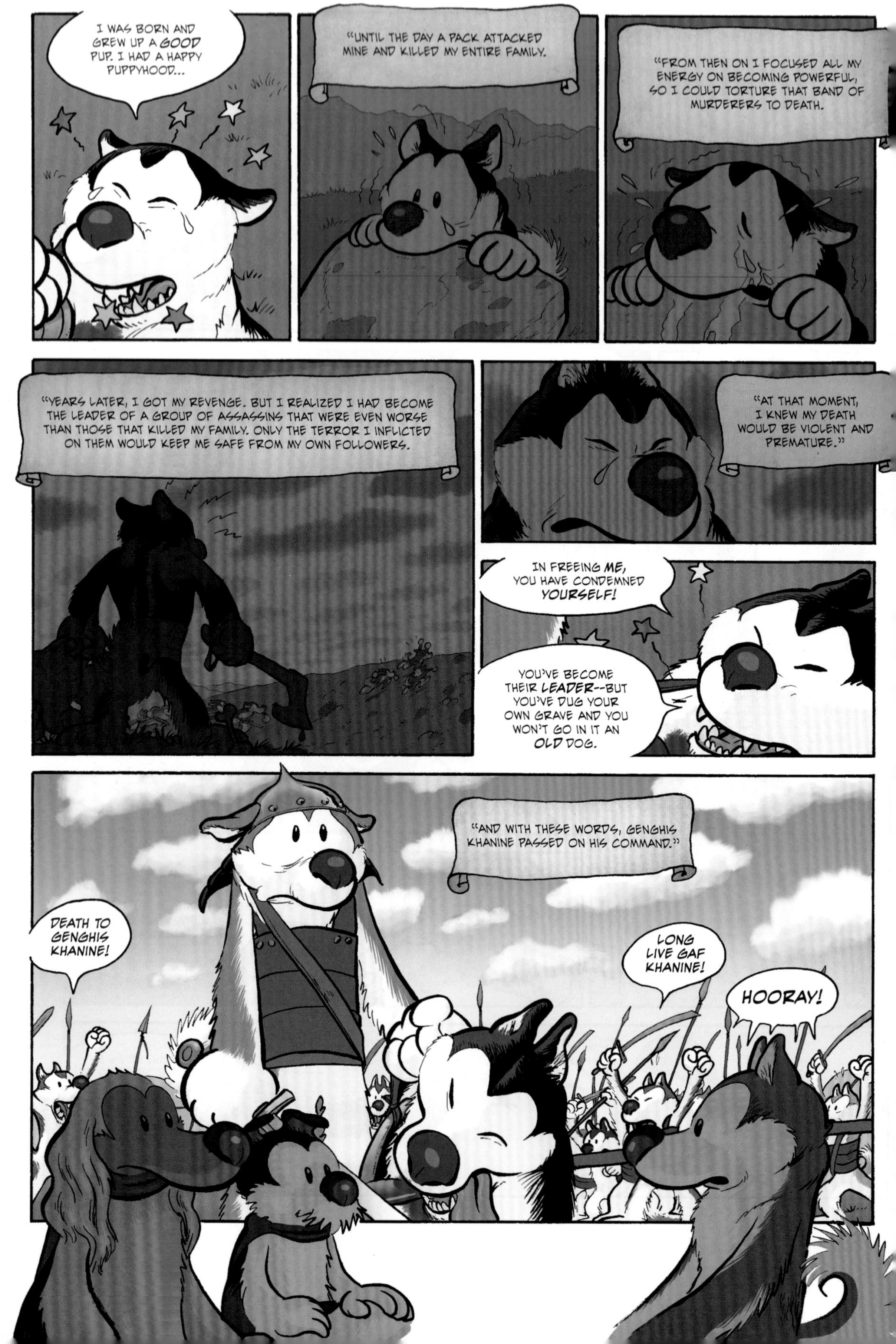
I WAS BORN AND GREW UP A GOOD PUP. I HAD A HAPPY PUPPYHOOD...
"UNTIL THE DAY A PACK ATTACKED MINE AND KILLED MY ENTIRE FAMILY.
"FROM THEN ON I FOCUSED ALL MY ENERGY ON BECOMING POWERFUL, SO I COULD TORTURE THAT BAND OF MURDERERS TO DEATH.
"YEARS LATER, I GOT MY REVENGE. BUT I REALIZED I HAD BECOME THE LEADER OF A GROUP OF ASSASSINS THAT WERE EVEN WORSE THAN THOSE THAT KILLED MY FAMILY. ONLY THE TERROR I INFLICTED ON THEM WOULD KEEP ME SAFE FROM MY OWN FOLLOWERS.
"AT THAT MOMENT, I KNEW MY DEATH WOULD BE VIOLENT AND PREMATURE."
IN FREEING ME, YOU HAVE CONDEMNED YOURSELF!
YOU'VE BECOME THEIR LEADER--BUT YOU'VE DUG YOUR OWN GRAVE AND YOU WON'T GO IN IT AN OLD DOG.
"AND WITH THESE WORDS, GENGHIS KHANINE PASSED ON HIS COMMAND."
DEATH TO GENGHIS KHANINE!
LONG LIVE GAF KHANINE!
HOORAY!

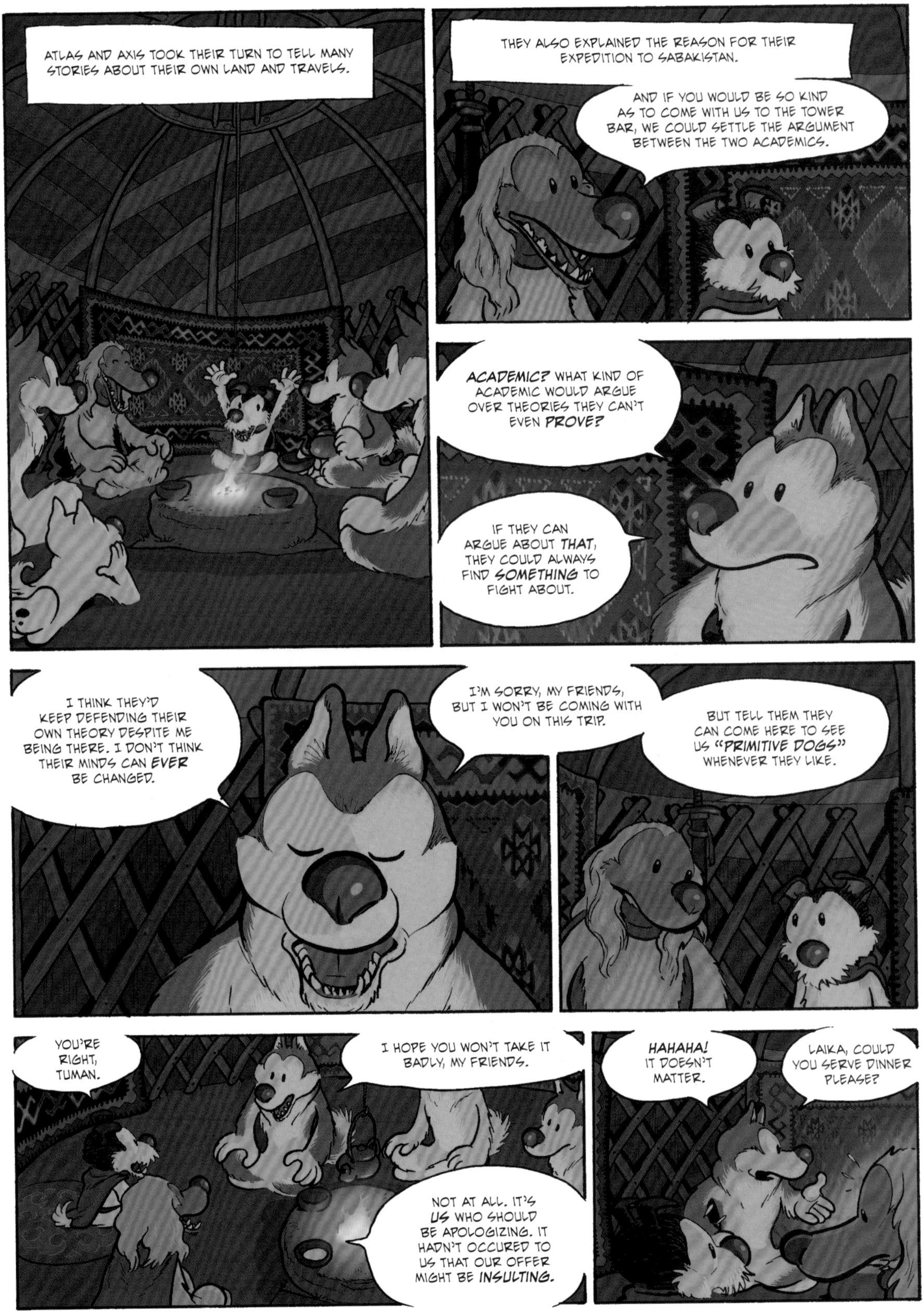
ATLAS AND AXIS TOOK THEIR TURN TO TELL MANY STORIES ABOUT THEIR OWN LAND AND TRAVELS.
THEY ALSO EXPLAINED THE REASON FOR THEIR EXPEDITION TO SABAKISTAN.
AND IF YOU WOULD BE SO KIND AS TO COME WITH US TO THE TOWER BAR, WE COULD SETTLE THE ARGUMENT BETWEEN THE TWO ACADEMICS.
ACADEMIC? WHAT KIND OF ACADEMIC WOULD ARGUE OVER THEORIES THEY CAN'T EVEN PROVE?
IF THEY CAN ARGUE ABOUT THAT, THEY COULD ALWAYS FIND SOMETHING TO FIGHT ABOUT.
I THINK THEY'D KEEP DEFENDING THEIR OWN THEORY DESPITE ME BEING THERE. I DON'T THINK THEIR MINDS CAN EVER BE CHANGED.
I'M SORRY, MY FRIENDS, BUT I WON'T BE COMING WITH YOU ON THIS TRIP.
BUT TELL THEM THEY CAN COME HERE TO SEE US "PRIMITIVE DOGS" WHENEVER THEY LIKE.
YOU'RE RIGHT, TUMAN.
I HOPE YOU WON'T TAKE IT BADLY, MY FRIENDS.
NOT AT ALL. IT'S US WHO SHOULD BE APOLOGIZING. IT HADN'T OCCURED TO US THAT OUR OFFER MIGHT BE INSULTING.
HAHAHA! IT DOESN'T MATTER.
LAIKA, COULD YOU SERVE DINNER PLEASE?

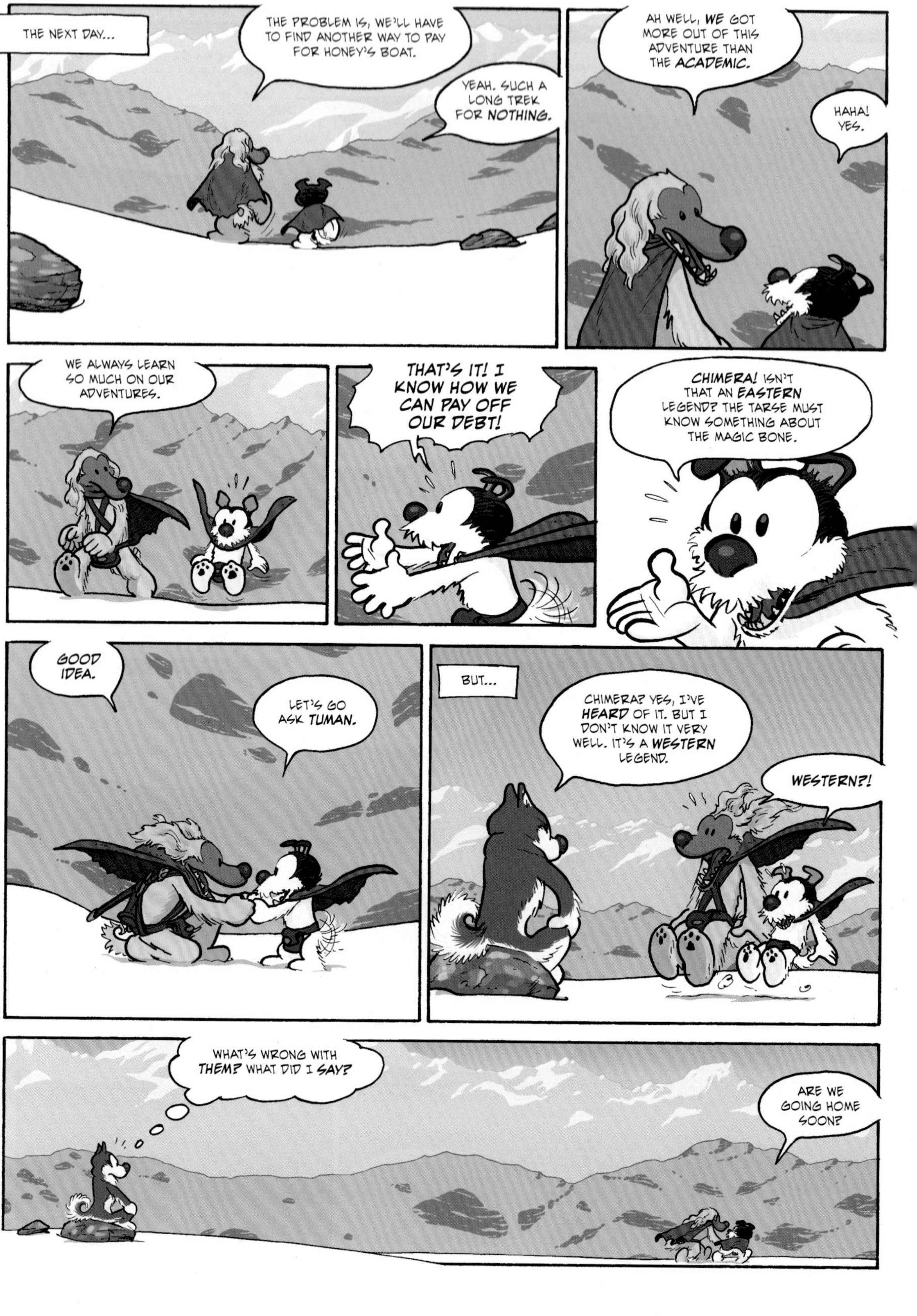

THE NEXT DAY...
THE PROBLEM IS, WE'LL HAVE TO FIND ANOTHER WAY TO PAY FOR HONEY'S BOAT.
YEAH. SUCH A LONG TREK FOR NOTHING.
AH WELL, WE GOT MORE OUT OF THIS ADVENTURE THAN THE ACADEMIC.
HAHA! YES.
WE ALWAYS LEARN SO MUCH ON OUR ADVENTURES.
THAT'S IT! I KNOW HOW WE CAN PAY OFF OUR DEBT!
CHIMERA! ISN'T THAT AN EASTERN LEGEND? THE TARSE MUST KNOW SOMETHING ABOUT THE MAGIC BONE.
GOOD IDEA.
LET'S GO ASK TUMAN.
BUT...
CHIMERA? YES, I'VE HEARD OF IT. BUT I DON'T KNOW IT VERY WELL. IT'S A WESTERN LEGEND.
WESTERN?!
WHAT'S WRONG WITH THEM? WHAT DID I SAY?
ARE WE GOING HOME SOON?

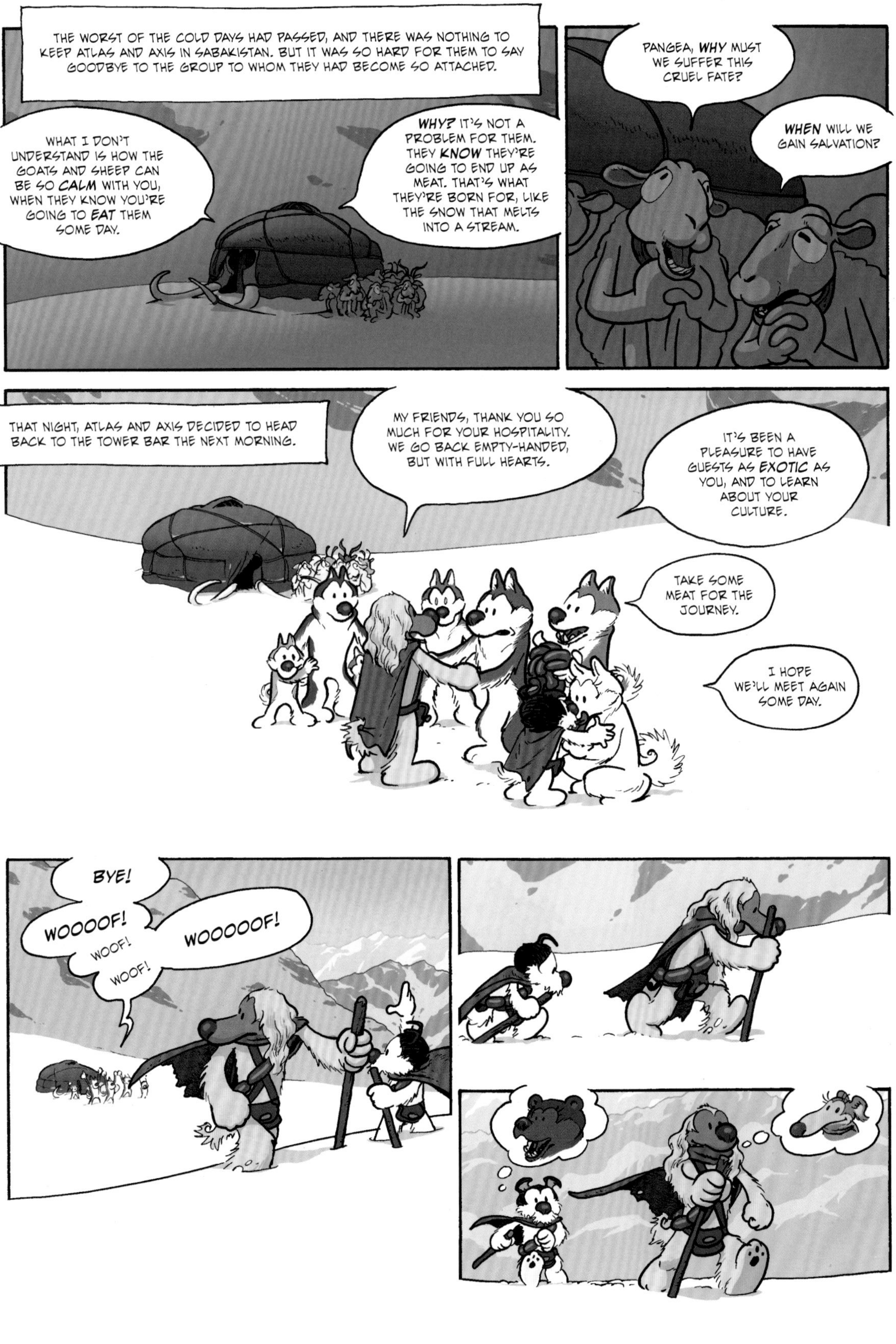
THE WORST OF THE COLD DAYS HAD PASSED, AND THERE WAS NOTHING TO KEEP ATLAS AND AXIS IN SABAKISTAN. BUT IT WAS SO HARD FOR THEM TO SAY GOODBYE TO THE GROUP TO WHOM THEY HAD BECOME SO ATTACHED.
WHAT I DON'T UNDERSTAND IS HOW THE GOATS AND SHEEP CAN BE SO **CALM** WITH YOU, WHEN THEY KNOW YOU'RE GOING TO **EAT** THEM SOME DAY.
WHY? IT'S NOT A PROBLEM FOR THEM. THEY **KNOW** THEY'RE GOING TO END UP AS MEAT. THAT'S WHAT THEY'RE BORN FOR, LIKE THE SNOW THAT MELTS INTO A STREAM.
PANGEA, **WHY** MUST WE SUFFER THIS CRUEL FATE?
WHEN WILL WE GAIN SALVATION?
THAT NIGHT, ATLAS AND AXIS DECIDED TO HEAD BACK TO THE TOWER BAR THE NEXT MORNING.
MY FRIENDS, THANK YOU SO MUCH FOR YOUR HOSPITALITY. WE GO BACK EMPTY-HANDED, BUT WITH FULL HEARTS.
IT'S BEEN A PLEASURE TO HAVE GUESTS AS **EXOTIC** AS YOU, AND TO LEARN ABOUT YOUR CULTURE.
TAKE SOME MEAT FOR THE JOURNEY.
I HOPE WE'LL MEET AGAIN SOME DAY.
BYE!
WOOOOF!
WOOF!
WOOF!
WOOOOOF!

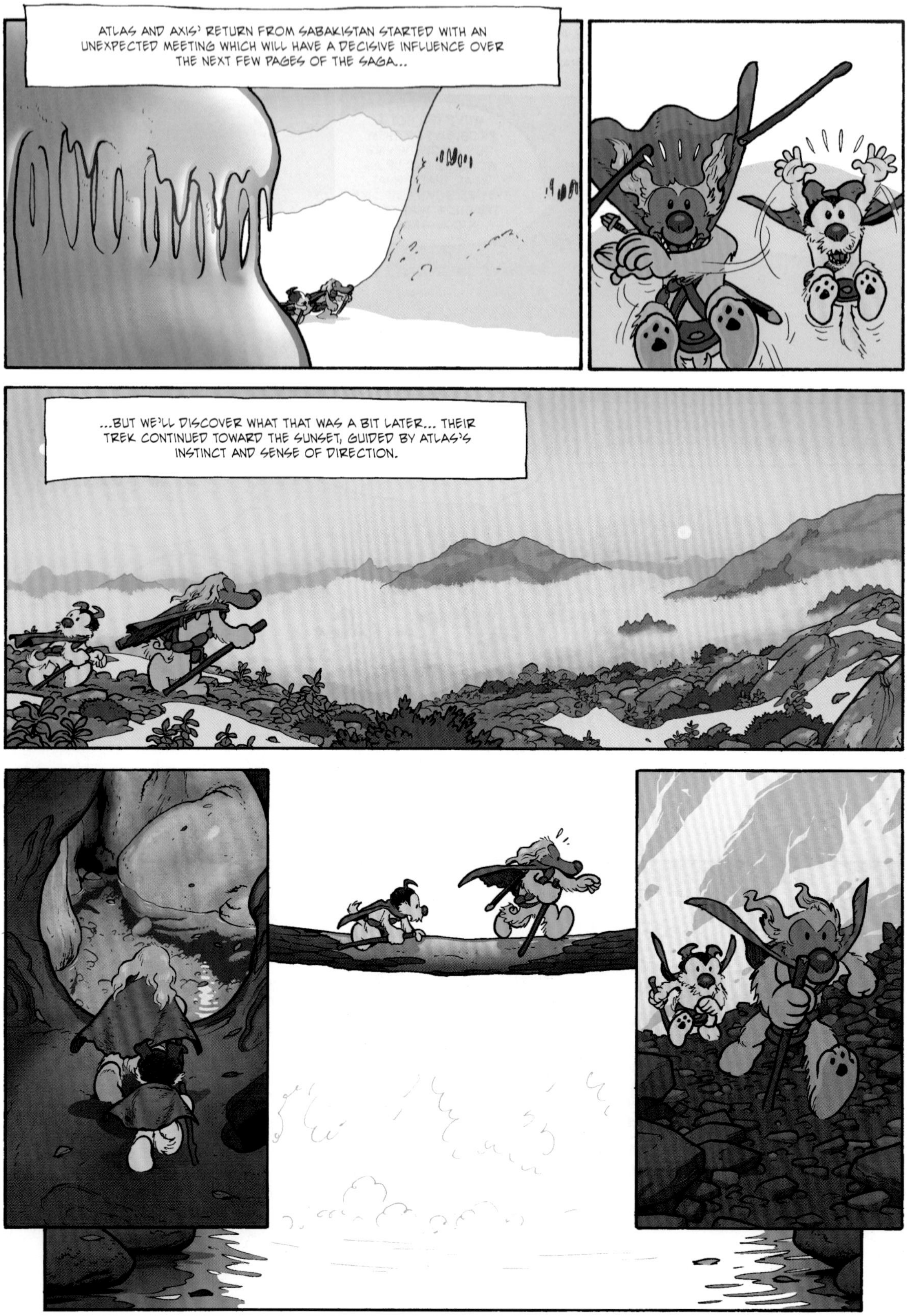
ATLAS AND AXIS' RETURN FROM SABAKISTAN STARTED WITH AN UNEXPECTED MEETING WHICH WILL HAVE A DECISIVE INFLUENCE OVER THE NEXT FEW PAGES OF THE SAGA...
...BUT WE'LL DISCOVER WHAT THAT WAS A BIT LATER... THEIR TREK CONTINUED TOWARD THE SUNSET, GUIDED BY ATLAS'S INSTINCT AND SENSE OF DIRECTION.

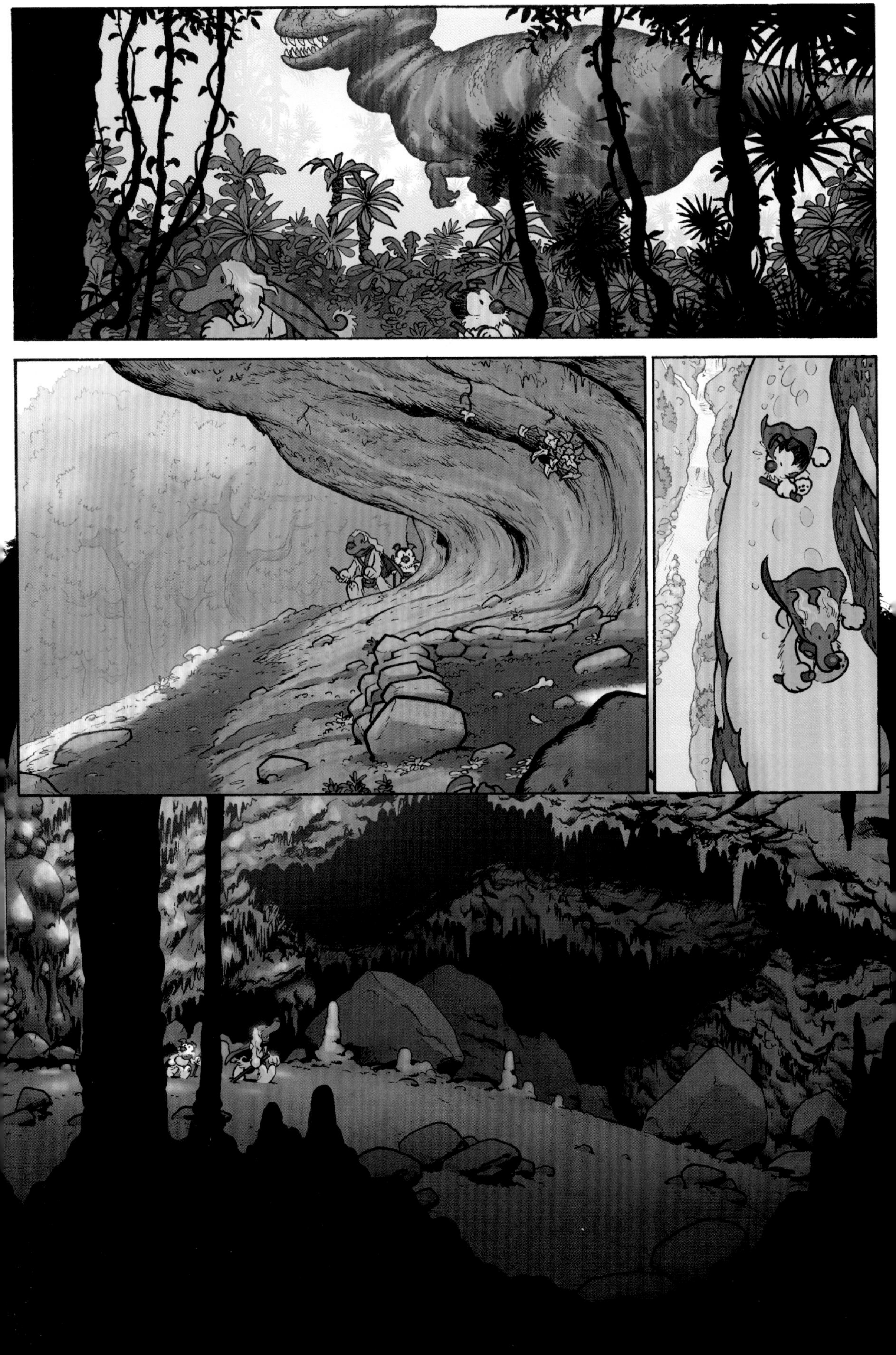

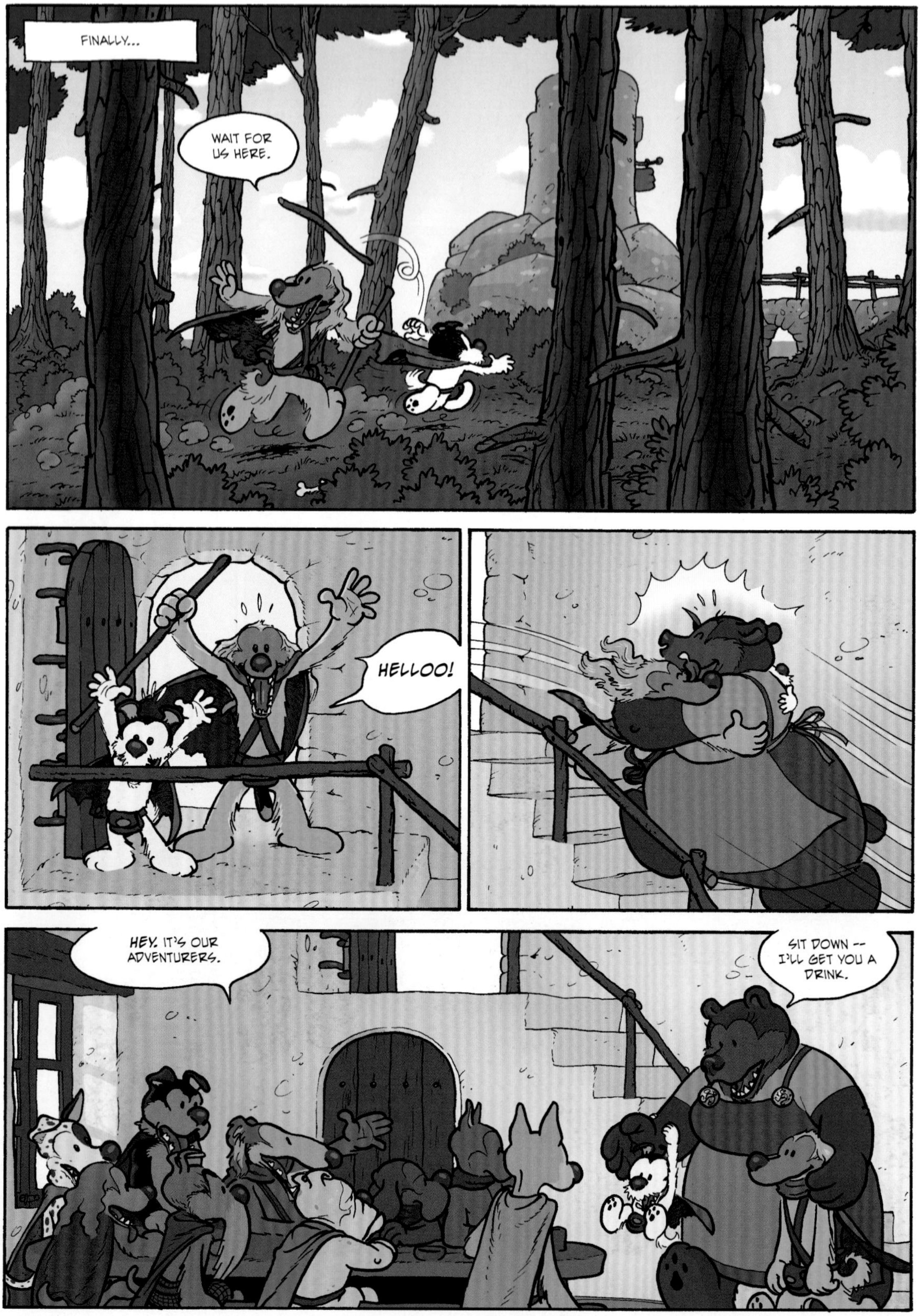
FINALLY...
WAIT FOR US HERE.
HELLOO!
HEY. IT'S OUR ADVENTURERS.
SIT DOWN -- I'LL GET YOU A DRINK.

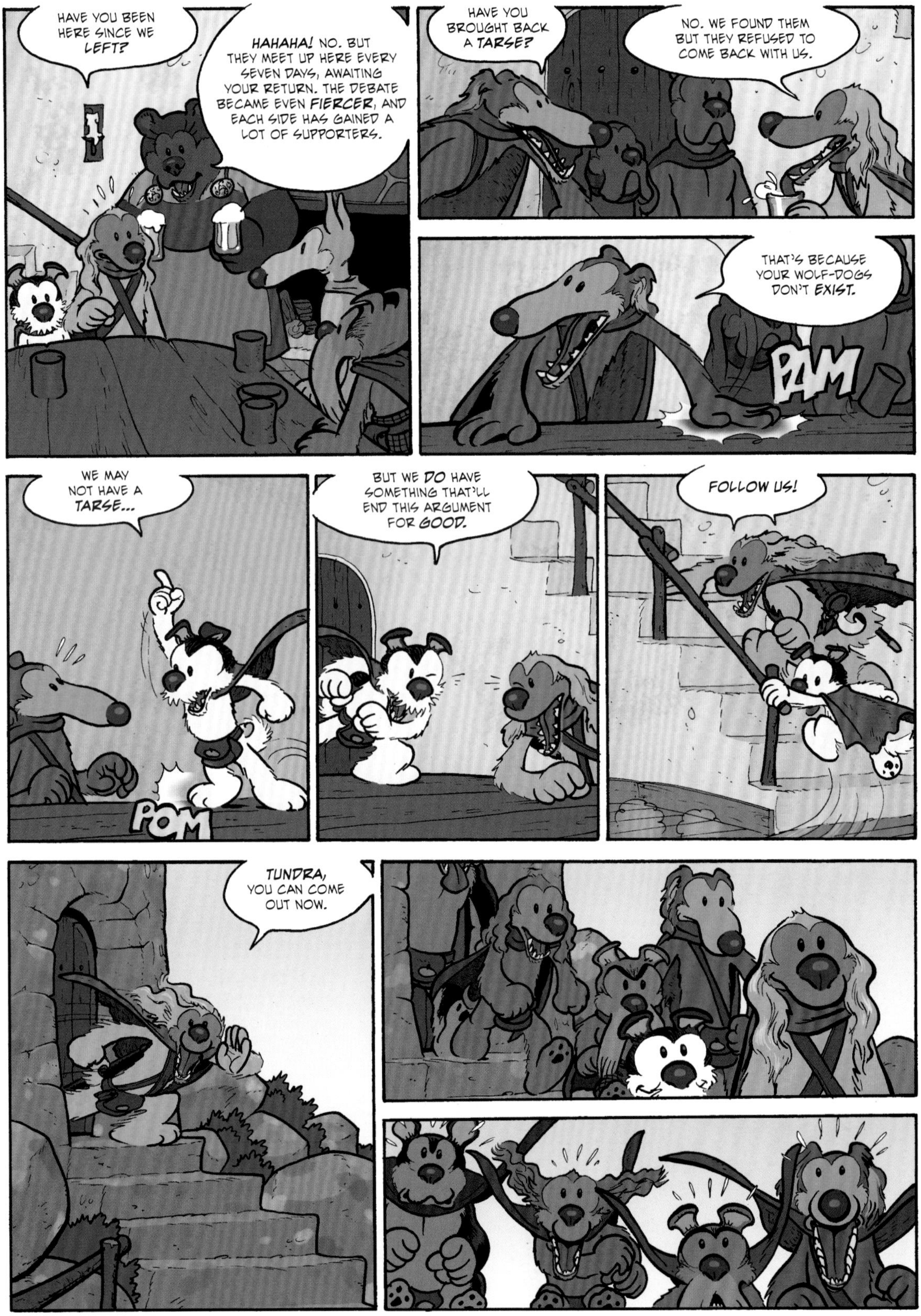

HAVE YOU BEEN HERE SINCE WE LEFT?
HAHAHA! NO. BUT THEY MEET UP HERE EVERY SEVEN DAYS, AWAITING YOUR RETURN. THE DEBATE BECAME EVEN FIERCER, AND EACH SIDE HAS GAINED A LOT OF SUPPORTERS.
HAVE YOU BROUGHT BACK A TARSE?
NO. WE FOUND THEM BUT THEY REFUSED TO COME BACK WITH US.
THAT'S BECAUSE YOUR WOLF-DOGS DON'T EXIST.
BAM
WE MAY NOT HAVE A TARSE...
POM
BUT WE DO HAVE SOMETHING THAT'LL END THIS ARGUMENT FOR GOOD.
FOLLOW US!
TUNDRA, YOU CAN COME OUT NOW.

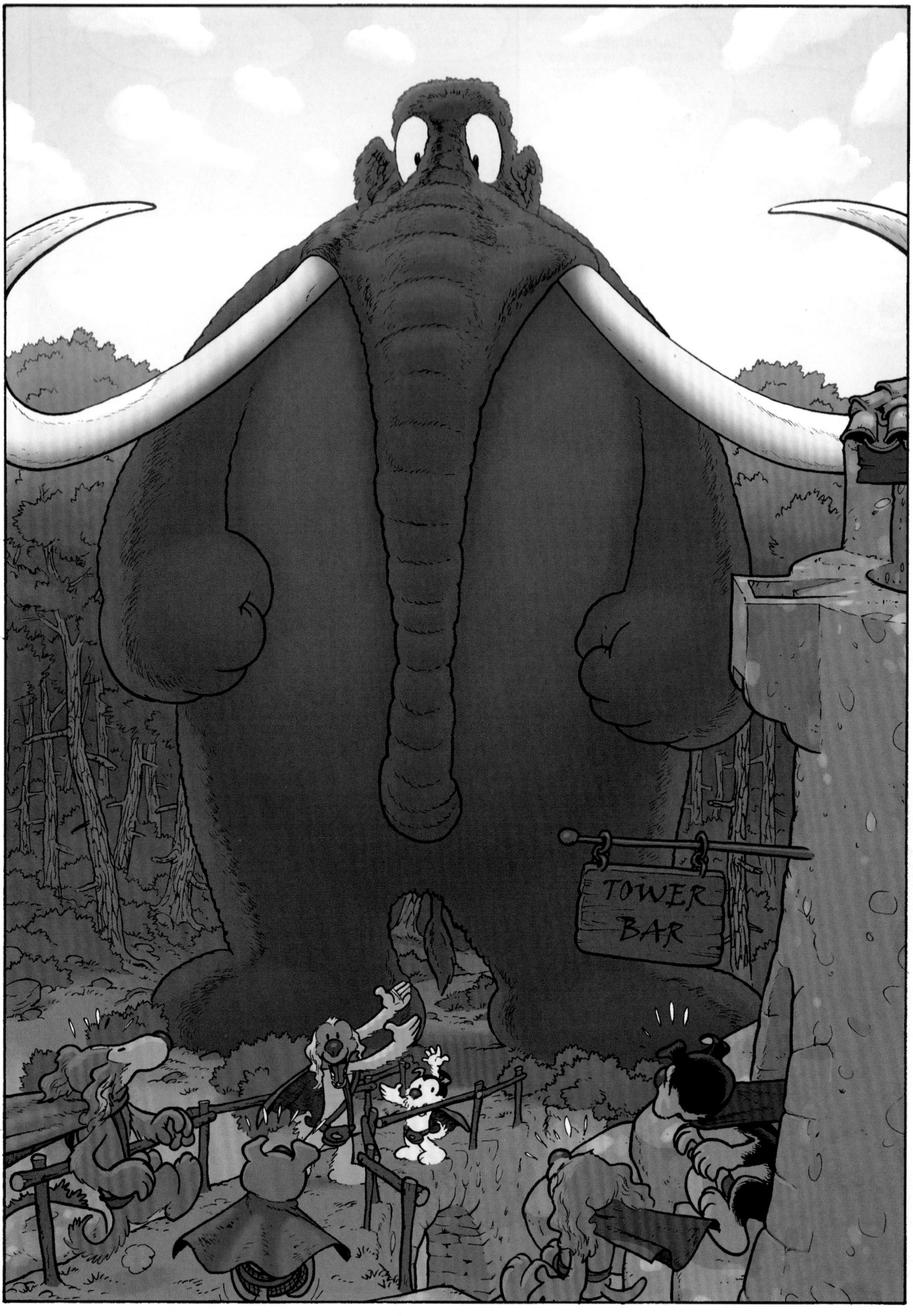
TOWER BAR

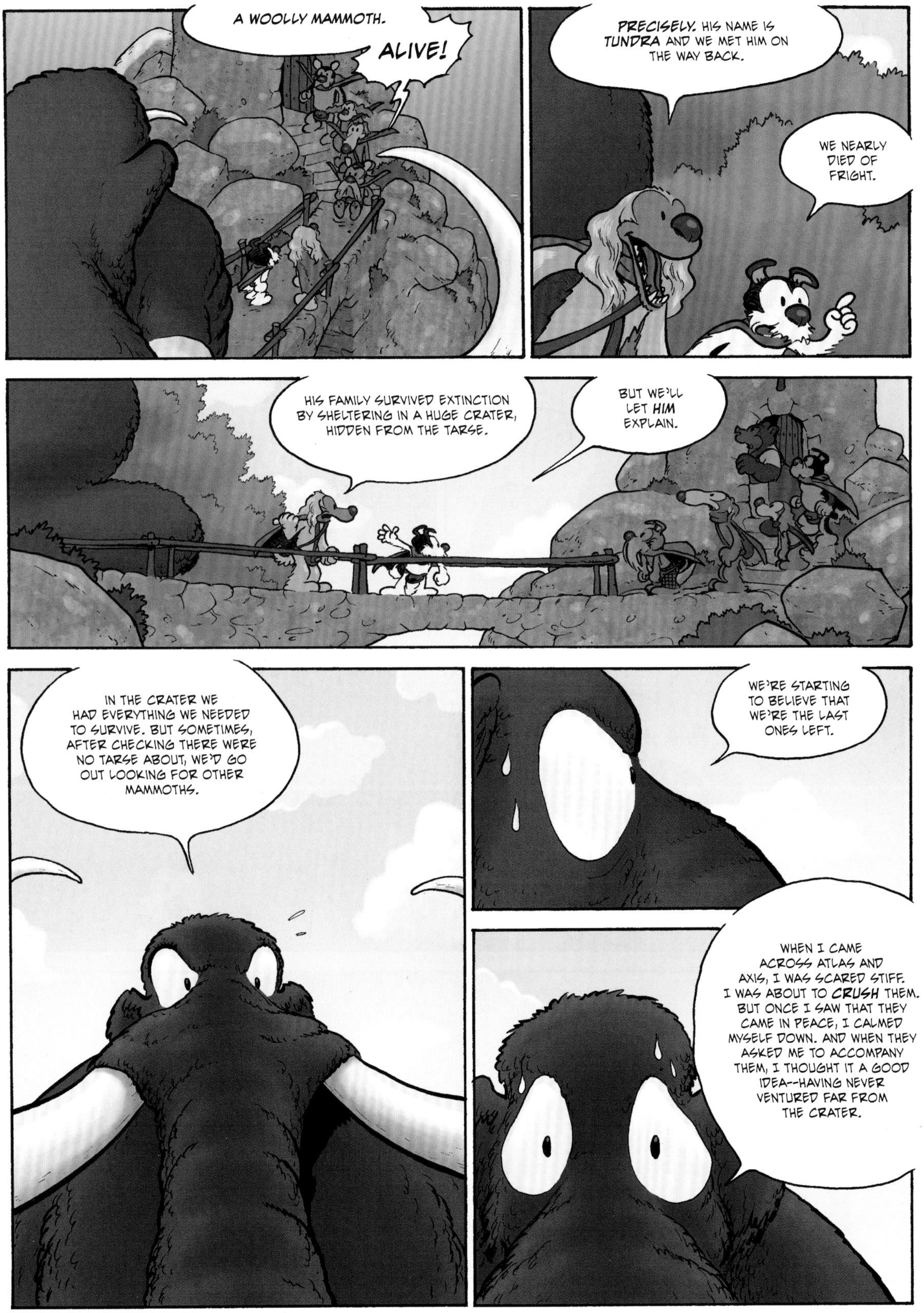
A WOOLLY MAMMOTH.
ALIVE!
PRECISELY. HIS NAME IS TUNDRA AND WE MET HIM ON THE WAY BACK.
WE NEARLY DIED OF FRIGHT.
HIS FAMILY SURVIVED EXTINCTION BY SHELTERING IN A HUGE CRATER, HIDDEN FROM THE TARSE.
BUT WE'LL LET HIM EXPLAIN.
IN THE CRATER WE HAD EVERYTHING WE NEEDED TO SURVIVE. BUT SOMETIMES, AFTER CHECKING THERE WERE NO TARSE ABOUT, WE'D GO OUT LOOKING FOR OTHER MAMMOTHS.
WE'RE STARTING TO BELIEVE THAT WE'RE THE LAST ONES LEFT.
WHEN I CAME ACROSS ATLAS AND AXIS, I WAS SCARED STIFF. I WAS ABOUT TO CRUSH THEM. BUT ONCE I SAW THAT THEY CAME IN PEACE, I CALMED MYSELF DOWN. AND WHEN THEY ASKED ME TO ACCOMPANY THEM, I THOUGHT IT A GOOD IDEA--HAVING NEVER VENTURED FAR FROM THE CRATER.

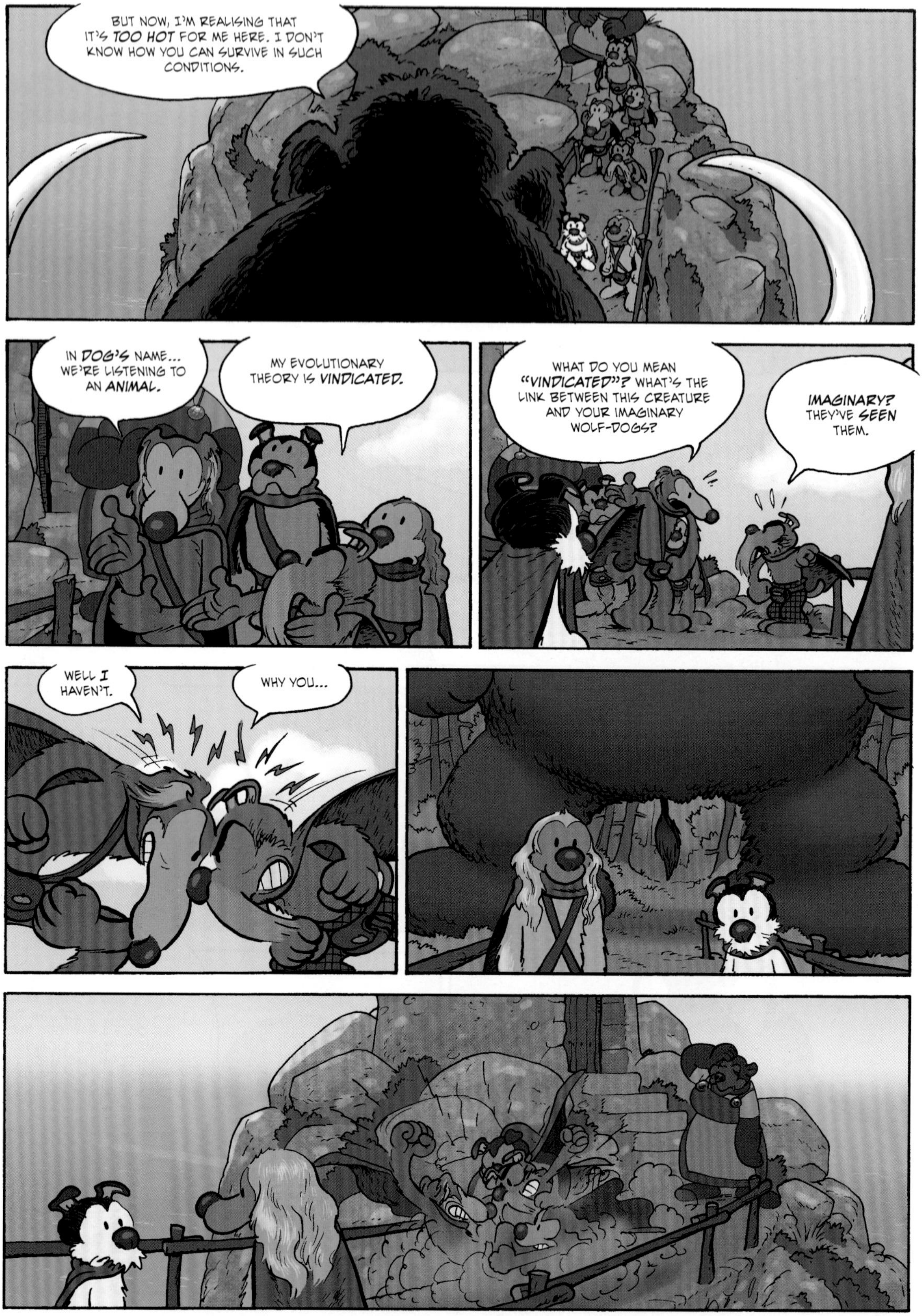
BUT NOW, I'M REALISING THAT IT'S TOO HOT FOR ME HERE. I DON'T KNOW HOW YOU CAN SURVIVE IN SUCH CONDITIONS.
IN DOG'S NAME... WE'RE LISTENING TO AN ANIMAL.
MY EVOLUTIONARY THEORY IS VINDICATED.
WHAT DO YOU MEAN "VINDICATED"? WHAT'S THE LINK BETWEEN THIS CREATURE AND YOUR IMAGINARY WOLF-DOGS?
IMAGINARY? THEY'VE SEEN THEM.
WELL I HAVEN'T.
WHY YOU...

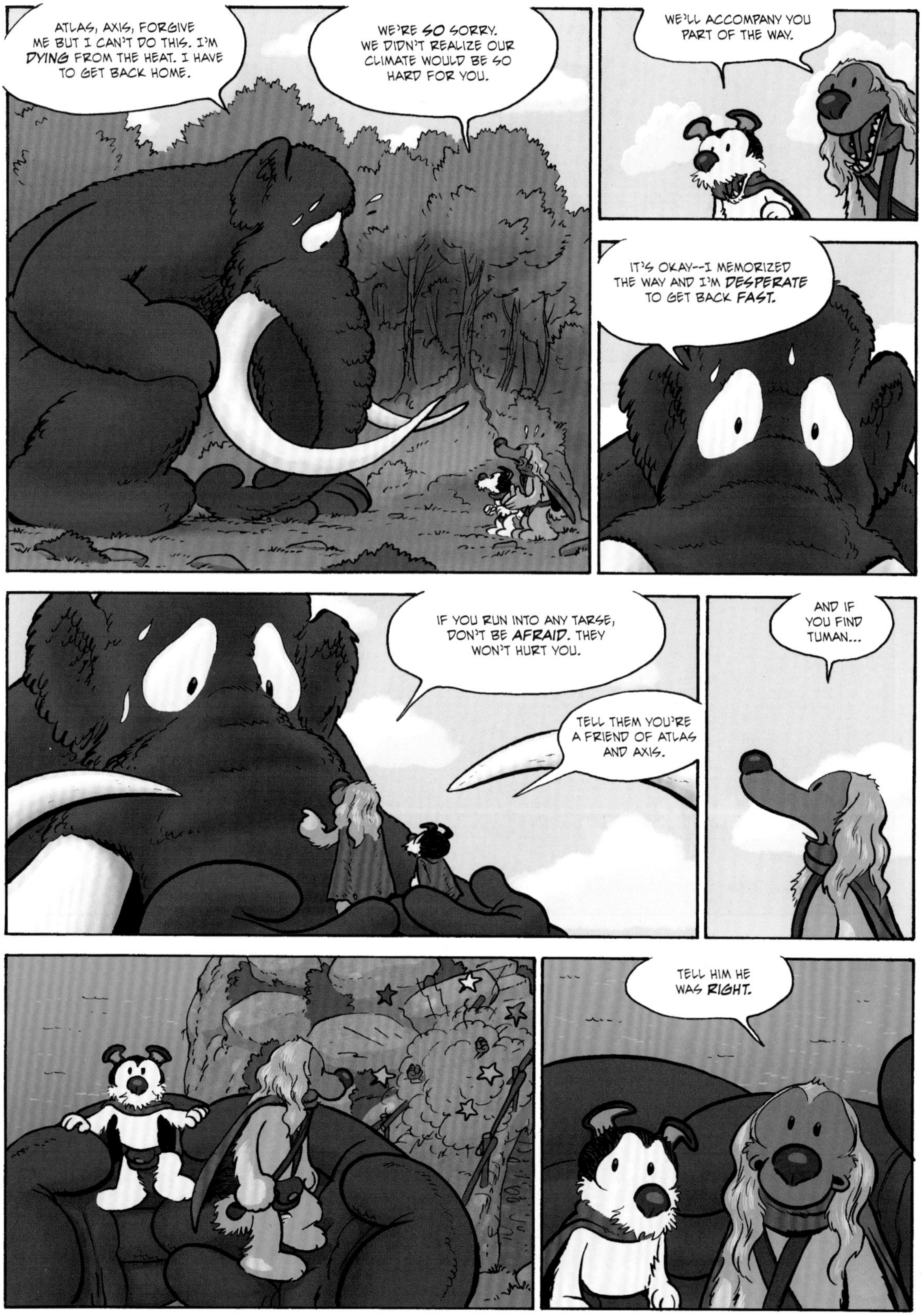
ATLAS, AXIS, FORGIVE ME BUT I CAN'T DO THIS. I'M DYING FROM THE HEAT. I HAVE TO GET BACK HOME.
WE'RE SO SORRY. WE DIDN'T REALIZE OUR CLIMATE WOULD BE SO HARD FOR YOU.
WE'LL ACCOMPANY YOU PART OF THE WAY.
IT'S OKAY--I MEMORIZED THE WAY AND I'M DESPERATE TO GET BACK FAST.
IF YOU RUN INTO ANY TARSE, DON'T BE AFRAID. THEY WON'T HURT YOU.
TELL THEM YOU'RE A FRIEND OF ATLAS AND AXIS.
AND IF YOU FIND TUMAN...
TELL HIM HE WAS RIGHT.

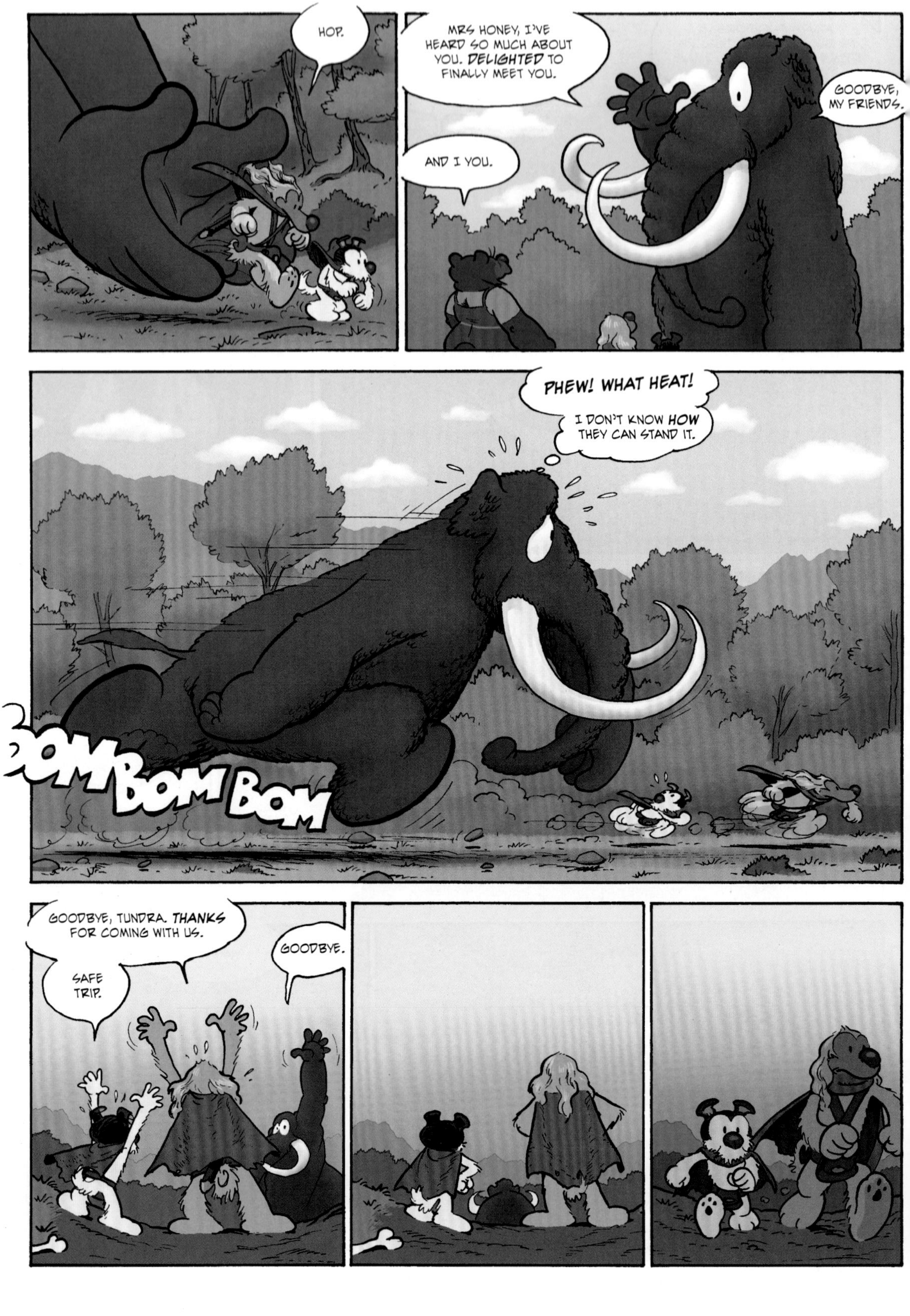
HOP.
MRS HONEY, I'VE HEARD SO MUCH ABOUT YOU. DELIGHTED TO FINALLY MEET YOU.
AND I YOU.
GOODBYE, MY FRIENDS.
PHEW! WHAT HEAT!
I DON'T KNOW HOW THEY CAN STAND IT.
BOM BOM BOM
GOODBYE, TUNDRA. THANKS FOR COMING WITH US.
SAFE TRIP.
GOODBYE.

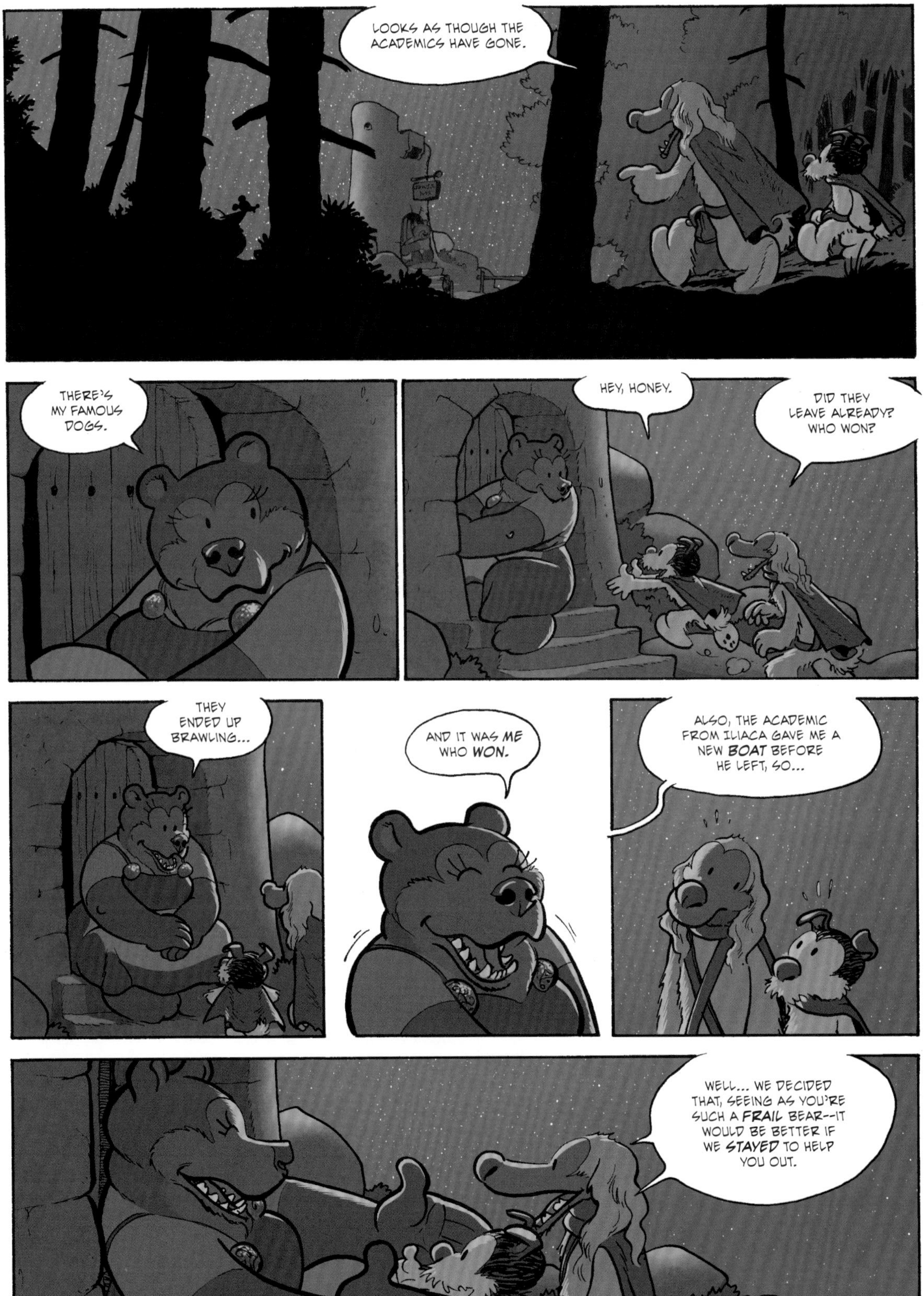
LOOKS AS THOUGH THE ACADEMICS HAVE GONE.
THERE'S MY FAMOUS DOGS.
HEY, HONEY.
DID THEY LEAVE ALREADY? WHO WON?
THEY ENDED UP BRAWLING...
AND IT WAS **ME** WHO **WON.**
ALSO, THE ACADEMIC FROM ILIACA GAVE ME A NEW **BOAT** BEFORE HE LEFT, SO...
WELL... WE DECIDED THAT, SEEING AS YOU'RE SUCH A **FRAIL** BEAR--IT WOULD BE BETTER IF WE **STAYED** TO HELP YOU OUT.

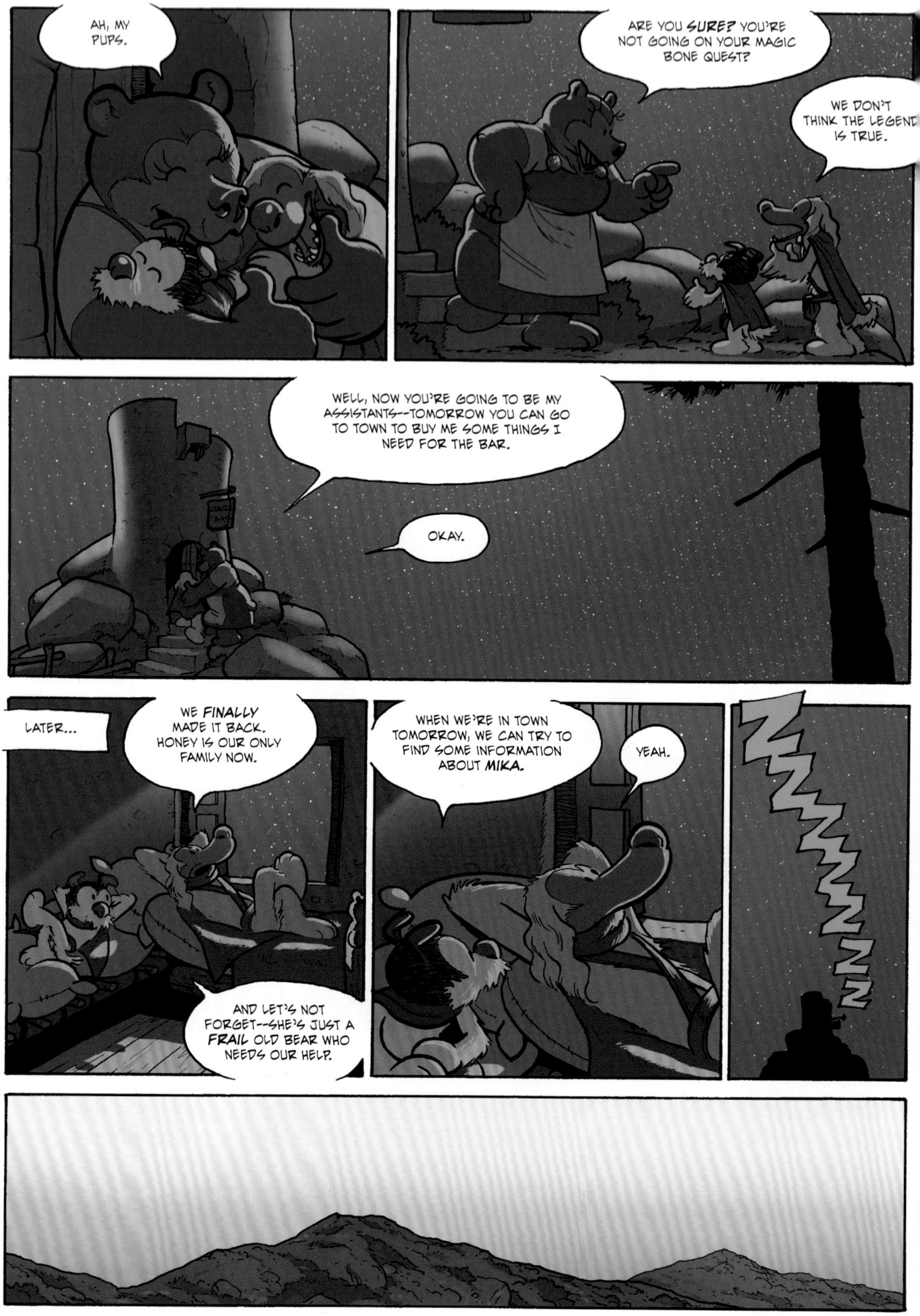
AH, MY PUPS.
ARE YOU SURE? YOU'RE NOT GOING ON YOUR MAGIC BONE QUEST?
WE DON'T THINK THE LEGEND IS TRUE.
WELL, NOW YOU'RE GOING TO BE MY ASSISTANTS--TOMORROW YOU CAN GO TO TOWN TO BUY ME SOME THINGS I NEED FOR THE BAR.
OKAY.
LATER...
WE FINALLY MADE IT BACK. HONEY IS OUR ONLY FAMILY NOW.
AND LET'S NOT FORGET--SHE'S JUST A FRAIL OLD BEAR WHO NEEDS OUR HELP.
WHEN WE'RE IN TOWN TOMORROW, WE CAN TRY TO FIND SOME INFORMATION ABOUT MIKA.
YEAH.
ZZZZZZZ

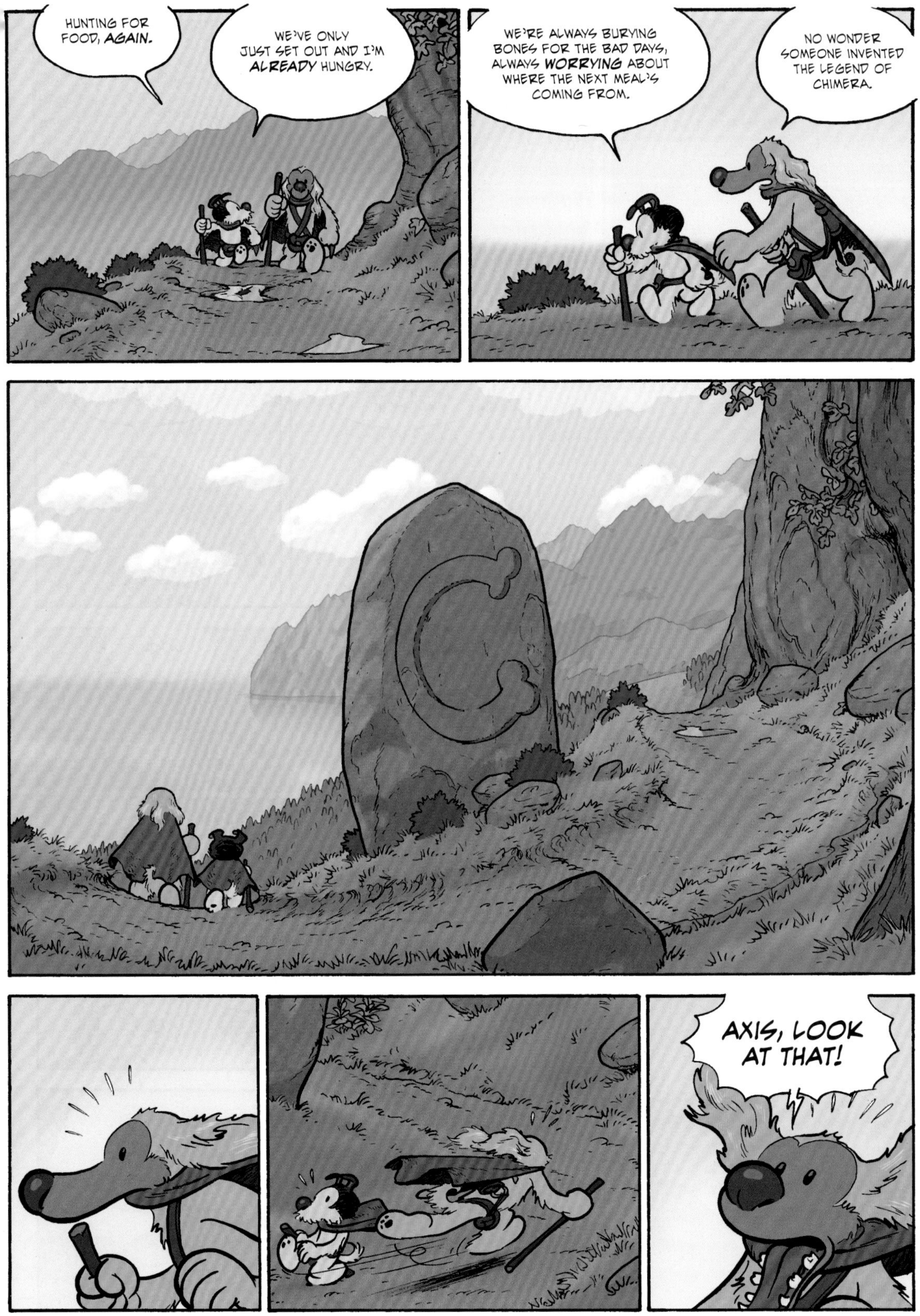
HUNTING FOR FOOD, **AGAIN.**
WE'VE ONLY JUST SET OUT AND I'M **ALREADY** HUNGRY.
WE'RE ALWAYS BURYING BONES FOR THE BAD DAYS, ALWAYS **WORRYING** ABOUT WHERE THE NEXT MEAL'S COMING FROM.
NO WONDER SOMEONE INVENTED THE LEGEND OF CHIMERA.
AXIS, LOOK AT THAT!

WHAT IS IT?

THERE.

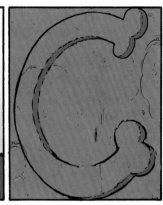

WHAT? A ROCK?

THAT SYMBOL IS WRITTEN ON CANUTO'S PARCHMENT.

IS IT A CLUE?!

LOOK.

THAT CAPE--IT'S IN THE SHAPE OF AN ARROW!

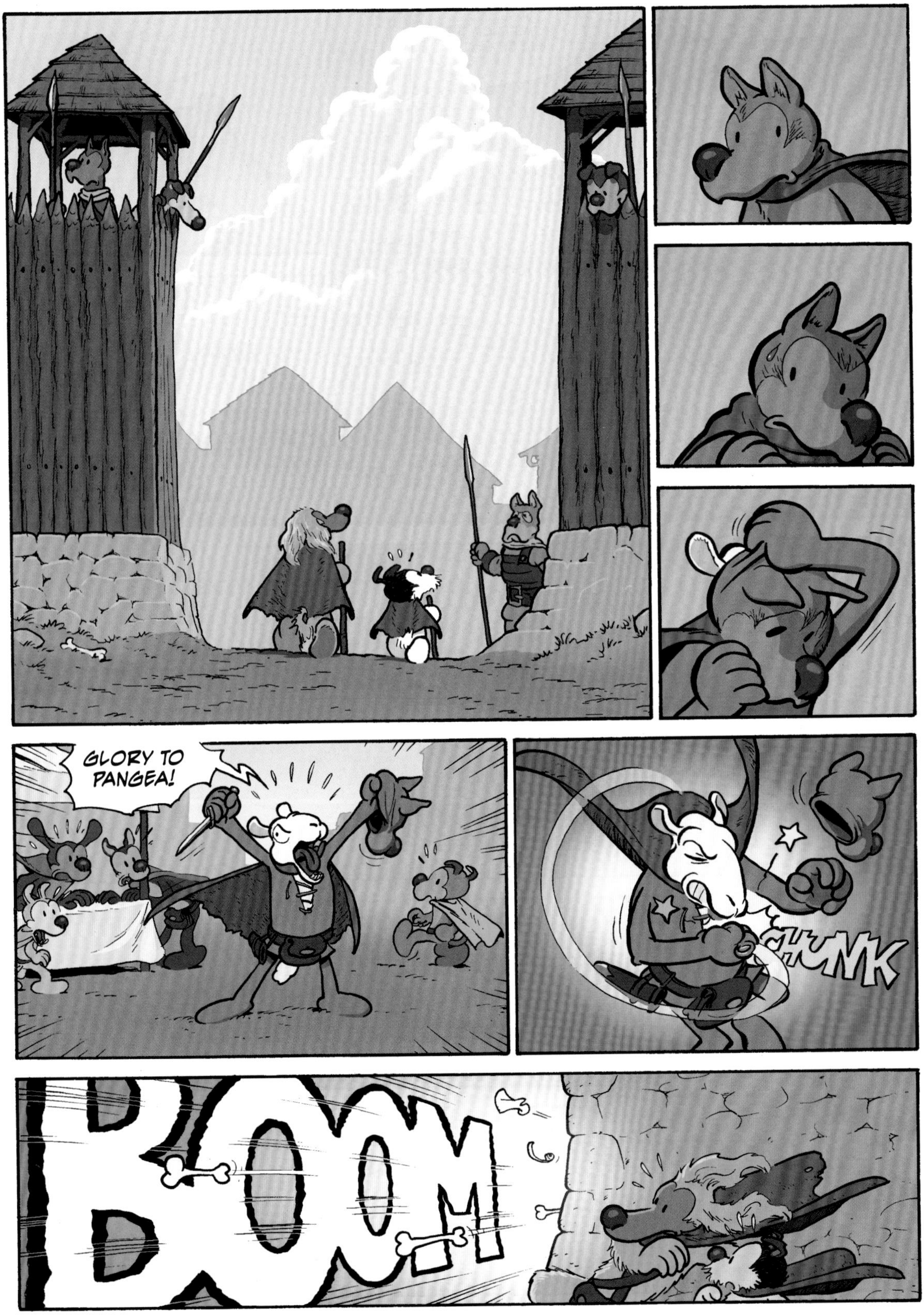
GLORY TO PANGEA!
CHUNK
BOOM

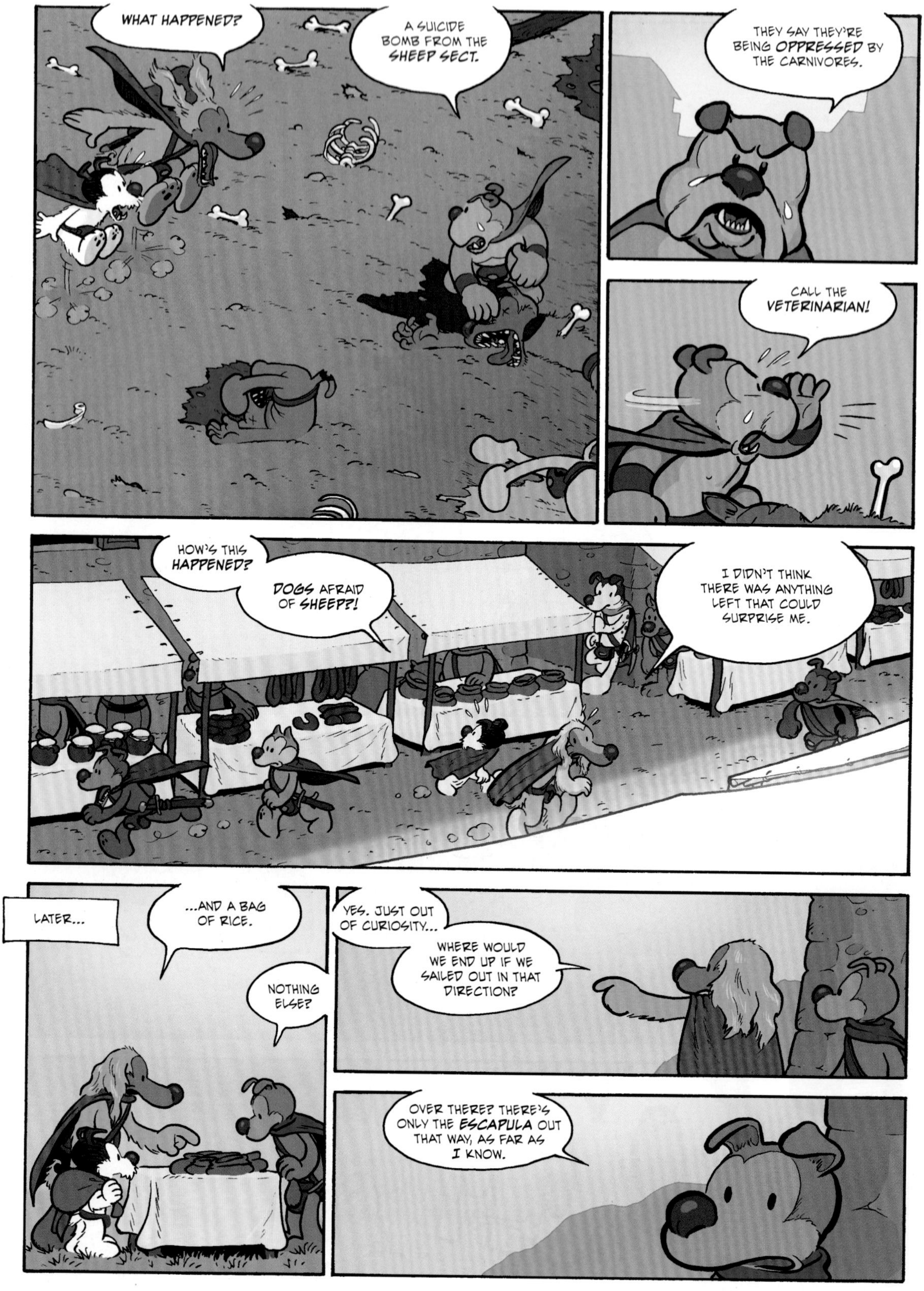
WHAT HAPPENED?
A SUICIDE BOMB FROM THE SHEEP SECT.
THEY SAY THEY'RE BEING OPPRESSED BY THE CARNIVORES.
CALL THE VETERINARIAN!
HOW'S THIS HAPPENED?
DOGS AFRAID OF SHEEP?!
I DIDN'T THINK THERE WAS ANYTHING LEFT THAT COULD SURPRISE ME.
LATER...
...AND A BAG OF RICE.
NOTHING ELSE?
YES. JUST OUT OF CURIOSITY...
WHERE WOULD WE END UP IF WE SAILED OUT IN THAT DIRECTION?
OVER THERE? THERE'S ONLY THE ESCAPULA OUT THAT WAY, AS FAR AS I KNOW.

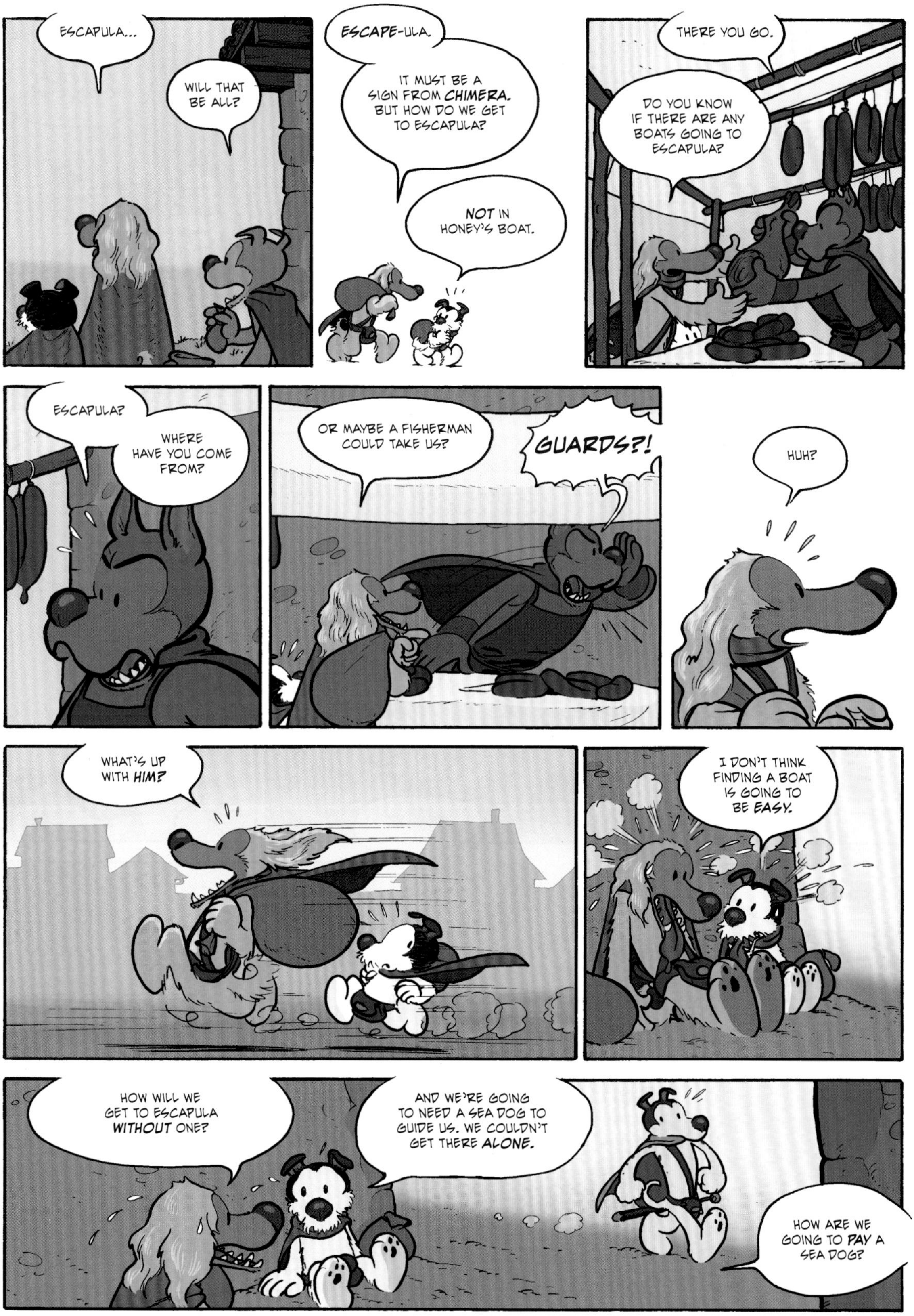
ESCAPULA...
WILL THAT BE ALL?
ESCAPE-ULA.
IT MUST BE A SIGN FROM CHIMERA. BUT HOW DO WE GET TO ESCAPULA?
NOT IN HONEY'S BOAT.
THERE YOU GO.
DO YOU KNOW IF THERE ARE ANY BOATS GOING TO ESCAPULA?
ESCAPULA?
WHERE HAVE YOU COME FROM?
OR MAYBE A FISHERMAN COULD TAKE US?
GUARDS?!
HUH?
WHAT'S UP WITH HIM?
I DON'T THINK FINDING A BOAT IS GOING TO BE EASY.
HOW WILL WE GET TO ESCAPULA WITHOUT ONE?
AND WE'RE GOING TO NEED A SEA DOG TO GUIDE US. WE COULDN'T GET THERE ALONE.
HOW ARE WE GOING TO PAY A SEA DOG?

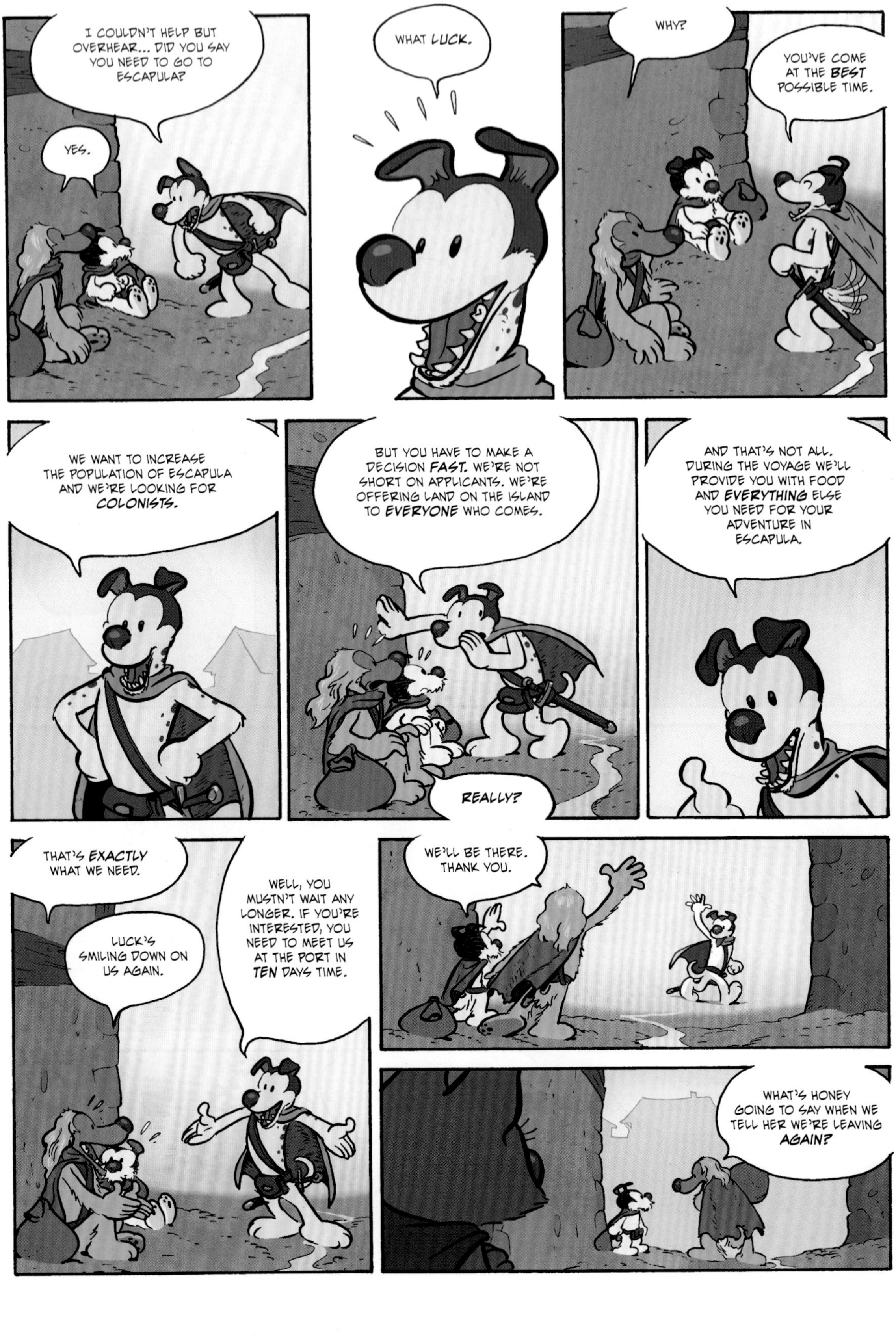
I COULDN'T HELP BUT OVERHEAR... DID YOU SAY YOU NEED TO GO TO ESCAPULA?
YES.
WHAT LUCK.
WHY?
YOU'VE COME AT THE BEST POSSIBLE TIME.
WE WANT TO INCREASE THE POPULATION OF ESCAPULA AND WE'RE LOOKING FOR COLONISTS.
BUT YOU HAVE TO MAKE A DECISION FAST. WE'RE NOT SHORT ON APPLICANTS. WE'RE OFFERING LAND ON THE ISLAND TO EVERYONE WHO COMES.
REALLY?
AND THAT'S NOT ALL. DURING THE VOYAGE WE'LL PROVIDE YOU WITH FOOD AND EVERYTHING ELSE YOU NEED FOR YOUR ADVENTURE IN ESCAPULA.
THAT'S EXACTLY WHAT WE NEED.
LUCK'S SMILING DOWN ON US AGAIN.
WELL, YOU MUSTN'T WAIT ANY LONGER. IF YOU'RE INTERESTED, YOU NEED TO MEET US AT THE PORT IN TEN DAYS TIME.
WE'LL BE THERE. THANK YOU.
WHAT'S HONEY GOING TO SAY WHEN WE TELL HER WE'RE LEAVING AGAIN?

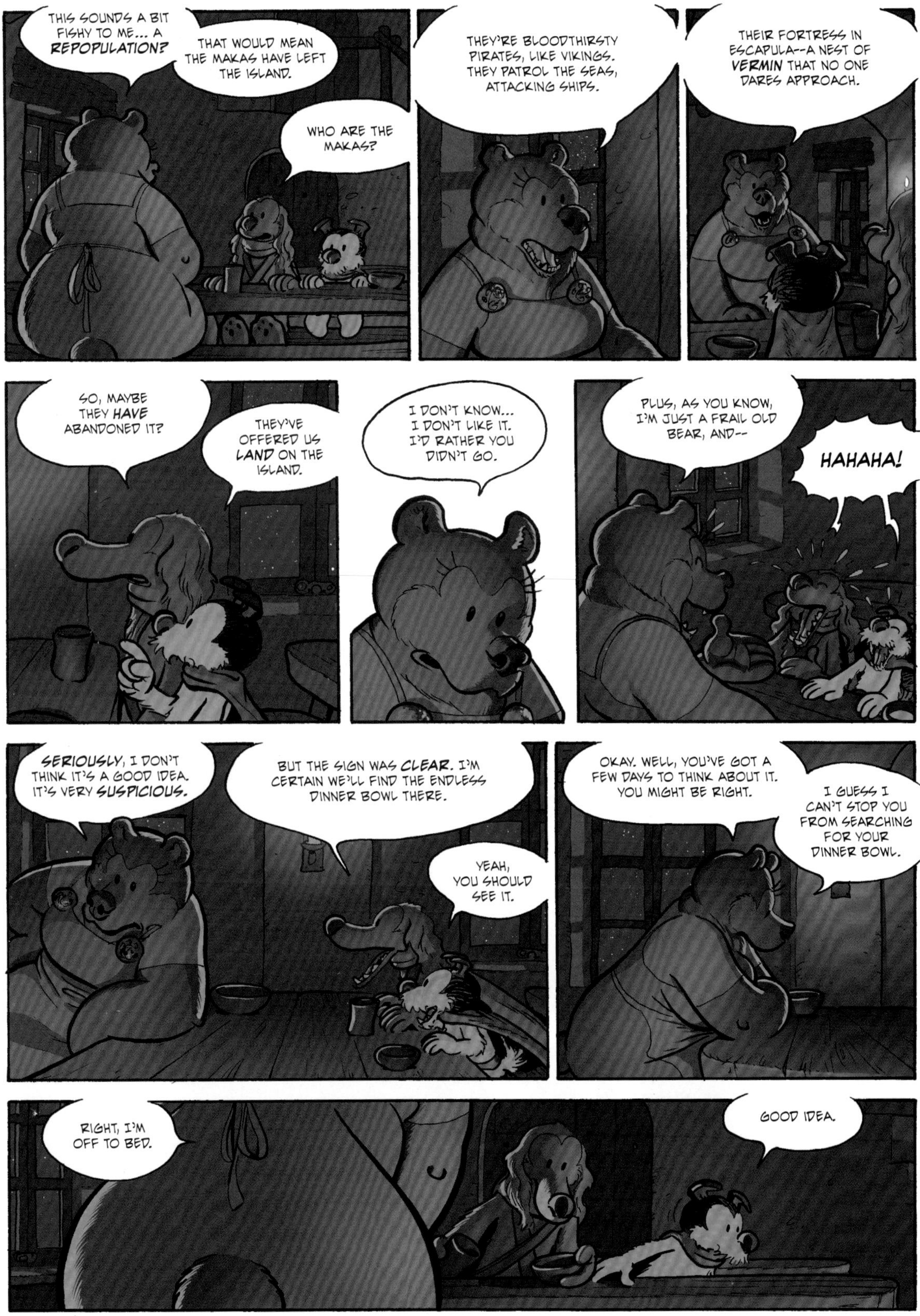
THIS SOUNDS A BIT FISHY TO ME... A REPOPULATION?
THAT WOULD MEAN THE MAKAS HAVE LEFT THE ISLAND.
WHO ARE THE MAKAS?
THEY'RE BLOODTHIRSTY PIRATES, LIKE VIKINGS. THEY PATROL THE SEAS, ATTACKING SHIPS.
THEIR FORTRESS IN ESCAPULA--A NEST OF VERMIN THAT NO ONE DARES APPROACH.
SO, MAYBE THEY HAVE ABANDONED IT?
THEY'VE OFFERED US LAND ON THE ISLAND.
I DON'T KNOW... I DON'T LIKE IT. I'D RATHER YOU DIDN'T GO.
PLUS, AS YOU KNOW, I'M JUST A FRAIL OLD BEAR, AND--
HAHAHA!
SERIOUSLY, I DON'T THINK IT'S A GOOD IDEA. IT'S VERY SUSPICIOUS.
BUT THE SIGN WAS CLEAR. I'M CERTAIN WE'LL FIND THE ENDLESS DINNER BOWL THERE.
YEAH, YOU SHOULD SEE IT.
OKAY. WELL, YOU'VE GOT A FEW DAYS TO THINK ABOUT IT. YOU MIGHT BE RIGHT.
I GUESS I CAN'T STOP YOU FROM SEARCHING FOR YOUR DINNER BOWL.
RIGHT, I'M OFF TO BED.
GOOD IDEA.

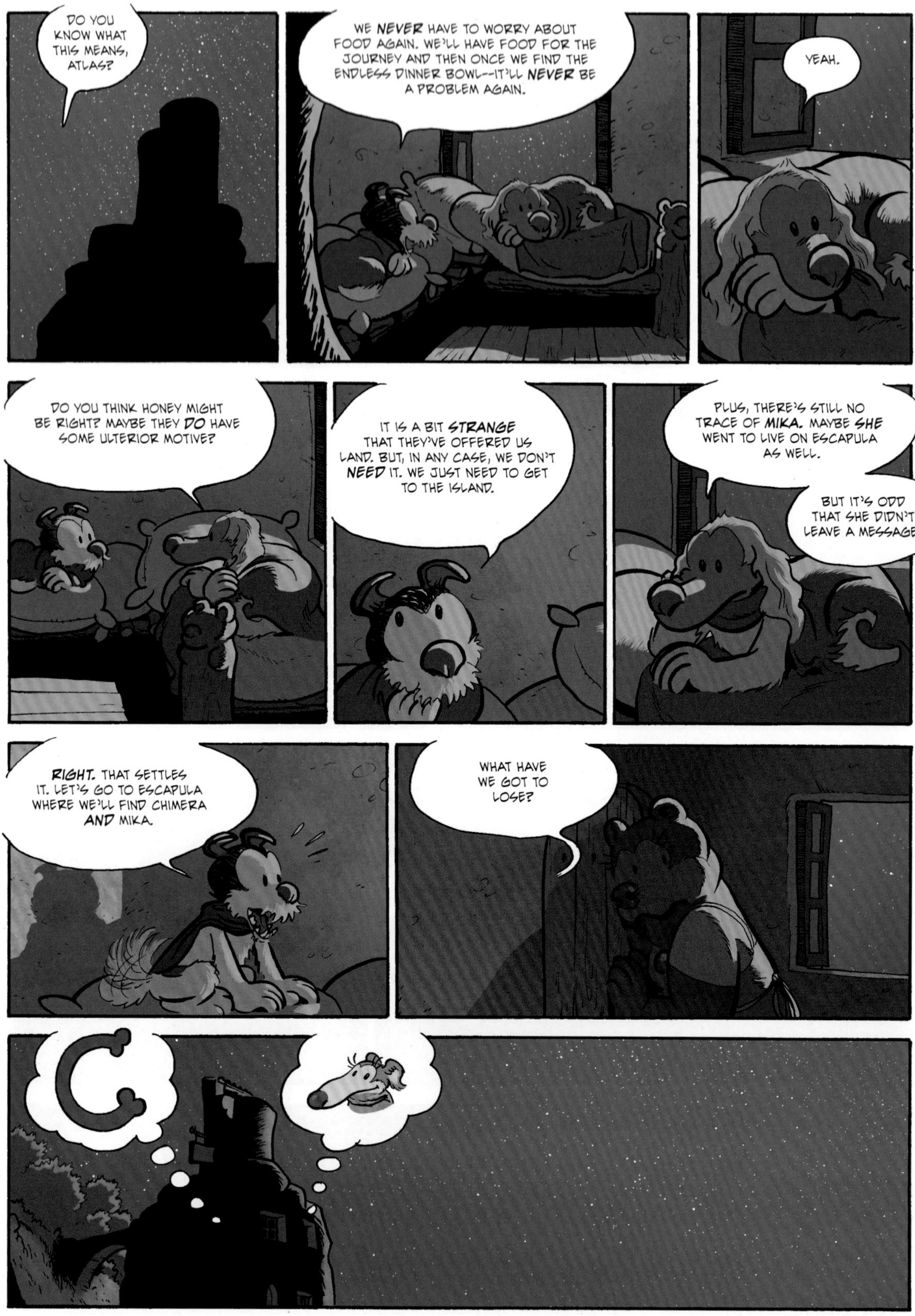
DO YOU KNOW WHAT THIS MEANS, ATLAS?
WE NEVER HAVE TO WORRY ABOUT FOOD AGAIN. WE'LL HAVE FOOD FOR THE JOURNEY AND THEN ONCE WE FIND THE ENDLESS DINNER BOWL--IT'LL NEVER BE A PROBLEM AGAIN.
YEAH.
DO YOU THINK HONEY MIGHT BE RIGHT? MAYBE THEY DO HAVE SOME ULTERIOR MOTIVE?
IT IS A BIT STRANGE THAT THEY'VE OFFERED US LAND. BUT, IN ANY CASE, WE DON'T NEED IT. WE JUST NEED TO GET TO THE ISLAND.
PLUS, THERE'S STILL NO TRACE OF MIKA. MAYBE SHE WENT TO LIVE ON ESCAPULA AS WELL.
BUT IT'S ODD THAT SHE DIDN'T LEAVE A MESSAGE.
RIGHT. THAT SETTLES IT. LET'S GO TO ESCAPULA WHERE WE'LL FIND CHIMERA AND MIKA.
WHAT HAVE WE GOT TO LOSE?

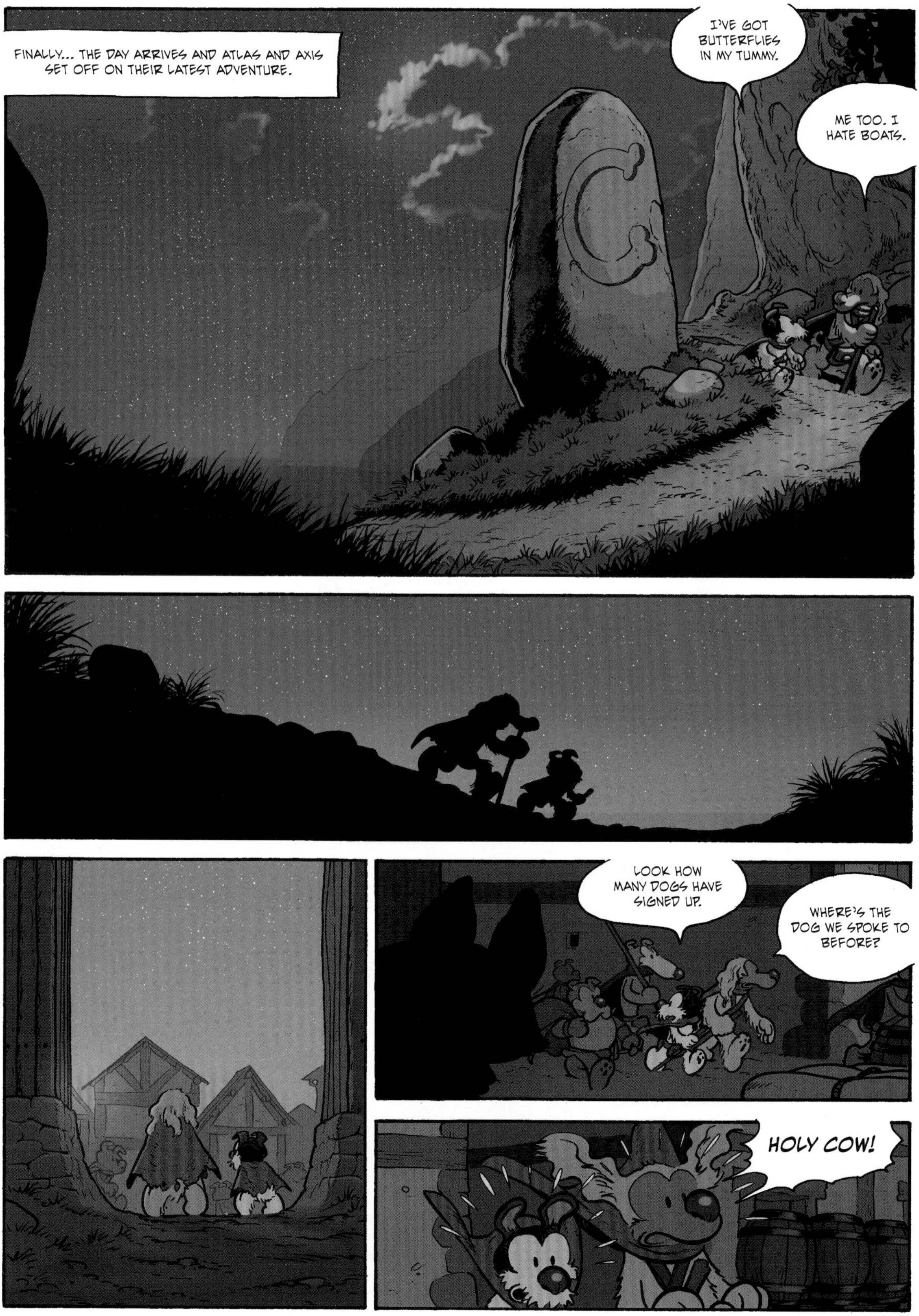
FINALLY... THE DAY ARRIVES AND ATLAS AND AXIS SET OFF ON THEIR LATEST ADVENTURE.
I'VE GOT BUTTERFLIES IN MY TUMMY.
ME TOO. I HATE BOATS.
LOOK HOW MANY DOGS HAVE SIGNED UP.
WHERE'S THE DOG WE SPOKE TO BEFORE?
HOLY COW!

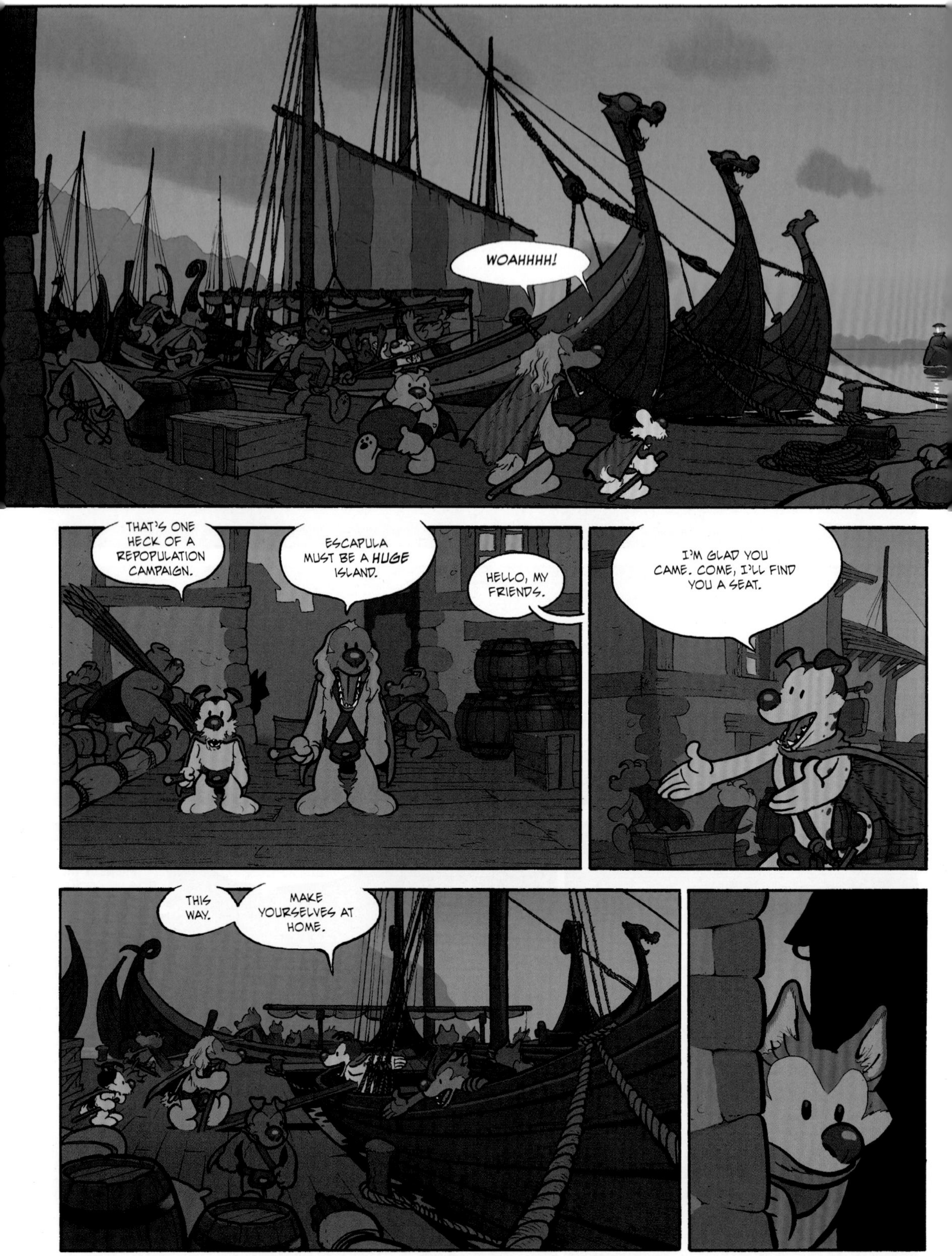
WOAHHHH!
THAT'S ONE HECK OF A REPOPULATION CAMPAIGN.
ESCAPULA MUST BE A HUGE ISLAND.
HELLO, MY FRIENDS.
I'M GLAD YOU CAME. COME, I'LL FIND YOU A SEAT.
THIS WAY.
MAKE YOURSELVES AT HOME.

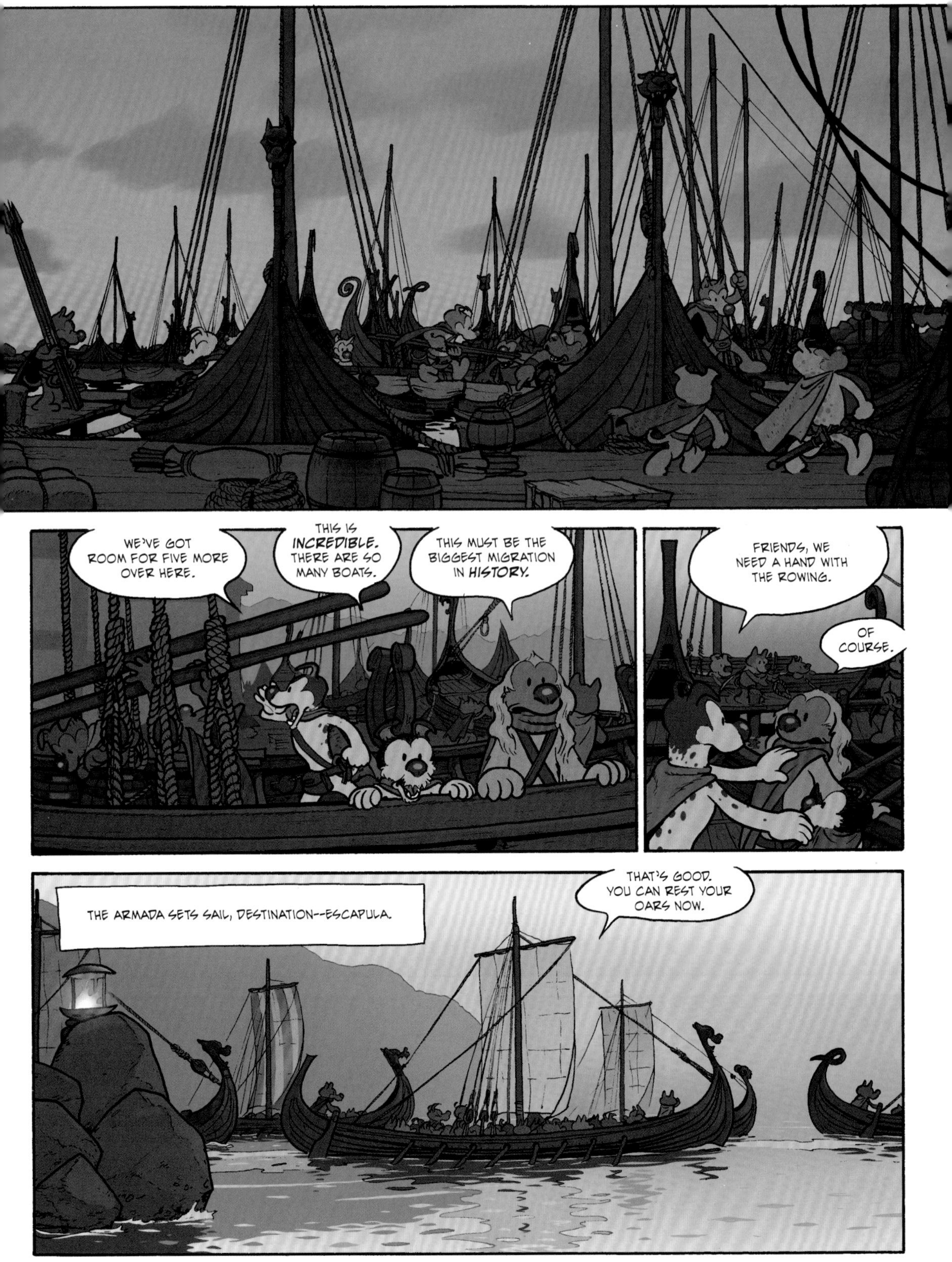
WE'VE GOT ROOM FOR FIVE MORE OVER HERE.
THIS IS INCREDIBLE. THERE ARE SO MANY BOATS.
THIS MUST BE THE BIGGEST MIGRATION IN HISTORY.
FRIENDS, WE NEED A HAND WITH THE ROWING.
OF COURSE.
THE ARMADA SETS SAIL, DESTINATION--ESCAPULA.
THAT'S GOOD. YOU CAN REST YOUR OARS NOW.

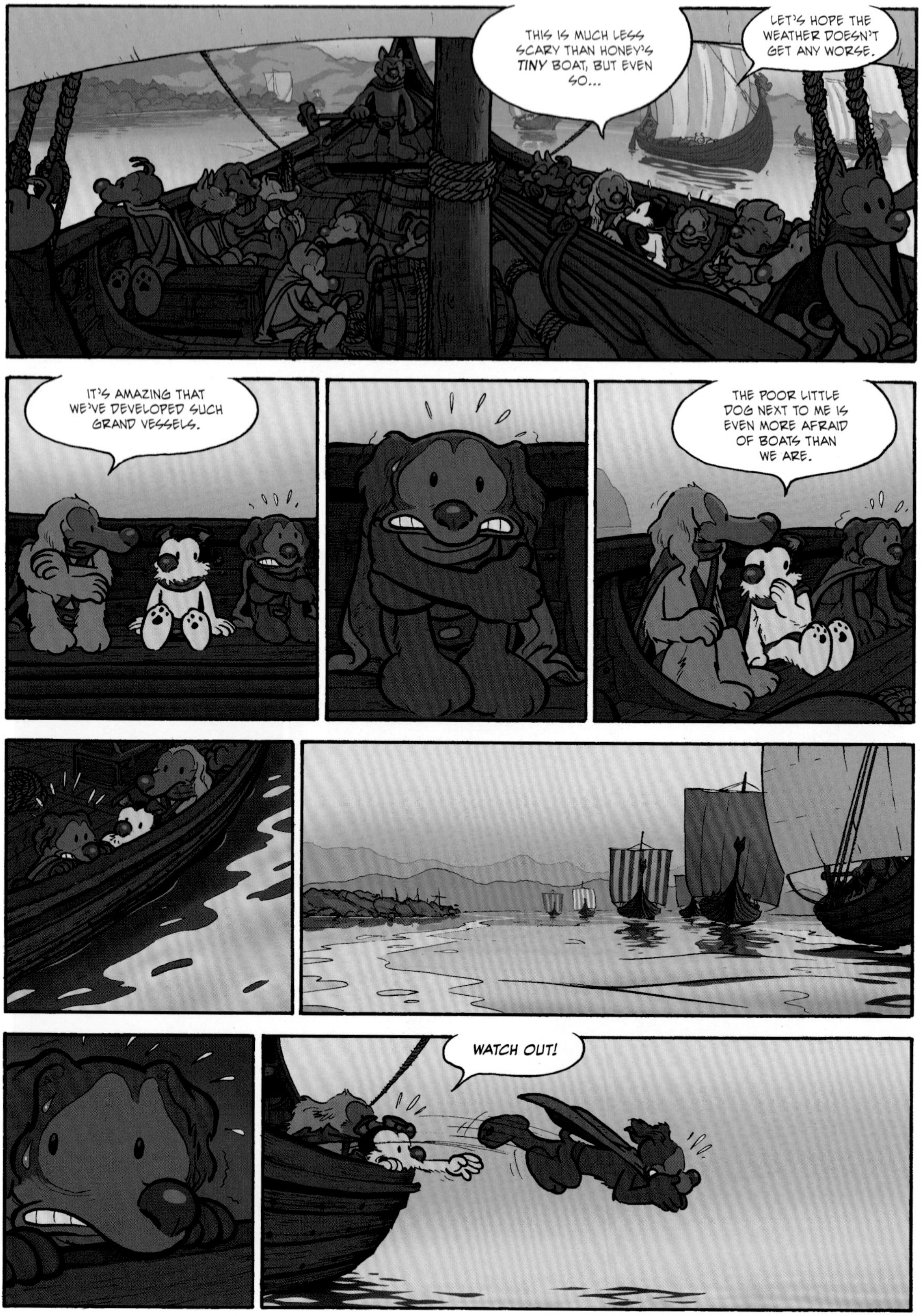
THIS IS MUCH LESS SCARY THAN HONEY'S *TINY* BOAT, BUT EVEN SO...
LET'S HOPE THE WEATHER DOESN'T GET ANY WORSE.
IT'S AMAZING THAT WE'VE DEVELOPED SUCH GRAND VESSELS.
THE POOR LITTLE DOG NEXT TO ME IS EVEN MORE AFRAID OF BOATS THAN WE ARE.
WATCH OUT!

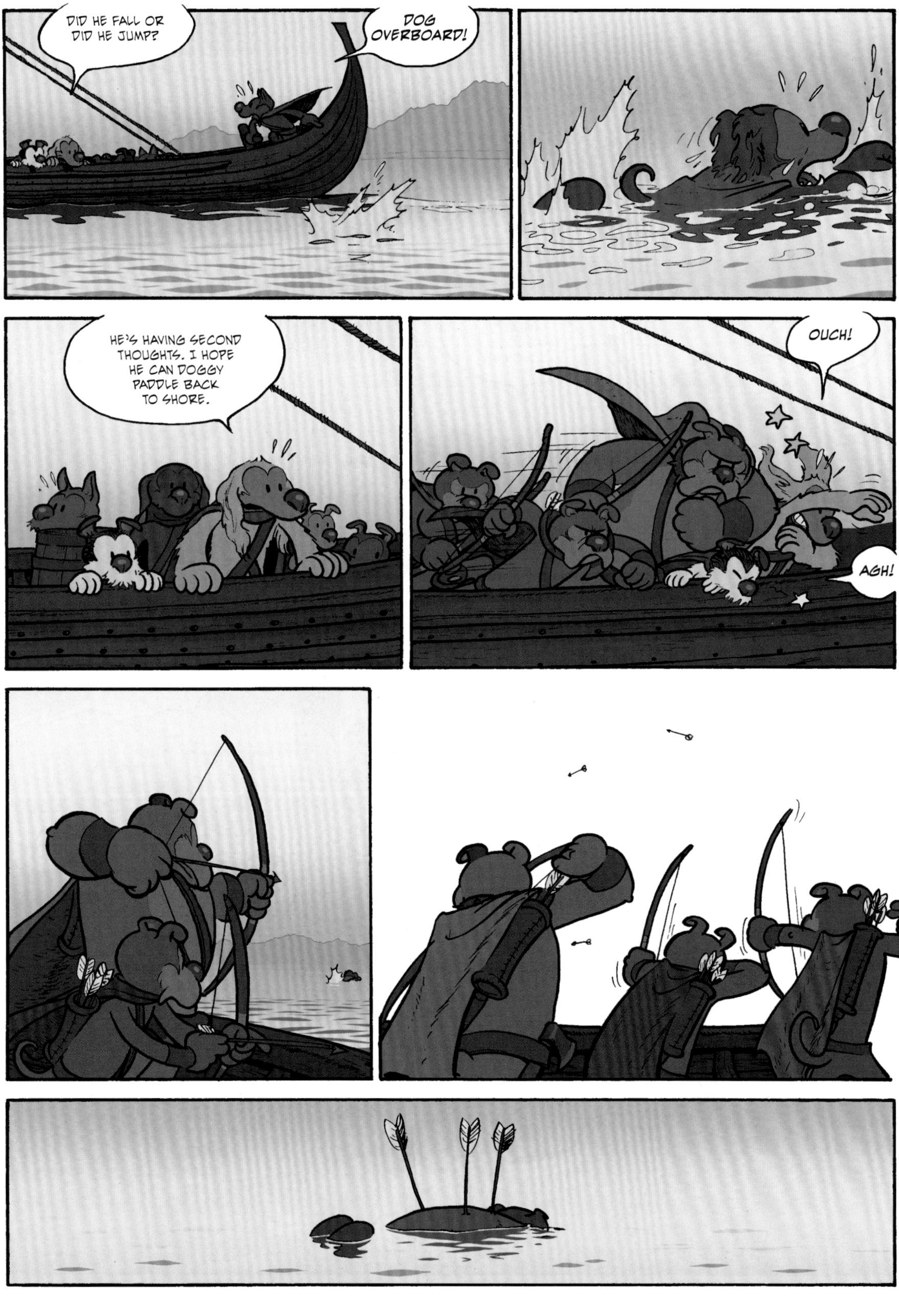
DID HE FALL OR DID HE JUMP?
DOG OVERBOARD!
HE'S HAVING SECOND THOUGHTS. I HOPE HE CAN DOGGY PADDLE BACK TO SHORE.
OUCH!
AGH!

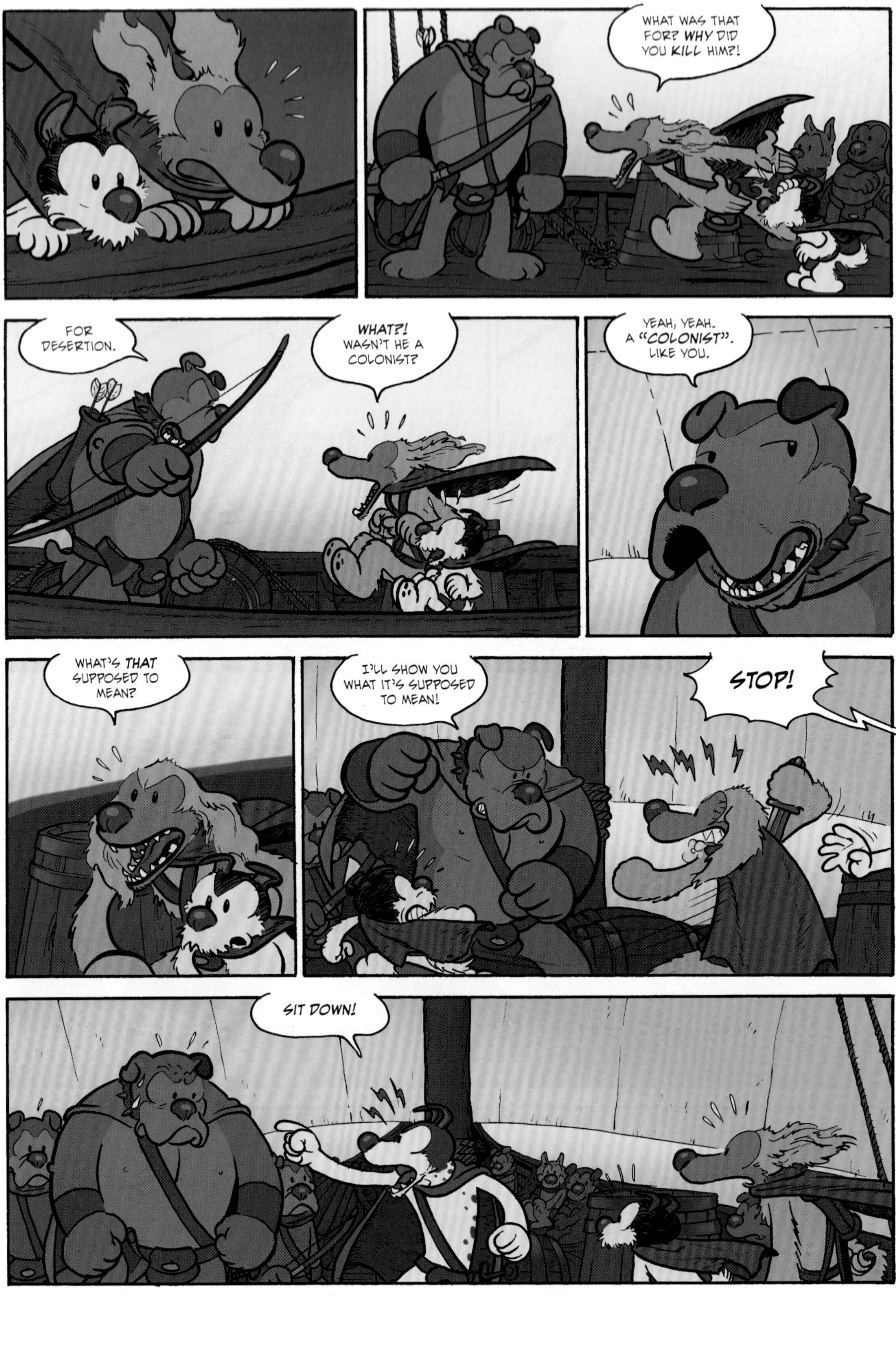
WHAT WAS THAT FOR? WHY DID YOU KILL HIM?!
FOR DESERTION.
WHAT?! WASN'T HE A COLONIST?
YEAH, YEAH. A "COLONIST". LIKE YOU.
WHAT'S THAT SUPPOSED TO MEAN?
I'LL SHOW YOU WHAT IT'S SUPPOSED TO MEAN!
STOP!
SIT DOWN!

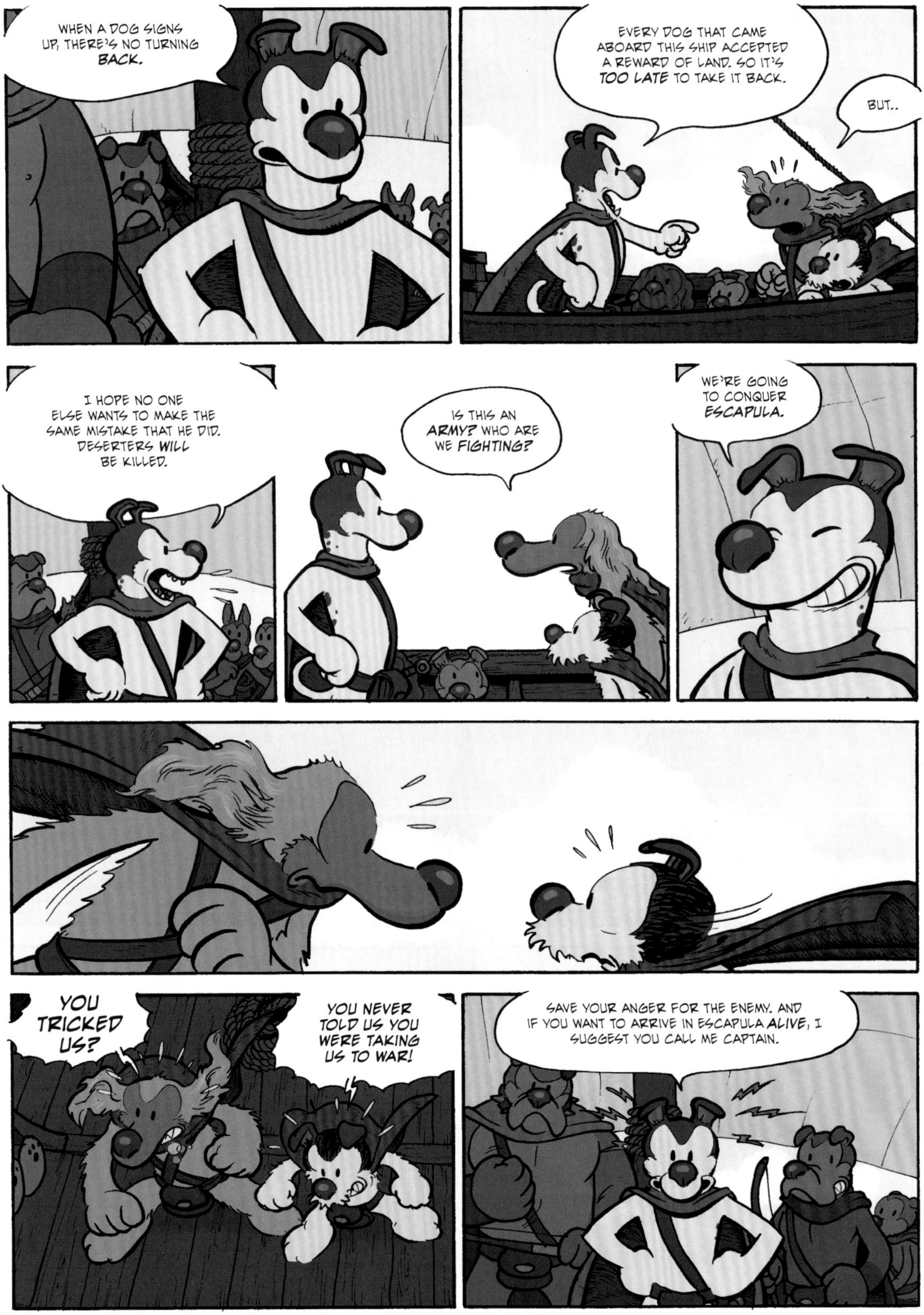
WHEN A DOG SIGNS UP, THERE'S NO TURNING BACK.
EVERY DOG THAT CAME ABOARD THIS SHIP ACCEPTED A REWARD OF LAND. SO IT'S TOO LATE TO TAKE IT BACK.
BUT..
I HOPE NO ONE ELSE WANTS TO MAKE THE SAME MISTAKE THAT HE DID. DESERTERS WILL BE KILLED.
IS THIS AN ARMY? WHO ARE WE FIGHTING?
WE'RE GOING TO CONQUER ESCAPULA.
YOU TRICKED US?
YOU NEVER TOLD US YOU WERE TAKING US TO WAR!
SAVE YOUR ANGER FOR THE ENEMY. AND IF YOU WANT TO ARRIVE IN ESCAPULA ALIVE, I SUGGEST YOU CALL ME CAPTAIN.

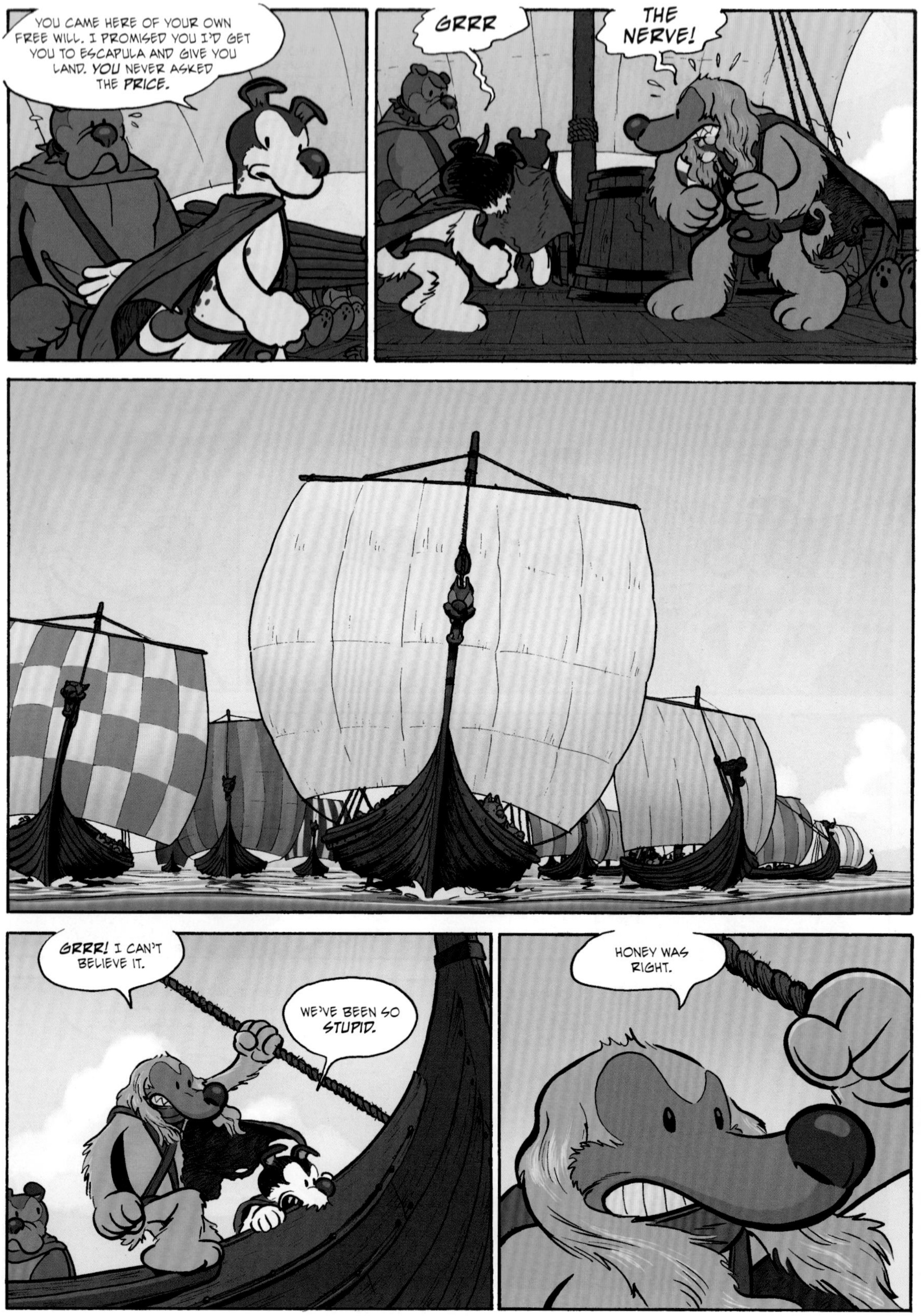
YOU CAME HERE OF YOUR OWN FREE WILL. I PROMISED YOU I'D GET YOU TO ESCAPULA AND GIVE YOU LAND. YOU NEVER ASKED THE PRICE.
GRRR
THE NERVE!
GRRR! I CAN'T BELIEVE IT.
WE'VE BEEN SO STUPID.
HONEY WAS RIGHT.

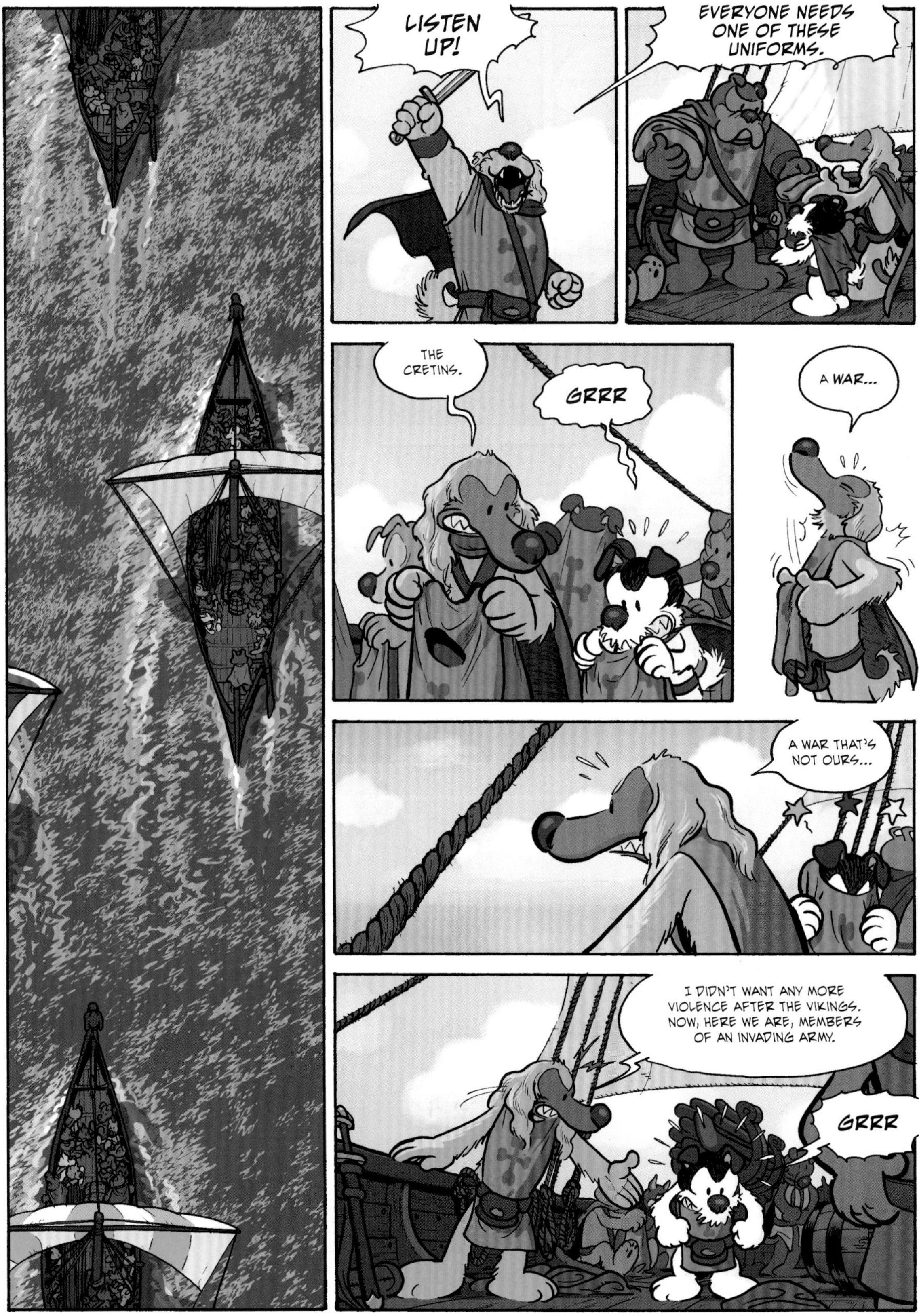
LISTEN UP!
EVERYONE NEEDS ONE OF THESE UNIFORMS.
THE CRETINS.
GRRR
A WAR...
A WAR THAT'S NOT OURS...
I DIDN'T WANT ANY MORE VIOLENCE AFTER THE VIKINGS. NOW, HERE WE ARE, MEMBERS OF AN INVADING ARMY.
GRRR

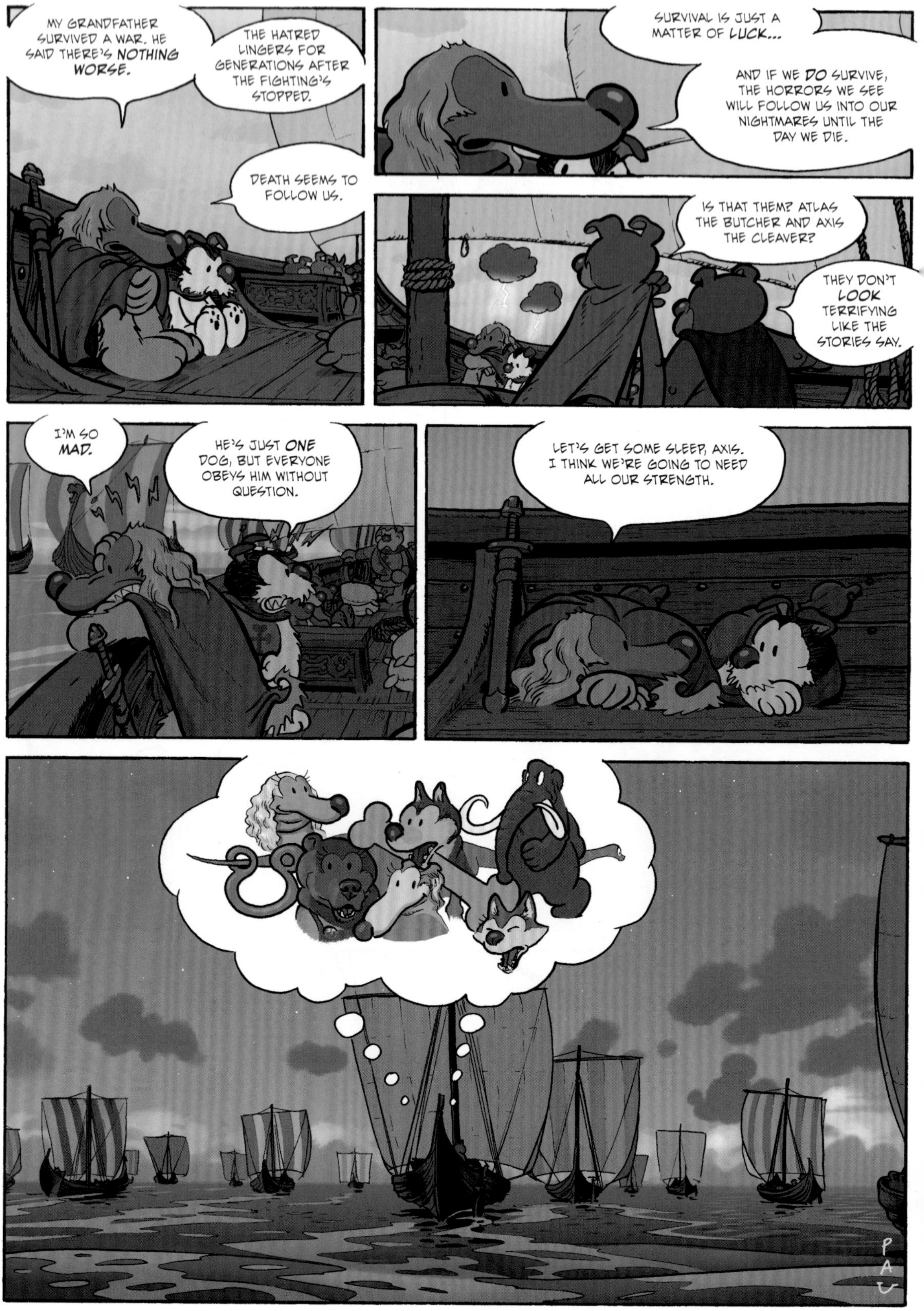
MY GRANDFATHER SURVIVED A WAR. HE SAID THERE'S **NOTHING WORSE.**
THE HATRED LINGERS FOR GENERATIONS AFTER THE FIGHTING'S STOPPED.
DEATH SEEMS TO FOLLOW US.
SURVIVAL IS JUST A MATTER OF **LUCK...**
AND IF WE **DO** SURVIVE, THE HORRORS WE SEE WILL FOLLOW US INTO OUR NIGHTMARES UNTIL THE DAY WE DIE.
IS THAT THEM? ATLAS THE BUTCHER AND AXIS THE CLEAVER?
THEY DON'T **LOOK** TERRIFYING LIKE THE STORIES SAY.
I'M SO **MAD.**
HE'S JUST **ONE** DOG, BUT EVERYONE OBEYS HIM WITHOUT QUESTION.
LET'S GET SOME SLEEP, AXIS. I THINK WE'RE GOING TO NEED ALL OUR STRENGTH.
PAU

THE END... FOR NOW!

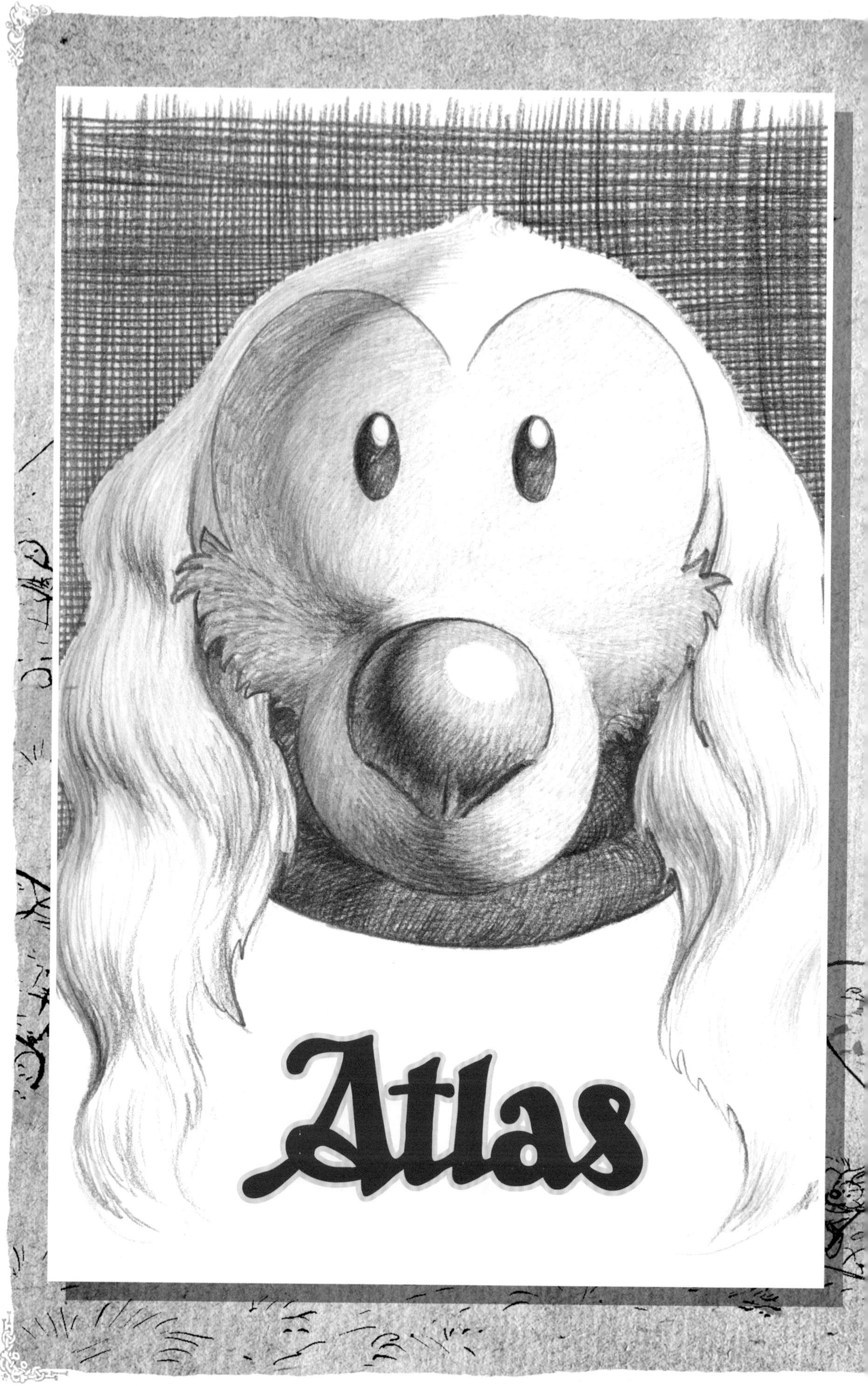
Atlas

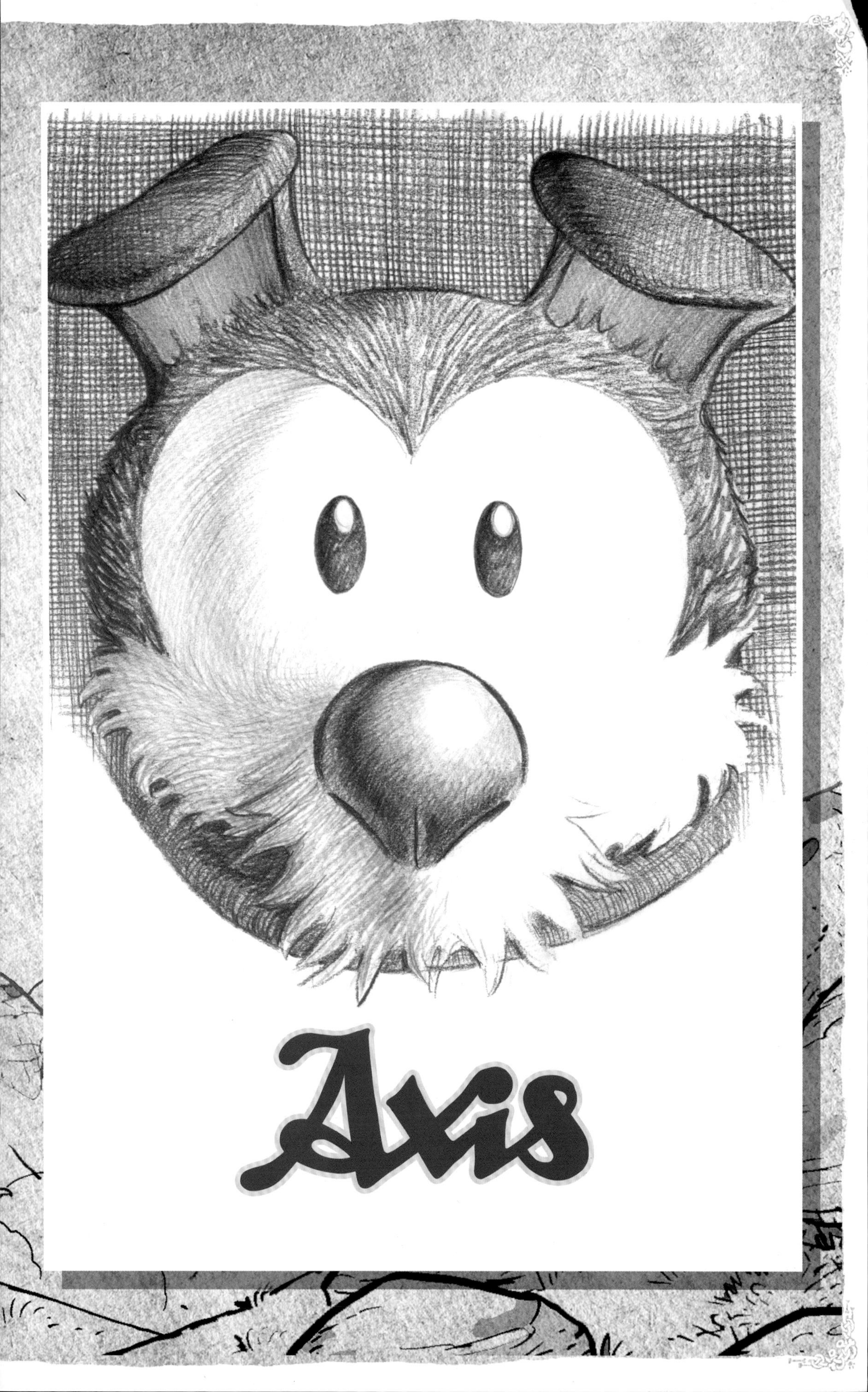
Axis

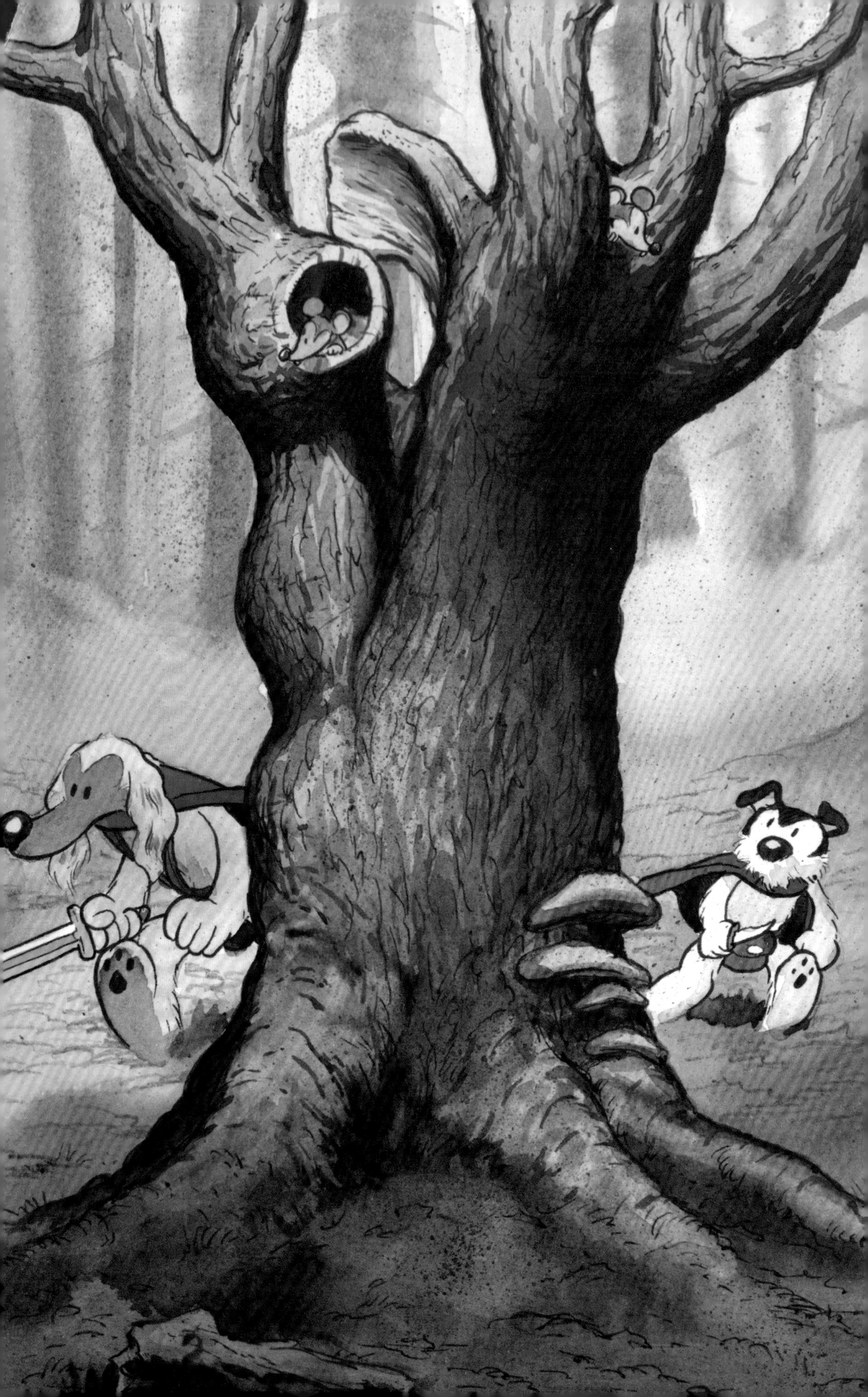

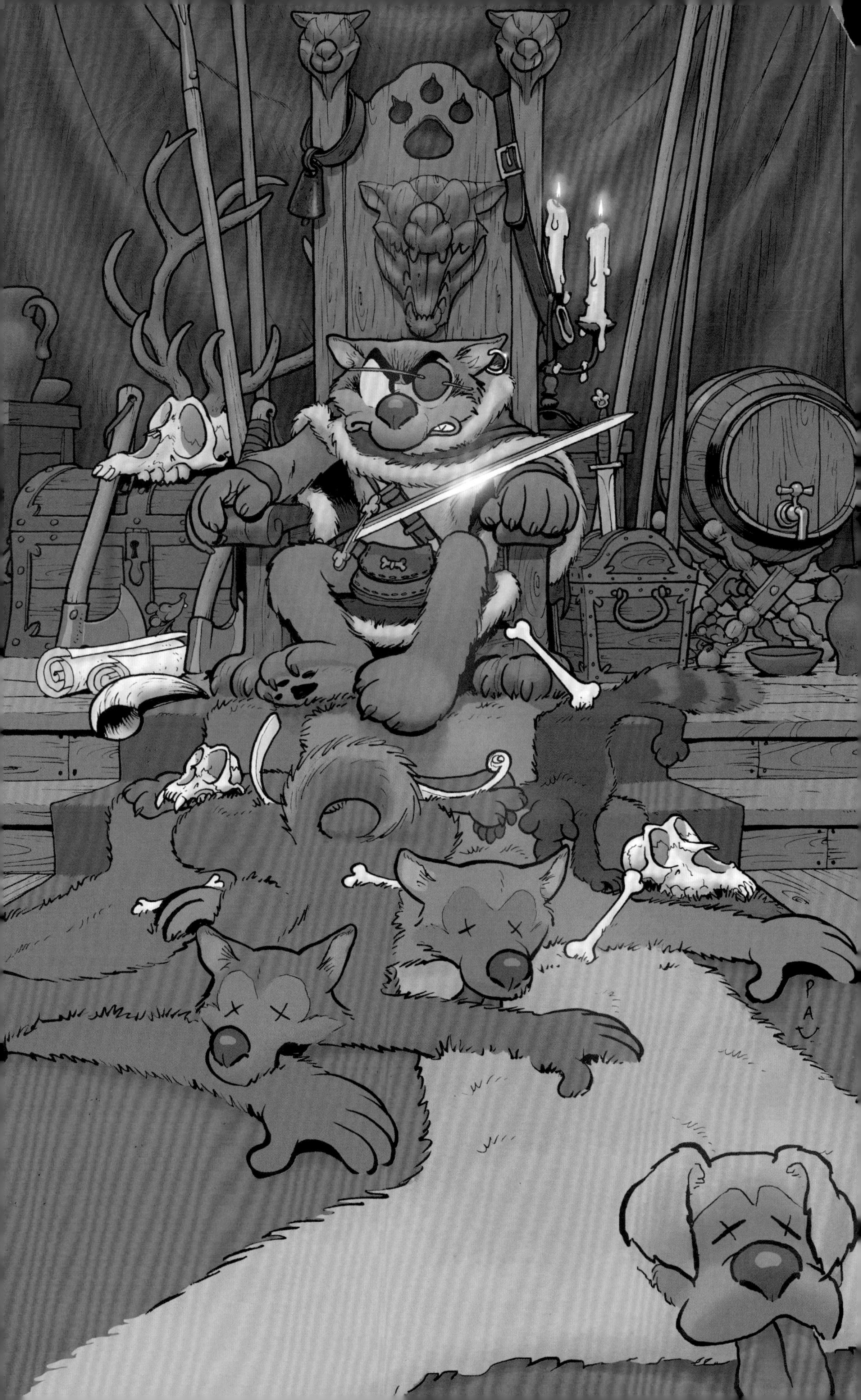

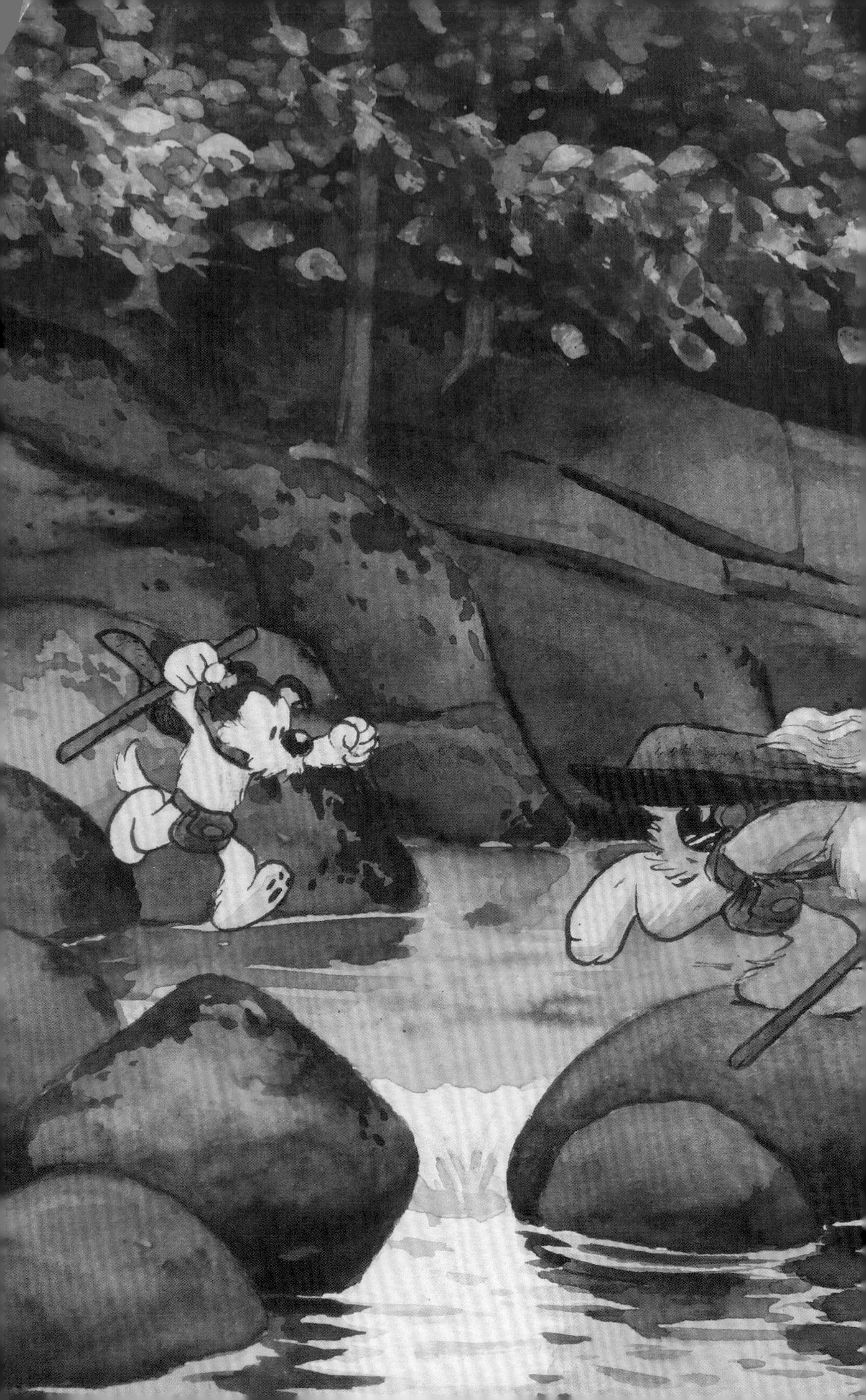

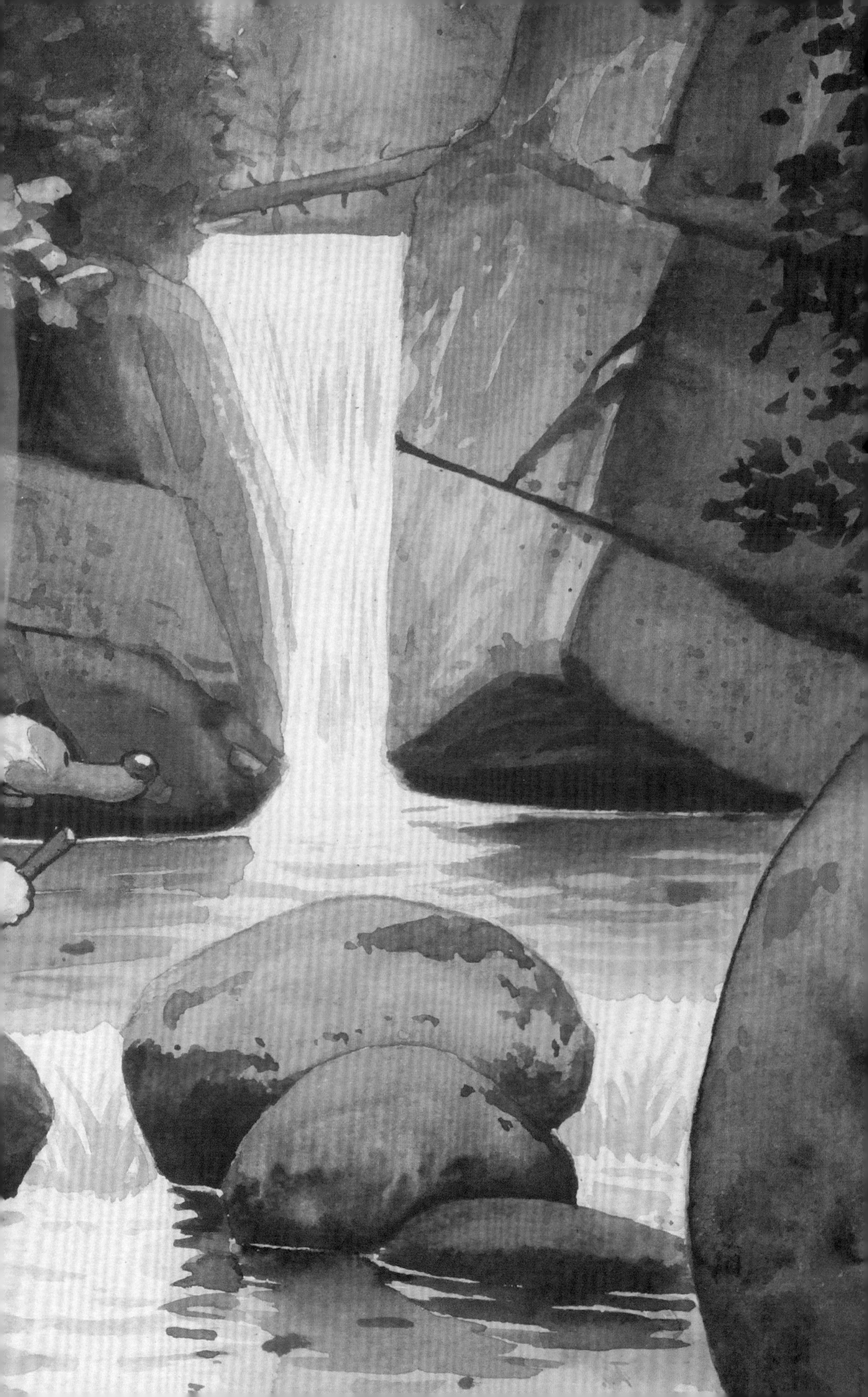

COVER GALLERY

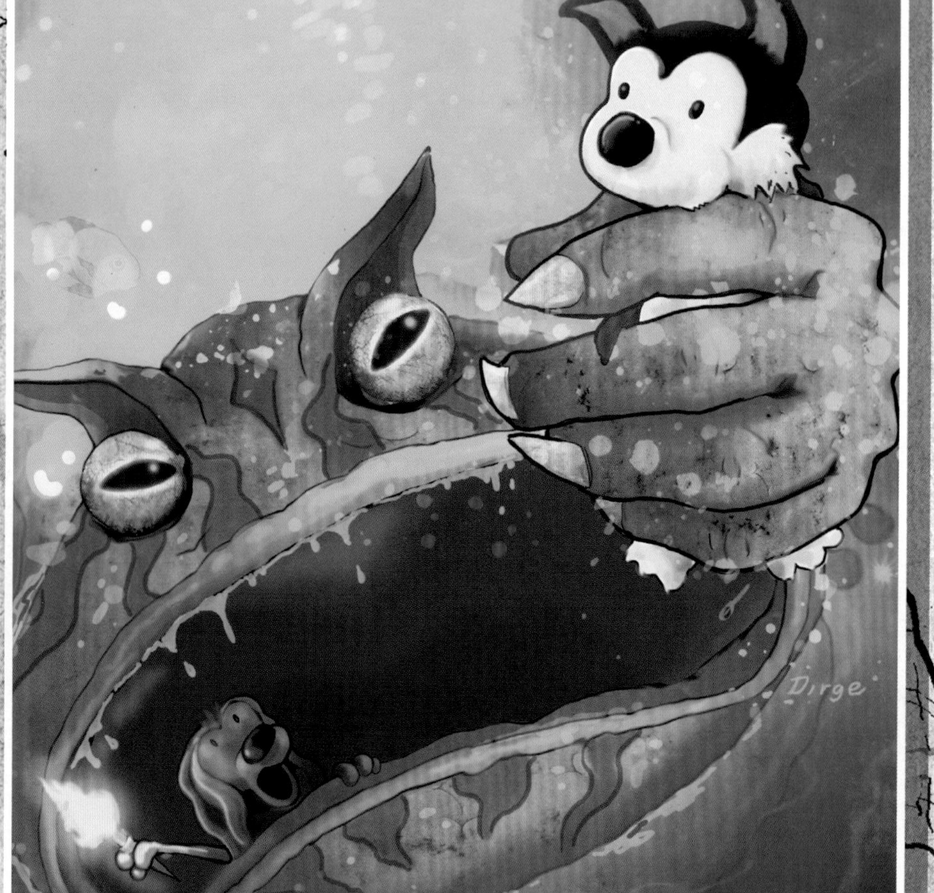
Dirge

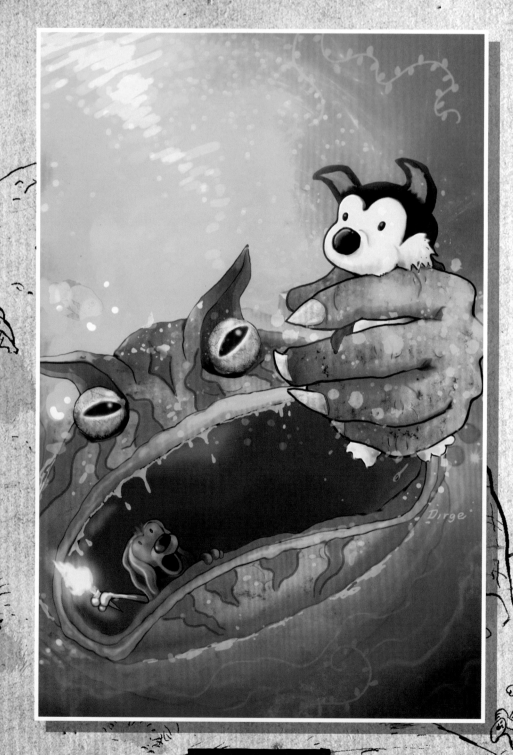

COVER #1A
ROMAN DIRGE

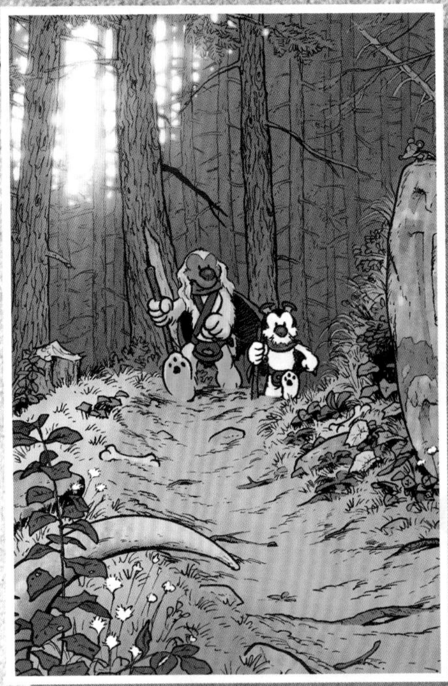

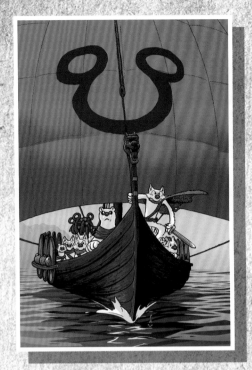

COVER #1B
PAU

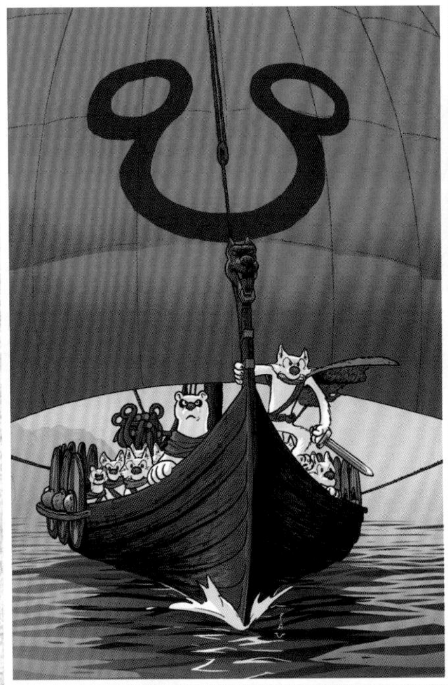

COVER #2
PAU

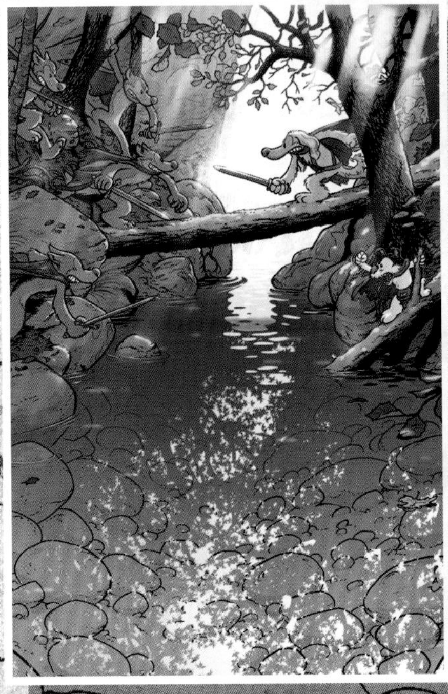

COVER #3
PAU

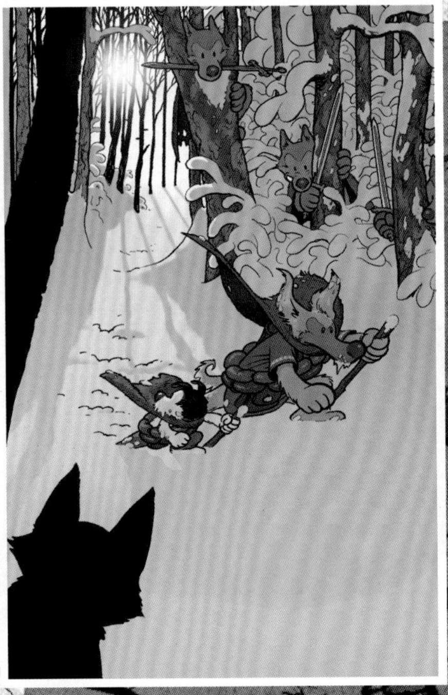

COVER #4
PAU